THE MYSTIC ROSE

THE MYSTIC ROSE

A Study of Primitive Marriage

By

ERNEST CRAWLEY

GYAN

Published by

GYAN

Gyan Publishing House
5, Ansari Road
Daryaganj, New Delhi-110002
Phone: 011-47034999, 9811692060
E-mail: books@gyanbooks.com

Distribution Network
gyanbooks.com
India, USA, Canada, UK, Australia, France

ISBN : 978-81-212-6224-8 (PB)
First Published, 1902

2nd Impression 2022

Printed at: Gyan Press, Delhi.

THE MYSTIC ROSE
Author: ERNEST CRAWLEY

THE MYSTIC ROSE

A STUDY OF PRIMITIVE MARRIAGE

BY

ERNEST CRAWLEY, M.A.

τὸ μυστήριον τοῦτο μέγα ἐστίν
Sacramentum hoc magnum est

1902

TO

J. G. FRAZER

IN

GRATITUDE AND ADMIRATION

PREFACE

The present theory was outlined about seven years ago, and a preliminary portion was published in the *Journal of the Anthropological Institute* for 1895 (vol. xxiv.). In that paper the main lines of the argument were laid down, and it was suggested that the explanation of marriage ceremonies and systems was to be developed thereon. The subsequent loss of a good deal of my materials, not yet all recovered, has been balanced by the publication of Messrs. Spencer and Gillen's valuable researches amongst the Central Australian natives, which confirm my conclusions in many ways.

These conclusions were originally completed without reference to the prevalent doctrines, originated by Bachofen and McLennan, and developed by Morgan, Bastian, Lubbock, G. A. Wilken, Robertson Smith, Giraud-Teulon, Fison, Howitt, Tylor, Post, Lippert, and others, concerning the origin and development of marriage, such as the Matriarchate (Bachofen), Marriage by Capture (McLennan), Primitive Promiscuity and Communal Marriage, comprising the hypotheses that some marriage ceremonies are intended to make the husband and wife of the same tribal or blood-kinship, and that others are "expiation for marriage" (Sir J. Lubbock); that is to say, these ceremonies are a compensation to the tribe or kin, individual marriage being an infringement of communal rights. These theories had to be taken into consideration. Previous study of the psychology of the lower races, starting from Professor Tylor's *Primitive Culture*, and Dr. Frazer's *Golden Bough*, to both of which I owe a great intellectual debt, made it evident that these prevalent theories of marriage origins were based on an imperfect understanding of primitive custom and thought. It also appeared a mistake, in view of the undifferentiated character of early thought, to separate the study of marriage systems and marriage ceremonies. I have here attempted to supply a more adequate basis for the enquiry by an analysis of the simplest and most elemental aspects in which the individual appears in relation to society. The ultimate appeal in these questions is to universal facts of human physiology and psychology. In illustration, it is perhaps worth mentioning that I was led from a general study of primitive culture to the study of marriage, by an investigation into the curious custom of exchange of dress between men and women, which occurs in the most dissimilar connections and the strangest places. I found that all cases of the custom yielded on analysis the same psychological components as do the relations of the sexes generally, and marriage in particular.

In 1889 Professor E. B. Tylor first applied statistics to the study of these questions (*Journ. Anthrop. Inst.* vol. xviii.). This was an important departure. It is first necessary, however, thoroughly to analyse every custom and its adhesions in the light not only of the whole culture of the given peoples, but of all primitive and elemental psychology; otherwise, tabulation leads to the pruning of facts, and a resulting neglect of essential characteristics which are apparently accidents. As MM. Langlois and Seignobos, our highest authorities on the methods of history, observe, the defect of statistical methods is that "they do not rest on a knowledge of the whole of the conditions under which the facts occur" (*Introduction to the Study of History*, p. 291, Eng. Trans.). So far as the data are correctly assigned and analysed, Professor Tylor's main results are, that there is a causal connection between (1) the mother-in-law avoidance custom and residence of the husband with the wife's family, (2) these and the custom of teknonymy (naming the parents after the child), (3) the couvade (the custom by which the husband pretends to lie-in) and temporary residence of the husband with the wife's family, (4) this temporary residence and marriage by capture. The cause, however, which he provisionally assumes is still the old Maternal system, arising out of communism, with marriage by capture intervening to produce individual marriage. As will be seen, the cause which I suggest also serves to explain all these connections, and these statistical results, so far as they correctly represent the facts, supply a corroboration of the present theory. Many of the tables, however, when the customs are analysed, present a very different appearance.

The valuable series of fresh data, collected from the Dutch East Indies, did not lead the distinguished Dutch ethnologist, the late Professor G. A. Wilken, to any new line of enquiry.

The late Professor Robertson Smith in 1885 first put one part of the problem, the question of the origin of bars to marriage, in a new light, by suggesting that whatever their origin, they are very early associated with the idea that it is not decent for housemates to intermarry (*Kinship and Marriage in Early Arabia*).

In 1890 Dr. J. G. Frazer, in his monumental work *The Golden Bough* (second edition, 1900), which, like Professor Tylor's *Primitive Culture*, marks an epoch in the study of man, referred to the existence of a mass of facts showing that the origin of the marriage system was to be found in some primitive conception of danger attaching to the sexual act. This statement is the most important contribution yet made to the study of these questions. As will be seen, however, I do not confine the issue so narrowly.

In 1891 appeared Dr. E. Westermarck's *History of*

Human Marriage (third edition, 1901), which revolutionised the study of the origins and development of marriage. His most valuable contributions are that he weakened or destroyed several positions of the old theory of primitive communism and the matriarchate, and gave an excellent account of human marriage in its biological aspects. He, however, carries the biological method too far when he "applies biological analogies (selection, struggle for existence, inherited habits, and so on) to the explanation of social evolution, which is not produced by the operation of the same causes as animal evolution" (Langlois and Seignobos, *op. cit.* p. 321), and not only takes no account of primitive psychology but neglects the importance of marriage ceremonies, of which he treats in one short chapter, without connecting them with other data. The general study not only of marriage ceremonies as a whole, which hitherto has not been systematically attempted, but of the whole question of marriage origins, is to be developed, as I have suggested, from that primitive religious mental habit, the characteristics of which have been so well analysed by Professor Tylor and in further issues by Dr. Frazer.

I am much indebted to my friend Mr. A. L. Bowley, one of our highest authorities on the methods of statistics, for working out for me some statistical problems.

E. C.

CONTENTS

CHAPTER I

INTRODUCTORY

THE TABOO IMPOSED, CHAPTERS II.—IX.

CHAPTER II

TABOO

CHAPTER III

SEXUAL TABOO

CHAPTER IV

HUMAN RELATIONS

CHAPTER V

HUMAN RELATIONS

CHAPTER VI

HUMAN RELATIONS

CHAPTER VII

COMMENSAL RELATIONS

CHAPTER VIII

SEXUAL RELATIONS

CHAPTER IX

SEXUAL RELATIONS

THE TABOO REMOVED, CHAPTERS X.—XIV.

CHAPTER X

THE BREAKING OF TABOO

CHAPTER XI

THEORY OF UNION

CHAPTER XII

THEORY OF CHANGE AND EXCHANGE

CHAPTER XIII

CONFIRMATION AND ENGAGEMENT

CHAPTER XIV

MARRIAGE AND ITS CEREMONIES

SECONDARY TABOO, CHAPTERS XV.—XVII.

CHAPTER I

All study of the origins of social institutions must be based on what ethnology can teach us of the psychology of the lower races and on the primitive conceptions of human relations which are thus established. It is only in early modes of thought that we can find the explanation of ceremonies and systems which originated in primitive society; and, if ceremony and system are the concrete forms in which human relations are expressed, an examination, ethnological and psychological, of human relations, is indispensable for enquiry into human institutions. It is necessary to lay stress upon this principle, for students of the history of marriage have hitherto ignored it, or rather, while using the facts of ethnology, have shown no sympathy with primitive thought. They have interpreted primitive custom by ideas which are far from primitive, which, in fact, are relatively late and belong to the legal stage of human culture. The attribution of legal conceptions to primitive thought has had the usual effect of *a priori* theory, and has checked enquiry.

In his *History of Human Marriage*[1] Dr. Westermarck made a much-needed protest, and refuted several of these pseudo-syntheses. In the constructive portion of his work he uses the biological argument. This was

[1] E. Westermarck, *The History of Human Marriage* (1891).

also necessary; the facts of biology must supply the preliminaries of investigation. But he goes too far with biology in one direction, and in another not far enough. The latter line of enquiry is sex. One of the most remarkable defects of the legal school of anthropology is its neglect to take sexual relations into account when discussing a sexual relation like that of marriage.

In the following pages I have followed the principle that marriage, both in ceremony and in system, is grounded in primitive conceptions of sexual relations. Many collateral phenomena will be discussed, which illustrate and are themselves explained by these conceptions; and though the lines of the argument lead from human relations through sexual relations to meet in marriage, yet by the way they will touch upon the connection of morality and religion with the social life of mankind.

At the outset it may be well to bring forward a few striking facts of custom, as types of the problems to be solved, and as a help towards clearness. Such are the following, which may be put, after the fashion of Plutarch, as questions:—

(1) Why, according to a very general custom, are husbands and wives, brothers and sisters, respectively, required to avoid each other in one or more ways, and, in particular, may not eat together?

(2) Why do engaged couples also, as is frequently the case, avoid each other with religious caution?

(3) Why, again, do men and women generally, practise the same religious avoidance of each other?

(4) Why, according to a common custom, is it necessary for the bridegroom to take his bride by violence? ("Marriage by capture.")

(5) Why are the bride and bridegroom in Bengal first married to two trees?

(6) Why did the bride in ancient Argos wear a beard in the bridal chamber, and why in Kos was the bridegroom arrayed in women's clothes when he received his bride?

(7) Why, according to a widely spread custom, which, like the next, has excited the laughter of mankind, should a man and his mother-in-law religiously avoid each other, to the extent of hiding the face and of being "ashamed"?

(8) Why, as is the practice in several parts of the world, and as was reported of the Tibarenoi by Greek writers and of the King of Torelore by the *jogleor* who wrote *Cest Daucassin et Nicolete*, does the husband lie-in and pretend to be a mother when his wife is confined? (*Couvade.*)

The primitive mental habit in its general features is best described negatively by the term *unscientific*, and positively by *religious*, in the ordinary connotation of that term. *Superstitious* would be preferable, were it not too narrow; as to *magic*, I do not here distinguish —magic being simply the superstitious or religious *method* as opposed to the scientific. This primitive thinking does not distinguish between the natural and the supernatural, between subjective and objective reality. Primitive man regards the creations of his own imagination as being no less real than the existences for which he has the evidence of sense-perception, in a sense more real, precisely because they elude sense-perception, though dealt with in the same way as objective reality; and, while the latter is always changing, these ideal existences, like the ideas of Plato, never pass away. Objective reality also takes on some properties of ideal reality, so that for primitive man the supernatural and the natural interchange, or rather, are not distinguished. This philosophy is truly monistic, and is neither materialist nor idealist, but undifferentiated. "Matter" is spiritual, and "spirit" is material, though sometimes invisible. Primitive logic corresponds to this metaphysic; it is likewise undifferentiated, and is chiefly guided by "material fallacies" and a Realism more pronounced than that of the Schoolmen. Such inference necessarily includes true results, inductive and deductive, but no less necessarily these results were not distinguished from the false; inextricably confused with fallacy, which often owed its continuance to the association, truth was held but was not recognised as a distinct species. As to "survivals" of primitive speculation and custom into civilised periods, the term is misused when it is implied that these are dead forms, surviving like fossil remains or rudimentary organs; the fact is that human nature remains potentially primitive, and it is not easy even for those most favoured by descent to rise above these primitive ideas, precisely because these ideas "spring eternally" from permanent functional causes. Every one would still be primitive were it not for education, and the importance of education in the evolution of the soul can hardly be over-estimated.

The undifferentiated character of primitive culture, its reference of all departments of thought and practice to one psychological habit, the superstitious or religious, may be illustrated from higher stages. "The political and religious Governments of the Kaffir tribes are so intimately connected that the one cannot be overturned without the other; they must stand or fall together."[1]

[1] Maclean, *Compendium of Kaffir Laws and Customs*, 107.

The great pagan civilisations show exactly the same homogeneity. The ideal society of early Christians and Puritans alike, was one where there should be no separation between Church and State, where public and private life and thought, politics and domestic affairs, individual and social morality, speculation and science, should all be subsumed under religion, and directed by the religious method. Such an ideal differs in degree only from the actual condition of primitive society; whatever term be used to describe this, it is homogeneous and monistic in practice and theory; one method is applied to its philosophy of nature and of man, its politics and public life, its sociology and human relations, domestic and social, its medical science and practice, its ethics and morality, its ordinary thought and action in everyday life, its behaviour and etiquette. Thus, as will also be shown by the way, there is a religious meaning inherent in the primitive conception and practice of all human relations, which is always ready to become actualised; and the same is true of all individual processes of sense and emotion and intellection and, in especial, of those functional processes that are most easily seen in their working and results. Not only "the Master knot of Human Fate," but all human actions and relations, all individual and social phenomena, have for primitive man, always potentially and often actually, a full religious content. So it is with that sub-division of human nature and human life caused by *sex*; all actions and relations, all individual and social phenomena conditioned by sex, are likewise filled with a religious meaning. Sexual relations and sexual processes, as all human relations and human processes, are religious to the primitive mind. The conception of danger, neither material nor spiritual, but both, which is the chief characteristic of early religious thought and practice, and is due to the unscientific character of early speculation, is here intensified by the importance, psychical and physiological, of the sexual life. As we proceed, this characteristic of sexual relations and sexual life will be made clear; it is seen in the phenomena of the individual life and of social relations, both in ordinary circumstances and, naturally intensified, in sexual crises. Thus, birth and baptism, confirmation and marriage, are attended by religious ceremonies. There is indeed a tendency amongst enquirers, due to the legal method of investigation, to ignore the religious character of the marriage ceremony; but it is only in later culture that marriage is a "civil act," and though in early Catholic times marriage was not necessarily performed by the Church, it was still in essence a religious rite, and had been so before Christianity, as it was so in the earliest ages. One of the crudest modes of marriage known, that of the Arunta and other Central Australian tribes, is proved by a note of Messrs. Spencer and Gillen to be a religious act,[1] though to all appearance this would seem impossible. As we shall see, even the ordinary intercourse of man with woman has for primitive man this religious meaning.

The primitive conception of danger, which leads to those precautions, religious or superstitious, so characteristic of early ritual, appears in two main forms, the predication of evil influences and the imposition of taboos. Let us take a few instances, from ordinary life and sexual crises.

In the Marquesas Islands, the use of canoes is prohibited to the female sex by *tabu*; the breaking of the

[1] B. Spencer and F. J. Gillen, *The Native Tribes of Central Australia*, 93.

rule is punished with death. *Tapa*-making belongs exclusively to women; and it is *tabu* for men to touch it.[1] The Kaffirs will not from superstitious motives allow women to touch their cattle.[2] Amongst the Dacotas custom and superstition ordain that the wife must carefully keep away from all that belongs to her husband's sphere.[3] In New Zealand, a man who has any important business on hand, either in peace or war, is *tapu*, and must keep away from the female sex.[4]

The fear of evil spirits shows itself from time to time during the long and wearisome marriage ceremonies of South Celebes, and methods are used to frustrate their evil intentions against the happiness of the young pair. There is also a fear that the soul of the bridegroom may fly away for sheer happiness.[5] In China, a new bride is apt to be attacked by evil spirits causing her to be ill; hence the figure of "a great magician" (a Taoist priest), brandishing a sword, is painted on the sedan-chair she uses on the wedding-day.[6] The sedan-chair in which a Manchu bride goes to the house of the bridegroom is "disinfected" with incense, to drive away evil spirits, and in it is placed a calendar containing the names of idols who control the spirits of evil.[7] The Druses "have a superstition that leads them to suppose that Gins or evil spirits are more than usually busy on the occasion of marriage" and may interfere with the happiness of the pair.[8] In English folklore "the malevolence of witchcraft seems to have taken the greatest pleasure in subtle assaults

[1] H. Melville, *The Marquesas Islands*, 13, 245.

[2] *Journal of the Anthropological Institute*, x. 11; xvi. 119.

[3] Waitz-Gerland, *Anthropologie der Naturvölker*, iii. 100.

[4] *Id.* vi. 349.

[5] B. F. Matthes, *Bijdragen tot de Ethnologie van Zuid-Celebes*, 30, 39, 33; van Eck, in *De Indische Gids* for 1881, 1038.

[6] Doolittle, *Social Life of the Chinese*, i. 95.

[7] Lockhart, in *Folk-Lore*, i. 487.

[8] G. W. Chasseaud, *The Druses of the Lebanon*, 168.

upon those just entering the married state."[1] In Russia, all doors, windows, and even the chimney, are closed at a wedding, to prevent malicious witches flying in and hurting the bride and bridegroom.[2] The Chuvashes honour their wizards (*iemzyas*) and always invite them to weddings, for fear that an offended *iemzya* might destroy the bride and bridegroom.[3]

Savages and barbarians, and, we may add, mankind in general, are very secretive concerning their functional life. This attitude is naturally emphasised when the sexual act is in question. Thus amongst the natives of the Ceramlaut Archipelago, between Celebes and Papua, where there is a veneer of Islam, it is the custom for both man and wife to say the well-known formula of good Moslems before the sexual act.[4] This is a general rule in Islam, especially on the first night of marriage.[5] The old Romans similarly invoked *Dea Virginensis*, while ceremonially loosing the zone.[6] The natives of Amboina believe in a witch, *Pontianak*, who steals away not only infants, but the genital organs of men.[7] In South Celebes, the evil spirit most feared by the male sex is one that makes a man incapable of performing his marital duties.[8] A similar belief is very common in European folklore.

Again, as soon as a Nicobarese woman shows signs of pregnancy, dancing and singing are interdicted in the village.[9] Pregnant women in the island Kisar, or Makiser, take a knife with them, when they leave the

[1] Brand, *Popular Antiquities*, iii. 305.
[2] W. Ralston, *Songs of the Russian People*, 381.
[3] *Journal of the Anthropological Institute*, xxiv. 156.
[4] J. G. F. Riedel, *De sluik- en kroesharige rassen tusschen Selebes en Papua*, 173.
[5] A. Bastian, *Der Mensch in der Geschichte*, iii. 293.
[6] Augustine, *De Civitate Dei*, iv. 11.
[7] Riedel, *op. cit.* 58.
[8] Matthes, *op. cit.* 97.
[9] A. Featherman, *Social History of the Races of Mankind*, ii. 246.

house, in order to frighten away evil spirits.[1] The same practice is found in Amboina, and the Watubella Islands.[2] In the Ceramlaut Islands, pregnant women use charms to protect themselves against evil influences, and in Ceram (Nusaina) they dread the evil spirit *Pusiana* or *Pontianak*.[3] Among the Basutos pregnant women are subject to witchcraft, and they wear skin-aprons to protect them.[4] In New Zealand and New Caledonia, for instance, they are *tabu*;[5] amongst the latter people also, and in Siam, the Marianne, Gilbert and Marshall Islands, amongst the Pshawes and some Transcaucasian tribes[6] they are "unclean," *i.e.* taboo. Turning to the other side of the taboo state, we find that amongst the natives of Costa Rica, a woman who is for the first time pregnant, "infects the whole neighbourhood"; all deaths are laid to her charge, and the husband pays the damages. This remarkable influence "seems to be an evil spirit, or rather a property acquired" by women in that state.[7]

At child-birth, more than at any other functional crisis, woman is taboo, and in that state where religion develops evil spirits. Amongst the Alfoers, before a birth, the husband sets a naked sword in front of the house, to keep off evil spirits who might bring ill-luck to the delivery.[8] In the Philippine Islands, there is an evil spirit, which causes painful labour. It is to be recognised by its voice, and when the husband hears it, he locks up the house, closing every chink, and goes round with a sword thrusting and parrying all night. In the morning he takes a well-earned rest, because "he

[1] Riedel, *op. cit.* 417. [2] *Id.* 71, 207. [3] *Id.* 173-74, 134.
[4] E. Casalis, *The Basutos*, 251. [5] H. Ploss, *Das Kind*, i. 20.
[6] H. Ploss u. M. Bartels, *Das Weib*, ii. 603.
[7] W. M. Gabb, *Transactions of the American Philosophical Society* for 1875, 505.
[8] J. G. F. Riedel, in *Zeitschrift für Ethnologie* for 1871, 403.

has saved his wife."[1] Amongst the Ovaherero the woman at child-birth, and the special hut which she occupies, are both *zera*, holy.[2] More often, women in child-bed and for some time after, are called "unclean," frequently *tabu*, but "holy," *tabu* and unclean are so far not differentiated. Amongst peoples who use special terms like *tapu*, as the Polynesians, she is *tapu*; elsewhere, as a rule, "unclean."

Especially is this the case after child-birth. The infant also is taboo, and comes under the same category.[3] In the islands Amboina and Uliasser the new-born babe is subject to the attacks of evil spirits, and is put by the fire to protect him.[4] In East Central Africa, when the child is seven days old, the parents believe that it is past its greatest dangers, and in order to prevent evil spirits from doing it further mischief, they strew the place with dressed victuals by way of appeasing them.[5]

At puberty also, religious ideas are found. Amongst the Kurnai of Gippsland "the initiatory ceremony, which introduced the young of both sexes to membership in the community, is a commemoration—even a species of rude worship—by the tribe, of the eponymous ancestors, Yeerung and Djeetgun. It forms the great central idea of Kurnai society."[6] Amongst the Narrinyeri boys at initiation are *narumbe*, sacred in a special sense, of which more hereafter.[7] Amongst the Chiriguanos the girl at puberty fasts, and is secluded, while women beat the floor and walls with sticks, by way of

[1] Bowring, *The Philippines*, 120; A. Bastian, *Die Völker des Östlichen Asien*, v. 270.

[2] *South African Folklore Journal*, ii. 63.

[3] Ploss, *Das Kind*, i. 51.

[4] Riedel, *De sluik- en kroesharige rassen tusschen Selebes en Papua*, 75.

[5] D. Macdonald, *Africana*, i. 224.

[6] L. Fison and A. W. Howitt, *Kamilaroi and Kurnai*, 199.

[7] *Native Tribes of South Australia*, 18.

finding and driving away "the snake that has wounded the girl."[1] The Siamese, who imagine that evil spirits swarm in the air, believe that these enjoy the first fruits of their girls, and that they cause the "wound" which renews itself every month.[2] On the religious state of girls at puberty Dr. Frazer gives many details.[3]

The same religious fears are connected with menstruation generally. Amongst the Vedahs of Travancore the wife at her monthly periods is secluded for five days in a hut, a quarter of a mile away, which is also used by her at child-birth. The next five days are passed in a second hut, half-way between the first and the house. On the ninth day the husband holds a feast, sprinkles his floor with wine, and invites his friends. Until this evening he has not dared to eat anything but roots, for fear of being killed by "the devil."[4] Here, as in the next case, the dangerous side of taboo is prominent. Amongst the Maoris, if a man touched a menstruous woman, he would be *tapu*; if he had connection with her, or ate food cooked by her, he would be "*tapu* an inch thick."[5]

In all these relations and functional crises connected with sex, a religious state is, as it were, entered upon. There is not needed, to prove this, the major premiss, that all primitive practice and belief are essentially religious; the particular instances themselves point clearly to a connection with religion. Though further evidence of this is to be found in most races from China to Peru, and even in higher civilisations, while European folklore is full of such evidence, yet a few typical examples may suffice.

[1] *Lettres édifiantes et curieuses*, viii. 333; J. G. Frazer, *The Golden Bough*[2], iii. 214.
[2] Loubere, *Siam*, i. 203.
[3] Frazer, *op. cit.* iii. 204 ff.
[4] F. Jagor, in *Zeitschrift für Ethnologie*, xi. 164.
[5] E. Tregear, in *Journ. Anthrop. Inst.*, xix. 101.

It may be objected that the presence of evil spirits in some of the above cases proves nothing. But all I wish to point out just now is the actual presence of evil or danger. I am far from wishing to imply that the evil spirits or dangerous influences present on all these occasions are those against which the ceremonies of marriage, baptism, and the like were instituted as safeguards. In some of these cases the evil influence stated is that which has caused the rite or the taboo; in others it is not so; other cases again are selected as examples of a belief in the process of crystallisation into ceremony, superimposed upon an already crystallised ceremony of similar origin, such as the cases of marriage taken from South Celebes, Manchuria, and Russia; whilst others show an original ceremony in the process of development from belief, as in the case of the Indian girl at puberty and the Vedahs at menstruation, and in those of the Muhammadan and Roman bridegrooms, where the Roman ceremony is obviously the crystallisation of an idea similar to the Muhammadan. In the higher stages of culture it is hardly necessary to quote instances to prove that marriage, baptism, confirmation, and "the churching of women" are religious ceremonies, but it is important to mark the continuity of these with the ritual of early man. A long array of facts might be given to show that the main line of development in ritual is from the propitiation or insulation of evil influences to the conciliation of beneficent powers. The change is effected in this way: the dangers feared are originally insulated before and during the progress of the function, as is the natural course, then at the end of the function, the expulsion of the dangers is performed for the last time, and often shows a twofold character, purification and propitiation, such as, to take the case of child-birth, the purification of the woman with water, and the propitiation of the spirits by food. The practice of performing the chief ceremony at the end of a functional crisis was more sure of continuance, precisely because the danger is then usually over, and the ceremony therefore cannot be discredited. Further, keeping the same instance, purification after child-birth, the deliverance from danger is naturally ascribed to some beneficent spirit, and the water with which the woman is purified of that danger takes on the character of "holy" accordingly. The examples drawn from the Vedahs, and from an East Central African tribe, are here instructive, as showing the necessary components of a ceremony and illustrating its origin.

We must next point out the fact that the rules and restrictions (taboos) imposed in these sexual relations or sexual crises, some of which are expressly called *tabu*, are identical with those imposed in other *tabu* states, such as hunting, war and the preparation therefor, mourning, also in the case of those sacred persons, priest-kings, incarnate gods, at once more and less than man, of whom Dr. Frazer treats in his great work. But the plurality of causes, which makes it unsafe to infer similarity of cause from similar effects, necessitates an analysis of particular results.

The ideas underlying the above-cited examples of taboo are in some cases connected with "spiritual" dangers, and, to that extent, are religious. In the further analysis of these and other cases, the religious character of practice and belief will be made more clear, and the precise nature of the danger will be investigated. For the present, let us take one or two of the above cases, which might be multiplied indefinitely, to show the identity of the ideas underlying Polynesian *tabu* and similar religious states elsewhere. A Maori woman at menstruation is *tapu*, and any one touching her is *tapu*. Now, according to the Siamese belief about this function, the danger is due to evil spirits which cause a wound, of which the menstrual blood is the result and proof, and it is contact with this blood of which the Maori male is so afraid. Add to this the fact that the Maoris themselves not only identify menstrual blood with an evil spirit, *Kahukahu*, but also hold that the *tapu* state generally is due to the influence of ancestral spirits,[1] and identification of taboo and "spiritual" influence is so far complete.

Now, if behind any sexual relation or sexual functional crisis and the relations between the sexes resulting in connection with it, there are found ideas identical with those underlying any taboo or religious condition, we may infer for all such ideas in primitive thought, not only correlation but identity of origin.

As we proceed we shall find evidence not only for identifying this religious state of "spiritual" danger with the dangers underlying taboo, and with those proceeding from evil agencies, material, spiritual, or both, but also for ascribing this state to the functional crises of sex and the ensuing sexual attitude, and even to the ordinary relations of the sexes.

[1] E. Shortland, *Southern Districts of New Zealand*, 67, 68.

CHAPTER II

We have seen reason to suppose that men and women at marriage, women during menstruation, pregnancy, and child-birth, infants, boys and girls at puberty, not to mention other critical conditions, are regarded by early man as being in that mysterious religious state which necessitates the imposition of restrictions and safeguards, or taboos, and to which mourners and kings, warriors and priests alike are called. In the last case cited from the Maoris we see very clearly the twofold nature of the state in which these *sacræ personæ* find themselves. They are dangerous and are themselves in danger. Dr. Frazer has here applied most happily the language of electricity. The person charged with this electric force, which is both dangerous and beneficent, must be insulated by various taboos.

The Polynesian *tabu*, especially in Hawaii and New Zealand, was the basis of society; it was the support of all religious, moral, and social institutions, for all of which it supplied a supernatural sanction. The system was indeed a good example of the religious character of early society. Used by priests and nobles for their own ends and no less for the good of the community, it early divided into religious, political, and social *tabu*. Every priest and every gentleman was *tabu*, "sacred." The opposite state was *noa*, "common." This was the system after a long development.

Here I wish to deal rather with the ideas underlying taboo, in its human aspect. These are universal human ideas, arising directly from the simplest human relations and physical functions, and I therefore propose, after having shown cause why the identity should be recognised, to apply the term taboo to all similar phenomena throughout mankind, and not only to the restrictions but to the whole series of persons, beliefs, and practices. All these are potentially what the Polynesian *tabu* was actually. Also, as will be seen, taboo as thus extended is identical with a considerable part of religion in the sense already described as characteristic of primitive culture. I am, of course, far from wishing to imply that these ideas underlying taboo have developed the whole of religion; and, as in this enquiry we have to discuss the relations of man with man and of man with woman, that is, Taboo in its social aspect, the terms Social Taboo and Sexual Taboo may well be used. They will serve both to avoid misconceptions as to religion in general, and to mark the fact that here we meet with some fundamental religious ideas which lie beneath the relations of man with man and the system of morality derived from those relations. In these ideas may be seen the basis of Evolutionary Ethics.

Primitive Taboo exists now in all its pristine strength, though it has split into religious, moral, and social habits, each distinguished by a more or less different terminology. To illustrate the continuity of culture and the identity of the elementary human ideas in all ages, it is sufficient to point to the ease with which the Polynesian word *tabu* has passed into modern languages. There is no more interesting or more important study than to trace the continuity of culture, and when we take any taboo custom of early man and follow it up to modern times, we generally find at this end not a mere survival but a living duplicate, often identical in form and content with its prototype. Many cases of this will appear in the following pages. As an example I may quote a common feature of primitive *tabu* in its social aspect, the placing of a cloth or stick or other mark on a piece of property to show that it belongs to some one and is therefore sacred. This widely spread custom shows the religious basis of the rights of property. Well, at our end of the chain, we find the same thing in the familiar piece of unwritten law which respects the seat thus tabooed in a railway carriage. The only difference is that in the Polynesian case there was a deep religious meaning behind the form and a terrible supernatural sanction to support it, while behind the modern custom there is human courtesy only; behind both, there is the universal sense of human nature. Indeed, as we shall see later, such an example points to the fact that ordinary universal human ideas, chiefly connected with functional needs, produce the same results in all ages; and many so-called survivals, which have on the face of them too much vitality to be mere fossil remains, at once receive a scientific explanation which is more than antiquarian.

Having found that the persons with whom we have to deal are, so far, taboo, in danger and dangerous, and concern us in their human relations, social taboo, we now proceed to investigate the nature of this danger other than the vague but ubiquitous evil spirits. The omnipresence of evil spirits according to early thought has been illustrated by Dr. Frazer, but to point the case, I may give some evidence of this here.

An excellent observer says of the Indian of British Guiana that his "whole world swarms with beings. He is surrounded by a host of them, possibly hurtful. It is therefore not wonderful that the Indian fears to be without his fellow, fears even to move beyond the light from his camp-fire, and when obliged to do so carries a firebrand with him, that he may have a chance of seeing the beings among whom he moves. Nor is it wonderful that occasionally the neighbourhood of their settlement seems to the Indians to become so oppressively full of gathering beings, that the *peaiman* who has the power of frightening those beings, even when they are invisible, is employed to effect a general clearance of the air."[1] Amongst the Sonthals evil spirits are ubiquitous, and offerings of grain are placed on the paths to appease them.[2] In Egypt the *Ginn* pervade everything; they inhabit rivers, ruined houses, wells, baths, ovens, and latrines. When pouring water or anything on the ground, it is the custom to exclaim, "Permission," by way of craving pardon of any *Ginnee* that may be there.[3] The Karalits believe that the air is peopled with invisible "spectres," which the angekoks only can discern and catch while they are hovering about.[4] The New Caledonians imagine that demon-agencies pervade the universe, and that they haunt their huts to trouble their sleep and are the original cause of sickness and death.[5] In Siam evil spirits are thought to swarm in the air. The people believe that they enjoy the first fruits of their girls.[6] "In one respect the life of the Kurnai was a life of dread. He

[1] E. F. im Thurn, *Among the Indians of Guiana*, 372.
[2] V. Ball, *Jungle Life in India*, 235.
[3] E. W. Lane, *Manners and Customs of the Modern Egyptians*, i. 284.
[4] Featherman, *op. cit.* iii. 444.
[5] *Id.* ii. 91.
[6] Loubere, *op. cit.* i. 203.

lived in fear of the visible and invisible. He never knew the moment when the lurking *Brajerak* might not spear him from behind, and never knew the moment when some secret foe among the Kurnai might not succeed in passing over him some spell, against which he could not struggle, or from which the most potent counter-charms given him by his ancestors could not free him."[1] The natives of Hatam in New Guinea had a great dread of poison infused in the atmosphere.[2] The last two cases form a link between the natural and the supernatural.

We thus see that in the thought of some peoples, man's whole environment is more or less full of the agencies or influences of evil, and as we may presuppose the same psychological material for all mankind, we infer a similarity of psychological result, potential if not actual, for all peoples at a certain stage of culture. The term "evil spirit" is often misused; many evil influences, which are not anthropomorphic at all, are too readily called "spirits." Supernatural personifications will not cover all the cases of primitive spiritualism. These dangers are still undifferentiated and combined in one *genus* in which there is no distinction between natural and supernatural, real and ideal, nor between persons and other existences or *entiæ*; these "spirits" are really material, though unseen, and many are simply "influences," states of matter, impersonal forces. The atmosphere is thus charged with "spiritual" electricity, with *bacteria* of invisible mischief. Man needs to walk warily; at any time he may be subjected to dangers coming from this hylo-idealistic force. The conduction or induction, contagion or infection, may result in death or sickness, spiritual or

[1] Fison and Howitt, *op. cit.* 259. [2] L. M. D'Albertis, *New Guinea*, i. 122.

material danger, real or but vaguely apprehended, the subjective notion being often stronger than objective presentation from its very elusiveness.

These influences are of the kind which produce the state of religious peril, or Taboo. When we take our attention from the mysterious force of taboo and analyse its subject, we find first that it is the "spiritual" danger which makes him taboo and dangerous to others, as soon as it descends upon him and fills him with virus or electric force. It is no inconsistency that a man is often taboo before the danger attacks him, for he is expecting it, or that people like Dr. Frazer's incarnate gods, or even the ordinary Maori gentleman, are always taboo. These *sacræ personæ* have the religious condition imposed upon them every day, they are *cottidie feriatæ*. It is a natural extension with persons on whom the safety of the world depends, as in the case of the incarnate gods, and no less with persons like the Maori, who has been led by the development of a system which combined the characteristics of Roman Catholicism with those of Feudalism, to believe, like many a modern aristocrat, that he is somewhat more than the salt of the earth.

The next commonest form in which the danger, resulting in taboo, is presented, is that of contagion of a *sickness* neither real nor imaginary, neither natural or supernatural, but both. This predication of "spiritual" sickness, though almost universal, and, as will be seen later, of very great importance in the history of human relations, does not cover all the facts, and we want to know the origin of this idea also. We have found the danger to come from the environment of the individual, and then to settle upon him. We may then look for its original character in the actual environment, not as it may really be, but as it is conceived to be, that is, conditioned by the individual's conception thereof; and secondly, where the environment is humanity, in the characteristics attributed to such persons by the individual. Now we find, after examining the facts, that there is one characteristic which inheres in all these manifold dangers. Things and persons are potentially dangerous, acts and functions are potentially liable to danger, which are strange, unfamiliar, unusual, abnormal, in a word, more or less unknown. Man's ignorance is the occasion of his fears, and he fears anything or everything which he does not understand. Of the savage it may most truly be said, *omnia exeunt in mysterium*. Man's superstitious fears are found to be in the exact ratio of man's ignorance. To all these potential dangers he naturally ascribes the results which he knows to ensue from real physical danger, and of course this wide generalisation includes cases of real injury inextricably confused with a thousand empty terrors. As man's earliest thinking is anthropomorphic and in terms of himself, he attributes to agencies which he does not understand, not only the conscious power and methods of human beings, but the involuntary influence or deleterious properties of dangerous men, such as enemies or diseased persons; and these imaginary results coming from things and persons feared because they are not understood, are actually accentuated by the very fact that the persons or things do not harmonise with man's knowledge of himself. Wonder becomes uneasiness, and eventually produces an attitude of religious caution. Again, man's fears are for himself, and especially for those parts and functions of his organism which are most important for life and health and are actually most liable to injury. Here there falls to be considered what may be called *physiological thought*, subconsciously arising from and concentrating upon physiological functions. Especially important in human psychology is the physiological thought arising from the two chief physical functions of nutrition and sex. For these and other complex and delicate functions, man's ignorance creates many potential dangers, and this leads to various attitudes of religious caution in their performance.

Let us take some cases which illustrate this potentiality of danger, inhering, through man's subjective conceptions, in things and acts and states which are different from what is usual and ordinary, which more or less break the comfortable routine of life, or which he cannot explain. From this point of view, the original idea behind the Maori term *noa*, for instance, which means *common* as opposed to *tapu*, is what we should call normal or regular. In South Celebes the Buginese word *pemâli* (*i.q.* Polynesian *tabu*) denotes all things unusual, and such are supposed to bring evil consequences in their train.[1] In the Marquesas anything different from ordinary custom is called taboo.[2] The Dyaks perform mystic ceremonies "for the most frivolous causes; when they have a bad dream, if a tree falls, or a basket of rice be upset." *Pamali* (*tabu*) is imposed on practically any occasion when something unusual or important is about to or has taken place.[3] Strangeness, potential danger, and spiritual power go together in the savage mind. "The Masai conception of deity (*ngai*) is vague," as Joseph Thomson pointed out. "I was *ngai*; my lamp was *ngai*; whatever struck them as strange or incomprehensible they supposed to

[1] Matthes, *op. cit.* 108. [2] Melville, *The Marquesas Islands*, 248.
[3] Featherman, *op. cit.* 278, 282.

have some connection with *ngai*."[1] The Cadiacks believed that every act was under the influence of some object, stone, or the like, especially if the said object was curious in appearance.[2] Of the Guiana Indian, Mr. im Thurn states that, "he always sees a spirit in any instrument which does him harm. When he falls on a rock, he attributes the injury to it. If he sees anything in any way curious or abnormal, and if soon after an evil befall him, he regards the thing and the evil as cause and effect. Just as some rocks, viz. the more peculiar, are more malignant than others, so it is not every river, but every bend and portion of a river that has a spirit; spirits of falls and rapids are still more dreaded, therefore people are more frequently drowned there. Spirits consist of harmless and harmful. The former are quite inactive. The good that befalls an Indian he takes as a matter of course, as the result of his own exertions, and all the evil as the work of evil-wishing spirits. He performs no acts to attract the goodwill of spirits, but he constantly does act or avoid action to arrest the ill-will of other spirits."[3] When animals act contrary to their ordinary habits, the Kaffirs regard them as omens.[4] So in Chinese and European folklore, the crowing of a hen is ominous of something unusual about to happen.[5] Amongst the Patagonians any unfamiliar object was supposed to possess an evil spirit; and any boy or girl who was odd or peculiar, was marked out for the profession of wizard.[6] So the Kaffirs of Natal honoured persons who were subject to fits, but they refused to eat out of such a person's

[1] J. Thomson, *Through Masai Land*, 260.
[2] U. Lisiansky, *A Voyage Round the World*, 243.
[3] im Thurn, *op. cit.* 370, 377, 379. [4] J. Shooter, *The Kaffirs of Natal*, 165.
[5] Doolittle, *op. cit.* ii. 328.
[6] G. C. Musters, *At Home with the Patagonians*, 181, 182.

vessels.[1] Kaffirs begin the career of diviner or doctor by being ill, and especially the appearance of epileptic symptoms in a Kaffir show that he is becoming a seer.[2] Neuropaths are much honoured in the islands of Leti, Moa, and Lakor.[3] The Bakgalagali, a weak and timorous race, are protected by the notion that it is uncanny to meddle with them.[4] Amongst the commonest cases are those where potentiality of danger is ascribed to strangers. The Guaranis suspected every stranger of hostility.[5] D'Albertis was requested by the Alfoers opposite Ramoi to leave their village because his presence brought bad luck. "The people began to die," they complained, "as soon as you looked at us. Five have died in three days."[6] The Samoans fear evil influence from strangers.[7] On entering a strange country the Maoris perform a ceremony to make it *noa*, as it may have been *tapu*, that is, potentially dangerous.[8] When an Australian tribe approaches another that is unknown, they carry burning sticks "to purify the air."[9] Strange meats, such as are for instance non-indigenous, are feared by the Indians of Guiana, and they are rendered eatable by the *peaiman*, or even occasionally an old woman blowing on them certain times, so as to expel the "spirit."[10] In German folklore there is the custom of blowing thrice into a strange spoon, before eating with it.[11] The Indians of Guiana are afraid of the food of strangers, or of anything belonging

[1] Shooter, *op. cit.* 218.
[2] Callaway, *The Religious System of the Amazulu*, 299; Shooter, 191.
[3] Riedel, *op. cit.* 378.
[4] *South African Folklore Journal*, ii. 32.
[5] Dobrizhoffer, *The Abipones*, 163.
[6] D'Albertis, *op. cit.* i. 53.
[7] G. Turner, *Samoa a Hundred Years Ago*, 291.
[8] Shortland, *Traditions and Superstitions of the New Zealanders*, 103.
[9] R. Brough Smyth, *The Aborigines of Victoria*, i. 134.
[10] im Thurn, *op. cit.* 368.
[11] F. Panzer, *Beitrag zur Deutschen Mythologie*, 257.

to such.[1] The Zulus taboo all foods that are strange or unknown.[2] A similar idea underlies the common diffidence about beginning an act or doing something for the first time, or handselling a new object. Before shooting a cataract for the first time, on the first sight of any new place, striking rocks, etc., the Guiana Indian arrests the ill-will of the spirits. The dreaded objects are not mentioned, are not looked at more than is necessary, and artificial means of blinding the eyes with pepper juice are used to avoid the dreaded sight.[3] The Sandwich Islanders prayed before they ate, before tilling the ground, before building houses, launching boats, or casting nets.[4] Before starting on a hunting expedition, the Hurons consulted their tutelar spirits to ascertain whether the time was propitious.[5] This kind of thing is world-wide. In the Luang Sermata Islands enquiries are made as to whether the new house will be unlucky. In the Babar Islands, before entering a new house, offerings are thrown inside, that the spirit, *Orlou*, may not make the inmates ill.[6] In the Sandwich Islands, before the owner entered a new house, the priest performed ceremonies and slept in it, to prevent evil spirits resorting thereto, and to secure the inmates from the effects of incantation.[7] A similar practice is found in Persia and China.[8] Amongst the Nicobarese sorcerers are employed to drive away evil spirits from the site selected for the building of a house. When a new boat is launched, a fire is lighted round it to expel the evil spirits.[9] Similarly, when an interval has elapsed,

[1] W. H. Brett, *The Indian Tribes of Guiana*, 363.
[2] D. Leslie, *Among the Zulus and Amatongas*, 197.
[3] im Thurn, *op. cit.* 380.
[4] W. Ellis, *Polynesian Researches*, i. 350.
[5] Featherman, *op. cit.* iii. 54.
[6] Riedel, *op. cit.* 318, 343.
[7] W. Ellis, *A Tour in Hawaii*, 295; *Polynesian Researches*, iv. 322.
[8] Pinkerton's *Voyages and Travels*, ix. 260; Doolittle, *op. cit.* ii. 325.
[9] Featherman, *op. cit.* ii. 250.

dwelling-houses become dangerous. Thus the Bashkirs, on returning from their nomadic life of the summer to their winter-quarters, approach these dwellings with reluctance, believing that *Sheitan* has taken up his abode there. The women therefore are sent forward first, armed with sticks, with which they strike the doors, uttering curses; when they have made their round, the men ride forward at full speed, with terrific shouts, to banish the dreaded demon from his hiding-place.[1] We may also compare the common belief that danger attaches to the first of any fruits or meats, as in the ceremony of first-fruits amongst the Kaffirs[2] and many other peoples, such "holiness" as attaches thereto being undistinguished from any kind of potential danger. Again, there is an almost universal belief that sickness and death are unnatural and abnormal. Being strange conditions of which the savage cannot solve the mystery, he often attributes them to the influence of evil spirits. Amongst the Zulus no one is believed to die a natural death except in battle or a row.[3] Among most Congo tribes death is seldom regarded in the light of a natural event.[4] Amongst the Dieri and neighbouring tribes of South Australia, "no native contracts a disease or complaint from natural causes; the disease is supposed to be caused by some enemy." In any serious case, the Koonkies or doctors are called in, to beat "the devil" out of the camp. "This is done by the stuffed tail of a kangaroo, by beating the ground in and out of the camp, chasing him away for some distance."[5] The Kurnai could not conceive of death by disease. It was regarded as due to the magical

[1] A. Erman, *Reise um die Erde*, i. 103.
[2] Shooter, *op. cit.* 25, 27.
[3] Leslie, *op. cit.* 48.
[4] H. Ward, in *Journ. Anthrop. Inst.* xxiv. 287.
[5] S. Gason, in *Journ. Anthrop. Inst.* xxiv. 170.

influence of enemies or evil spirits. Death, according to their ideas, could only occur through accident, open violence, or secret magic.[1] Amongst the tribes of Central Australia "no such thing as natural death is realised by the native; a man who dies has of necessity been killed by some other man, or perhaps even by a woman, and sooner or later that man or woman will be attacked. However old or decrepit a man or woman may be when death takes place, it is at once supposed that it has been brought about by the magic influence of some enemy."[2] All deaths, sicknesses, and calamities are attributed by the Andamanese to evil spirits.[3] The Navajos ascribe death to *Chinde*, "the devil," who remains in the vicinity of the dead. Those who perform the burial protect themselves from the evil influence by smearing their naked bodies with tar.[4] Death has always been a mystery, and it is no wonder that savage and barbarous peoples should have regarded it as an abnormal event. This conception is illustrated by the numerous myths invented to explain the abnormality of death. An interesting case, repeating the idea of "death and his brother sleep," is the myth of the Yaos and Wayisa of East Central Africa. They say that death is largely caused by wizards; it was originally brought into the world by a woman, who taught two men to go to sleep. One day, while they slumbered, she held the nostrils of one of them, till his breath ceased and he died.[5] Sickness, in a lesser degree, is also mysterious. With such unusual states, as is generally the case, we find connected evil spirits or taboo or both, and may trace these predications back to man's

[1] Fison and Howitt, *op. cit.* 251, 258. [2] Spencer and Gillen, *op. cit.* 48, 476.

[3] E. H. Man, in *Journ. Anthrop. Inst.* xi. 288, 289.

[4] *First Report of the Bureau of Ethnology* (Washington), 123.

[5] J. Macdonald, in *Journ. Anthrop. Inst.* xxii. 111, 112.

conceptions of what is unusual and not understood, in combination with his instinctive desire for life, health, and strength. All illness and bodily evil in British Guiana is the work of spirits, occasionally supposed to act in human form, but generally not, "therefore disease is more common than assault by bodily foes."[1] Amongst the Basutos sickness is attributed to ill-wishers who bewitch one.[2] In the last examples, we see how human and supernatural agencies may meet.

Again, in the case of normal functions, which are unusual in so far as they are periodic, it is natural that danger from spiritual agencies should be thought of chiefly when the crisis is worse than usual. Thus in the Aru Islands it is at difficult labour that means are taken against evil spirits, for instance, the banging of drums; so in the island Wetar and the Ceramlaut Archipelago.[3] If labour is difficult, the Chinese suppose it is due to an evil spirit that prevents the child's appearance;[4] and in the Philippines, when the birth is delayed, witches are supposed to be responsible, and are driven away by exploding gunpowder from a mortar improvised out of a bamboo.[5] If the new-born child howls, the Babar natives attribute it to the influence of an evil spirit, and food is spread for it outside the house.[6] This case is somewhat surprising, but perhaps it is excessive squalling that is referred to. More naturally, if a Chinese child will not suck nor cry and appears lifeless, the belief is that it is exposed to evil influences.[7]

The Andamanese and Maoris ascribe internal pains to evil spirits; and amongst the latter people, when a

[1] im Thurn, *op. cit.* 366.
[2] Casalis, *op. cit.* 277.
[3] Riedel, *op. cit.* 265, 449, 175.
[4] Doolittle, *op. cit.* i. 118.
[5] Bowring, *op. cit.* 144.
[6] Riedel, *op. cit.* 354.
[7] Doolittle, *op. cit.* i. 120.

chief is in pain, he is thereby accounted *tapu*.[1] Also when a Maori warrior was afraid, the *tohunga* invoked a friendly spirit to repulse the evil spirit causing the fear.[2] It will be remembered that the Maori *tapu* implies that one is under the influence of the ancestral spirits; and the apparent inconsistency, that a Maori gentleman, who is always *tapu*, can become *tapu* at various crises, and, as will be seen later, can contract such *tapu* as to injure his inherent *tapu*, is quite natural and needs no explanation. Further, the Battas attribute not only diseases, but such phenomena as anger, to evil spirits, which also force men to do murder and commit crimes.[3] Such states as idiocy, hysteria, and various forms of neurosis are, as is well known, explained by savages in the same way. We still have the phrase "an inspired idiot." Intoxication is similarly explained, also such apparently irregular conditions as ecstasy and enthusiasm. In the same way, popular thought and language prove this to be so with love, no less than with other periodic emotional crises. Both the Yoruba and the Ewe-speaking peoples attribute sexual desire to possession by the god of love (*Legba*).[4] It is very natural that savage ignorance should ascribe to possession by supernatural influences those strong impulses which carry a man away and render him for the moment a blind automaton. The very word "passion" preserves the primitive idea that such states are due to external agency; yet these facts limit still further primitive man's knowledge of himself.

Again, if we survey the whole of human life and human relations, we find that all states in which there

[1] Man, *op. cit.* xl. 84; Shortland, *op. cit.* 82; W. Yate, *New Zealand*, 104.

[2] Shortland, *Southern Districts of New Zealand*, 67, 68.

[3] F. Junghuhn, *Die Battaländer auf Sumatra*, ii, 156.

[4] A. B. Ellis, *The Ewe-speaking Peoples of West Africa*, 41.

is danger to be apprehended or something unusual or unusally important to be done or suffered are taboo. Every one is taboo in time of war, at the arrival of strangers, at the planting of the new seed, and at other periodic performances. Dr. Frazer has given examples of these. We shall also find later that occasions, where the performance of bodily functions is in question, are frequently taboo, and practically always when the functions are sexual or nutritive. We have also seen that even emotional states, such as pain, anger, fear, and love, which are apparently so abnormal, are ascribed to supernatural agencies and are taboo states; and at last the remarkable fact becomes clear, that in primitive thought, most of what a man or woman does is actually, and all is potentially taboo. It is not merely the incarnate god, the king and the priest, the sick and the mourner, the warrior and hunter, the boy and girl at puberty, the infant, the mother in child-bed, and the like, that are in this religious condition, but all human beings, as such, are potentially taboo, dangerous and in danger, all alike are, as it were, kings and priests. This tendency arising from subjective conceptions as to the danger of acts and things unfamiliar, out of the routine, or not understood, grows out of man's egoistic sensibility, that animal form of the instinct of self-preservation and the will to live, which causes the individual to insulate himself from potential danger. Such danger centres in particular upon the organs of sense and function, the mysterious and complex working of which produces in the thinking organism a subconscious impulse, in the ratio of their importance and complexity, towards their preservation, and thereby the preservation of the individual himself. This subconscious impulse develops into ideas, which are religious in their character, and in their turn suggest the various methods of taboo. These ideas are religious in their content of "spiritual," as not distinguished from material danger, and these dangers are conceived of materially and dealt with as such. In all these facts, also, the identity of the taboo state and the dangerous condition caused by evil spirits can be seen between the lines. Turning now to the other side of these states, in which the person concerned is dangerous as well as in danger, we are told by Messrs. Spencer and Gillen that they "were constantly impressed with the idea that one black fellow will often tell you that he can and does do something magical, whilst all the time he is perfectly well aware that he cannot, and yet firmly believes that some other man can really do it. In order that his fellows may not be considered in this respect as superior to himself, he is obliged to resort to what is really a *fraud*; but in course of time he may even come to lose sight of the fact that it is a fraud which he is practising upon himself and his fellows."[1] In fact amongst savages it is not only professional sorcerers who possess magic power and influence, every man has this more or less. For instance, most of the old men amongst Australian natives are sorcerers, and a sorcerer "is able both to cause and cure, disease, rain, wind, thunder, and hail."[2]

Thus, all persons are potentially dangerous to others, as well as potentially in danger, in virtue simply of the distinction between a man and his fellows. The individual *quâ* individual is potentially in danger from other individuals and dangerous to them. This egoistic sensibility and caution is intensified when things or

[1] Spencer and Gillen, *op. cit.* 130.

[2] E. J. Eyre, *Journals of Expeditions of Discovery into Central Australia*, ii. 359, 384.

persons present some unexplained strangeness, and we may conclude that the mere fact of sexual differentiation is enough to form the basis of a similar religious caution between men and women. In the second place, functional crises are accentuated forms of this sexual differentiation, and their apparent abnormality causes uneasiness to the individual and to the other sex also. The following case sums up the argument; the Indians of Costa Rica believe that the ceremonial "uncleanness" called *bu-ku-ru* is very virulent. It is most dangerous from a woman in her first pregnancy. "She infects the whole neighbourhood, and all deaths are laid at her door." Also, "a place which has not been visited for a long time, or one approached for the first time, is infected with *bu-ku-ru*."[1] Here then we have an ultimate origin for the religious precautions used not only at birth, puberty, and pregnancy, but at the entering upon a new relation, and that a sexual relation, such as marriage.

The whole series of phenomena, as may especially be seen in the ideas and practices concerned with things new and unusual, with the handselling of such, and with the entering upon strange or important acts and functions, illustrates well a characteristic of early man in the animistic stage, which may be described as diffidence, lack of initiative and incapacity for responsibility, and is the general result of ignorance and inexperience. This mental and moral habit has, as the material on which it works, the very ignorance with which it is associated in origin. Later, this interesting stage of human development will be shown to have developed moral ideas which have profoundly influenced the progress of man.

[1] W. M. Gabb, *op. cit.* 504.

CHAPTER III

"IN the beginning, when Twashtri came to the creation of woman, he found that he had exhausted his materials in the making of man, and that no solid elements were left. In this dilemma, after profound meditation, he did as follows. He took the rotundity of the moon, and the curves of creepers, and the clinging of tendrils, and the trembling of grass, and the slenderness of the reed, and the bloom of flowers, and the lightness of leaves, and the tapering of the elephant's trunk, and the glances of deer, and the clustering of rows of bees, and the joyous gaiety of sunbeams, and the weeping of clouds, and the fickleness of the winds, and the timidity of the hare, and the vanity of the peacock, and the softness of the parrot's bosom, and the hardness of adamant, and the sweetness of honey, and the cruelty of the tiger, and the warm glow of fire, and the coldness of snow, and the chattering of jays, and the cooing of the *kókila*, and the hypocrisy of the crane, and the fidelity of the *chakrawáka*, and compounding all these together, he made woman and gave her to man. But after one week, man came to him and said: Lord, this creature that you have given me makes my life miserable. She chatters incessantly and teases me beyond endurance, never leaving me alone; and she requires incessant attention, and takes all my time up, and cries about nothing, and is always idle; and so I have come to give her back again, as I cannot live with her. So Twashtri said: Very well; and he took her back. Then after another week, man came again to him and said: Lord, I find that my life is very lonely, since I gave you back that creature. I remember how she used to dance and sing to me, and look at me out of the corner of her eye, and play with me, and cling to me; and her laughter was music, and she was beautiful to look at, and soft to touch; so give her back to me again. So Twashtri said: Very well; and gave her back again. Then after only three days, man came back to him again and said: Lord, I know not how it is; but after all I have come to the conclusion that she is more of a trouble than a pleasure to me; so please take her back again. But Twashtri said: Out on you! Be off! I will have no more of this. You must manage how you can. Then man said: But I cannot live with her. And Twashtri replied: Neither could you live without her. And he turned his back on man, and went on with his work. Then man said: What is to be done? for I cannot live either with her or without her."[1]

This extract from a beautiful Sanscrit story illustrates a conception of the relations of man and woman, which often recurs in literature. The same conception, due ultimately to that difference of sex and of sexual characters which renders mutual sympathy and understanding more or less difficult, is characteristic of mankind in all periods and stages of culture. Woman is one of the last things to be understood by man; though the complement of man and his partner in health and sickness, poverty and wealth, woman is different from man, and this difference has had the same religious results as have attended other things which

[1] *A Digit of the Moon*, trans. by F. W. Bain, 13-15.

man does not understand. The same is true of woman's attitude to man. In the history of the sexes there have been always at work the two complementary physical forces of attraction and repulsion; man and woman may be regarded, and not fancifully, as the highest sphere in which this law of physics operates; in love the two sexes are drawn to each other by an irresistible sympathy, while in other circumstances there is more or less of segregation, due to and enforced by human ideas of human relations.

The remarkable facts which follow show the primitive theory and practice of this separation of the sexes. Both in origin and results the phenomena are those of Taboo, and hence I have applied to these facts the specific term of Sexual Taboo. At first sight this early stage of the relations of men and women may cause surprise, but when one realises the continuity of human ideas, and analyses one's own consciousness, one may find there in potentiality, if not actualised by prejudice, the same conception, though perhaps emptied of its religious content.

In Nukahiva if a woman happens to sit upon or even pass near an object which has become *tabu* by contact with a man, it can never be used again, and she is put to death.[1] In Tahiti a woman had to respect those places frequented by men, their weapons and fishing implements; the head of a husband or father was *sacred* from the touch of woman, nor might a wife or daughter touch any object that had been in contact with these *tabued* heads, or step over them when their owners were asleep.[2] In the Solomon Islands a man will never pass under a tree fallen across the path, because a woman may have stepped over it before him.[3] In Siam it is

[1] D'Urville, *Voyage pittoresque autour du Monde*, i. 505.
[2] C. Letourneau, *Sociologie*, 173.
[3] H. B. Guppy, *The Solomon Islands*, i. 4.

considered unlucky to pass under women's clothes hung out to dry.[1] It is *degrading* to a Melanesian chief to go where women may be above his head; boys also are forbidden to go underneath the women's bed-place.[2] Amongst the Karens of Burmah going under a house when there are females within is avoided; and in Burmah generally it is thought an *indignity* to have a woman above the head; to prevent which the houses are never built with more than one storey.[3] This explanation of an architectural peculiarity is doubtless *ex post facto*. Amongst the people of Rajmahal, if a man be detected by a woman sitting on her cot and she complains of the impropriety, he pays her a fowl as fine, which she returns; on the other hand, if a man detects a woman sitting on his cot, he kills the fowl which she produces in answer to his complaint, and sprinkles the blood on the cot to purify it, after which she is pardoned.[4] In Cambodia a wife may never use the pillow or mattress of her husband, because "she would hurt his happiness thereby."[5] In Siam the wife has a lower pillow "to remind her of her inferiority."[6] This reason is possibly late. Amongst the Barea man and wife seldom share the same bed, the reason they give is, that if they sleep together the breath of the wife will render her husband weak.[7] Amongst the Lapps no grown woman may touch the hinder part of the house, which is sacred to the sun.[8] No woman

[1] Bastian, *op. cit.* iii. 230.

[2] R. H. Codrington, *The Melanesians*, 233.

[3] *Journal of the American Oriental Society*, iv. 312; Bastian, *op. cit.* ii. 150.

[4] Colebrooke in *Asiatick Researches*, iv. 88.

[5] E. Aymonier, *Les coutumes et croyances superstitieuses des Cambodgiens*, 162. The Cambodians also say that a used pillow should be washed at once, or taken care of, for sorcery is easily performed by its means against one who has used it.

[6] Pinkerton, *op. cit.* ix. 585.

[7] W. Munzinger, *Ostafrikanische Studien*, 526.

[8] Ploss, *Das Kind*, ii. 435.

may enter the house of a Maori chief.[1] Amongst the Kaffas of East Africa husband and wife see each other only at night, never meeting during the day. She is secluded in the interior portion of the house, while he occupies the remainder. "A public resort is also set apart for the husband, where no woman is permitted to appear. A penalty of three years' imprisonment attaches to an infringement of this rule."[2] Observers have noted "the haughty contempt" shown by Zulus for their wives. Men and women rarely are seen together; if a man and his wife are going to the same place, they do not walk together.[3] In some Redskin tribes and amongst the Indians of California a man never enters his wife's wigwam except under cover of the darkness; and the men's club-house may never be entered by women.[4] The Bedouin tent is divided into two compartments for the men and women respectively. No man of good reputation will enter the women's part of the tent or even be seen in its shadow.[5] In Nukahiva the houses of important men are not accessible to their own wives, who live in separate huts.[6] Amongst the Samoyeds and Ostyaks a wife may not tread in any part of the tent except her own corner; after pitching the tent she must fumigate it before the men enter.[7] In Fiji husbands are as frequently away from their wives as with them; it is not, in Fijian society, thought well for a man to sleep regularly at home.[8] Another account

[1] R. Taylor, *Te Ika a Maui*, 165; Tregear, in *Journ. Anthrop. Inst.* xix. 118; *id. Maori Comparative Dictionary*, s.v. *Kokohitu*; Shortland, *Maori Religion*, 101; *id. Southern Districts of New Zealand*, 295.

[2] J. L. Krapf, *Eighteen Years in Eastern Africa*, 58.

[3] Shooter, *op. cit.* 81, 82.

[4] Lafitau, *Mœurs des sauvages Amériquains*, i. 576; S. Powers, *The Tribes of California*, 24.

[5] Featherman, *op. cit.* v. 357.

[6] D'Urville, *op. cit.* i. 504.

[7] J. Georgi, *Les nations Samoyèdes*, 15, 137.

[8] T. Williams, *Fiji and the Fijians*, i. 137.

states that "it is quite against Fijian ideas of delicacy that a man ever remains under the same roof with his wife or wives at night." He may not take his night's repose anywhere except at one of the public *bures* of his town or village. The women and girls sleep at home. "*Rendezvous* between husband and wife are arranged in the depths of the forest, unknown to any but the two." All the male population, married and unmarried, sleep at the *bures*, or club-houses, of which there are generally two in each village. Boys till of age have a special one.[1] From another account we learn that women are not allowed to enter a *bure*, which is also used as a lounge by the chiefs.[2] In New Caledonia a peculiarity of conjugal life is that men and women do not sleep under the same roof. The wife lives and sleeps by herself in a shed near the house. "You rarely see the men and women talking or sitting together. The women seem perfectly content with the companionship of their own sex. The men, who loiter about with spears in a most lazy fashion, are seldom seen in the society of the opposite sex.[3] No Hindu female may enter the men's apartments.[4] In New Guinea the women sleep in houses apart, near those of their male relatives. The men assemble for conversation and meals in the *marea*, a large reception-house, which women may not enter.[5] Amongst the Nubians each family has two dwelling-houses, one for the males, the other for the females.[6] In the Sandwich Islands there were six houses connected with every great establishment; one for worship, one for the men to eat in,

[1] B. Seeman, *Viti*, 110, 191.
[2] Wilkes, *U.S. Exploring Expedition*, iii. 97, 352.
[3] J. Garnier, *Océanie*, 186; J. W. Anderson, *Fiji and New Caledonia*, 232.
[4] Ploss, *Das Kind*, ii. 441.
[5] D'Albertis, *op. cit.* i. 282, 320, 390, 391.
[6] Waitz-Gerland, *op. cit.* ii. 485.

another for the women, a dormitory, a house for *kapa*-beating, and one where at certain intervals the women might live in seclusion.[1] In the Caroline Islands a chief's establishment has one house for the women, a second for eating, and a third for sleeping.[2] In the Admiralty Islands there is a house reserved in each village for the use of women, both married and single, while the single men live together in a separate building.[3] The Shastika Indians of California have a town-lodge for men and another for women. Other Californian tribes possess the first institution; the women may not enter the men's lodges.[4] The centre of Bororo life is the *Baitó*, the men's house, where all the men really live; the family huts are nothing more than a residence for the women and children. Amongst the Bakairi and the Schingú tribes generally, women may never enter the men's club-house, where the men spend most of their time.[5] In the Solomon Islands women may not enter the men's *tambu* house, nor even cross the beach in front of it.[6] In Ceram women are forbidden to enter the men's club-house.[7] In New Britain there are two large houses in each village, one for men, the other for women: neither sex may enter the house of the other.[8] In the Marquesas Islands the *ti* where the men congregate and spend most of their time is taboo to women, and protected by the penalty of death from the imaginary pollution of a woman's presence; the chiefs never trouble about any domestic affairs.[9] In the Pelew Islands there is "a remarkable

[1] J. J. Jarves, *The Hawaiian or Sandwich Islands*, 208.
[2] C. E. Meinicke, *Die Inseln des Stillen Oceans*, ii. 370.
[3] *Journ. Anthrop. Inst.* vi. 413. [4] Powers, *op. cit.* 244, 24.
[5] K. von den Steinen, *Unter den Naturvölkern Zentral-Brasiliens*, 480.
[6] Guppy, *op. cit.* i. 67. [7] Riedel, *op. cit.* 110.
[8] W. Powell, *Wanderings in a Wild Country*, 84.
[9] Melville, *op. cit.* 101, 210.

separation of the sexes." Men and women hardly live together, and family life is impossible. The segregation is political as well as social.[1] In the Society and Sandwich Islands the female sex was isolated and humiliated by *tabu*, and in their domestic life the women lived almost entirely by themselves.[2] In Uripiv (New Hebrides) there is a curious segregation of the sexes, beginning, at least in one respect, soon after a boy is born.[3] In Rapa (Tubuai Islands) all men are *tabu* to women.[4] In Seoul, the capital of Corea, "they have a curious curfew law called *pem-ya*. A large bell is tolled at about 8 P.M. and 3 A.M. daily, and between these hours only are women supposed to appear in the streets. In the old days men found in the streets during the hours allotted to women were severely punished, but the rule has been greatly relaxed of late years." "Family life, as we have it, is utterly unknown in Corea."[5] The Ojebway, Peter Jones, thus writes of his own people: "I have scarcely ever seen anything like social intercourse between husband and wife, and it is remarkable that the women say little in the presence of the men."[6] In Senegambia the negro women live by themselves, rarely with their husbands, and their sex is virtually a clique.[7] In Bali to speak *tête-à-tête* with a woman is absolutely forbidden.[8] In Egypt a man never converses with his wife, and in the tomb they are separated by a wall, though males and females are not usually buried in the same vault.[9]

[1] J. S. Kubary, *Journal des Museum Godeffroy*, iv. 43, 53; *id. Die socialen Einrichtungen der Pelauer*, 33, 148; Meinicke, *op. cit.* ii. 380; K. Semper, *Die Palau Inseln*, 318, 319, 366.

[2] W. Ellis, *op. cit.* i. 129; *id. Tour Through Hawaii*, 369.

[3] B. T. Somerville, in *Journ. Anthrop. Inst.* xxiii. 4.

[4] Letourneau, *op. cit.* 174.

[5] H. S. Saunderson, in *Journ. Anthrop. Inst.* xxiv. 305, 306.

[6] P. Jones, *History of the Ojebway Indians*, 60.

[7] L. J. B. Bérenger-Féraud, *Les peuplades de la Sénégambie*, 373.

[8] Junghuhn, *op. cit.* ii. 340.

[9] Ploss, *op. cit.* ii. 455.

Some cases of this complementary result, solidarity of sex, have been noticed, and others will occur in various connections. It is practically universal in all stages of culture, even the highest. Amongst the Bedouins of Libya women associate for the most part with their own sex only.[1] In Morocco women are by no means reserved when by themselves, nor do they seek to cover their faces.[2] Amongst the Gauchos of Uruguay women show a marked tendency to huddle together.[3] Sexual solidarity is well brought out in the following. Amongst the extinct Tasmanians, if a wife was struck by her husband, the whole female population would come out and bring the "rattle of their tongues to bear upon the brute."[4] When ill-treated, the Kaffir wife can claim an asylum with her father, till her husband has made atonement. "Nor would many European husbands like to be subjected to the usual discipline on such occasions. The offending husband must go in person to ask for his wife. He is instantly surrounded by the women of the place, who cover him at once with reproaches and blows. Their nails and fists may be used with impunity, for it is the day of female vengeance, and the belaboured delinquent is not allowed to resist. He is not permitted to see his wife, but is sent home, with an intimation of what cattle are expected from him, which he must send before he can demand his wife again."[5] Amongst the Kunama the wife has an agent who protects her against her husband, and fines him for ill-treatment. She possesses considerable authority in the house, and is on equal

[1] Featherman, *op. cit.* v. 645.
[2] A. Leared, *Morocco and the Moors*, 119.
[3] D. Christison, in *Journ. Anthrop. Inst.* xi. 43.
[4] J. Bonwick, *Daily Life and Origin of the Tasmanians*, 73.
[5] Munzinger, *op. cit.* 53.

terms with her husband.[1] Amongst the Beni-Amer women enjoy considerable independence. To obtain marital privileges, the husband has to make his wife a present of value. He must do the same for every harsh word he uses, and is often kept a whole night out of doors in the rain, until he pays. The women have a strong *esprit de corps*; when a wife is ill-treated the other women come in to help her; it goes without saying that the husband is always in the wrong. The women express much contempt for the men, and it is considered disgraceful in a woman to show love for her husband.[2]

The first of these examples shows the length to which religious ideas may carry this segregation, the last is one of many cases in which the solidarity of sex is seen. This is well brought out in examples of club-life, and there is here a close parallel to be found, not merely humorous, in the institution and etiquette of the modern club. The same biological tendency is behind both the modern and the primitive institution, though the later one is no longer supported by religious ideas. Again, sexual differentiation often develops into real antagonism. The attempts of the Indians of California to keep their women in check show how the latter were struggling up to equality.[3] An account of the Hottentots represents that the women, though ill-treated and forced to do harder work, can defend themselves and avenge their wrongs.[4] A Poul (Fulah) governs his wives by force, but they recoup themselves when they get the chance.[5] The Indian of Brazil has a wholesome dread of his wives, and "follows the

[1] Munzinger, *op. cit.* 387.
[2] *Id.* 324, 325.
[3] Powers, *op. cit.* 406.
[4] Waitz-Gerland, *op. cit.* ii. 341.
[5] *Histoire universelle des voyages*, xxviii. 439.

maxim of *laissez faire* with regard to their intrigues."[1] Amongst the Wataveita fire-making is not revealed to women, "because," say the men, "they would then become our masters."[2] The Miris will not allow their women to eat tiger's flesh, lest it should make them too strong-minded.[3] The Fuegians celebrate a festival, *Kina*, in commemoration of their revolt against the women, "who formerly had the authority, and possessed the secrets of sorcery."[4] In the Dieri tribe of South Australia men threaten their wives, should they do anything wrong, with the "bone," the instrument of sorcery, which, when pointed at the victim, causes death; "this produces such dread among the women, that mostly instead of having a salutary effect, it causes them to hate their husbands."[5] The Pomo Indians of California "find it very difficult to maintain authority over their women." A husband often terrifies his wife into submission by personating an ogre; after this she is usually tractable for some days.[6] Amongst the Tatu Indians of California, the men have a secret society, which gives periodic dramatic performances, with the object of keeping the women in order. The chief actor, disguised as a devil, charges about among the assembled squaws.[7] The Gualala and Patwin Indians have similar dances, performed by the assembled men, to show the women the necessity of obedience.[8] In Africa the anxious attempts of the men to keep the women down have been noted.[9] The adult males in South Guinea have a secret association, *Nda*, whose object is to keep the women, children, and slaves in

[1] Ploss u. Bartels, *Das Weib*, ii. 424.
[2] *Journ. Anthrop. Inst.* xv. 10.
[3] E. T. Dalton, *Ethnology of Bengal*, 33.
[4] Giraud-Teulon, *Les origines du mariage et de la famille*, 148.
[5] *Native Tribes of South Australia*, 276.
[6] Powers, *op. cit.* 154, 161.
[7] *Id.* 141.
[8] *Id.* 193, 224.
[9] Bastian, *San Salvador*, 182.

order.[1] The *Mumbo-Jumbo* of the Mandingos is well known. The same performer, who represents Mumbo-Jumbo, has also the duty of keeping the sexes apart for the forty days after circumcision.[2] Other instances of associations to keep the women in subjection are the *Egbo* in Calabar, *Oro* in Yoruba, the *Purro*, *Semo*, and varieties of *Egbo* on the west coast, the *Bundu* amongst the Bullamers.[3] Women in their turn form similar associations amongst themselves, in which they discuss their wrongs and form plans of revenge. Mpongwe women have an institution of this kind, which is really feared by the men.[4] Similarly amongst the Bakalais and other African tribes.[5]

The way in which each sex is self-centred is also illustrated by the natural practice that women worship female, and men male deities. This needs no illustration, but a very instructive case may be quoted, which comes from ancient Roman life. When husband and wife quarrelled, they visited the shrine of the goddess *Viriplaca* on the Palatine. After opening their hearts in confession, they would return in harmony. This "appeaser of the male sex" was regarded as *domesticæ pacis custos*.[6] Similarly, Bakalai women have a tutelar spirit, which protects them against their male enemies and avenges their wrongs.[7] According to the Greenlanders, the moon is a male and the sun a female spirit; the former rejoices in the death of women, while the latter has her revenge in the death of men. All males, therefore, keep within doors during an eclipse of the

[1] J. L. Wilson, *Western Africa*, 396.

[2] Waitz-Gerland, *op. cit.* ii. 118.

[3] Bastian, *op. cit.* 179; Waitz-Gerland, *op. cit.* ii. 118; *Journ. Anthrop. Inst.* vi. 121.

[4] Bastian, *op. cit.* 180; *id. Der Mensch in der Geschichte*, iii. 294; *id. Loango Küste*, ii. 24; J. L. Wilson, *op. cit.* 397.

[5] P. B. Du Chaillu, *Equatorial Africa*, 296.

[6] Valerius Maximus, ii. 16.

[7] Du Chaillu, *op. cit. loc. cit.*

sun, and all females during an eclipse of the moon.[1] In the Pelew Islands the *kalids* of men are quiet and gentlemanly; it is those of women that make disturbances, and inflict disease and death on members of the family.[2] The same hostility makes use of the system of sex-totems. In the Port Lincoln tribe a small kind of lizard, the male of which is called *Ibirri*, and the female *Waka*, is said to have divided the sexes in the human species, "an event which would appear not to be much approved of by the natives, since either sex has a mortal hatred against the opposite sex of these little animals, the men always destroying the *Waka* and the women the *Ibirri*."[3] In the Wotjobaluk tribe it is believed that the "life of *Ngunungunut* (the bat) is the life of a man, and the life of *Yartatgurk* (the nightjar) is the life of a woman"; when either is killed, a man or woman dies. Should one of these animals be killed, every man or every woman fears that he or she may be the victim; and this gives rise to numerous fights. "In these fights, men on one side, and women on the other, it was not at all certain who would be victorious, for at times the women gave the men a severe drubbing with their yam-sticks, while often the women were injured or killed by spears."[4] In some Victorian tribes the bat is the man's animal, and they "protect it against injury, even to the half-killing of their wives for its sake." The goatsucker belongs to the women, who protect it jealously. "If a man kills one, they are as much enraged as if it was one of their children, and will strike him with their long poles." The *mantis* also belongs to the men and no woman dares kill it.[5]

[1] Crans, *Greenland*, i. 213.

[2] J. S. Kubary in Bastian's *Allerlei aus Volks- und Menschenkunde*, i. 22.

[3] *Native Tribes of South Australia*, 241.

[4] *Journ. Anthrop. Inst.* xviii. 58.

[5] Dawson, *Australian Aborigines*, 53.

Such segregation of the sexes has influenced language. In Madagascar there are terms proper for a woman to use to her own sex, others for women to men, and for men to women.[1] Amongst the Guaycurus the women have many words and phrases peculiar to themselves, and never employed by men; the reason being that the women are "barred" by the men.[2] So in Surinam.[3] The proper Fijian term for a newly circumcised boy is *teve*, which may not be uttered when women are present, in which case the word *kula* is used; and there are many words in the language which it is *tambu* to utter in female society.[4] In Micronesia many words are tabooed for men when conversing with women.[5] In Japan female writing has quite a different syntax and many peculiar idioms; the Japanese alphabet possesses two sets of characters, *katakana* for the use of men, and *hiragana* for women.[6] In Fiji, again, women make their salutations in different words from those of the men.[7] In the language of the Abipones some words vary according to sex.[8] The island Caribs have two distinct vocabularies, one used by men and by women when speaking to men, the other used by women when speaking to each other, and by men when repeating in *oratio obliqua* some saying of the women. Their councils of war are held in a secret dialect or jargon, in which the women are never initiated.[9] It has been suggested that this inconvenient custom, according to which a Carib needs to know, like Ennius, three languages, is due to

[1] J. Sibree in *Journ. Anthrop. Inst.* ix. 48.

[2] Waitz-Gerland, *op. cit.* iii. 472.

[3] Ploss u. Bartels, *op. cit.* i. 110.

[4] Williams, *op. cit.* i. 167; Anderson, *op. cit.* 89.

[5] Waitz-Gerland, *op. cit.* v. 147.

[6] I. Bird, *Unbeaten Tracks in Japan*, i. 133; Siebold, *Manners and Customs of the Japanese*, i. 299.

[7] Wilkes, *op. cit.* iii. 326.

[8] Dobrizhoffer, *op. cit.* ii. 197.

[9] im Thurn, *op. cit.* 186; Brett, *op. cit.* 131.

exogamy, husband and wife retaining the languages of their original tribes respectively. This explanation, however, does not account for the martial dialect, and has been refuted by Mr. im Thurn on other grounds.[1] Even in cases where this explanation may hold, this cause is not the ultimate origin of the custom, but merely carries on an existing practice. Thus in some tribes of Victoria, the marriage-system is organised exogamy, but the inconvenience of sexual taboos has led to the use of an artificial language or "turn-tongue."[2] Similar phenomena occur in all stages of culture, and in modern Europe sexual separation to some extent still influences popular language, women and men respectively using certain terms peculiar to each sex.

In connection with names, sexual taboo has developed a prohibition which has had a particular influence upon many languages. A Hindu wife is never allowed to mention the name of her husband. She generally speaks of him, therefore, as "the master" or "man of the house."[3] Amongst the Barea the wife may not utter her husband's name.[4] Amongst the Kirgiz the women may not utter the names of the male members of the household, to do so being "indecent."[5] A Zulu woman may not call her husband by his name, either when addressing him or when speaking of him to others; she must use the phrase "father of so-and-so." This particularly applies to the *i-gama* (real name). Further, the women may not use the interdicted words in their ordinary sense. Consequently they are obliged to alter words and phrases which contain the prohibited sounds. This has had considerable influence upon the language, and the women have a

[1] *Loc. cit.*
[2] Dawson, *op. cit.* 40.
[3] Ward, *The Hindoos*, ii. 337.
[4] Munzinger, *op. cit.* 526.
[5] Ploss u. Bartels, *op. cit.* i. 111.

large vocabulary of their own. Any woman transgressing the rule is accused of witchcraft by the "doctor," and punished with death. This prohibition on names belongs to the *hlonipa* system, and the altered vocabulary of the women, which is unintelligible to the men, is called *ukuteta kwabapzi*, "women's language."[1] In the Solomon Islands men show considerable reluctance to give the names of women, and when prevailed upon to do so, pronounce them in a low tone, as if it were not proper to speak of them to others.[2] In the Pelew Islands men are not allowed to speak openly of married women, nor to mention their names.[3] Amongst the Todas there is some delicacy in mentioning the names of women at all; they prefer to use the phrase "wife of so-and-so."[4] A Servian never speaks of his wife or daughter before men.[5] Amongst the Nishinams of California a husband never calls his wife by name on any account; should he do so she has the right to get a divorce. In this tribe no one can be induced to divulge his own name.[6] Dr. Frazer has explained this widespread reluctance[7]; the name is a vital part of a man, and often regarded as a sort of soul. Sexual taboo has used this idea to form a special duty as between men and women, especially husbands and wives. In one or two cases feelings of proprietary jealousy have doubtless had some influence, but as a rule the religious fears as to sexual relations have played the chief part in the prohibition.

[1] Callaway, *op. cit.* 316; Shooter, *op. cit.* 221, 222; Waitz-Gerland, *op. cit.* ii. 388.

[2] Guppy, *op. cit.* i. 47.

[3] J. S. Kubary in Bastian's *Allerlei aus Volks- und Menschenkunde*, i. 20; *id. Die socialen Einrichtungen der Pelauer*, 90.

[4] Marshall, *A Phrenologist amongst the Todas*, 73.

[5] Maxwell in *Folklore*, ii. 71.

[6] Powers, *op. cit.* 315.

[7] J. G. Frazer, *The Golden Bough*[2], i. 403 *sq.*

Evidence drawn from the respective occupations of the two sexes throws further light upon sexual taboo. Sexual differentiation in primary and secondary sexual characters necessitates some difference of occupation, and the religious ideas of primitive man have emphasised the biological separation.

Amongst the Dacotas custom and superstition ordain that the wife must carefully keep away from all that belongs to her husband's sphere of action.[1] The Bechuanas never allow women to touch their cattle, accordingly the men have to plough themselves.[2] So amongst the Kaffirs, "because of some superstition."[3] Amongst the Todas women may not approach the *tiriëri*, where the sacred cattle are kept, nor the sacred *palâls*.[4] In Guiana no women may go near the hut where *ourali* is made.[5] In the Marquesas Islands the use of canoes is prohibited to the female sex by *tabu*; the breaking of the rule is punished with death. Conversely, amongst the same people, *tapa*-making belongs exclusively to women; when they are making it for their own head-dresses it is *tabu* for men to touch it.[6] In Nicaragua all the marketing was done by women. A man might not enter the market or even see the proceedings, at the risk of a beating.[7] In New Caledonia it is considered *infra dig*. for the men to perform manual labour, at any rate in the neighbourhood of the settlement; such work is done by women only.[8] In Samoa, where the manufacture of cloth is allotted solely to the women, it is a degradation for a man to engage in any detail of the process.[9] In the Andaman Islands

[1] Waitz-Gerland, *op. cit.* iii. 100.
[2] *Journ. Anthrop. Inst.* x. 11.
[3] *Id.* xvi. 119.
[4] Marshall, *op. cit.* 137.
[5] im Thurn, *op. cit.* 311.
[6] Melville, *op. cit.* 13, 245.
[7] H. H. Bancroft, *Native Races of the Pacific States*, iii. 145.
[8] Anderson, *op. cit.* 231.
[9] W. T. Pritchard, *Polynesian Reminiscences*, 131.

the performance by men of duties supposed to belong to women only, is regarded as *infra dig.*[1] An Eskimo thinks it an indignity to row in an *umiak*, the large boat used by women. The different offices of husband and wife are also very clearly distinguished; for example, when he has brought his booty to land, it would be a stigma on his character if he so much as drew a seal ashore, and, generally, it is regarded as scandalous for a man to interfere with what is the work of women.[2] In British Guiana cooking is the province of the women; on one occasion when the men were perforce compelled to bake, they were only persuaded to do so with the utmost difficulty, and were ever after pointed at as old women.[3] Exactly the same feelings subsist in the highest civilisations.

The chief occupations of the male sex in those stages of culture with which we have principally to deal are hunting and war. The supreme importance of these occasions has been referred to above, and is expressed by such terms as the Polynesian *tabu*. These terms generally imply rules and precautions intended to secure the safety and success of the warrior or hunter, which form sometimes a sort of system of "training." Among these regulations the most constant is that which prohibits every kind of intercourse with the female sex. Thus in New Zealand a man who has any important business on hand, either in peace or war, is *tapu* and must keep from women. On a war party men are *tapu* to women, and may not go near their wives until the fighting is over.[4] In South Africa before and during an expedition men may have no

[1] Man, in *Journ. Anthrop. Inst.* xii. 286.

[2] F. Nansen, *The First Crossing of Greenland*, 192; Cranz, *op. cit.* i. 138, 154.

[3] im Thurn, *op. cit.* 256.

[4] Waitz-Gerland, *op. cit.* vi. 349; Tregear, in *Journ. Anthrop. Inst.* xix. 111.

connection with women.[1] Nootka Indians before war abstain from women.[2] In South-East New Guinea for some days before fighting the men are "sacred," *helega*, and are not allowed to see or approach any woman.[3] A Samoyed woman is credited with the power of spoiling the success of a hunt.[4] Amongst the Ostyaks harm befalls the hunter either from the ill-wishes of an enemy or the vicinity of a woman.[5] Amongst the Ahts whale-fishers must abstain from women.[6] A Motu man before hunting or fishing is *helega*; he may not see his wives, else he will have no success.[7] North American Indians both before and after war refrain "on religious grounds" from women. "Contact with females makes a warrior laughable, and injures, as they believe, his bravery for the future." Accordingly the chiefs of the Iroquois, for instance, remain as a rule unmarried until they have retired from active warfare.[8] The Damaras may not look upon a lying-in woman, else they will become weak and consequently be killed in battle.[9] In the Booandik tribe if men see women's blood they will not be able to fight.[10] In some South American tribes the presence of a woman lately confined makes the weapons of the men weak,[11] and the same belief extends amongst the Tschutsches to hunting and fishing implements.[12] Amongst the Zulus women may not go near the army when about to set out. Old women, however, who are past child-bearing may do so; for such "have become men" and "no longer

[1] Macdonald, in *Journ. Anthrop. Inst.* xix. 284.
[2] Bancroft, *op. cit.* i. 189.
[3] Chalmers, *Pioneering in New Guinea*, 65.
[4] Ploss u. Bartels, *op. cit.* ii. 433.
[5] Erman, *op. cit.* ii. 55.
[6] G. M. Sproat, *Scenes and Studies of Savage Life*, 227.
[7] Chalmers, *op. cit.* 186.
[8] Waitz-Gerland, *op. cit.* iii. 158, 159.
[9] *South African Folklore Journal*, ii. 63.
[10] J. Smith, *The Booandik Tribe*, 5.
[11] Ploss u. Bartels, *op. cit.* i. 26.
[12] *Id.*, *op. cit. loc. cit.*

observe the customs of *hlonipa* in relation to the men."[1]

Woman has generally been debarred more or less from the public life and civil rights of men. This is an extension of the biological difference of occupation, sometimes exaggerated into seclusion amongst polygamous races, and into somewhat of inferiority in martial and feudal societies. We may instance, to go no further, the Australian natives, the Fijians, who have religious grounds for the exclusion, the Sumatrans, the Hindus and Muhammadans, and most civilised nations.[2]

Again, women are more often than not, excluded from the religious worship of the community. The Arabs of Mecca will not allow women religious instruction, because "it would bring them too near their masters." According to some theologians of Islam, they have no place in Paradise.[3] The Ansayrees consider woman to be an inferior being without a soul, and "therefore compel her to do all the drudgery and exclude her from religious services."[4] In the Sandwich Islands women were not allowed to share in worship or festivals, and their touch "polluted" offerings to the gods.[5] If a Hindu woman touches an image, its divinity is thereby destroyed and it must be thrown away.[6] The Australians are very jealous lest women or strangers should intrude upon their sacred mysteries: it is death for a woman to look into a *bora*.[7] In Fiji women are kept away from all worship; dogs are excluded from some temples, women from all.[8] In the

[1] Callaway, *op. cit.* 441-43.

[2] Waitz-Gerland, *op. cit.* vi. 775, 627; Junghuhn, *op. cit.* ii. 57.

[3] Letourneau, *op. cit.* 180.

[4] Featherman, *op. cit.* v. 495.

[5] W. Ellis, *op. cit.* i. 129; Meinicke, *op. cit.* ii. 300.

[6] Ward, *op. cit.* ii. 13.

[7] Ridley, in *Journ. Anthrop. Inst.* ii. 271.

[8] Williams, *Fiji and the Fijians*, i. 232, 238; Waitz-Gerland, *op. cit.* vi. 627.

Gilbert and Marshall Islands and in Tonga, women are excluded from worship.[1] The women of the hill tribes near Rajmahal may not sacrifice nor appear at shrines, nor take part in religious festivals.[2] Amongst the Tschuwashes women dare not assist at sacrifices.[3] Bayeye women may not enter the place of sacrifice, which is the centre of tribal life.[4] Amongst the Gallas women may not go near the sacred *woda*-tree where worship is celebrated.[5] On the east of the Gulf of Papua women are not allowed to approach the temple.[6] In New Ireland women may not enter the temples.[7] In the Marquesas Islands the *hoolah-hoolah* ground, where festivals are held, is *tabu* to women, who are killed if they enter or even touch with their feet the shadow of the trees.[8]

Festivals and feasts, dances and entertainments of various character, are similarly often prohibited to women. In the Schingú tribes of Brazil women may not be present at the dances and feasts.[9] In New Britain women are not allowed to be present at the festivals, and when men are talking of things which women may not hear, the latter must leave the hut.[10] Amongst the Ahts women are never invited to the great feasts.[11] Amongst the Aleuts the women have dances from which the men are excluded; the men have their dances and exclude women. It is regarded as a fatal mischance to see on these occasions

[1] Meinicke, *op. cit.* ii. 338; Waitz-Gerland, *op. cit.* vi. 348.
[2] *Asiatick Researches*, iv. 51, 101.   [3] M. P. S. Pallas, *Voyages*, i. 135.
[4] *South African Folklore Journal*, ii. 36.
[5] W. C. Harris, *The Highlands of Æthiopia*, iii. 56.
[6] Chalmers and Gill, *New Guinea*, 140, 150.
[7] H. H. Remilly, *The Western Pacific and New Guinea*, 44.
[8] Melville, *op. cit.* 100.   [9] *Von den Steinen*, *op. cit.* 214.
[10] R. Parkinson, *Im Bismarck Archipelago*, 300; Romilly, *op. cit.* 29.
[11] G. M. Sproat, *op. cit.* 60.

one of the opposite sex.[1] Similar exclusion of women from what is regarded as not being their sphere is indeed very widely spread, and is of course found in the highest civilisations.

Where the prohibition is not needed to be carried out, the ideas which underlie these customs are satisfied by separating the sexes, as is the case still in many Catholic churches. Much in the same way the sexes never mingle together at the dances in the Hervey Islands.[2] Amongst the Nufoers of New Guinea men and women are separated on the same occasions;[3] and at entertainments of every kind amongst the Greenlanders men and women sit apart.[4]

In the next place we have to consider the very widely spread rule which insists upon the separation of the sexes, so far as is possible, at those functional crises with which sex is concerned. It is a special result of the ideas of sexual taboo applied to the most obvious sexual differences, primary sexual characters.

During pregnancy there is sometimes avoidance between the wife and the husband, as in the Caroline Islands, where men may not eat with their wives during pregnancy,[5] and in Fiji where a pregnant woman may not wait upon her husband.[6] Lenapé women as soon as they were pregnant separated from their husbands.[7] So also amongst the Coroados, Puris, and Coropos.[8]

At birth, though there are a few cases where the husband attends or assists his wife, the general rule throughout the peoples of the world is that only the

[1] W. H. Dall, *Alaska and its Resources*, 389; Bancroft, *op. cit.* iii. 145.
[2] W. W. Gill, *Life in the Southern Isles*, 65.
[3] Van Hasselt, in *Zeitschrift für Ethnologie*, viii. 186.
[4] Cranz, *op. cit.* i. 158.
[5] Waitz-Gerland, *op. cit.* vii. 106.
[6] Williams, *op. cit.* i. 137.
[7] Featherman, *op. cit.* iii. 107.
[8] Spix and Martius, *Travels in Brazil*, 247.

female sex may be present. Thus in Buru only old women may be in the room.[1] In South Africa the husband may not see his wife while she is lying-in.[2] Amongst the Basutos the father is separated from mother and child for four days, and may not see them until the medicine man has performed the religious ceremony of "absolution of the man and wife." If this were neglected, it is believed that he would die when he saw his wife.[3]

At puberty it is a widespread rule that neither sex may see the other. Amongst the Narrinyeri boys during initiation are called *narumbe*, *i.e.* sacred from the touch of women, and everything that they possess or obtain becomes *narumbe* also.[4] Amongst the Basutos no woman may come near the boys during initiation.[5] In New Ireland girls may not be seen by any males except relatives from puberty to marriage, during which time they are kept in cages.[6] No man may come near the girls of Ceram while they are being subjected to the ceremonies necessary at puberty.[7]

During menstruation generally, the separation of the sexes is most prominent, and is most widely spread. As examples, there are the Pueblo Indians, amongst whom women must separate from the men at menstruation, and before delivery, because if a man touch a woman at those times he will fall ill.[8] An Australian, finding that his wife had lain on his blanket during menstruation, killed her, and died of terror in a fortnight.[9]

[1] J. G. F. Riedel, *De sluik- en kroesharige rassen tusschen Selebes en Papua*, 24.

[2] Macdonald, in *Journ. Anthrop. Inst.* xix. 267.

[3] Grützner, in *Zeitschrift für Ethnologie* for 1877, 78.

[4] *Native Tribes of South Australia*, 69.

[5] K. Endemann, in *Zeitschrift für Ethnologie* for 1874, 37.

[6] B. Danks, in *Journ. Anthrop. Inst.* xviii. 284.

[7] Riedel, *op. cit.* 138.

[8] Bancroft, *op. cit.* i. 549.

[9] W. Ridley, in *Journ. Anthrop. Inst.* ii. 268.

Even at marriage there is a good deal of separation of the sexes, and actually of the bride and bridegroom for as long as possible. Thus in Amboina none but women may enter the room where the bride sits in state.[1] In the Watubella Islands the men stand on one side with the groom and the women on the other with the bride. The feast is in two parts; the groom and the men eat their "breakfast" separately, and then the bride and the women fall to.[2] At marriage-feasts amongst the Jews of Jerusalem the men sit on one side with the bridegroom, while the bride and the women occupy the opposite side of the room.[3] And generally, at marriage, the bride is escorted by women, and the bridegroom by men.

In these cases there is avoidance between the sexes at sexual crises, as a rule more emphasised than that during ordinary life. The question may be asked—is the latter prohibition merely an extension of the former? When we penetrate to the ideas lying behind both, we shall find these to be identical, and of such a specific character and universal extension that we must suppose the sex-taboos imposed at sexual crises to be simply emphasised results of these ideas, though, as always, such results become through the very continuance of the phenomena to which they apply, further causes for the support of these ideas. Not to anticipate what will be treated of later, it may be pointed out first that perhaps the most widely spread and the most stringent of all sex-taboos has nothing to do with sexual functions—this is the prohibition against eating together. In the second place, in order rightly to estimate the whole of the evidence, it must be borne in mind that these sexual

[1] A. S. Bickmore, *East Indian Archipelago*, 276.
[2] Riedel, *op. cit.* 205.
[3] Featherman, *op. cit.* v. 140.

functions are parallel to the various occupations of the respective sexes: in biology and in primitive thought child-bearing is as much a feminine occupation as is the preparation of meals, and the confirmation of a boy as much of a male occupation as is warfare or the chase. Also, it is clear from a survey of the various cases of sexual taboo, first, that the avoidance is of the religious and taboo character; secondly, that men and women are afraid of dangerous results from each other—the fact that we see more of the man's side of the question is an instance of the way in which the male sex has practically monopolised the expression of thought; and thirdly, that where one sex or the other is particularly liable to danger, as men at war, or women at child-birth, more care is naturally taken to prevent injury from the other sex.

In the taboos against eating together, we shall see an expression of that almost universal preference for solitude, while important physiological functions are proceeding, due ultimately to the instinct of self-preservation in the form of subconscious physiological thought arising from those functions; and in the taboos against one or the other sex in sexual crises the same preference is seen, commuted by sexual solidarity to a preference for the presence of the same sex; and in all forms of the taboo it is evident that to a religious regard for personal security, there has been applied a religious diffidence concerning persons who are more or less unknown, different from what is normal, different from one's self.

So far, then, we may take it that the complementary difference of sex, producing by physiological laws a certain difference of life no less than of function, came in an early stage of mental development to be accentuated by religious ideas, which thus enforced more strongly such separation as is due to nature. The separation thus accentuated by religious conceptions as to sexual difference, is assisted by the natural solidarity of each sex, until there is, as we find so very generally, a prohibition or sex-taboo more or less regularly imposed throughout life. Man and woman, as such, are ignorant of each other, as if they were different species; they are constantly tending to become, what they never can become, two divided castes; every woman and every man are, as men and women, potentially taboo to each other.

All living religious conceptions spring from more or less constant functional origins, physiological and psychological. Now when we look at mankind in general, and in particular at civilised societies, we find that men as a rule prefer to associate with men, and women with women, except on those occasions when the functional needs of love, for instance, call for union and sympathy between the sexes. We may thus realise that the same biological causes, working through human ideas of primary and secondary sexual difference, produce this subconscious preference which we find in the civilised man, and with more primitive expression in the modern boy, no less than the religious segregation we find amongst early peoples.

CHAPTER IV

Before passing on to the discussion of primitive ideas of human relations, there is the problem of the connection of human persons with the spiritual agencies of taboo in its social aspect to be considered.

Primitive science is materialistic, and the fact is evident in every case cited, that evil or harm—even when due to evil spirits—is of a material nature. Evil spirits in the first place are warded off by material methods. Thus the Khonds prevent the approach of *Joogah Pennu*, the goddess of small-pox, by barricading the paths with thorns and ditches, and boiling caldrons of stinking oil.[1] Amongst the Bechuanas, to arrest disease or prevent it from entering a village, a pointed stone is planted at the middle of the entrance, or a cross-bar smeared with "medicine."[2]

In the next place, there is a vagueness as to the distinction between spirits and material evil influence. Amongst the natives of Central Australia *Arungquiltha* is the term applied to persons or things possessed of magical power. For instance, "a pointing stick used by a medicine man is *Arungquiltha*; it is applied indiscriminately to the magical influence itself, and to the object in which it is resident. It is a vague term, and sometimes can be best expressed by saying that a thing

[1] Macpherson, *Memorials of Service in India*, 370.

[2] *South African Folklore Journal*, i. 34.

is possessed by an evil spirit."[1] In the Luang Sermata Islands sickness is caused by bad food, "bad wind," the influence of evil persons or evil spirits.[2] Amongst the Indians of Costa Rica there are two kinds of ceremonial uncleanness, *nya* and *bu-ku-rü*. The former is connected with death, the latter, which is the more virulent, is most dangerous from a woman in her first pregnancy. She infects the whole neighbourhood, and all deaths are laid at her door. People going from her house carry the contagion with them. Arms and utensils transmit it, and therefore the people beat things with a stick before using, or sweep the house. A place which has not been visited for a long time, or one approached for the first time, is infected with *bu-ku-rü*. "It is an evil spirit, or rather a property acquired."[3] The personification of various evils and of diseases and plagues is so well known as to need no illustration. In the following cases there is a confusion between evil spirits and contagious matter, real or imaginary. Amongst the Dieri and neighbouring tribes of South Australia, no one is believed to contract a disease or complaint, or even to die, from natural causes. The disease or death is caused by some enemy, of their own or neighbouring tribe, and in any serious case the Koonkies or doctors are called in, to beat out the devil, *Cootchie*. "This is done by beating the ground in and out of the camp, chasing him away for some distance." Also, "many an innocent man has been condemned to death through this superstition, being believed to have in his possession the small bone of a human leg."[4] Amongst the Vedahs of Travancore,

[1] Spencer and Gillen, *The Native Tribes of Central Australia*, 548.

[2] Riedel, *op. cit.* 327.

[3] W. M. Gabb, *op. cit.* 504.

[4] Gason, in *Journ. Anthrop. Inst.* xxiv. 170.

the wife at menstruation lives in a separate hut for five days, at a good distance from the home. The next five days she spends in another, half-way distant. During these ten days, the husband dares not eat in his house anything but roots, for fear of being killed by "the devil."[1] The Maoris believed that the spirits of dead ancestors could send a *kahukahu* to a man; this would enter his body and feed on vital parts. In a Maori poem the statement occurs, "should the *kahukahu* gnaw spitefully, it will be certain death." The *kahukahu* is the personification of the germs of a human being, supposed to be contained in the *menses*, and the Maoris avoid contact with menstrual blood as if it were a poison.[2] Again, in Manchuria the sedan-chair in which the bride goes to the home of the groom is "disinfected" with incense, to drive away "evil spirits."[3] They seem therefore to be regarded as material influences resembling germs of a disease. The properties of the taboo state are in fact always material and transmissible, and are removed by material methods as if they were a physical secretion or emanation. Thus in Fiji, when *tabu* is removed, the tabooed persons wash in a stream; they then take an animal, a pig or turtle, on which they wipe their hands, and this animal becomes sacred to the chief. The *tabu* is now off, and they are free to work, to feed themselves, and to live with their wives.[4] In Borneo and South Celebes evil spirits, after a funeral for instance, cling to one's body "like a burr."[5] The Friar Roman Pane described a native sorcerer in the West Indies "pulling the disease off the

[1] Ploss, *Das Kind*, ii. 435.

[2] Shortland, *Southern Districts of New Zealand*, 294-95.

[3] Lockhart, in *Folklore*, i. 487.

[4] Wilkes, *op. cit.* ii. 99.

[5] M. J. F. Perelaer, *Ethnographische Beschrijving der Dajaks*, 44, 54, 252; Matthes, *op. cit.* 49.

patient's legs as one pulls off a pair of trousers."[1] In the New Hebrides, ceremonial "uncleanness," for instance from death or child-birth, is taken off by sweeping a branch over the body.[2] To cure a sick person, the Navajo priest pressed bundles of stuff to different parts of the body from head to foot. Each time after pressing them on the body, he "held them up to the smoke-hole, and blew on them in that direction a quick puff, as if blowing away some evil influence which the bundles were supposed to draw from the body." They were then buried.[3]

We see then that evil spirits are not always clearly distinguished from the transmissible properties of matter. The latter are no doubt often regarded logically enough as the emanations of the "evil spirit," the trail or slime of the serpent; but the points to be stressed are, first, that where evil spirits are predicated of tabooed persons the evil can be transmitted by contagion and infection; secondly, that many so-called "evil spirits" are not supernatural persons at all, but evil material properties of natural things or of human persons. Further, this latter notion is a factor in the process of anthropomorphic personification, of which more is to be said; and the whole set of phenomena illustrates the importance of material contact as leading to transmission of material evil.

In fact, the inherent materialism of human thought, which so hardly allows of progress to idealism, is even more in evidence among primitive men than it is now. Primitive man believes in the supernatural, but supernatural beings and existences are to him really material —the supernatural is a part of and obeys the laws of

[1] E. B. Tylor, *Primitive Culture*[3], ii. 129. [2] D. Macdonald, *Oceania*, 184.
[3] Washington Mathews, in *Fifth Report of the Bureau of Ethnology*, 420.

nature. How difficult it is to conceive of immaterial existence, except by a negation of thought, is well seen in popular conceptions of the nature of the soul, especially those of modern spiritualism. In the last analysis of these conceptions, the soul is generally found to be simply attenuated or etherealised matter. Similar are the conceptions of early man, not only of the soul, but of all supernatural beings, existences, and influences; and they are well illustrated by the methods used in dealing with such, being generally those that would be used in dealing with matter.

In the next place, there are the familiar facts of anthropomorphism. "Man never knows how anthropomorphic he is." Goethe's epigram applies most completely to early man, for he is more anthropomorphic in his ideas, and is less aware of the fact. He thinks of everything in terms of himself, and his ideal creations of supernatural beings are generally in his own image, or in the image of animals which for him are man-like as possessing such close similarities of structure and function. The modern theory of descent would have been easily understood in its general outline by early man, who has, by the way, several conceptions which foreshadow it. The Digger Indians of California say that their ancestors derived their existence from *coyotes*; these became Indians, but as one died the body was changed into a number of little creatures which were gradually developed into deer, elks, and antelopes; others took wings and flew about in the air. Men originally went on all fours, and gradually progressed to a higher organisation. While in a state of transition, they were in the habit of sitting upright, and from this cause, having worn off their tails, they now appear without this appendage.[1] The Central Australians have the theory of man's descent from animals.[2]

There is often a natural confusion between the person who is possessed or obsessed by spirits and the spirits themselves, as in the case of him whose name was Legion. Thus, according to the Cambodians, the *Arak* are spirits, dwelling in trees or houses. *Grou* are sorcerers, men or women, who invoke the *Arak*, and are possessed by them. During the period of possession they are themselves called *Arak*, the latter being incarnate in them.[3] The Nickol Bay natives believe in an evil spirit, *Juno*, who kills men; when a man of the tribe prowls about seeking to kill other blacks, he is said to be a *Juno* for the time.[4]

A priori it would be expected that in cases where a dangerous condition or taboo state arises in close connection with a man's fellow-men, he should have inferred from his experience of all human relations that the danger was due to one or more of his fellows, and psychology bears this out.

In the psychology of personification there are two processes to be observed. First, there are the phenomena of ideation, especially when visualised. The fact that the memory-image is formed below the threshold of consciousness, and suddenly emerges complete in outline, is one of great importance for the origin and development of animistic thought. As a simple illustration, let us take the case of a man who is in fear of another. For this, by the way, we often use the instructive phrase "bodily fear." Such a man will chiefly avoid personal contact, as likely to result in personal injury, and all ill that happens to him he will ascribe to

[1] Featherman, *op. cit.* iii. 215.
[2] Spencer and Gillen, *op. cit.* 392.
[3] Aymonier, *op. cit.* 176.
[4] E. M. Curr, *The Australian Race*, i. 298.

the influence of his enemy; while in the secret depths of his soul, the image of his foe, impressed upon his brain, is lying dormant, ready at any moment to rise above the threshold. Whenever he closes his eyes to shut out the thought of his enemy, the image of him appears. His brain is, in a word, "obsessed" by the image of his foe. This memory-image, presented to complete consciousness, I believe to be a factor in the origin of anthropomorphic animism, of no less importance than its subconscious appearance in sleep. The man's own soul has thus acquired an image of his foe, a tiny but evil spirit, which appears within him, he knows not how nor whence. Its presence helps to explain "possession," and certain conceptions of personal influence and of the supernatural powers of man. The actual result to the subject, apart from actual violence at his enemy's hands, might be illness from fear. There are many cases on record where similar fear has killed a man. If the man did fall ill in this way, he would be perfectly justified in inferring his enemy to have caused the illness; there are besides numerous cases where illness is attributed to potential, in default of knowledge of actual human foes. Early man knows little of bacteriology, but he has the great principle of contagion very strongly outlined and extended all round the circle of human relations. If a man who is sick is conscious of having made an enemy, he generally attributes his sickness to him; for to his mind man can do everything, and everything he does is potentially transmissible. In cases such as drowning, injury from lightning, and from various natural forces or objects other than man, of course other agencies are inferred, though many such are anthropomorphic; but where a man, as in social relations is generally the case, can ascribe his troubles to human agency, he does so.

Again, our supposed subject does not distinguish the real and the ideal, and from this would arise a crowd of ideas and precautionary measures against the ubiquitous evil image of his foe, as well as against his actual self. And there will be thus a constant interchange between his natural and supernatural dangers. Now, fear is the main cause of the precautions of taboo, and though I do not insist that ideas concerning contact obtained a religious connotation before the creation of evil spirits, yet there is no doubt that the two sets of ideas are, in reference to human relations, correlative, and work together. Just as in artistic criticism one comes back in the end to the personality behind a work, so in human relations the beginning and the ending is personality and personal contact. In these relations the danger, which is both real and ideal, proceeds from man and to man returns—the link between, say, the first meeting with an enemy, and the second, being that veritable Erinys, the visualised image of him in the other's brain.

I now proceed to give actual cases from the relations of man with man, in which ideas of physical and spiritual danger combine in persons. There is a large mass of such facts, and we find that the attribution of human ills and sicknesses to human agency is more pronounced in the lower and less in the higher stages of culture, while modern science brings us back to the view of the lower races.

In Ceram-laut sickness is caused through the influence of evil spirits or "poisoning" by evil persons, *suwanggi*. The two methods are practically interchangeable, and appear throughout the islands between Celebes and New Guinea.[1] In the Aru Islands such

[1] Riedel, *op. cit.* 178, 265, 304, 305, 341.

persons are able to extract men's souls. They can make themselves invisible, or take the shape of bats, pigs, dogs, crocodiles, or birds.[1] Amongst the Dieri, Auminie, Yandrawontha, Yarawuarka, and Pilladapa tribes of Australia, "no person dies a natural death, death is supposed to be caused by some evil-disposed person of their own or neighbouring tribe; they religiously believe this superstition, it is called '*Mookoo-ellieduckuna*,' (translation: *Mookoo*, 'bone'; *duckuna*, 'to strike,' *i.e.* struck by a bone). Many an innocent man has been condemned to death through this superstitious custom, believing that he had in his possession the small bone of a human leg."[2] Amongst the tribes of North-West Australia, no man can die unless he has been bewitched. "Some one is supposed to come at night and take away the fat out of the man's belly; and his friends must find out who did it, to kill him."[3] The natives in the district of Powell's Creek, in the northern territory of South Australia, ascribe "death or illness to some strange black-fellow, belonging to another tribe, who has doomed a certain man or woman to die or suffer from ill-health. It is not unusual, such is their superstitious belief, that a man, apparently in good health, will in a very short time lose condition and die, under the impression that he has been doomed by a member of some other tribe;"[4] the people of the Belyando tribe believe that no strong man dies except as the consequence of witchcraft. "That should A and B, two strong blacks of the same tribe who were quite friendly, go out hunting together, and A, on returning to the camp, be suddenly taken ill and die,

[1] Riedel, 253, 327.
[2] Gason, *op. cit.* xxiv. 170.
[3] Bassett Smith, in *Journ. Anthrop. Inst.* xxiii. 327.
[4] *Journ. Anthrop. Inst.* xxiv. 178.

the tribe would believe that B had killed him by means of witchcraft, and demand his life accordingly." [1] Amongst the Murray River natives, at the funeral of a dead person, some relative generally attempted to spear some one, till it was explained that the deceased did not die by sorcery.[2] Messrs. Spencer and Gillen remark of the Central Australians, "the undercurrent of anxious feeling, which, though it may be stilled, and indeed forgotten for a time, is yet always present. In his natural state the native is often thinking that some enemy is attempting to harm him by means of evil magic, and, on the other hand, he never knows when a medicine-man in some distant group may not point him out as guilty of killing some one else by magic. It is, however," they add, "easy to lay too much stress upon this. . . . It is not right to say that the Australian native lives in constant dread of the evil magic of an enemy. The feeling is always, as it were, lying dormant, and ready to be called up by any strange or suspicious sound." [3] "All ailments of every kind, from the simplest to the most serious, are without exception attributed to the malign influence of an enemy in either human or spirit shape." [4] "Amongst most Congo tribes death is seldom regarded in the light of a natural event. In most cases the charm doctor accuses an old person, or a slave, of having been the cause. The accused is forthwith secured, and at an appointed time is submitted to a poison ordeal." [5] In Tongareva death is ascribed to witchcraft.[6] The Kurnai believed that death only occurred from accident, open violence, or secret magic. The magical influence of enemies was

[1] Curr, *op. cit.* iii. 27, 28.

[2] Eyre, *op. cit.* ii. 349, 353.

[3] Spencer and Gillen, *op. cit.* 53, 54.

[4] *Id.* 530.

[5] H. Ward, in *Journ. Anthrop. Inst.* xxiv. 287.

[6] W. W. Gill, *Jottings from the Pacific*, 225.

the ordinary cause of natural death, though sometimes attributed to evil spirits.[1] The Abipones thought that no one would die if the jugglers and Spaniards were banished. They attributed every death to these. Man could only die by magic, and a sick man often suspected some person of making him ill, and accordingly would go for him.[2] Amongst the Bongos old women are especially suspected of alliance with wicked spirits, and are accused if sudden death occurs.[3] Amongst the Gonds the fear of witchcraft and the evil eye is so great, that "there is nothing they will not do to guard themselves against these influences."[4] "So deeply rooted in the Indian's bosom is the belief concerning the origin of diseases" (from sorcery) "that they have little idea of sickness arising from other causes." The Indians of Guiana attribute all disease to sorcery. The sorcerer is credited with the power of causing as well as curing illness.[5] Amongst the Yorubas witchcraft is the chief cause of sickness and death.[6] Amongst the tribes of East Central Africa disease and sudden death are attributed to witchcraft. The notorious "smelling out" of the guilty person follows, and if found he is put to death.[7] In Hawaii disease could be caused by the prayers of an enemy.[8] The Chiquitos often attributed disease to the female "jugglers" or lady-doctors.[9] The Guarani magicians could inflict or ward off disease and death.[10] In Siam disease is attributed to sorcery.[11] When a death occurs among

[1] Fison and Howitt, *op. cit.* 251, 258.
[2] Dobrizhoffer, *op. cit.* ii. 84, 223, 227.
[3] G. Schweinfurth, *The Heart of Africa*, 307.
[4] H. B. Rowney, *Wild Tribes of India*, 15.
[5] W. H. Brett, *The Indian Tribes of Guiana*, 365.
[6] A. B. Ellis, *The Yoruba-speaking Peoples of the Slave Coast of West Africa*, 118.
[7] Macdonald in *Journ. Anthrop. Inst.* xxii. 104.
[8] Ellis, *Tour in Hawaii*, 258.
[9] Dobrizhoffer, *op. cit.* ii. 264.
[10] *Id.* i. 71.
[11] Loubere, *op. cit.* i. 206.

the Dacotas that cannot be reasonably accounted for, it is supposed to have been caused by the mischievous action of a neighbouring clan by sorcery. Constant feuds are thus caused.[1] When a sudden death occurs, the people of the New Hebrides ascribe it to sorcerers.[2] Amongst the Bannars every misfortune is attributed to the malice of persons who have the power of influencing their fate.[3] Among the Maoris a belief in witchcraft almost universally prevailed. If a chief, or his wife or child fell ill, it was attributed to witchcraft. Those possessing the art were often hired to bewitch people.[4] In the Babar Islands evil persons make others ill by magic. When such are found out they are put to death.[5] Reality and imagination sometimes coincide, as in East Central Africa, where "the doctor" who can kill by magic will administer real poison for a fee.[6] There are also interesting cases showing how zoomorphism and reality correlate. In Tenimber and Timor-laut various illnesses are due to evilly disposed persons or evil spirits, taking the form of birds.[7]

In the following cases, we may see the actual meeting-place and reconciliation of two theories as to the origin of the moral law, from supernatural and human sanctions. For these are cases where, behind the spiritual, there is a human agent at work. Amongst the Yorubas the god Egungun becomes incarnate from time to time, in this way: a man dressed up like the god goes about, and carries off people who are troublesome to their neighbours. "He is thus a kind of supernatural inquisitor, who appears from time to time to inquire into the conduct of people, particularly of women, and

[1] Featherman, *op. cit.* iii. 290.
[2] *Id.* ii. 77.
[3] H. Mouhot, *Travels in Indo-China*, ii. 28.
[4] Yate, *op. cit.* 95.
[5] Riedel, *op. cit.* 358.
[6] *Journ. Anthrop. Inst.* xxii. 105.
[7] Riedel, *op. cit.* 305.

to punish misdeeds. Although it is well known that Egungun is only a disguised man, yet it is popularly believed that to touch him, even by accident, causes death."[1] In British Guiana blood-revenge is closely connected with the system of sorcery. If a man dies, and it is supposed that an enemy has killed him by means of an evil spirit, they employ a sorcerer to find him. A near relative is then charged with the duty of vengeance; he becomes a *Kanaima*, *i.e.* he is possessed by the destroying spirit so called, and has to live apart, according to strict rules, and to submit to many privations, till the deed of blood is done. When the man is killed, the murderer must pass a stick through his body, to taste the victim's blood. Not until this is done does he become an ordinary man once more, but wanders about, and madness comes upon him through the agency of the disappointed spirit. The family of the victim, to prevent the *Kanaima* getting at the body, sometimes manage to bury it in a secret place, or take out the liver and put a red-hot axe in its place. Then, if the *Kanaima* visit the corpse, the heat of the axe-head will pass into his body and consume him. Sometimes they put *ourali* poison on the body, for the purpose of destroying the *Kanaima*. In cases of secret enmity poison is used, and, in consequence of all this, the Indians seldom consider themselves safe. He against whom or whose near relative wrong has been done, becomes a *Kanaima*, and all injury which befalls an Indian is the work of such. The *Kanaima* may assume any shape, often that of the jaguar (which by the way is the most dangerous animal the Indian knows), often an inanimate shape; for instance, the *peaiman* will extract from his patient a stick or stone, which is the

[1] Ellis, *op. cit.* 107.

bodily form of the *Kanaima* causing illness.[1] Very similar is the practice of *Kurdaitcha* amongst the Central Australians.[2]

Is there any similar correlation of "spirits" and human beings, or spiritual and human influence, in the relations of the one sex with the other? We may well expect that there should be, and there are facts which show it.

The Pomo Indians find it difficult to maintain authority over their women. A husband often terrifies his wife into submission by personating an ogre.[3] Amongst the Tatu Indians of California the men have a secret society which gives periodic dramatic entertainments with the object of keeping the women in order. The chief actor, disguised as a devil, charges about among the assembled squaws.[4] The *Mumbo Jumbo* of the Mandingoes is a well-known case. The periodic impersonation is intended to frighten the women. The same performer who represents *Mumbo Jumbo* has also the duty of keeping the sexes apart for the forty days after circumcision.[5] Amongst the Krumen, when a wife dies, the husband is believed to have caused her death by witchcraft.[6] In Congo widows and widowers are charged with the same.[7] In Loango, when a man is ill, his wife is accused of causing the illness by witchcraft, and must undergo the *cassa* ordeal.[8] The Chiquitos used to kill the wife of a sick man, believing her to be the cause of his illness.[9] In Luzon wives are sometimes bewitched by their husbands.[10] In China a man's illness is often attributed to the spirit of a former wife.[11] In

[1] Brett, *op. cit.* 357-60; im Thurn, *op. cit.* 368.

[2] Spencer and Gillen, *op. cit.* 47.

[3] Powers, *op. cit.* 154, 161.

[4] *Id.* 141.

[5] Waitz-Gerland, *op. cit.* ii. 118.

[6] J. L. Wilson, *Western Africa*, 115.

[7] Waitz-Gerland, *op. cit.* ii. 120.

[8] Bastian, *Loango-Küste*, i. 46.

[9] Dobrizhoffer, *op. cit.* ii. 264.

[10] De Tavera, in *Globus*, xlviii. 314.

[11] Doolittle, *op. cit.* i. 146.

Halmahera women who die in child-bed are supposed to become evil spirits, *oputiana*, who emasculate men, and cause injury to pregnant women.[1] This belief is found among the Malays.[2] Among the Kei islanders if a woman dies in child-bed they kill the unborn babe, to prevent the woman becoming a *Pontianak*, in which case she would haunt her husband and emasculate him.[3] It is easy to see how this sort of belief correlates with, if it does not arise from, a common phase of sexual fear.

In the next examples there is no hint of spiritual influence at all, human influence alone has the deleterious result. The Cambodians have the following belief in the case of a young married pair, neither of whom have been married before. When the wife is *enceinte* for the first time, the husband is able to take from her the fruit of her womb, by magic influence over her. Accordingly, the parents of the bride never trust their son-in-law, and will not let the young couple go out of their sight. In Cambodia the married pair live with or near the bride's parents.[4] When a Halmahera woman is three months pregnant, she uses protective charms to prevent evil men destroying the babe. She may not eat the remains of her husband's food, "because that would cause difficult labour."[5] In Amboina and the Aru Islands men are not allowed to see a woman confined, because "their presence would hinder the birth."[6] Conversely, at the feast to celebrate the birth in the Luang Sermata Islands, only women may be present. If men partook of even the slightest morsel they would be unlucky in all their

[1] J. G. F. Riedel, in *Zeitschrift für Ethnologie*, xvii. 85.
[2] W. W. Skeat, *Malay Magic*, 434.
[3] Riedel, *De sluik- en kroesharige rassen tusschen Selebes en Papua*, 259.
[4] Aymonier, *op. cit.* 187.
[5] Riedel, in *Zeitschrift für Ethnologie*, xvii. 79.
[6] *Id. De sluik- en kroesharige rassen tusschen Selebes en Papua*, 73, 263.

undertakings.[1] Next there is an extension of the idea, which has had much influence upon morality in the theory that sickness is due to sin. The people of Luang Sermata believe that prolonged pains in child-birth are due to the woman having had forbidden intercourse.[2] In Cambodia, if a child is born with two locks of hair, husband and wife suspect each other of infidelity.[3] In Wetar sickness may be caused to the injured person, wife, husband, or lover, by infidelity.[4] If birth is difficult, the Samoyeds suspect the woman of adultery.[5]

Lastly, this kind of magical deleterious human influence is clearly seen in all the various phenomena of sexual taboo, such as those already reviewed, and others to be dealt with later.

Thus in the phenomena of social taboo, human and spiritual agencies meet in persons. With the special cases described, we may compare the facts of incarnation, the evidence of ghost phenomena (in which the ghost possesses the form and characteristics of the person it once tenanted, in more or less exact resemblance), the ideas which led to the preservation of the dead body, as by the Egyptians, in order to save the soul, and the evidence of the psychology of ideation. We have reached the conclusion, then, that in social taboo the "spiritual" dangers feared come from a man's fellow-men, and thus of the evil "spirits" or influences which surround him some are simply spiritualised persons or their qualities; and in sexual taboo the "spiritual" dangers feared come from the other sex, and the evil "spirits" or influences connected with sexual acts and functions are spiritualised persons of their own sex or their sexual characters materialised. The connection, of

[1] Riedel, 326. [2] *Id.* 325. [3] Aymonier, *op. cit.* 169.
[4] Riedel, *op. cit.* 451. [5] Georgi, *op. cit.* 14.

course, is mostly subconscious, but the importance of subconscious thought can hardly be over-estimated, though man cannot trace back the origin of his own ideas into their various associations. With the great mass of mankind in any age, this direct connection of sexual danger with actual living influence of the other sex, has perhaps never risen into consciousness; with the majority of human beings such danger is and has been attributed to external vague "spiritual" agencies; but the patent evidence of biology upon the complementary nature of sex, and that of psychology as to the development of emotional attitudes from functional phenomena, especially in connection with sex, prove conclusively that we are to find the ultimate origin of idea and practice relating to sex in actual sexual difference embodied in persons. And conversely, there is the romantic fact that human persons who are mysterious or not understood, as is the case with woman and man in their mutual aspect, *i.e.* potentially dangerous, can be regarded as spiritual persons, supernatural existences: indeed with primitive man there is often no clear distinction drawn between those who are made lower than the angels and the angelic hosts themselves. These considerations assist us to see not only the correlation of taboo and "spiritual," or rather hylo-idealistic, danger, but also the religious character, whether magical or superstitious, of human relations in primitive thought.

CHAPTER V

GENERAL ideas concerning human relations are the medium through which sexual taboo works, and these must now be examined. If we compare the facts of social taboo generally or of its subdivision, sexual taboo, we find that the ultimate test of human relations, in both *genus* and *species*, is *contact*. An investigation of primitive ideas concerning the relations of man with man, when guided by this clue, will lay bare the principles which underlie the theory and practice of sexual taboo. Arising, as we have seen, from sexual differentiation, and forced into permanence by difference of occupation and sexual solidarity, this segregation receives the continuous support of religious conceptions as to human relations. These conceptions centre upon contact, and ideas of contact are at the root of all conceptions of human relations at any stage of culture; contact is the one universal test, as it is the most elementary form, of mutual relations. Psychology bears this out, and the point is psychological rather than ethnological.

As I have pointed out before and shall have occasion to do so again, a comparative examination, assisted by psychology, of the emotions and ideas of average modern humanity, is a most valuable aid to ethnological enquiry. In this connection, we find that desire or willingness for physical contact is an animal emotion, more or less subconscious, which is characteristic of similarity, harmony, friendship, or love. Throughout the world, the greeting of a friend is expressed by contact, whether it be nose-rubbing, or the kiss, the embrace, or the clasp of hands; so the ordinary expression of friendship by a boy, that eternal savage, is contact of arm and shoulder. More interesting still, for our purpose, is the universal expression by contact, of the emotion of love. To touch his mistress is the ever-present desire of the lover, and in this impulse, even if we do not trace it back, as we may without being fanciful, to polar or sexual attraction inherent in the atoms, the φιλία of Empedocles, yet we may place the beginning and ending of love. When analysed, the emotion always comes back to contact. As Clough puts it:—

"Well, I know, after all, it is only juxtaposition. Juxtaposition, in short, and what is juxtaposition?"

Further, mere willingness for contact is found universally when the person to be touched is healthy, if not clean, or where he is of the same age or class or caste, and we may add, for ordinary humanity, the same sex.

On the other hand, the avoidance of contact, whether consciously or subconsciously presented, is no less the universal characteristic of human relations, where similarity, harmony, friendship, or love is absent. This appears in the attitude of men to the sick, to strangers, distant acquaintances, enemies, and in cases of difference of age, position, sympathies or aims, and even of sex. Popular language is full of phrases which illustrate this feeling.

Again, the pathology of the emotions supplies many curious cases, where the whole being seems concentrated upon the sense of touch, with abnormal desire or disgust for contact; and in the evolution of the emotions from physiological pleasure and pain, contact plays an important part in connection with functional satisfaction or dissatisfaction with the environment.

In the next place there are the facts, first, that an element of thought inheres in all sensation, while sensation conditions thought; and secondly, that there is a close connection of all the senses, both in origin, each of them being a modification of the one primary sense of touch, and in subsequent development, where the specialised organs are still co-ordinated through tactile sensation, in the sensitive surface of organism. Again, and here we can see the genesis of ideas of contact, it is by means of the tactile sensibility of the skin and membranes of sense-organs, forming a sensitised as well as a protecting surface, that the nervous system conveys to the brain information about the external world, and this information is in its original aspect the response to impact. Primitive physics, no less than modern, recognises that contact is a modified form of a blow. These considerations show that contact not only plays an important part in the life of the soul, but must have had a profound influence on the development of ideas, and it may now be assumed that ideas of contact have been a universal and original constant factor in human relations, and that they are so still. The latter assumption is to be stressed, because we find that the ideas which lie beneath primitive taboo are still a vital part of human nature, though mostly emptied of their religious content; and also because, as I hold, ceremonies and etiquette such as still obtain, could not possess such vitality as they do, unless there were a living psychological force behind them, such as we find in elementary ideas which come straight from functional processes.

These ideas of contact are *primitive* in each sense of the word, at whatever stage of culture they appear. They seem to go back in origin and in character to that highly developed sensibility of all animal and even organised life, which forms at once a biological monitor and a safeguard for the whole organism in relation to its environment. From this sensibility there arise subjective ideas concerning the safety or danger of the environment, and in man we may suppose these subjective ideas as to his environment, and especially as to his fellow-men, to be the origin of his various expressions of avoidance or desire for contact.

Lastly, it is to be observed that avoidance of contact is the most conspicuous phenomenon attaching to cases of taboo when its dangerous character is prominent. In taboo the connotation of "not to be touched" is the salient point all over the world, even in cases of permanent taboo such as belongs to Samoan and Maori chiefs, with whom no one dared come in contact; and so we may infer the same aversion to be potential in all such relations.

In connection with the phenomena of ideation and with the next question, there comes in the familiar piece of elementary metaphysics which has played so great a part in religion from the days of primitive man, the idea of substance and accidents. The distinction is quite familiar to savages; they can tell you how the god eats only the essence of a sacrifice, leaving behind the properties of colour, shape, taste, and the like for the priest or worshippers. In East Central Africa the people give an offering of flour to the ancestral spirits, when a person is ill. The spirits regale themselves with the "essence" of the flour.[1] The Galelas and

[1] Macdonald, in *Journ. Anthrop. Inst.* xxii. 104.

Tobelorese of Halmahera hold that spirits eat the "essence" of food.[1] The Hill Dyaks place choice morsels before their gods, who extract the "essence" of the food.[2] Amongst the Yorubas evil spirits are supposed to cause illness in young children. They enter them and eat their food, so that they pine away. The spirit is supposed to eat the "spiritual" part of the food.[3]

So with regard to man's ideas of his fellow-men. The visual image and similar appearances, such as a man's shadow, are his essence, soul or second-self, and the ideas a man forms of another's characteristics are the properties. On the other hand, the reference of all the characteristics of a man to him, as so many predicates to one subject, forms a correlative method by which the soul or essence of a man is thought of. For instance, in the New Hebrides the word for soul connotes the essence of a man;[4] the Wetarese poetically liken the soul to the smell of a flower.[5] Here again we see the materialism of early thought; even "essence" is material, and is sometimes visible. There is no distinction between the substantial nature of "soul," a man's properties, physical and spiritual, magical influence whether of man or spirit, the contagious properties of disease, the mystical character of "taboo," the wholesome or deleterious influence of men and evil spirits—they are all alike material and transmissible.

Now it is this material transmissibility that makes contact of such importance, and it is transmission of

[1] J. G. F. Riedel, in *Zeitschrift für Ethnologie*, xvii. 67.
[2] H. Low, *Sarawak*, 251.
[3] A. B. Ellis, *op. cit.* 111, 113.
[4] D. Macdonald, *Oceania*, 180.
[5] J. G. F. Riedel, *De sluik- en kroesharige rassen tusschen Selebes en Papua*, 453.

properties, whether of nature, man, or spirits, that lies behind the avoidance or desire for contact.

Potentially always and actually often, it is true of all men and conditions of men and natural objects, that their properties can be transmitted by all possible material methods, and even by *actio in distans*. For practical purposes we may speak of *contagion*, and in so far as the properties transmitted are evil, all contact is contagion. The wide generalisation of early man, of course, covered real cases of infection of disease, or transmission of strength, and the affirmative instances, as usual, helped to perpetuate the negative, though what Messrs. Spencer and Gillen state of the Central Australians, applies to all early peoples. In connection with the disease *Erkincha* and its contagion, the natives do not reason "from a strictly medical point of view; their idea in a case of this kind is, that a man suffering from *Erkincha* conveys a magic evil influence, which they call *Arungquiltha*, to the women, and by this means it is conveyed as a punishment to other men." This *Arungquiltha* is a typical example of the primitive ideas of contact, and may preface a set of cases which show the meaning and application of these ideas. The same people say when the sun is eclipsed, that "*Arungquiltha* has got into it," this being an "evil or malignant influence, sometimes regarded as personal and at other times as impersonal." Here the idea is applied to a strange, unusual phenomenon. They have also a tradition of a thin, emaciated man; "where he died arose a stone, the rubbing of which may cause emaciation in other people. This stone is charged with *Arungquiltha*, or evil influence." Again, there is a myth of an old man who plucked boils from his body, each of which turned into a stone. This group of stones is still to be seen, and they are called stone-sores. Men who desire to harm others, hit these stones with spears; which are then thrown in the direction of the victim. The spears carry away with them *Arungquiltha* from the stones, and this produces an eruption of painful boils in the victim. And similarly, any stones marking the spot where men died from magical influence, are themselves credited with magical powers.[1] This principle may be illustrated from Maori and Red Indian science. The latter say that "Nature has the property to transfuse the qualities of food, or of objects presented to the senses, into men."[2] The former hold that anything placed in contact with a sacred object acquires the sacred nature of that object, and anything thus made sacred cannot be eaten or used for cooking.[3] "Uncleanness" attaches to mourners, enchanters, and murderers, amongst the Kaffirs. The murderer washes to remove the contagion of his guilt, the mourner to remove the contagion of death, and the enchanter washes when he renounces his art.[4] This "uncleanness" is the contagious property of *taboo* and is not distinguished from "sacredness," whether in the case of kings, priests, Maori gentlemen, infants, women during pregnancy, child-birth, and menstruation, boys and girls at puberty, or other especially *taboo* characters. The Polynesian word *parapara* means, "first, a sacred place; secondly, the first fruits of fish; thirdly, a tree; fourthly, defiled or unclean, from having touched sacred food; *cf. para*, dross, sediments; *parapara*, dirt, soilure, stain; *parare*, food."[5] It is noticeable that Kaffir words for "un-

[1] Spencer and Gillen, *op. cit.* 412, 566, 441, 550, 552.
[2] J. Adair, *History of the American Indians*, 133.
[3] Shortland, *Southern Districts of New Zealand*, 292-94.
[4] H. Lichtenstein, *Travels in Southern Africa*, i. 257.
[5] E. Tregear, *Maori Dictionary*, s.v.

cleanness" connote "rubbing" and that which is "rubbed off."[1] Lucian, speaking of the sacred pigs of Hierapolis, the touch of which rendered one "unclean," says that some thought they were "unclean," others "sacred."[2] In other words, they were *taboo*. When lightning strikes a Kaffir *kraal* or individual or object, the persons connected therewith are "unclean." Animals struck by lightning are never eaten.[3] Amongst the Malays "not only is the king's person considered sacred, but the sanctity of his body is believed to communicate itself to his regalia, and to slay those who break the royal taboos." Again, "the theory of the king as the divine man, is held perhaps as strongly in the Malay region as in any other part of the world, a fact which is strikingly emphasised by the alleged right of Malay monarchs to slay at pleasure without being guilty of a crime."[4] So with the materialised dignity of chiefs and the like persons. No one in Samoa dared come in contact with a chief,[5] and in New Zealand such contact caused transmission of *tapu*.[6] Again, in Melanesia, where we see ideas of taboo attaching to men generally, a fact which shows its derivation from subjective conceptions of a man's own importance and power, and in more primitive form, his egoistic caution, *mana*, which combines personal ability, influence, strength, and luck, is the regular term for any result of such, and is of a supernatural character. *Mana* comes from communication with spirits, and from eating human flesh. All men of any importance have large supplies of *mana*. To give a

[1] Döhne, *Zulu-Kaffir Dictionary*.

[2] Lucian, *De dea Syria*, 54.

[3] Maclean, *op. cit.* 86, 121.

[4] W. W. Skeat, *Malay Magic*, 23.

[5] Wilkes, *op. cit.* ii. 103.

[6] R. Taylor, *Te Ika a Maui*, 165; Shortland, *Southern Districts of New Zealand*, 292-94.

boy a start in the world, a kind man will put his hand on the boy's head to impart the mysterious force.[1] The transmission of "virtue" ends in the laying-on of hands, as it began in man's ideas connected with contact. The civilised man still subconsciously gains solace, comfort, and strength, from the contact of a friend, and at the other end of the chain, the same is true of animals.

In the Solomon Islands, again, inland people are thought to have more *mana* than coast people. When they go down to the coast, they avoid spreading out their fingers, for to point the fingers at a man is to shoot him with a charm.[2] In this example, we may note the extension of the idea that a man's qualities are transmitted by touch; the outstretched hand and spreading of the fingers signify "intention," and the hand is the organ of touch, *par excellence*. The last religious phase of this idea is seen in the Catholic gesture of benediction.

"*Badi* is the name given to the evil principle which, according to the view of Malay medicine-men, attends (like an evil angel) everything that has life, and inert objects also, for these are regarded as animate." It is also described as "the enchanting or destroying influence which issues from anything, *e.g.* from a tiger which one sees, from a poison-tree which one passes under, from the saliva of a mad dog, from an action which one has performed; the contagious principle of morbid matter." It is applied to "all kinds of evil influences or principles such as may have entered into a man who has unguardedly touched a dead animal or bird, from which the *badi* has not yet been expelled, or who has met the

R. H. Codrington, in *Journ. Anthrop. Inst.* 279, 285, 305.

[2] *Id. op. cit.* 301.

Wild Huntsman in the forest." There are one hundred and ninety of these "mischiefs." Mr. Skeat compares the English word "mischief" in the phrase "it has the mischief in it." Illness is ascribed by the Malays to accidental contact with *badi*. A man also contracts *badi* when another practises magic on him by means of a wax image.[1] In Malay medicine neutralising ceremonies are used to destroy the evil principle, and also expulsory ceremonies to cast it out. The Malays also use counter-charms to neutralise the active principle of poison, and this is "extended to cover all cases where any evil principle (even for instance a familiar spirit) is believed to have entered the sick person's system."[2] Amongst the Arunta, when a man is ill, "he will sometimes have a stone *churinga* belonging to his totem brought from the storehouse. With the flint flake of his spear-thrower, he will scrape off some of the edge of the *churinga*, mix the dust with water and drink it, the mixture being supposed to be very strengthening. The idea evidently is, that in some way he absorbs part of the essence of the stone, thereby gaining strength, as it is endowed with the attributes of the individual whom it represents."[3] The Iroquois believed that sorcerers used an impalpable, invisible poison that carried infection through the air and produced death.[4] The Kurnai were afraid of white men, and believed that their eyes possessed a supernatural power. One would say to another, "Don't look, or he will kill you!" A white man could "flash death" upon a man. Death could only occur from accident, open violence, or secret magic. The last was met by counter-charms. "Every individual, though doubtful

[1] Skeat, *op. cit.* 427-29, 432.

[2] *Id.* 410, 425.

[3] Spencer and Gillen, *op. cit.* 135.

[4] Featherman, *op. cit.* iii. 43.

of his own magic powers, has no doubt about the possible powers of any other person. If the individual himself fails, he supposes that he is not strong enough. Nearly every one carries a round black pebble of magic power. For instance, if it is buried with a man's excreta, that person receives the magic *bulk* in his intestines and dies. The touch of it is supposed to be highly injurious to any but its owner. It is believed that a *bulk* has the power of motion; for instance a man once saw a *bulk*, in the shape of a bright spark of fire, cross over a house. From all this we may infer that some secret influence passes from the magic substance to the victim." Further, the magic influence, "may, they suppose, be communicated from this to some other substance, as a throwing-stick, spear, or club. Death also occurred through a combination of sorcery and violence: this combination was called *barn*." It is clear from the above that subjective hate and malice, the influence or will of a person, is regarded as materalised and visible.[1]

The material character of these properties is evident in all cases, and the last quotation gives a remarkable instance of magical property or human "intention" being visible. The common method of curing illness by cupping, or sucking out the "bad" blood, as used by the people of the Kei Islands,[2] is scientific in a way, but not to be distinguished from other early methods. Some curious developments of the materialistic conception are these. The Laplanders attributed disease to spiritual birds. They flew to the *shaman* (*noid*) and shook out of their feathers a multitude of poisonous insects, like lice, called magic flies, *lon*. If these flies

[1] Fison and Howitt, *Kamilaroi and Kurnai*, 248-49, 251-52.
[2] Riedel, *op. cit.* 419.

fell on men or beasts, they brought sickness and other misfortunes. The *noids* carefully gathered up these insects, but never touched them with bare hands; they kept them in boxes, using them to do injury.[1] This is a curious coincidence with the fact that germs of disease are known to be carried about by flies. They also used a magic axe, with which they touched people, and a disease thus caused could only be cured by the *noid* who caused it.[2] In the same way, the Encounter Bay tribes believed that if a person was lightly tapped upon the breast with the magic knobbed-stick, he would sicken and die. A similar magic weapon was a hatchet of black stone, of which the sharp end was used to bewitch men, and the obtuse end was only efficacious when women were the victims.[3] Again, Australian sorcerers extract from their own bodies by passes and manipulations a magical essence called *boylya*, which they can make to enter the patient's body.[4] The East Central Africans practice counter-irritation by making incisions in which ashes and roots are rubbed. This is called "killing the disease."[5] These ideas have produced the "sucking cure," with which the "cupping" of the Kei Islanders may be compared, and the conception, such as is found in Australia, that pain in any part of the body is due to the presence of some foreign substance. The Central Australians not only project into a sick man crystals to counteract the evil influence, but extract things from his body by sleight-of-hand. Avengers carry *churinga* like those kept as sacred objects, filled with souls of ancestors; "they are supposed, as usual, to impart to them strength, courage, accuracy

[1] *Journ. Anthrop. Inst.* xxiv. 149. [2] *Id. l.c.*
[3] Featherman, *op. cit.* ii. 179. [4] E. B. Tylor, *Primitive Culture*[3], ii. 146.
[5] *Journ. Anthrop. Inst.* xxii. 104.

of aim, and also to render them invisible to their enemies, and in addition they act as charms to prevent their wearers being wounded." A man injured by an avenger, was cured by a doctor extracting from his body a number of pieces of a *churinga*, which is used as the magical weapon, actually thrown. The stick has been "sung over" and is charged with magic and evil influence (*Arungquiltha*).[1]

Again, amongst the Maoris, a slave entering a sacred place, *wahi tapu*, had to take off his clothes first, else they would be rendered useless.[2] In this case we see that the sanctity of taboo is contagious, but does not agree with one of low rank. In Efate (one of the New Hebrides) the word *namim* means ceremonial "uncleanness." One sort is of death, another of child-birth. If a "sacred man" comes in contact with *namim*, it destroys his own "sacredness."[3] Again, amongst the modern Egyptians, if any one in a state of religious "uncleanness" enters a room where there is a person afflicted with ophthalmia, the incident aggravates the disease.[4] Many other cases of this cross-contagion could be mentioned. All the various sorts are the taboo force, while the fact that there are different varieties and that these sometimes cross, gives an opportunity of inferring their special origin. The Indians of Costa Rica, as we have noted before, know two kinds of ceremonial "uncleanness," *nya* and *bu-ku-rú*. Death and its concomitants are *nya*. *Bu-ku-rú* is the more dangerous and can kill. The worst kind of *bu-ku-rú* is that of a woman in her first pregnancy. She infects the whole neighbourhood. People think of it as an

[1] Spencer and Gillen, *op. cit.* 531, 480, 485-88, 489.
[2] Shortland, *op. cit.* 293.
[3] Macdonald, *Oceania*, 181.
[4] Lane, *op. cit.* i. 333.

evil spirit, or a property acquired. Any one going from her house carries the infection, and all deaths are laid to her charge; her husband pays the damages. *Bu-ku-rú* is also found in new houses and places visited after an interval, or for the first time.[1] The Zulu word *unesisila* means "you have dirt" or "are dirty," that is to say, you have done or said something, or some one has said or done something to you, which has bespattered you with metaphorical filth. Mr. Leslie compares the Scriptural "defile," and our expression "his hands are not clean." If a woman has been called the worst possible thing, viz. *omka ninazala*, *i.e.* "you will bear children to your father-in-law," she makes a great to-do; she goes to the hut of the person who used the phrase, and kills an animal, which is eaten by old women or little children, but by none of marriageable age. It takes over the *insila* which has now left the woman who was abused.[2] The Zulus, again, use two kinds of "medicine," black and white. Black wipes off "the black," which causes a man to be disliked, white causes him to be "bright," and therefore liked. The black is drunk and the body washed with it. It is emetic, and is vomited into a fire, and thus the "badness" is burnt and consumed. Or the contents of the stomach may be ejected on pathways, that others may walk over it, and take away the "filth" that is the cause of the offence. The "white" is thus used: if a man has been rejected by a girl, he adds to it something which she has worn next her skin, especially beads. Then he drinks it after sprinkling it on his head and over his body. Homœopathy is the principle of this method.[3] We can clearly

[1] Gabb *op. cit. l.c.*

[2] Leslie, *op. cit.* 169, 174-75.

[3] Callaway, *op. cit.* 142-43.

see from this case how personal properties are regarded as transmissible.

In these miscellaneous examples there are combined many features of contact which will be developed hereafter, and it will be noticed that these various "influences" are essentially of the kind which underlies the phenomena of taboo; whether they are ceremonial "uncleanness," evil influence of man or spirit, or "sacredness," each may be the property of the taboo character, either in its specialised form or as belonging to the ordinary individual. All are simply results of human characteristics, properties, and states.

Personal properties are what others suppose them to be, according to their estimate of the person in question; or, on the other hand, they are what their possessor supposes them or himself to be. He believes that he can transmit himself or his properties to others, with results according to the estimate he holds of his character at the time, and either with or without "intention"; and his fellowmen also believe that he can transmit himself to them, with results according to their estimate of him. Thus, in love-charms we find that the lover believes he can transmit his feelings or rather himself, full of love as he is, to his mistress, an idea arising straight from animal contact and ideas about it; and in sorcery, we find that men transmit their feelings of envy, hatred, and malice to the person concerned. These ideas are justified to their holders by such phenomena of contact as are scientifically true. Accordingly, a man can transmit his strength, his ability, and his personal influence, his crimes and his degradation, his splendour or his shame, voluntarily or involuntarily.

As illustrating the continuity of culture we may point

out that similar ideas exist now, though considerably lightened of their crude religious materialism, which, however, is preserved in language. When we say that A and B cannot *abide* each other, we are at the bottom of such institutions as Caste, Club, Clique, and such emotional attitudes as prejudice and insularity. We avoid the company of "publicans and sinners"; we say, we do not wish to be *contaminated* by their presence; we speak of moral *influence* in terms which are still materialistic; we talk of being *poisoned* by a man or by a book. Such constant human ideas need only to be accentuated by religion to produce exactly the same results of subjective feeling which gave rise to the phenomena of social taboo.

Using the language of contagion, as more convenient, for primitive man does not distinguish between transmission of disease and transmission of all other states and properties, we find that practically every human quality or condition can be transferred to others. Where evil influence or dangerous properties are not differentiated, we have seen many cases of their contagion and infection. Very often the force of taboo, when thus vaguely conceived, has correspondingly vague results in transmission, such as sudden death, sickness, or other supernatural visitations. Similar vague results follow the ill-wishes of an enemy, unless he specifies the effect he desires, but this will, of course, be sickness or death as a rule. This vagueness of result is naturally found most in the conception of the persons who receive the contagion, as they do not know the "intention," to use the term in its liturgical sense, of the dangerous person.

Degradation, as is well seen in Caste countries, is contagious. Thus, in ancient India, a Brahmin became an outcast by using the same carriage or seat or by eating with an outcast.[1] The touch of an inferior still contaminates a high-caste Hindoo.[2] In Burma a man may be defiled by sitting or eating with a low-caste Sandala.[3] The black Jews of Loango are so despised that no one will eat with them.[4] In Travancore courtiers must cover the mouth with the right hand, lest their breath should pollute the king or other superior. Also at the temples, a low-caste man must wear a broad bandage over his nose and mouth, that his breath may not pollute the idols.[5] In Egypt the Jews are regarded as so unclean by the Moslems that their blood would defile a sword, and therefore they are never beheaded.[6] The name of the Rodiya caste in Ceylon means "filth." No recognised caste could deal or hold intercourse with a Rodiya. Their contact was shunned as "pollution," and they themselves acquiesced. On the approach of a traveller they would shout, to warn him to stop till they could get off the road, and allow him to pass without the risk of too close proximity to their persons. "The most dreadful of all punishments under the Kandyan dynasty was to hand over the offender, if a lady of high rank, to the Rodiyas. She was 'adopted' by the latter thus: a Rodiya took *betel* from his own mouth, placed it in hers, and after this till death her degradation was indelible. As if to demonstrate that within the lowest depths of degradation there may exist a lower still, there are two races of outcasts in Ceylon who are abhorred and avoided, even by the Rodiyas." The latter would tie up their dogs, to prevent them prowling in search of food to the

[1] *Laws of Manu* (ed. Bühler), xi. 181.
[2] Ward, *op. cit.* ii. 149; Colebrooke, in *Asiatick Researches*, vii. 277.
[3] D'Urville, *op. cit.* i. 173.
[4] Bastian, *Loango-Küste*, i. 278.
[5] S. Mateer, *Native Life in Travancore*, 129.
[6] Lane, *op. cit.* ii. 346.

dwellings of these wretches.[1] Dulness can be transmitted; thus the Red Indians will not eat animals of a gross quality, because such food conveys "dulness" to the system.[2] The Indians of Equador believe that eating "heavy" meats produces unwieldiness.[3] Timidity can be transferred, as amongst the Dyaks, where young men are forbidden to eat venison, because it would make them timid as deer.[4] The Hottentots will not eat the flesh of hares, because it would make them faint-hearted.[5] Stupidity, according to the people of Morocco, is the chief characteristic of the hyæna. A dull man is said to have eaten the brains of an hyæna. A woman can make her husband stupid by giving him hyæna meat.[6] Weakness is transmissible; amongst the Barea man and wife seldom share the same bed. The reason they give is, "that the breath of the wife weakens her husband."[7] Effeminacy is transmissible; amongst the Omahas if a boy plays with girls he is dubbed "hermaphrodite";[8] in the Wiraijuri tribe boys are reproved for playing with girls—the culprit is taken aside by an old man, who solemnly extracts from his legs some "strands of the woman's apron" which have got in.[9] Pain, also, can be transmitted or transferred. Thus the Australians apply a heated spear-thrower to the cheek of one who is suffering from toothache, and then throw it away, believing that the toothache is transferred to it.[10] In old Greek folklore, if one who had been stung by a scorpion sat on an ass, the pain was supposed to be transferred

[1] J. E. Tennent, *Ceylon*, 188-91.
[2] Adair, *op. cit.* 133.
[3] *Journ. Anthrop. Inst.* vii. 503.
[4] Spenser St. John, *Life in the Forests of the Far East*, i. 186.
[5] T. Hahn, *Tsuni-Goam*, 106.
[6] Leared, *op. cit.* 304.
[7] Munzinger, *op. cit.* 526.
[8] J. O. Dorsey, *Third Report of Bureau of Ethnology*, 266.
[9] *Journ. Anthrop. Inst.* xiii. 448.
[10] Dawson, *op. cit.* 59.

from him to the ass.[1] The taboo state resulting from sin and crime has material properties. At the purification ceremony of the Cherokees, they threw their old clothes into the river, supposing thus their impurities to be removed.[2] Similarly the Incas shook their clothes for the same purpose, and passed the hands over head and face, arms and legs, as if washing. It was done to drive evil and maladies away.[3] At the installation of a king in the Sandwich Islands, the priest struck him on the back with a sacred branch, by way of purifying him from all defilement and guilt he may have contracted.[4] Consequently, it is transmissible by contagion. Thus in East Central Africa, when a wife has been guilty of unchastity, her husband will die if he taste any food she has salted; when preparing his food, she asks a little girl to put the salt in it. A guilty wife may be forgiven by her husband, but in this case he cannot live with the faithless one till a third party has been with her.[5] Amongst the Falashas a visit to an unbeliever's dwelling is considered a sin, and subjects the transgressor to the penance of submitting to a thorough ablution before he is permitted to enter his home.[6] A Brahman embraced the Rajah of Travancore, undertaking to bear his sins and diseases.[7] The idea is well brought out in the familiar practice of "sin-eating." It is well known that the highest religions have found it difficult, and in view of the materialism of human thought not altogether desirable, to rise beyond a material conception of "sin." The savage conceives of the results of sin, such as breaking of taboo, as material, and clinging to his person, and

[1] *Geoponica*, xiii. 9; xv. 1.
[2] *Id. l.c.*
[3] Frazer, *op. cit.*[2], iii. 74.
[4] Ellis, *Polynesian Researches*, iii. 110.
[5] Macdonald, *Africana*, i. 173; *Journ. Anthrop. Inst.* xxii. 110.
[6] Featherman, *op. cit.* v. 635.
[7] Mateer, *op. cit.* 136.

at both ends of the chain of culture sin is washed away by water, and can be transmitted by "contagion" in early culture, by "influence" in later.

Early man is only too well aware of the contagion and infection of certain sicknesses and diseases. Of sickness we need no instances, but of the interesting fact that death not only causes sickness but is in itself contagious, we may cite illustrations.

Beginning with the correlation of evil spirits and dangerous human properties, we find that where spirits are thought of, the fear is that others may be attacked by them in the same way as the dead man. They are naturally supposed to hang about their quarry, and often the dead man is identified with the angel of death who killed him. In Halmahera after a death, fire is set round the house to keep the evil spirits from the body.[1] In Cambodia a dead body is carried away feet foremost that it may not see the house, in which event other sicknesses and other deaths would result.[2] On Teressa Island, one of the Nicobars, the mourners shave their heads, and drown their grief by drinking hard. On the day of death they are not allowed to go to the jungle, lest they might be killed by the demons, and they abstain from the food which was most relished by the deceased in his lifetime.[3] Amongst the Yorubas death is generally attributed to witchcraft. Enquiry is made whether any other member of the family is threatened with the like fate, and also whether the soul of the dead is likely to be further molested by the evil spirits.[4] The Navajos ascribe death to the devil, *Chinde*, who remains about the dead man. Those who bury him, protect their bodies from the evil influence by smearing themselves

[1] Riedel, in *Zeitschrift für Ethnologie*, xvii. 84.
[2] Aymonier, *op. cit.* 202.
[3] Featherman, *op. cit.* ii. 247.
[4] A. B. Ellis, *op. cit.* 155.

with tar.[1] The Kamchadales abandoned the cabin in which a man died, because the judge of the underworld had been there and might cause the death of others. Those who buried a corpse feared being pursued by death, and to avoid him they took certain precautions.[2] At Batta funerals men march behind the coffin brandishing swords to drive away the *begus* or demons.[3] Amongst the Clallams and Twanas there is a superstitious fear about going near the dead body, for fear the evil spirit who killed the man may kill them also.[4] Here we see how the idea of the contagion of death is connected with evil spirits. Men fear that they may meet with the same fate as the dead man. Amongst the Koosa Kaffirs there is a general fear that illness or misfortune may fall upon others if a dying person is not removed from the *kraal*. From the same motive if they see a person drowning, or in danger of his life in any way, particularly if he should utter a scream of terror, they always run away from him.[5] The latter idea is world-wide and obtains amongst ourselves.

Passing to transmission of the state or influence of death, we find that immediately after a death has occurred the Karalits carry out every movable article, "that it may not be contaminated and rendered unclean."[6] There is a Swiss superstition that the dress of a child that dies will kill any child it is given to.[7] Amongst the Talmud Jews "whenever a death occurs in a house, all the water is poured out; for it is supposed that the Angel of Death defiles the water by washing off the poison drops that adhere to his sword." The corpse is carefully

[1] *First Report of the Bureau of Ethnology*, 123.
[2] Georgi, *op. cit.* 91, 92.
[3] Featherman, *op. cit.* ii. 330.
[4] *First Report of the Bureau of Ethnology*, 176.
[5] Lichtenstein, *op. cit.* i. 258.
[6] Featherman, *op. cit.* iii. 437.
[7] Ploss, *Das Kind*, i. 240.

washed; and after the funeral the mourners wash their hands.[1] At a death all members of a Zulu *kraal* eat "medicine" to protect them from evil influences. When the king's mother died he was begirt with charms "to keep the evil from him."[2] "To prevent death from entering" the food and drink iron used to be put in them by the Northern Scots. Whisky has been spoiled by neglect of this.[3] In the Babar Islands after a burial no one may go back to his house until he has washed his hands and eaten some food.[4] The Northern Indians were "unclean" after murder; all concerned in it could not cook any kind of victuals for themselves or others. They could not drink out of any other dish, or smoke out of any other pipe than their own, and none other would drink or smoke out of theirs. For a long time they would not kiss their wives or children.[5] In Samoa those who attended upon a dead person were careful not to handle any food, and for days were fed by others, as if they were helpless infants; while the dead body was in the house, no food was eaten inside, the family took their meals out of doors.[6] Amongst the Central Eskimo, "when a child dies, women who carried it in their hands must throw their jackets away if the child has urinated on them."[7] Among the Navajos of New Mexico and Arizona the person who touches or carries the dead body takes off his clothes afterwards, and washes his body before mingling with the living.[8] The Ilavars of Travancore ascribe "pollution" to the house after a death.[9] The Greenlanders believe that if a man when whale-fishing

[1] Featherman, *op. cit.* v. 156.
[2] Leslie, *op. cit.* 197, 252.
[3] W. Gregor, *Folklore of the North-East of Scotland*, 206.
[4] J. G. F. Riedel, *De sluik- en kroesharige rassen tusschen Selebes en Papua*, 360.
[5] S. Hearne, *Journey to the Northern Ocean*, 204-5.
[6] Turner, *op. cit.* 145.
[7] F. Boas, *The Central Eskimo*, 612.
[8] *First Report of the Bureau of Ethnology*, 123.
[9] Mateer, *op. cit.* 90.

wears a dirty dress, especially one that is contaminated by touching a corpse, the whales will retire.[1] Amongst the Bechuanas death is believed liable to come upon all the cattle when a widow is mourning her husband.[2] In the Aru Islands the humours of a decaying corpse are used sometimes to make a man ill, by the help of the soul of the dead man. During the first night after getting rid of the dead body, no one will sleep in the house for fear of being made sick by meeting the soul of the dead man in their dreams.[3] The ceremonial "uncleanness," then, so generally ascribed to the dead, is the property of taboo, and is based on the ideas of contact which underlie social taboo.

Hence the custom of destroying the personal property of the dead. The Zulus burn this "because they are afraid to wear anything belonging to a dead man."[4] The Nicobarese never use any object belonging to one who has been murdered, unless it has been previously purified by the sorcerer.[5] The Greenlanders throw out of the house everything belonging to the dead man, else they would be polluted and their lives unfortunate; the danger remains until the smell of the corpse has passed away.[6] Here, as in other examples, there is seen the obvious connection of the idea of contagion with smell. The practice of cremation originated in the same way.

Another reason for this destruction of property, namely, to provide the dead man with utensils and furniture in the next world, is well known, and often combines with the present explanation, though probably it is later in origin.

Another result is the common practice of deserting

[1] Cranz, *op. cit.* i. 120.
[2] *South African Folklore Journal*, i. 34.
[3] Riedel, *op. cit.* 267.
[4] Callaway, *op. cit.* 13.
[5] Featherman, *op. cit.* ii. 250.
[6] Cranz, *op. cit.* i. 217.

the house, or destroying it, after sickness or death. A common reason for this practice in sickness is to mislead the evil spirits by removing the sick man to another house. With this may be compared the custom of pretending that the sick man is dead, by performing funeral rites over a dummy corpse. Burial places are notoriously of evil omen, because they are infected by death and by the dead. The Gorngai and Tungu are afraid to visit the places where the dead are buried, for fear the spirits may make them ill.[1] The ground is often regarded as a good conductor of evil and disease. In Tenimber and Timorlaut strangers are not buried, for fear that sickness may thus spread over the country.[2] From this idea comes the common objection to burial among early peoples, no less than in modern times when cremation is becoming fashionable. The Masai do not bury people, because, as they say, the body would poison the soil.[3] Exactly the same practice and belief is found in East Central Africa.[4] This idea, combined with fear of ghosts, has helped to form the relatively late phenomena of ancestral and Chthonian hierology. It is also one factor in the formation of the common idea that the ground is dangerous. We shall not, perhaps, be wrong in adding the multifarious dangers in the shape of snakes, scorpions, and other things that creep upon the ground. On this hypothesis we may explain the rule that people in certain taboo states may not touch the ground, because there is the abode of evil, material and spiritual. Combined with this is the other side of the idea, namely, that "virtue" is apt to be conducted into the soil by contact, as has been worked out by Dr. Frazer.[5] As to spirits there residing, in

[1] Riedel, *op. cit.* 271. [2] *Id.* 306. [3] Thomson, *op. cit.* 211, 259.
[4] *Journ. Anthrop. Inst.* xxii. 113. [5] *Op. cit.* iii. 202 sqq.

Ethiopia you should never throw fluid on the ground, lest you hurt the dignity of some unseen elf.[1] The natives of Kola and Kobroor fear the spirit who lives in the ground.[2] The Bedouins never throw an object to the ground without saying *Tesdur*, "Permission."[3] In the Punjab spirits are thought to be in the habit of upsetting bedsteads; accordingly, bride and groom may not sleep on bedsteads for several days before and after marriage.[4] In spiritualistic *séances* held by Guiana sorcerers, the rule is that one must not put one's feet to the ground, for the spirits are swarming there.[5]

From the belief in the contagion and infection of death, combined with the belief in and fear of the ghosts of the dead, the origin of which I would explain on the lines used above in the account of personal agents, arises the taboo upon mourners, who are, from their proximity, in danger from the dead and also dangerous to others. I would also attribute to this contagion of death the rule of the ancient Romans, that *patrimi* and *matrimi* only, boys and girls whose parents respectively both live, may be acolytes in ceremonies.

Turning to the beneficent side of the taboo state, where the individual is benevolent: he can transmit his beneficence or good qualities, and others believe that they can receive them from him, with the same limitations connected with "intention." Rajah Brooke was regarded by the Dyaks, because of what he had done for them, as a supernatural being. He was believed "to shed influence over them." Whenever he visited a village, the people used to bring some of the *padi* seed they were going to sow, for him to make it produc-

[1] Harris, *op. cit.* ii. 296.
[2] Riedel, *op. cit.* 271.
[3] Featherman, *op. cit.* v. 424.
[4] *Panjab Notes and Queries*, i. 214.
[5] Im Thurn, *op. cit.* 335.

tive; and women bathed his feet, preserving the water to put on the fields and make them fertile.[1] Here is the vague sort of beneficent influence materially transmitted. In Melanesia, *mana*, which is a man's character, ability, influence, and power combined, in other words, himself and his attributes materialised, can be transferred to young men or others by the laying-on of hands.[2] Amongst love-charms, the transmission by the lover of his loving qualities, of himself impregnated with love, to his mistress, to inspire her with affection, is world-wide. Thus in European folk-custom, a lover applies a piece of his hair, drops of his blood or sweat, or water in which he has washed his hands, to the garments of the girl whose affection he desires.[3] In this kind of thing we reach down to the origin of ideas of contact in physiological thought. Similarly, friendship and friendly feelings are transmissible, as will be seen in the ceremonies common at making peace or consolidating friendship.

Again, world-wide customs attest the belief that properties such as strength, courage, swiftness, and the like, can be transmitted by contact with those possessing them, or by assimilating separable parts of such persons. Hence, as is at last becoming well known, the origin and chief meaning of cannibalism. The flesh and blood of a man are, by a natural fallacy, regarded as the best means for transmission of his properties. The flesh of a slain enemy is eaten and his blood drunk by the savage in order to acquire his strength and courage. The Bechuanas have a solemn ceremony of eating the flesh of an enemy killed, "following the ancient superstition that eating human flesh inspires courage, and by

[1] Low, *op. cit.* 247, 259.

[2] Codrington, in *Journ. Anthrop. Inst.*, *l.c.*

[3] Ploss u. Bartels, *op. cit.* ii. 442 ff.

degrees renders the warrior invincible. So far from liking it, they feel abhorrence, and yield to it only from superstition."[1] The flesh of a slain enemy is eaten in Timorlaut to cure impotence.[2] The New Caledonians eat slain enemies to acquire courage and strength.[3] Before battle the Zulus "ceremoniously eat cattle to get their qualities, that they may be brave."[4] The Amaxosa drink the gall of an ox to make themselves fierce.[5] The notorious Matuana drank the gall of thirty chiefs, believing it would render him strong.[6] The Pinya, or armed band of the Dieri, by whom offences are punished, after putting a man to death, wash their weapons, "and, getting all the gore and flesh adhering to them off, mix it with some water; a little of this is given to each to swallow, and they believe that thereby they will be inspired with courage and strength. The fat of the murdered man is cut off and wrapped round the weapons of all the old men."[7] The people of Halmahera drink the blood of slain enemies, in order to become brave.[8] In Amboina warriors drink the blood of enemies they have killed, to acquire their courage.[9] The Muskogees ate the hearts of enemies to get courage, and their brains to get intellect.[10] The Battas greedily drink the blood and eat the flesh of prisoners of war and condemned criminals.[11] The people of Celebes drink the blood of enemies to make themselves strong.[12]

The idea is further generalised amongst the natives

[1] Lichtenstein, *op. cit.* ii. 290.
[2] Riedel, *op. cit.* 279.
[3] Garnier, *Nouvelle Calédonie*, 347.
[4] Callaway, *op. cit.* 438.
[5] Shooter, *op. cit.* 216.
[6] *Id. l.c.*
[7] Curr, *op. cit.* ii. 53.
[8] Riedel, in *Zeitschrift für Ethnologie*, xvii. 86.
[9] *Id. De sluik-en kroesharige rassen tusschen Selebes en Papua*, 52.
[10] J. Adair, *op. cit.* 135.
[11] Featherman, *op. cit.* ii. 335.
[12] Riedel, in *Bijdragen tot de Taal Land en Volkenkunde van Nederlandsch Indië*, xxxv. 5, i. 90.

of Central Australia. "When starting on an avenging expedition or *Atninga*, every man of the party drinks some blood, and also has some spurted over his body, so as to make him what is called *uchuilima*, that is, lithe and active. The elder men indicate from whom the blood is to be drawn, and the men so selected must not decline, though the amount drawn from a single individual is often very great; indeed, we have known of a case in which blood was taken from a young and strong man until he dropped down from sheer exhaustion."[1] In the Luritcha tribe of Central Australia "young children are sometimes killed and eaten, and it is not an infrequent custom, when a child is in weak health, to kill a younger and healthy one, and then to feed the weakling on its flesh, the idea being that this will give to the weak child the strength of the stronger one."[2] The natives of the Dieri and neighbouring tribes will eat a man and drink his blood in order to acquire his strength; the fat is rubbed on sick people.[3] In Tasmania a man's blood was often administered as a healing draught.[4] South Australian women will rub their gums till they bleed, and give the blood to be swallowed by their husbands, to cure sickness.[5] Many peoples, for instance the Yorubas, believe that the "blood is the life."[6] The Shoshones believed that they became animated by the spirit of a fallen foe if they partook of his flesh.[7] From this comes the idea that inspiration can be effected by drinking blood.

Similarly the flesh and blood of animals are taken to acquire their characteristics. Hottentots will not eat the flesh of hares, for fear it might make them timid,

[1] Spencer and Gillen, *op. cit.* 461.
[2] *Id.* 475.
[3] *Journ. Anthrop. Inst.* xxiv. 171, 178, 179, 182.
[4] Bonwick, *op. cit.* 89.
[5] Featherman, *op. cit.* ii. 178.
[6] A. B. Ellis, *op. cit.* 65.
[7] Featherman, *op. cit.* iii. 206.

but they will eat a lion's flesh and drink its blood, in order to get its courage and strength.[1] Among the Motu boys eat pigs and other animals to acquire their strength.[2] The men of Buru and the Aru Islands eat dogs to become bold and nimble.[3] In Morocco it is believed that eating lion's flesh makes cowards brave. On the same principle ants are given to lethargic people, an excellent practical application of the proverb. If a woman meets an hyæna she becomes stupid, for the hyæna is the most stupid of animals; of a dull man one says, "he has eaten the brains of an hyæna." A woman will sometimes administer such brain-sauce to her husband, who thus becomes stupid, and her ascendancy over him is rendered complete.[4]

Every part of a man's body is regarded by primitive science as impregnated with his properties; but such parts are especially so considered which themselves are held to have a special connection with the life and soul; and these are chiefly important organs and centres. From each and any of these parts of the organism, transmission of properties can be effected, with beneficent or maleficent results according to circumstances or the subjective estimate held at the time. Instructive examples are found in folk-medicine.[5]

Various modes of transmission have appeared already. Others will be seen in the following examples. The most certain method of acquiring properties is by eating and drinking, but any mode of contact will suffice, and in such modes primitive thought includes sight, proximity, and similar connections; "intention" even can form the link by *actio in distans*. We have also

[1] Hahn, *op. cit.* 106.
[2] Chalmers, *Pioneering in New Guinea*, 166.
[3] Riedel, *De sluik- en kroesharige rassen tusschen Selebes en Papua*, 10, 262.
[4] Leared, *op. cit.* 281, 304.
[5] W. Black, *Folk Medicine*, *passim*.

seen cases of transmission by the most obvious vehicle, flesh and blood, and we now proceed to pass others in review. The people of Wetar make especial use of the blood and the head of slain enemies to acquire their properties.[1] The head is naturally supposed sacred by most peoples, the Siamese and the Maoris, for instance; if a Maori touched his head he had to put his fingers to his nose "and snuff up the sanctity which they had acquired by the touch, and thus restore it to the part from which it was taken." Also he could not blow the fire, for his breath being sacred communicated sanctity to the fire, and any one using it for cooking might die.[2] The Malays still regard the head as "sacred."[3] A New Zealand chief would eat the eyes of a dead enemy to improve himself.[4] In the island Wetar the men during war eat the tongue, heart, and liver of slain enemies, believing that in these parts the soul resides. They also drink their blood mixed with *kalapa* water.[5] In Buru they eat the hearts of dogs in order to become brave and swift.[6] After the Italones of Luzon have killed an enemy, they drink his blood and eat raw the lungs, brain, etc., supposing that this gives them spirit and courage.[7] The Kamilaroi ate the heart and liver of a brave man in order to obtain his courage.[8] In Uganda the liver is regarded as the seat of the soul, and by eating liver one may improve one's powers.[9] The Shiré Highlanders eat the heart of a brave man to acquire his courage.[10]

Another mode of transmission is rubbing the stuff into the skin or anointing. Australians rub themselves

[1] Riedel, *op. cit.* 445. [2] Loubere, *op. cit.* i. 175; R. Taylor, *Te ika a Maui*, 165.
[3] Skeat, *op. cit.* 43. [4] Taylor, *op. cit.* 352. [5] Riedel, *op. cit. l.c.*
[6] *Id.* 10. [7] Featherman, *op. cit.* ii. 501. [8] Fison and Howitt, *op. cit.* 160.
[9] Felkin, *Transactions of the Royal Society of Edinburgh*, xiii. 218.
[10] J. Buchanan, *The Shiré Highlands*, 138.

with the fat of a slain enemy, believing that his qualities are thus transferred to themselves; they rub sick persons also with it. Human fat is used to grease weapons, which thus gain additional power.[1] The fat of a pig is melted and poured over and rubbed into the body of the Andamanese boy at puberty; this "makes him strong."[2] We may compare such cases as that in the Homeric hymn, where Demeter anointed Demophoon with ambrosia, "breathed sweetness over him, and held him in her arms" and "he waxed like a god."[3] Another method of the Andamanese is mere pressure of the animal on to the person's body.[4] Or again, a powder may be made of the substance. The Yorubas sacrifice a slave to ensure success in war. The heart is made into a powder, which mingled with rum is sold to those who "wish to be endowed with courage." They drink this, believing that the "heart is the seat of courage, and the qualities with which it is inspired can be taken into the system."[5] Amongst the Northern Indians the genital organs of any beast killed are eaten by men and boys; they must not be cut with an edge tool, but are torn to pieces with the teeth. They believe that if a dog should eat any part of them, it would have the same effect on their success in hunting that a woman crossing their hunting track at an improper period would have. The same ill-success is supposed to attend them if a woman eat any of those parts.[6] Primitive thought by a natural fallacy attributes *strength* to these parts and their secretions, just as it attributes *life* to blood. The Central Australians

[1] Brough Smyth, *op. cit.* ii. 313; *Journ. Anthrop. Inst.* xxiv. 178; Eyre, *op. cit.* ii. 315.
[2] E. H. Man, *The Aborigines of the Andaman Islands*, 66.
[3] *Hymn to Demeter*, 236.
[4] Man, in *Journ. Anthrop. Inst.* xii. 134.
[5] A. B. Ellis, *op. cit.* 69.
[6] Hearne, *op. cit.* 319.

administer blood from the genital organs in cases of severe sickness.[1] The people of Mowat believe that the penis of great warriors slain in battle possesses "virtue," and it is therefore worn by the victor to increase his strength.[2] In South Africa during a protracted war, the soldiers are frequently "doctored" in order to stimulate their courage. The heart, liver, and testicles of the slain enemies are made into a broth, which is taken internally, and also used as a war-paint.[3] The Woloffs carry the prepuce, removed at circumcision, as an amulet, believing that it will make them strong in procreation.[4]

Here may be mentioned a common case of primitive argument from analogy, the idea, namely, that any object resembling a part of the body, may possess the virtues of such part. In this is probably to be found the origin of the beliefs concerning beans and vegetables of similar shape. Their obvious resemblance to the *testes* is perhaps the ultimate explanation of the well-known taboo, as enforced by the Pythagoreans. The frequent prohibition against the eating of snakes, eels, and similarly shaped animals has a similar origin.

In Devon and Scotland, to cure whooping-cough, a hair from the child's head is put between slices of bread and butter and given to a dog. If the dog cough while eating it, the whooping-cough is transferred to the animal and the child is cured.[5] In Devonshire you can give a neighbour ague by burying a dead man's hair under his threshold.[6] Pliny mentions the use of hair to cure various sicknesses.[7] The Kaffir charm, *isiko lobulunga*, consists in tying the long hair

[1] Spencer and Gillen, *op. cit.* 464.
[2] *Journ. Anthrop. Inst.* xix. 462.
[3] *Id.* xix. 416.
[4] *Revue d'Anthropologie* for 1882, 292.
[5] Black, *op. cit.* 35.
[6] *Id.* 27.
[7] Pliny, *Historia Naturalis*, xxviii. 20.

drawn from the tail of a cow round one's neck, to prevent any kind of evil. "Each family has certain cattle set apart for this purpose, and which are to a certain extent considered sacred." When a woman is married, she takes with her the ox which has been consecrated for her protection, and from the tail of which the *lobulunga* or long hair was taken which is tied round her neck.[1] After circumcision a Dieri boy has wrapped round his waist a rope of hair taken from the heads of the men, women, and children.[2] Amongst the Central Australians the use of the hair of others is a developed system; every one is entitled to acquire hair from some one else, and the claim is arranged according to relationship. The intention of this use of hair is shown clearly by the following practice. The natives, when "avenging blood," "wear round the waist the *kirra-urkna* or girdle made from the hair which has been cut from a warrior after his death, and which is supposed to add to the wearer all the warlike virtues of the dead man."[3]

Amongst many peoples bones are used for healing diseases and preventing danger, and for causing such. The idea is that human virtue permanently resides in them. Amongst the extinct Tasmanians the ashes of a burnt body, human bones attached to the parts affected, a child's skull hung round the neck, were all efficacious means to stop the progress of disease.[4] In order to be invulnerable in war, the men of Timorlaut wash in holy water, and use amulets. By way of protection in battle, they use the *epistropheus* of a slain enemy. The water in which it is placed is drunk and

[1] Maclean, *op. cit.* 92, 93.

[2] Curr, *op. cit.* ii. 56.

[3] Spencer and Gillen, *op. cit.* 480, 539.

[4] Featherman, *op. cit.* ii. 106; J. G. Bourke, *Scatalogic Rites of all Nations*, 378-79.

the body washed with it.[1] Pliny mentions the custom according to which the first tooth shed by a child was worn as an amulet, and protected him from pain; sometimes this cured toothache.[2]

Finger-nail clippings are used in folk-medicine to transmit strength. Human skin, flesh, and "mummy" are used for the same purpose.[3] The Manicheans sprinkled their eucharistic bread with human semen, a custom followed by the Albigenses.[4] Human semen, as medicine, is used by many peoples, as by the Australians, who believe it an infallible remedy for severe illness.[5] It is so used in European folk-custom, where we also find it used as a love-charm,[6] on the principle of transmission of qualities.[7] Menstrual blood is also used in medicine and as a love-charm.[8] Pliny states that if door-posts are touched with menstrual fluid, all spells of witchcraft are dissolved.[9] The menstrual fluid is used in Angola to cure bites of centipedes.[10] The Ovaherero believe that to add one's urine, even unintentionally, to the food of another, bewitches that person and does him grievous harm.[11] Urine is very commonly used in folk-medicine.[12] Amongst the extinct Tasmanians the urine of women was thought to possess specific virtues.[13] Amongst most Australians aspersion of female urine was held to be a panacea for nearly all ailments.[14]

The Kaffirs hold it a capital crime to ease nature in a cattle-fold, or in a river, as it pollutes the water.[15] In

[1] Riedel, *op. cit.* 298.
[2] Pliny, *op. cit.* xxviii. 7, 12.
[3] Bourke, *op. cit.* 256, 346-47; Pliny, *op. cit.* xxviii. 10.
[4] Picart, *Coutumes et cérémonies religieuses*, viii. 79.
[5] Beveridge, *The Aborigines of Victoria and Riverina*, 55; Bourke, *op. cit. l.c.*
[6] *Id.* 343, 355.
[7] *Id.* 219.
[8] *Id.* 354.
[9] Pliny, xxviii. 24.
[10] Bourke, *op. cit.* 351-52.
[11] *Id.* 376.
[12] *Id.* 300, 338; Eyre, *op. cit.* ii. 300.
[13] Featherman, *op. cit.* ii. 106.
[14] *Id.* ii. 177.
[15] Lichtenstein, *op. cit.* i. 289.

this case we see the deleterious aspect of a taboo substance, and the action of disgust.

Again, the smell of a man contains his properties. Thus when a Central Australian black-fellow is eating, he must take care that certain relatives by marriage do not see what he is eating, lest they should spoil it by what is called *Equilla timma*, which means "projecting their smell into it." Should a man eat meat which has been killed or seen by any of these persons, the food would disagree with him, and he would sicken and suffer severely.[1]

Human qualities are transmitted by the breath. Chiquito doctors fill themselves with dainties, chickens, hens, and partridges, etc., to render their health wholesomer and stronger, for blowing the body of patients.[2] Healing by the breath is a common idea in the East.[3] Blowing on a person is a common method of "bewitching" him. A Maori could not blow the fire, for his breath being sacred, communicated his sanctity to it, and some one might use the fire for cooking and be thus injured.[4] Health is transmitted by breathing amongst the Columbians.[5] The common people of Timor place the hand before the mouth when they address the Rajah, that their profane breath may not pollute him.[6]

Pliny notes that the Greeks used the scrapings of the bodies of athletes to cure rheumatism, sprains, and uterine troubles.[7]

Folk-medicine has examples of the transference of disease by putting one's sweat on a dog.[8] The Nubians

[1] Spencer and Gillen, *op. cit.* 469.

[2] Dobrizhoffer, *op. cit.* ii. 263.

[3] Ploss, *Das Kind*, i. 200; Skeat, *op. cit.* 430; R. F. Burton, *The Arabian Nights*, v. 30.

[4] Taylor, *op. cit.* 165.

[5] Bancroft, *op. cit.* i. 286.

[6] Featherman, *op. cit.* ii. 465.

[7] Pliny, *op. cit.* xxviii. 18.

[8] Bourke, *op. cit.* 349.

"suppose it will give them strength to apply the sweat of their horses to their own bodies. After a ride they scrape off the sweat from their horses' backs with the hand, and rub it about their persons as if it were one of their ordinary greasy ointments. A horse is not an unclean animal, and cannot defile." These people have a practice which shows well the ideas of transmission of properties. Before the tongue of any animal is eaten, the tip is cut off; on human analogy they believe that "here is the seat of curses and ill-wishes."[1]

Some Queensland tribes used to flay a slain enemy and preserve the skin as powerful "medicine." They would cover their patients with it as with a blanket.[2] This case forms a link with those in which a man's garments contain his properties, and accordingly can transmit them through the bodily exhalations remaining therein. In early thought a man's dress is a real part of him, and can be used as a substitute for him. Thus in Tonga, when the office of high priest was vacant, his dress was put on his chair, and yams were offered to it. It was supposed to be an exact equivalent.[3] The Zulus call in "the lightning-doctor" to avert hail-storms. If he is not at home, they take his blanket, and spread it out before the storm. It is regarded as an equivalent.[4] On the principle of transmission, the Mikado's clothes, if worn by any one else, would cause the wearer pain and produce swellings. His taboo "sanctity" was such that his eating and drinking vessels were destroyed after being used once; any one eating from them would be seriously injured.[5]

Transmission of properties for good or evil, and

[1] Schweinfurth, *op. cit.* ii. 326, 327.

[2] Fison and Howitt, *op. cit.* 223.

[3] S. S. Farmer, *Tonga and the Friendly Islands*, 130.

[4] Callaway, *op. cit.* 378.

[5] Frazer, *op. cit.*[2] iii. 233.

assimilation of various kinds, are effected by eating food which a person has touched with his hands or any part of his body, or by eating with him or in his presence, or even by using the same kind of food and drink. This is a large subject, and will be separately discussed later. The connection of saliva with eating leads up to the next vehicle of transmission. The Masai asked Joseph Thomson to spit on them, believing his saliva to "have sovereign virtues." With these people spitting is a regular "expression of goodwill," and is customary at meetings and partings.[1] A curious instance, showing how this method of transmission can be extended, is found amongst the Zulus. The *Amatongo* (ancestral spirits) cause men to be sick; if a man dreams of one, the "doctor" tells him to spit out the spittle which is in his mouth when he dreams, and throw it behind his back; should he look behind him, the dream will recur.[2] The practice of using saliva for healing purposes and for love-charms is very common.[3] The transmission or projection of hatred, contempt, and other feelings by spitting is world-wide, and leads back to an animal practice. To spit in a man's face is the grossest form of insult throughout mankind,[4] and, like similar acts of animals, it is physically the modification of a blow, as is all contact itself.

Woman's milk is often used in folk-medicine to transmit health and strength. Conversely, a Bondei infant may not drink any milk but that of relatives, for fear of *usawi* witchcraft;[5] and the Garos abhor milk as "diseased matter."[6] A similar fear of human contagion is seen in the Kaffir custom. Milk is the chief article

[1] Thomson, *op. cit.* 165, 166.
[2] Callaway, *op. cit.* 161.
[3] Bourke, *op. cit.* 348.
[4] Riedel, *op. cit.* 259, 295, 406.
[5] G. Dale, in *Journ. Anthrop. Inst.* xxv. 183.
[6] H. B. Rowney, *Wild Tribes of India*, 193.

of food for all classes among the Kaffirs. One man only is allowed to touch the milk-bag.'[1]

Again, remoter forms of connection can effect transmission. The natives of the Mary River and Bunya-Bunya country had a great fear of persons stepping over their bodies while lying down. "When camping out with a black boy I have unthinkingly stepped over him, and have known him involuntarily to cry out with fear and to denounce the ignorance and stupidity of white people." They also "had a strange dread of passing under a leaning tree or even under the rails of a fence. Their reason for this was that a female might have been upon the tree or fence, and that some blood from her might have fallen upon it, and might fall from it on them."[2] Amongst other Australian tribes, a woman stepping over a man whilst asleep on the ground raises serious apprehensions.[3] The Bedouins believe that a person stepping over another who lies prostrate on the ground transfers to him all the maladies to which he is subject, or from which he may be suffering at the time.[4] When the son of Bábar was lying at the point of death, and the doctors could do nothing, "it was suggested that nothing could save him but some supreme sacrifice to God. Bábar eagerly caught at the hope, and resolved at once to lay down his life for his son. He entered his son's chamber, and, going to the head of the bed, walked gravely three times round the sick man, saying the while: 'On me be all that thou art suffering.' 'I have prevailed,' at last he was heard to cry, 'I have taken it.'"[5] In Tenimber it is a great insult to step over a man who is lying on the ground. As an insult

[1] Maclean, *op. cit.* 152.

[2] *Id.* i. 50.

[3] Curr, *op. cit.* iii. 179.

[4] Featherman, *op. cit.* v. 424.

[5] Lane Poole, *Bábar: the Founder of the Mughal Dynasty.*

it is coupled with spitting in a man's face.[1] In Ceram, when passing by a person who is sitting down, one must bow.[2] Mere touch or proximity even is quite enough. The sensitive part of a Kaffir "doctor" is his shoulders. No one may touch him there. If a man merely stands behind a doctor, he sends him off with the cry, "Get away! you are hurting me; it is as if you sat upon me."[3]

Further, in Ethiopia disease can be caused by the shadow of an enemy falling upon one.[4] Amongst the Hawaiians people may not let their shadows fall upon the chief.[5] The Malays and West Africans regard a man's shadow as a soul.[6]

The mere act of sight can also transmit qualities. Thus Kolosh women during menstruation and child-birth live in a special hut. They are avoided by the men, and wear at menstruation a peculiar hat, that they "may not defile heaven with a look."[7] Similarly amongst the Aleuts.[8] When Kaffirs have killed the "sacred" lion, to avert "danger" they rub their eyes with his skin, before they look at his dead body.[9] The natives of Borneo are afraid lest Europeans, by looking at them, should make them ill.[10] Some Papuans complained to an explorer that they began to die "as soon as you looked at us."[11] Guiana Indians, before approaching a dangerous place, rub their eyes with pepper to make them fill with water, by way of not seeing the dreaded object.[12]

1 Riedel, *op. cit.* 295.
2 *Id.* 129.
3 Callaway, *op. cit.* 159.
4 Harris, *op. cit.* ii. 158.
5 C. de Varigny, *Quatorze Ans aux Iles Sandwich*, 13.
6 Skeat, *op. cit.* 575; W. Reade, *Savage Africa*, 539.
7 Erman, *op. cit.* ii. 318.
8 Ploss, *Das Kind*, ii. 434.
9 Arbousset and Daumas, *Tour to the North-East Colony of the Cape of Good Hope*, 214.
10 Schwaner, *Borneo*, ii. 167.
11 D'Albertis, *op. cit.* 53.
12 im Thurn, *op. cit.* 369.

Similar phenomena are connected with the sense of sight throughout the world. As are all the senses, so sight is a form of contact, both in modern physics, primitive belief, and still to some extent in ordinary civilised ideas. The "power of the human eye" is a case of this, and we still fear "influence" by being looked at or by seeing persons and things. We prevent a child from seeing a dead person for sentimental reasons—early man did so for the more practical purpose of avoiding contagion.[1] So I would explain the common rule which forbids one to look back; after performing a dangerous thing or visiting a dangerous place. An interesting feature of these beliefs appears in the above-cited cases; to the savage, the same result ensues from seeing a dangerous thing and from being seen by it. The sense of sight is both active and passive, and contact through it can be effected from either end. The myth of the ostrich, which is supposed to bury its head in the sand in the idea that it thus becomes invisible, is repeated in human thought, both when the savage shuts his eyes to avoid seeing a dreaded thing, as an equivalent to not being seen by it, and when we shut our eyes to escape from a sight we are afraid of, or a thought that we would expel. The world-wide belief in the "evil eye," and the fact that psychical influence is most easily exerted by the look, illustrate these ideas. It is especially envy that is here transmitted. Lane mentions the case of an Egyptian refusing to buy meat from a well-patronised butcher's shop, because it would be poisonous to eat meat which had hung in the street before the eyes of the public, so that every beggar who passed envied it.[2]

Lastly, a man's words—heard, reported, or read—can

[1] Riedel, *op. cit.* 361.

[2] Lane, *op. cit.* i. 326.

transmit his "influence," both in our sense and in the primitive material sense of the word; and here we have another curious illustration of the really scientific materialism of early men. A man's kind words transmit his kind feelings; the civilised man and the uncivilised alike recognise the result in their own consciousness when they hear such words, but in the latter case material transmission has been effected. In the same way, a man's hatred is projected by a curse, and a man's general character can be transmitted, as will be seen hereafter, by taking his name. The name in savage thought is a real part of a man, or rather it is his "essence," the "real" sum of his characteristics. But so it is to us, if we consider the matter; the only difference is that to the savage the idea is "real" in the scholastic sense, to us it is "nominal."

Modern Egyptians cure sickness by writing a passage from the Koran on the inside of an earthern bowl; water is poured in and stirred till the writing is worked off; the patient drinks the water with the sacred words thus infused.[1] The Malays write charms on paper or cloth and wear them on the person; sometimes they are written on the body itself, especially on the part to be affected; occasionally they are written on a cup, which is then used for drinking purposes.[2] These cases serve to show what is a natural extension, transmission of properties effected from objects such as fetishes and charms, which are endowed by man's ideas with virtue and power, a conception well illustrated by the people of Surinam who wear iron, the "strong substance," in order to acquire strength,[3] or from things

[1] Lane, *op. cit.* i. 328. [2] Skeat, *op. cit.* 567.

[3] Martin, in *Bijdragen tot de Taal Land en Volkenkunde van Nederlandsch Indië*, xxxv. 5, t. 24

which have a connection with gods or sacred objects, such as holy water and consecrated substances. The Andamanese, before leaving home, get a medicine man to give them charms to keep off harm at the hands of those they are going to visit. He applies an ointment to their bodies and weapons. Hence they bear a charmed life, and their weapons are sure to kill.[1] When going to war, the Tenimberese are sprinkled with holy water; they also eat snakes in order to be brave. As charms against danger in war, they wear the *vertebræ* of a slain foe, as a necklace; also they steep this in water, then drink, and wash their bodies with it.[2]

Transmission of properties can thus be effected by any portion of the organism, or by anything that, in the wide view taken by the savage, belongs to the personality; but, conversely, as each and all of these are instinct with the life and character of the possessor, it follows that any result produced upon any of them, is regarded as done to the whole man. In primitive thought, the individualistic conception of personality is so sensitive, and so materialistic, that anything which has once formed part of the man, or anything that has been in but momentary contact with him, is held to retain its connection, and, when acted upon, to affect the original owner, whose substance it still preserves. From this derive two widely spread ideas, which are, like so many early thoughts, complementary to each other. The first is that of the external soul, as to which I need but refer to Dr. Frazer's account;[3] the second is the common belief that a part of one's self may be used as a substitute for the whole, or sacrificed to preserve the rest of the personality. The Fijians

[1] *Journ. Anthrop. Inst.* xii. 275.
[2] Riedel, *op. cit.* 298.
[3] J. G. Frazer, *The Golden Bough*[2], iii. 353 ff.

performed acts of devotion at mourning. They cut their hair short, burned the skin, and lopped off the end joints of the little toe and little finger.[1] To secure success in an undertaking the Mandans lop off one of the *phalanges* of their fingers, and preserve it in a bundle of *absinthium*.[2]

The idea that detachable portions of the organism retain the substance and life of the possessor, and, as such, bring upon him any injury they may receive, explains a common set of beliefs and practices concerned with the placenta, umbilical cord, and the "caul." In Amboina the placenta is hidden away in a tree.[3] In the Babar Islands women hang it in a tree; on their way they carry weapons, "because evil spirits might, if they got hold of the placenta, make the child ill."[4] The remains of the umbilical cord are sacred in New Zealand, Tahiti, Fiji, and many parts of the world.[5] In Iceland the caul is supposed to contain a part of the child's soul. It is kept safe, therefore, and sometimes buried under the threshold. Whoever destroys it, "robs the child of its soul."[6] The sacred character of the caul is well known in European folklore.[7] A particular point in connection with these appurtenances of the new-born child is, that as they preserve the substance of the possessor, they can give him health and strength in after-life. If a child is born with a caul, Amboinese women preserve this, and when the child is ill, dip it in water and give this water to the child to drink.[8] In Ceram the remains of the umbilical cord are kept, and hung round the child's neck to keep off sickness, or are otherwise used when the child is ill.[9]

1 Featherman, *op. cit.* ii. 205.
2 *Id. op. cit.* iii. 303.
3 Riedel, *op. cit.* 23.
4 *Id.* 355.
5 Ploss, *Das Kind*, i. 15.
6 *Id.* i. 13.
7 *Id.* i. 14.
8 Riedel, *op. cit.* 74.
9 *Id.* 135.

In the Watubela Islands the placenta is buried under a tree. The remains of the umbilical cord are preserved, to be used as medicine for the child.[1] In the islands Leti, Moa, and Lakor the child's navel-string is kept, and used by him later as an amulet in war or when travelling.[2] It is used as an amulet by the Somalis, Kalmucks, Chinese, Soongars, and Alfoers of Celebes.[3] In Greenland it cures the child's sicknesses. In ancient Peru and modern Europe it cures the child to whom it is given to suck.[4] Similarly with the "caul" with which an infant is sometimes born.[5] The Central Australians work the navel-string into a necklace which the child wears round its neck. "This makes it grow, keeps it quiet, and averts illness."[6] The connection, already noticed, between these appurtenances and the idea of the external soul, is also seen in the following cases: the Fijians buried the umbilical cord with a cocoa-nut, the last being intended to grow up by the time the child reached maturity.[7] It is interesting to compare the modern custom of planting a tree as a record of the birth of a child. The navel-string and the placenta are in South Celebes called the "brother" and "sister" of the child.[8]

We have seen the transmission, chiefly involuntary, of a man's properties through contact with him or with any part of him, or object that has had connection with him, and we now come to what is a development of these ideas of contact, in cases where the individual transmits his own properties or his feelings by means of contact with himself or by putting detachable parts of himself in contact with others, by an act of will or

[1] *Id.* 208.
[2] *Id.* 391.
[3] Ploss, *Das Kind*, i. 16, 17.
[4] *Id.* 17, 18.
[5] *Id.* 392.
[6] Spencer and Gillen, *op. cit.* 461.
[7] Williams, *op. cit.* i. 175.
[8] Matthes, *op. cit.* 57.

"intention." To impart "virtue" or ability, the Melanesian who is full of it (*mana*) lays his hands on the recipient.[1] The latter, of course, consciously or subconsciously would here perform an act of faith. So the lover imparts his love to his mistress by all kinds of methods—he sends a lock of hair, or food he has touched, in the hope that his personality contained therein will soften her heart, that is, that she may be assimilated to him by contact with him.

Enemies, on the other hand, can do the same by all these methods, but it is not surprising that they seldom use them. The reason is that they would thus put themselves in the power of the very man they wish to hurt, by giving to him a part of themselves, for he may injure them by magic treatment of it, which his own *virus* contained in the part might not be strong enough to overcome. The best course is then naturally found to be, either to use the mere act of will, or to get hold of some detachable part of the man, or anything that has been in contact with him, and by working the "intention" on that, to do him hurt. The idea is, as stated above, a man is not distinguished from his separate parts, and injury done to them is done to him. The easy analogy which leads the savage to "make-believe," assists him here. It will be convenient to give to this widely spread method and theory the name it has in Australia, where its development is very complete, that of *ngadhungi*. Both the act of will, assisted sometimes by a make-believe process, and also the method of *ngadhungi* are, as will be obvious, developments of the ideas of contact; and both, it is hardly necessary to premise, are often used for benevolent purposes. The following cases show how

[1] *Supra*, 83, *sq*.

the "intention", or subjective attitude may produce the various results connected with taboo. In order to ward off a danger from themselves, or to send evil to another person, the Zulus squirt water containing medicine from the mouth.[1] To cause a person to become thin and weak, the Arunta puts spittle on the tips of his fingers, which are then bunched together and jerked in the direction of the victim. This is called *Puliliwuma* or spittle-throwing.[2] A string-whip associated with magic is carried by Central Australian men. "The sight of one is alone enough to cause the greatest fright to a woman who has offended her husband, while the stroke is supposed to result in death, or at least in maiming for life. In addition to this use, the *ililika* is sometimes unwound and cracked like a whip in the direction of any individual whom it is desired to injure, when the evil influence is supposed to travel through the air, and so to reach the victim."[3] In many Amboina villages there are persons who anoint their eyes daily with certain ingredients, in order to increase their keenness of sight, and to acquire "a warm eye." Such are greatly feared, for they can by concentration of a look make any one ill and poison food.[4] Amongst the Nicobarese there are sorcerers, who possess the power not only of curing diseases but of afflicting people with various ailments, and can even cause death by a mere act of power.[5] Sorcerers are very dangerous in Cambodia, in that they can enchant people by a mere act of will.[6] Hidatsa sorcerers can injure persons at a distance.[7] In Tenimber and Timor-laut a common method of causing a man to be

[1] Callaway, *op. cit.* 435.
[2] Spencer and Gillen, *op. cit.* 552.
[3] *Id.* 540.
[4] Riedel, *op. cit.* 61.
[5] Featherman, *op. cit.* ii. 248.
[6] Aymonier, *op. cit.* 182.
[7] Featherman, *op. cit.* iii. 322.

ill is to place objects, such as thorns and sharp stones, on the ground where he is likely to pass. Over these curses have been muttered. The person walking over these objects will fall ill. Another method is to use curses, and blow in a special way under a man's house.[1] This illustrates a principle of savage "make-believe," viz. a fear of direct action. Amongst the Orang Benuas are sorcerers who have the art of *tuju*, which is the power of killing an enemy at a distance; this is done by pointing a dagger or a *sumpitan* in his direction.[2] The Australians have a well-known method of injuring persons at a distance, by pointing a bone at them.[3] Being the bone of a dead man, it has in it both human qualities and the contagion of death, but apart from these accidents, the essence of the practice is this; the man first sings curses and evil wishes over it, *e.g.* "may your heart be rent asunder," and his will or "intention" of hatred and malice enters materially into the bone, and veritably "informs" it. As the natives explain, "any bone, stick, spear, etc., which has been 'sung,' is endowed with *Arungquiltha*, magical poisonous properties," but these are the man's temporary characteristics of hate materially conceived.[4] There are actual cases where a man who has been hit by a "sung" spear, or knows that a man has pointed "the bone" at him, has pined away and died of fear.[5] For a very different object, that of inspiring love, the same method is used. Women "sing" over necklets of fur, which they place round the man's neck, or "sing" over some food which they then give him to eat.[6] They transfuse, in fact, their "intention" of love

[1] Riedel, *op. cit.* 304.
[2] Featherman, *op. cit.* ii. 441.
[3] *Journ. Anthrop. Inst.* xxiv. 188.
[4] Spencer and Gillen, *op. cit.* 534, 537.
[5] *Id. l.c.*
[6] *Id.* 548.

into the substance, and thus it passes to the person intended.

The same conception is the essential feature of a common class of oaths and ordeals, which in primitive practice are identical. The formula of the oath passes materially into the thing sworn by, which, as Greek reminds us, was the original *oath*, and as the following cases show, is of such a character as to do that injury to the perjurer which he invokes upon himself. The "oath" is held, or eaten or drunk, so as to ensure assimilation, and if perjury or treachery results, the wish has its effect and renders the substance of the "oath" deleterious. Thus in Madagascar parties taking an oath pray that the liquor drunk, which is the material "oath," may turn into poison for him who breaks it.[1] In Ceram an oath is taken by eating food in which a sword has been placed.[2] In Tenimber the oath-taker invokes death, and drinks his own blood in which a sword has been dipped.[3] The Tunguses drink the blood of a dog, which is then burned, and the wish made is "may I burn as this dog if I break my oath."[4] When the Timorese take an oath they drink water mixed with gunpowder and earth, saying, "May I die of sickness, by powder or the sword, if I swear falsely."[5] Amongst the Malays, when swearing fidelity, alliance, etc., water in which daggers, spears, or bullets have been dipped, is drunk, the drinker saying, "If I turn traitor, may I be eaten up by this dagger or spear."[6] A Balinese when giving evidence takes in his hand a basin of water, and pronounces these words, "May I perish with my whole generation if what I say is not true," and in confirmation of this sacramental

[1] D'Urville, *op. cit.* 181. [2] Riedel, *op. cit.* 129. [3] *Id.* 284.
[4] Georgi, *op. cit.* 48. [5] Featherman, *op. cit.* ii. 466. [6] Skeat, *op. cit.* 528.

declaration he drinks the water.[1] The terms of a Sumatran oath are, "If what I now declare is truly and really so, may I be freed and cleared from my oath; if what I assert is wittingly false, may my oath be the cause of my destruction."[2] The same material transmission of "intention" is the motive power behind the practice of setting *tabu*-marks on property. The indignation of the injured party *informs* the notice, just as the power of the law is behind the name on a modern warning to trespassers. For the security of property in the Luang-Sermata Islands, they place marks thereon to warn people from trespassing. Any person found trespassing, becomes ill or dies. They are of various kinds: a notice made of hen-feathers causes pains in the thief's back; one sort causes him to be struck by lightning, another to be eaten by sharks.[3] Similarly, sickness follows trespassers on property thus protected in the island Makiser.[4]

The method of *ngadhungi* is well known. On the principle stated above, a man can work injury or any result according to his "intention" on another, by treating parts of him in various ways. It will be remembered that a man's food is especially connected with him, from the mere fact of the important results of food to the organism, and it will be noticed that such detachable portions of personality as food, hair, nail-parings, clothes, and the like, are peculiarly easy to get hold of. Amongst the aborigines of Queensland any food left over from the meal is always burnt, to prevent the possibility of sorcerers getting hold of it and injuring them by means of the food.[5] The western tribes of Victoria "believe that if an enemy gets

[1] Featherman, *op. cit.* ii. 408.
[2] W. Marsden, *Sumatra*, 238.
[3] Riedel, *op. cit.* 317.
[4] *Id.* 414.
[5] C. Lumholtz, *Among Cannibals*, 298.

possession of anything that has belonged to them, even such things as bones of animals which they have eaten, broken weapons, feathers, portions of dress, pieces of skin, or refuse of any kind, he can employ it as a charm to produce illness in the person to whom they belonged. They are, therefore, very careful to burn up all rubbish or uncleanness before leaving a camping-place. Should anything belonging to an unfriendly tribe be found at any time, it is given to the chief, who preserves it as a means of injuring the enemy. This *wuulon* is lent to any one of the tribe who wishes to vent his spite against any one belonging to the unfriendly tribe. When used as a charm, the *wuulon* is rubbed over with emu fat mixed with red clay, and tied to the point of a spear-thrower, which is stuck upright in the ground before the camp-fire. The company sit round watching it, but at such a distance that their shadows cannot fall on it. They keep chanting imprecations on the enemy till the spear-thrower turns round and falls in his direction."[1] "The whole community of the Narrinyeri is influenced by disease-makers. Their method is called *ngadhungi*, and is practised in the following manner. Every adult black-fellow is constantly on the look-out for bones of ducks, swans, or other birds, or fish, the flesh of which has been eaten by anybody. When a man has obtained a bone, he supposes that he possesses the power of life and death over the man, woman, or child who ate its flesh. Should circumstances arise calculated to excite the resentment of the disease-maker towards the person who ate the flesh of the animal from which the bone was taken, he immediately sticks the bone in the ground near the fire, firmly believing that it will produce disease in the person for

[1] Dawson, *op. cit.* 54.

whom it was designed, however distant he may be. Death also may result. All the natives, therefore, are careful to burn the bones of the animals which they eat, so as to prevent their enemies from getting hold of them. When a person is ill, he generally regards his sickness as a result of *ngadhungi*, and tries to discover who is the disease-maker. When he thinks that he has discovered him, he puts down a *ngadhungi* to the fire, for the purpose of retaliating, that is, if he possesses one made of an animal from which his enemy has eaten. And if he has not, he tries to borrow one. Frequently, when a man has got the *ngadhungi* of another, he will go to him and say, 'I have your *ngadhungi*, what will you give me for it?' Perhaps the other man will say that he has one belonging to the person who asks him, and in that case they will make an exchange, and each destroy the *ngadhungi*. The constant seeking for revenge caused by this belief produces an atmosphere of suspicion among the natives. It is often the case that they will trust none but relatives; all others are regarded as possible enemies."[1] In the Encounter Bay tribe the same superstition is rampant. If a man has not been able to get a bone of an animal eaten by his foe, he takes an animal, and cooks and offers the meat in a friendly manner to his intended victim, having previously taken from it a piece of bone.[2] In Tanna the disease-makers injure a man by burning his *nahak*, that is, the refuse of his food, or any article that has been in close contact with his body. When a person is taken ill, he believes that it is occasioned by some one who is burning his *nahak*; and if he dies, his friends ascribe it to the disease-maker as having burnt the refuse to the end. All the Tannese carry small baskets about with

[1] *Native Tribes of South Australia*, 24, 25, 26, 136. [2] *Id.* 196.

them, into which they put banana skins, cocoanut husk, or any refuse from that which they may have been eating, in order to avoid its discovery by an enemy, until reaching and crossing a stream of running water, which alone has the power of annulling such contingency. "It is surprising how these men are dreaded, and how strong the belief is that they have in their hands the power of life and death." The belief "has so strong a hold in Tanna that all the continual fights and feuds are attributable to it."[1] The practice of burning a man's food in order to injure him flourishes in New Britain; the islanders are therefore careful to hide or burn their leavings.[2] In the Banks Islands one man can injure another by charming some bit of food, hair, or nail-parings, anything in fact that has been in close connection with his body; they are consequently at pains to hide all such.[3] In Pululaa (Solomon Islands) guests bring their own food to feasts, as they may not eat the food set out. The belief is that if a visitor should purposely or accidentally retain a morsel of food of his host, he can thereby exercise a mysterious influence over the giver of the feast. In such a contingency the host will redeem the lost fragment at as high a figure as he can afford.[4] In the Solomon Islands, again, an enemy will throw scraps of his victim's food into a sacred pool, of which he knows the spirit or Tindalo. If the food is eaten by a fish or snake the man will die.[5] Throughout Melanesia it is believed that one man may harm another by taking bits of his food into a sacred place, upon which the victim's lips will swell and his body break out with ulcers.[6] In the New Hebrides, when

[1] G. Turner, *Nineteen Years in Polynesia*, 89; R. T. Somerville, in *Journ. Anthrop. Inst.* xxiii. 19, 20.

[2] W. Powell, *Wanderings in a Wild Country*, 171.

[3] *Journ. Anthrop. Inst.* x. 283.

[4] Coote, *Wanderings South and East*, 177.

[5] *Journ. Anthrop. Inst.* x. 309.

[6] R. H. Codrington, *The Melanesians*, 188.

the *mae* snake carries away a fragment of food into the place sacred to a spirit, a man who has eaten of that will sicken as the fragment decays.[1] The Malays take great care in disposing of the clippings of hair, as they believe that "the sympathetic connection which exists between himself and every part of his body continues to exist, even after the physical connection has been severed, and that he will suffer from any harm that may befall the severed parts of his body, such as the clippings of his hair or the parings of his nails. Accordingly he takes care that these severed portions of himself shall not be left in places where they might either be exposed to accidental injury or fall into the hands of malicious persons who might work magic on them to his detriment or death." Charms are used by the Malays for an infinity of purposes. They are worked by "direct contact, sometimes by indirect, sometimes without." To charm a person, take soil from the centre of the foot-print of the person you wish to charm, and "treat it ceremonially" for about three days. Another Malay method of charming a person is to scrape off some of the wood of the floor from the place where your intended victim has been sitting; then mould it with wax into a figure resembling him; the figure is scorched over a lamp, while the following words are repeated, "It is not wax that I am scorching, it is the liver, heart, and spleen of so-and-so that I scorch." The Malays use clippings of the victim's hair, his saliva, and parings of his nails, etc., in making the well-known wax image, into which pins are stuck, and "which is still believed by all Malays to be a most effective method of causing the illness or death of an enemy." To work dissension between a husband and wife, a Malay makes

[1] R. H. Codrington, *The Melanesians*, 203.

two wax figures resembling them; he breathes upon them, and puts them back to back, so that they look away from one another.[1] The Mandans believe that a person at a distance may be injured or killed by sticking a needle in the heart of a figure made of clay or wood representing him.[2] In Luang-Sermata one can cause swellings of the head or hands of an enemy by burning his hair.[3] In Buru, as a love-charm, one "speaks over" oil the woman uses for her hair, or over a hair of her one finds. Or one buries a piece of ginger where she will pass.[4] The natives of the Mary River and Bunya-Bunya country believe that if you can procure some hair or excrement of an enemy, his life will decay while they are in your possession.[5] In the Babar Islands the method is used to make people ill, of burning their hair or *sirih* they have used. This is also done by rejected lovers.[6] Witchcraft prevailed amongst the Tasmanians. They procured some object belonging to the person, and, having enveloped it in fat, they laid it before the fire, and they supposed that as the fat was gradually melting, the health of their enemy would by degrees decline and that he would thus be doomed to perish.[7] The Cambodians say that a traveller must not throw away fragments of his garments when in a foreign country. If he does not wish to be unlucky, he must keep them.[8] The Gippsland tribes "practised sorcery, with a view to taking the lives of their enemies. The mode of proceeding was to obtain possession of something which had

[1] Skeat, *op. cit.* 44, also quoting Frazer's *Golden Bough*², i. 193; Skeat, 569, 570, 45, 573. The words of the Malay charm are identical with those used by the sorceress in Theocritus ii.

[2] Featherman, *op. cit.* iii. 303.

[3] Riedel, *op. cit.* 328.

[4] *Id. op. cit.* 10, 11.

[5] Curr, *op. cit.* iii. 179.

[6] Riedel, *op. cit.* 377.

[7] Featherman, *op. cit.* ii. 109.

[8] Aymonier, *op. cit.* 166.

belonged to the person whose death was desired, such as some of his hair, excrement, or food; or to touch him with an egg-shaped piece of stone which was called *bulk*, and was thought to be possessed of magic powers. At other times they would charm by means of the *makthar* (real name of the person); or several of them, retiring to some lonely spot, and drawing on the ground a rude likeness of the victim, would sit around it and devote him to destruction with cabalistic ceremonies. Such was their dread of proceedings of this sort that, not unfrequently, men and women who learnt that they had been made the subjects of incantation, quickly pined away and died of fright."[1] The Central Australians use the method of drawing a portrait of the intended victim, and stabbing it.[2] In Wetar one can make a man ill by getting hold of some of his saliva, hair, *betel* he has chewed, a piece of his clothes, or anything belonging to him. These objects are put in a place haunted by evil spirits, who are then called upon to kill the man or make him ill.[3] Sorcerers amongst the Karalits injure or slay persons by magic use of any part of the victim's body, or part of an animal killed by such.[4] Before a battle, a Zulu chief sits on a circlet of "medicines," containing some object belonging to the hostile chief, and he says, "I am overcoming him; I am now treading him down; he is now under me. I do not know by what way he will escape."[5] The Zulus also use a vessel of medicines which one churns like a Chinese praying-machine. A young man will use it as a love-charm; if it froths, he knows he has prevailed over the girl. Something belonging to her is

[1] Curr, *op. cit.* iii. 547.

[2] Spencer and Gillen, *op. cit.* 550.

[3] Riedel, *op. cit.* 451.

[4] Featherman, *op. cit.* iii. 437.

[5] Callaway, *op. cit.* 342.

put in it. The churn is used before war, with something in it belonging to the hostile chief, so as to kill or weaken him. Any disease may be caused by walking over "medicines" placed, to that end, in the path.[1] Another account of the Zulus says that before the army sets out, the king makes "medicine" in which is some personal article belonging to his enemy. "The belief in this is so strong, that when a chief is forced to retreat, the floor of his hut is scraped, and for this reason Dingan, when he fled from the Boers, burnt his hut."[2] The method is used with saliva, as well as other vehicles, in Ceylon and Nukahiva;[3] and throughout the islands between Celebes and New Guinea the method flourishes in many forms, both for injury and for producing love.[4] A very common form is the injuring of a person by means of his name. To injure a person, the Amboinese use some of his *sirih* he has thrown away, a piece of his hair, or clothing; also one writes his name on a piece of paper, which is put in a gun and fired off, or else one puts it in the highest branch of a tree.[5] The Gippsland blacks objected strongly to let any one outside the tribe know their names, lest their enemies, learning them, should make them vehicles of incantation, and so charm their lives away. As children were not thought to have enemies, they used to speak of a man as "the father, uncle, or cousin of so-and-so," naming a child, but on all occasions abstained from mentioning the name of a grown-up person.[6] In many Australian tribes "the belief obtains that the life of an enemy may be taken by the use of his name in incantations. The consequence of this idea is, that in the tribes in which

[1] Callaway *op. cit.* 343, 346, 35.
[2] Shooter, *op. cit.* 343.
[3] Tennent, *op. cit.* ii. 544; D'Urville, *op. cit.* i. 502.
[4] Riedel, *op. cit. passim.*
[5] *Id. op. cit.* 61, 79.
[6] Curr, *op. cit.* iii. 545.

it obtains, the name of the male is given up for ever at the time when he undergoes the first of a series of ceremonies which end in conferring the rights of manhood. In such tribes a man has no name, and, instead of calling a man by name, one addresses him as brother, nephew, or cousin, as the case may be, or by the name of the class to which he belongs."[1] Sorcery is one of the most heinous crimes in Bali. A man is guilty of it if he writes the name of any one on the winding-sheet of a corpse, or on a dead man's bier, or if he makes an image of paste of the person he intends to bewitch, or if he hangs from a tree a slip of paper on which his name is written, or if he buries such a paper in the ground, or in a haunted place.[2] In Abyssinia it is believed that the sorcerer can cause no injury to a person unless he knows his true name, and it is the custom for mothers to conceal the baptismal name of their children, and to substitute for it, Son of St. George, Slave of the Virgin, Daughter of Moses, and the like.[3] In modern Europe there is still to be found, especially amongst children, some diffidence about revealing the Christian name.

[1] Curr, *op. cit.* i. 46. [2] Featherman, *op. cit.* ii. 408. [3] *Id.* v. 6, 8.

CHAPTER VI

With this sensibility to contact there is always closely connected the instinctive care of functions and organs, which are, of course, but specialised channels of contact, both in use and origin, and this care is common to all highly organised life. It is a good instance of physiological thought. Throughout the world it is the general rule for the performance of human functions to take place in secret, and this secrecy is closer in primitive than in civilised custom.[1] As will be shown later, one important function, that of eating and drinking, though no longer secret in civilised periods, was so in early society. Prayer before such functions testifies to this caution, and the custom of the Babar islanders, who pray to the ancestral spirits before eating, drinking, and sleeping, or of the people of Timorlaut, who pray to *Dudilaa* before such functions as sexual intercourse, eating, and drinking, is typical of the generality of mankind.[2] Hence also the general ascription of the taboo character to the various functions, especially the nutritive and sexual. When called "unclean," the term originally is equivalent to taboo, still undifferentiated, though later it becomes specialised by other associations. The Hindu and Muhammadan rules of "uncleanness" in connection with physical functions,

[1] J. G. F. Riedel, *De sluik-en kroesharige rassen tusschen Selebes en Papua*, 96, 406.

[2] *Id.* 338, 281.

are examples of a general human practice.[1] The universal desire for solitude during the performance of certain physical functions, shared by man with the higher animals, is an extension of the organic instinct for safety and self-preservation. These functions, especially the nutritive, sexual, and excretory, are not only of supreme importance in organic life, but their performance exposes the individual to danger, by rendering him defenceless for the time being. Ideas formed straight from this instinct invest such functions at once with a potential sacredness, and assist towards a religious concealment of them. Again, this impulse for solitude is emphasised, as psychology proves, in illness and in critical states, a fact which shows the origin of many taboos on their subjective side.

In the development of these ideas, each principle of contact has its share, and the biological caution is intensified by religious conceptions. The very complexity and importance of functions intensifies both the biological and the religious care of them. The individual avoids, in the first place, the dangers resulting to himself from contact with others; and secondarily, from knowledge of these dangers, he concludes that the material secretions and emanations are in every case dangerous, even apart from personal properties, and accordingly avoids his own, for his own sake and, altruistically, for the sake of his fellows. This altruistic feeling is later, and is connected with disgust.

While it is the functions and external organs connected with nutrition and sex that are most guarded, and the senses of taste and touch that are here most sensitive, yet the instinct to preserve and insulate from danger all the channels of sense is seen in savage custom.

[1] Vambéry, *Sketches of Central Asia*, 190.

This insulation is effected sometimes by wearing amulets upon the external organs, sometimes by means of the painful processes of tattooing, boring, and scarification. It is erroneous to attribute these practices to the desire for ornament. There is ample evidence that "savage mutilation" is never due to this desire; the savage does not hold with the maxim—*il faut souffrir pour être belle*; on the contrary, he is extremely averse to pain, except for the purpose of preserving his life, health, and strength. Accordingly, when we find that the mouth and lips, the teeth, nose, eyes, ears, and genital organs are subjected to such processes, we may infer that the object is to secure the safety of these sense-organs, by what is practically a *permanent* amulet or charm.

The idea behind the mutilation of organs is complex. Let us take the common practices of piercing an organ, filing the teeth, knocking out a tooth, circumcision, and perforation of the hymen. The first part of the idea is to obviate possible difficulty in function, suggested by an apparent closure of the organ; this possibility of difficulty is to the savage a potentiality of evil, and is connected with the fear of doing a thing for the first time, a fear which, as we have seen, creates a material dangerous substance attaching to the thing in question, and needing removal before contact can safely take place. The Pepos state that the object of knocking out one or more teeth at puberty is to assist breathing.[1] Shortly after a birth the Malays administer to the child "the mouth-opener"; "first you take a green cocoa-nut, split it in halves, put a grain of salt inside one half of the shell, and give it to the child to drink, counting up to seven, and putting it up to the child's

[1] Ploss, *Das Kind*, ii. 424.

mouth at the word seven."[1] This account is important as suggesting that the first taking of food, the first employment of the mouth, is a dangerous crisis. When we take into account the importance of food in savage life, and the care of the mouth and teeth resulting, also the fact that this knocking out of teeth, like the similar process of teeth-filing, is regularly performed at puberty, when as a rule there are certain food taboos removed, and a boy is initiated to "man's food," it is a fair conjecture that its object is to secure in some way the safety of that important function. When a Dieri boy has had the teeth knocked out, he may not look at the men who performed the operation, or "his mouth would close up and he would be unable to eat."[2] Mr. Skeat was invariably told that the Malay practice of teeth-filing not only beautified but preserved the teeth from decay.[3] The idea of ornament is later. With the particular imaginary danger already mentioned all danger of material contact of course combines, including that of disease in the wide range of reality and imagination with which early man regards disease. Amongst the Cadiacks a hole is bored through the *septum* of the child's nose, when it is washed after birth. These people have also the practice of piercing the *septum* in cases where venereal disease attacks the nose.[4] The connection is obvious. The Yorubas call circumcision "the cutting that saves."[5] Amongst the Central Australians there is a causal connection between the practice of sub-incision and the common disease *Erkincha*. It is not, as has been proved, intended to prevent impregnation, nor does it have this result.[6]

[1] Skeat, *op. cit.* 337.

[2] Howitt, in *Journ. Anthrop. Inst.* xx. 82.

[3] Skeat, *op. cit.* 359.

[4] U. Lisiansky, *op. cit.* 200, 201.

[5] A. B. Ellis, *op. cit.* 66.

[6] Spencer and Gillen, *op. cit.* 405, 264.

The ceremony of head-biting performed on Central Australian boys at puberty is supposed to make the hair grow strong.[1] Now it is prevention of future harm, illness and weakness, and transmission of strength and life that are one special object of ceremonies at puberty. Again, it has been conclusively proved that circumcision does not prevent disease, and it is probable that there was no sanitary intention in its origin, except such as forms part of the explanation here given.[2] The ceremony amongst the Semites was originally "religious" in the primitive sense, but here, as elsewhere, when the religious habit becomes rational, the fallacy of sanitary intention in circumcision became prominent, and may often have been the reason for the continuance of the practice. The last factor in the principle behind these mutilations is one very closely connected with ideas of contact, and applies especially to such practices as circumcision. The deleterious emanation from strange or new things is identical in theory with human emanations, not only from strange or unhandselled beings, but from characteristic parts of such, and in later thought, from such parts of one's own personality. This dangerous emanation is any physical secretion religiously regarded, and its retention is prevented by cutting away separable parts which would easily harbour it, as the teeth retain morsels of food. This primitive notion is the same with those of personal cleanliness and of the removal of separable parts of a tabooed person. Dr. Frazer points out the idea of destroying separable parts of tabooed persons; thus, in Roti the first hair of a child "is not his own, and unless cut off will make him ill." When the part is cut off, there result the ideas, first of securing

[1] Spencer and Gillen, *op. cit.* 151.

[2] Joseph Jacobs, in *Journ. Anthrop. Inst.* xv. 32.

the safety of the rest by sacrificing a part, a practice well illustrated by the custom of cutting off the little finger; and secondly, of sacrificing such part to a deity so as to consecrate the rest, by making it less "impure" or "*taboo*." Thus, Sir A. B. Ellis infers that circumcision amongst the Yorubas and Ewe peoples is a sacrifice of a portion of the organ, which the god inspires, to ensure the well-being of the rest. The rite is there connected with the worship of *Elegbra*.[1] And for the earlier notion, the Jews and Egyptians regarded it as a "cleansing."[2]

Circumcision and artificial hymen-perforation thus originated in the intention both to obviate hylo-idealistic danger resulting from apparent closure, and to remove a separable part of a taboo organ, on the above-stated principles. This removal also explains the practice of excision. The other ideas follow later, and the safety both of the individual and of those who will have contact is the more necessary because that contact is with the other, the dangerous sex.

As to the insertion of plugs and sticks and the like, in the nose, lips, and ears, it is probable that the original object was to keep off evil from the organs by a mark, an idea connected with the widely spread belief that the attention of the evil influence is thus diverted from the organ as lightning is diverted from an object by the lightning-rod.

Here is to be considered the psychology of disgust. The emotion in its origin is caused by the presence or contact of what is dangerous or useless to the individual organism, chiefly in connection with the nutritive and sexual functions. It is part of the natural law of

[1] A. B. Ellis, *op. cit.* 66.

[2] Ploss, *Das Kind*, i. 345; Trusen, *Die Sitten u. Gebräuche der alten Hebräer*, 115.

economy, ultimately chemical, which produces an impulse for what one needs and an avoidance of what one does not need, or has cast away. Food that is needed is the object of man's fiercest desire, and, on the other hand, food after satiety or the excreta from food produce the strongest loathing; in each case the feeling is part of the primary nutritive impulse. The same desire and loathing belong to the sexual functions and emotions, the development and complement of the nutritive. The sensitive instinct of self-preservation and of self-realisation which insulates a man from other organisms, accentuates the emotion of disgust when the cast-off substances are from others, and makes those from himself more tolerable. Further, where there is no desire, there is potential disgust, especially at the sight of another's function. Disgust correlates with satiety and is the opposite pole to desire and satisfaction, and ultimately its connection is with the alimentary functions alone, from which the sexual and other are developed. Desire and disgust are the final expression of chemical laws of combination and rejection. Desire and disgust are curiously blended when with one's own desire unsatisfied one sees the satisfaction of another; and here we may see the altruistic stage beginning; this has two sides, the fear of causing desire in others, and the fear of causing disgust, in each case personal isolation is the psychological result.

The ideas of impurity and ceremonial "uncleanness" are closely connected with these phenomena, and in primitive thought are concerned with the nutritive no less than with other functions. Theoretically, if we carry primitive ideas to their logical conclusion, the perfectly "pure" person is one who should not only avoid contact with the functional effluvia of others, but all contact with persons also; and moreover, to obviate pollution from his own functions, should abstain not only from sexual but from nutritive processes as well. It is the ascetic ideal of the perfect Buddhist. This *practice* (ἄσκησις) has probably assisted man considerably towards attaining a higher than animal culture.

Again, the feeling of shame is closely connected with these functional phenomena; it is produced by ideas which arise from the importance and sensibility of functions, tending towards diffidence and mistrust of them, and is expressed originally upon any external interference with a function. Later it becomes altruistic. We may also observe that amongst early men it is also to an important extent concerned with alimentary processes. It is at first sight surprising to read the following statement, but a slight acquaintance with primitive habit shows how inevitable such facts are, and observation of the lower classes in modern times reveals the same phenomenon. Amongst the Bakairi every man eats by himself; when one eats in the presence of another, it is the custom to do so with head averted, while the other turns his back and does not speak till the meal is over. When the German explorer, not knowing of this, ate his lunch without giving notice, they hung their heads and showed on their faces real shame.[1]

All these emotions and the ideas connected therewith are part of the foundation of social and of sexual taboo. Closely connected as they are with contact and with functional sensitiveness, they at once, when in the altruistic stage in which one conceals or refrains from functions to avoid causing others to feel disgust or shame, vary in intensity according to the distance of the person whose feelings are being considered. A man

[1] K. von den Steinen, *Unter den Natur-Völkern Zentral-Brasiliens*, 66.

certainly would avoid performing such acts as involve these emotions before an entire stranger, for to primitive thought a stranger is a potential foe, and in such a case we see the original cause of such secrecy; but on the other hand, amongst acquaintances and friends, he is less ready to insist upon secrecy than he is with closer connections, such as those with whom he lives. The reason is the accentuation, first of the danger, and later of altruistic consideration, produced in each case by the very closeness of the contact. Add to this the religious caution between the two sexes, and we get a potential avoidance of all such functions in the presence of the other sex generally, and especially in the presence of those with whom a man is in closest daily contact. Not only civilised ideas and habits of decency and personal cleanliness, but human systems and institutions of the most important character are built on these foundations.

These ideas of contact, which are found all over the world, give to human relations generally a religious meaning, such as we can hardly realise by imagination. Every individual, as such, is surrounded by a taboo of personal isolation; and for communication between him and his fellows there is in theory needed a go-between. A type of this may be seen in the New Hebridean custom, where the last man to "take the book" (*i.e.* turn Christian), was a "sacred man," whose sanctity was such that anything given to him by a white man had to be passed through the hands of a go-between.[1] Secondly, to take the dangerous side of the taboo character, all human and sexual properties, states of mind and of emotion, even acts and thoughts, are so material that they exude, *sans phrase*, from the skin.

[1] *Journ. Anthrop. Inst.* xxiii. 12.

In civilised stages of society, moral and social systems which are themselves closely connected in origin with this early view of contact, have so defined and safeguarded human relations that these ideas have almost disappeared. They exist still, however, in one or two special forms, as in the still rampant belief in the evil eye throughout Southern Europe, and in the refinement always kept in civilisation, which reveals its material origin in more or less dainty avoidance of the lower classes, of "publicans and sinners."

Primitive man has some differences in his code of morals, but on the whole, he is more moral in the social sense than is civilised man. A few examples will illustrate this basis of early morality. The immaturity of the human "will" is a characteristic of early man. What is said of the Fijians applies still more to earlier peoples. "We have to bear in mind the absolute helplessness of the Fijian, in fact, the Polynesian generally, when anybody has acquired a moral ascendancy over him."[1] Death often occurs from this moral fear. Sorcery is so dreaded by Australians that individuals have been known to die through fear of it.[2] As we have seen, amongst the Australians a great motor power is the belief in sorcery or witchcraft. In the everyday life of the black, a pressure originating in this source may be said to be always at work.[3] Of the Kurnai it is said that "the gratification of self is choked in them, as in us, by a sense of duty or by affection. Speaking to a Kroatun young man about the food prohibited during initiation, I said, 'But if you were hungry and caught a female opossum, you might eat it if the old men were not there'; he replied, 'I could not do that: it would not be right.' Although I

[1] Seemann, *op. cit.* 190. [2] Curr, *op. cit.* i. 49. [3] *Id.* i. 45, 46.

tried to find out from him some other reason, he could give no other than that it would be wrong to disregard the customs."[1] In New South Wales the universal reprobation which followed a breach of ancient customs, preserved a strict observance of morality.[2] Amongst the Maoris *tapu* was law, and far more observed and feared than the latter, as such, ever has been in higher culture.[3] So it has been said of the Fijian *tambu*; "the taboo is a religion in itself, and without doubt has helped to prevent savages from allowing their naturally depraved natures to have full scope to carry out their intentions. The law-givers who introduced the *tambu* must have done so with the idea of promoting the happiness of the community, and of encouraging morality among the people."[4] The Leh-tas, according to the Karens, have no laws or rulers, and do not require any, as they never commit any evil among themselves or against other people. "The sense of shame amongst this tribe is so acute, that on being accused of any evil act by several of the community, the person so accused retires to a desolate spot, digs his grave and strangles himself."[5] Amongst the Hill Dyaks crime is so rare that its punishments are only known from tradition. They have a complete system similar to the Polynesian *tabu*.[6] In New Britain marriage within the totem-clan would bring instant destruction upon the woman, and the man's life would never be secure. Her relatives would be so ashamed, that only her death could satisfy them. "However, such a case never occurs in a thickly populated district. If a man should be accused of adultery or fornication with a woman, he would at

[1] Fison and Howitt, *op. cit.* 256, 257.
[2] Wilkes, *op. cit.* ii. 193.
[3] *Id.* ii. 383.
[4] Anderson, *op. cit.* 89.
[5] A. R. Colquhoun, *Among the Shans*, 76.
[6] Low, *op. cit.* 247, 248.

once be acquitted by the public voice, if he could say 'she is one of us'; *i.e.* she belongs to my totem."[1] In Timor "the custom of *pomali* is general, fruit-trees, houses, crops, and property of all kinds being protected from depredation by this ceremony, the reverence for which is very great. A palm branch stuck across an open door, showing that the house is tabooed, is a more effectual guard against robbery than any amount of locks and bars."[2] The same is true of most primitive races. In Hawaii a "wicked person" was one who broke *tabu*.[3] Amongst the Indians of Guiana any breach of the marriage system is "wicked."[4] Amongst the Zulus *umtakati* means "witch, wizard, or evil-doer," *i.e.* murderers, adulterers, one who violates rules of consanguinity; also one who does secret injury to another, by using "medicine," *e.g.* human remains, or poison. Evil-doers can injure health, destroy life, cause cows to become dry, prevent rain, occasion lightning.[5] Turning to the question of deterrents, amongst the Bangerang it was believed that the sorcery of other tribes could be counteracted by their own incantations. On the other hand, they sometimes feel that the incantations of their own doctors can be neutralised by stronger ones on the part of their enemies; and so they "frequently revenge a death in the tribe—which is of course attributed to sorcery, though in effect the result of sickness or accident—by attacking at night a hostile camp and massacring the sleepers."[6] In Hawaii violators of taboo were seized by the priests and killed.[7] Mr. Curr says of the Australian tribes with which he was

[1] B. Danks, in *Journ. Anthrop. Inst.* xviii. 282, 283.
[2] A. R. Wallace, *The Malay Archipelago*, 450.
[3] Ellis, *Tour in Hawaii*, 279.
[4] Brett, *op. cit.* 98.
[5] Shooter, *op. cit.* 141.
[6] Curr, *op. cit.* i. 47, 49.
[7] Wilkes, *op. cit.* iv. 40.

acquainted, "we find our blacks, male and female, submitting for years loyally and without exception to a number of irksome restraints, especially in connection with food, just as we Roman Catholics do to the fasts and abstinences imposed by the Church. Now the question is, what is the hidden power which secures the black's scrupulous compliance with custom in such cases? What is it, for instance, which prompts the hungry black boy, when out hunting with the white man, to refuse (as I have often seen him do) to share in a meal of emu flesh, or in some other sort of food forbidden to those of his age, when he might easily do so without fear of detection by his tribe? What is it that makes him so faithfully observant of many trying customs? The reply is, that the constraining power in such cases is not government, whether by chief or council, but *education*; that the black is educated from infancy in the belief that departure from the customs of his tribe is inevitably followed by one at least of many evils, such as becoming grey, ophthalmia, skin eruptions, or sickness; but above all, that it exposes the offender to the danger of death from sorcery."[1] The Luang Sermata islanders hold that sickness is due to "sin";[2] and this is a common human idea, a phase of which is the belief that evil physical results follow breaches of the system or principle of marriage, and, we may add, of sexual taboo generally. Amongst the Australians old people are mostly sorcerers; "and custom holds the weak and the young in willing subjection to the old."[3] In speaking of the power of the old men, and the enforcing of moral laws by them, Messrs. Spencer and Gillen show that the influence which supports custom is far from being impersonal.

[1] Curr, *op. cit.* i. 54, 55. [2] Riedel, *op. cit.* 325. [3] Eyre, *op. cit.* ii. 384.

In the Central Australian tribes which they examined, they found that offenders were regularly dealt with by the elder men, and that offending natives were perfectly well aware that they would "be dealt with by something much more real than an impersonal power." In reference to the dying-out of native races upon contact with Europeans, they remark of the Central Australian tribes, that "the young men under the new influence become freed from the wholesome restraint of the older men, who are all-powerful in the normal condition of the tribe. The strict moral code, which is certainly enforced in their natural state, is set on one side, and nothing is adopted in place of it."[1]

Early men have also an elaborate etiquette based on these ideas. Amongst the Northern Indians when two people met, they would stop when within twenty yards, and generally sit or lie down, without speaking for some minutes.[2] The origin of such may be seen in the Australian practice; when a tribe approaches another, that is unknown to it, they carry burning sticks to purify the air.[3] In the Dieri and neighbouring tribes, when a man reaches home, no notice at first is taken, until he sits down; then "the friends or relations sit around, and the news is whispered, whatever it may be, and repeated in a loud voice to the whole camp." Also, when an influential native arrives, he is received thus:—"On approaching the camp, the inmates close in with raised arms, as in defence; then the person of note rushes at them, making a faint blow as if to strike them, they warding it off with their shields; immediately after they embrace him and lead him into the camp, where

[1] Spencer and Gillen, *op. cit.* 15, 8.

[2] Hearne, *op. cit.* 332.

[3] Brough Smyth, *op. cit.* i. 134.

the women bring him food."[1] The Malay, says Mr. Wallace, is "particularly sensitive to breaches of etiquette, or any interference with the personal liberty of himself or another. As an example, I may mention that I often found it very difficult to get one Malay servant to waken another. He will call as loud as he can, but will hardly touch, much less shake his companion."[2] In the islands of Leti, Moa, and Lakor, and the Babar Islands no one may without important reason wake a sleeping man.[3] The greatest possible insult to a man in Tenimber and Timorlaut is to spit in his face, or to step over his body when on the ground.[4] In New Caledonia there is an elaborate system of etiquette. Politeness requires one to walk in front of the person to whom respect is due; to enter first on introducing him; to pass in front and not behind him.[5] The Fijians observe scrupulously certain rules of etiquette.[6] The Javanese are distinguished for the formal observance of etiquette.[7] The Tagalas of Luzon and Mindanao are remarkable for a sentiment of personal shamefulness, called *hya*, which renders them very susceptible of insult, and causes them to respect the feelings of others.[8] The same results of the taboo of personal isolation are constant in all stages of culture. The whole series of phenomena, lastly, helps to disprove the common idea that early society possessed a communistic and socialistic character. The "rights" of the individual in property, marriage, and everything else, were never more clearly defined than by primitive man.

[1] Gason, in *Journ. Anthrop. Inst.* xxiv. 173; *id.* in Curr, *op. cit.* ii. 50.
[2] Wallace, *op. cit.* 443.
[3] Riedel, *op. cit.* 378.
[4] *Id.* 295.
[5] Featherman, *op. cit.* ii. 85.
[6] *Id.* ii. 200.
[7] *Id.* ii. 382.
[8] *Id.* ii. 481.

CHAPTER VII

THERE are still to be described the two most important forms of contact, contact by means of food and by sexual intercourse. I have deferred their description because they have so close a connection with sexual taboo, the further developments of which chiefly take the lines marked out by ideas concerning these two functions of eating and of sexual congress.

Biologically, the sexual impulse is a development from the nutritive, and the primary close connection of the two functions is continued in thought, subconscious and physiological, and appears sometimes above the threshold of consciousness. We find further, that many primary human conceptions are not only based on the connection but express it clearly. One of the most obvious links between the two is the kiss, and much popular thought and language preserves similar conceptions.

Various rules attest the importance of "man's bread and oil and wine." The natives of the Baram district of Borneo feed alone; "they are very particular about being called away from their meals, and it takes a great deal to make a man set about doing anything before he has concluded his repast." To such an extent is this practice observed that it is considered wrong to attack even an enemy whilst he is eating, but the moment he has finished it is legitimate and proper to fall upon him.[1] The custom of eating in silence is found amongst the Ahts, Maoris, Siamese, and the ancient Hindoos.[2] The Arabs of Syria mutter a *bismillah* before eating, and take their meals in silence.[3] In Siam it is a maxim of the Buddhist priests that "to eat and talk at the same time is a sin."[4] The Tahitians offered a prayer before they ate their food.[5] The Mois of Cochin China invoke a superior power before eating and drinking.[6] The Malayalam Sudras of Travancore bathe and put sacred ashes on the forehead before each meal.[7] In origin, the custom of prayer before eating was not an expression of thankfulness. The object was to avert any deleterious influence that the food might possess. On this is superimposed the wish that the food may be good and beneficial, may be "blessed," which passes into an invocation to a superior power to so bless it, and also, for the older idea often remains, to cleanse the food from harmful properties.

The savage realises better than most civilised men that his life, his health and strength, and general well-being depend chiefly upon what is ultimately the most necessary of human functions. It is not surprising, therefore, that so many customs and beliefs attach to the processes of eating and drinking. "The procuring of food is the great business of the Australian's life," says a good observer, "and forms one of the principal topics of his conversation."[8] Custom and belief in this connection are based upon the egoistic physical

[1] *Journ. Anthrop. Inst.* xxiii. 160.

[2] Sproat, *op. cit.* 61; Thomson, *New Zealand*, 160; Bowring, *Siam*, i. 110; *Manu*, iii. 236, 237.

[3] Featherman, *op. cit.* v. 448, 451.

[4] Bowring, *op. cit.* i. 328.

[5] Ellis, *Polynesian Researches*, i. 350.

[6] *Cochinchine française*, viii. 12.

[7] Mateer, *op. cit.* 112.

[8] Curr, *op. cit.* i. 81.

sensibility of man, applied to the object of his fiercest desires, and with this there combine later all his conceptions of matter and of material and human contact. Thus the savage as a rule prefers to eat alone, as he prefers to be alone for the performance of similar functions, from egoistic caution and fear of interruption. The Karajas always eat by themselves, with back turned.[1] Amongst the Bakairi every man eats by himself; when one has to eat in the presence of another it is the custom to do so with head averted, while the other turns his back and does not speak till the meal is over. When von den Steinen ate before them they hung their heads and were "ashamed."[2] The Zafimanelos of Madagascar eat alone with locked doors.[3] The Maori gentleman eats in solitude.[4] The rule is common in Polynesia and Africa. It is naturally still more emphasised in the case of kings and chiefs. The King of Abyssinia always dines alone.[5] Amongst the Niam-niam the king takes his meals in private; no one may see the contents of his dish, and everything that he leaves is carefully thrown into a pit, set apart for the purpose. All that he handles is held as "sacred," and may not be touched; and a guest, though of higher rank, may not so much as light his pipe with embers from the king's fire.[6] A carved and gilt wooden screen was always placed in front of Montezuma at his meals, that no one might see him while eating.[7] In Loango the king is sacred; from his birth he is forbidden to eat with any one, and various foods are prohibited to him. He eats and drinks alone, in huts devoted to the purpose. The covered dishes containing his food are preceded by a crier, at whose

[1] K. von den Steinen, *Unter den Natur-Völkern Zentral-Brasiliens*, 67.
[2] *Id.* 66.
[3] *Antananarivo Annual*, ii. 219.
[4] Yate, *op. cit.* 20.
[5] Harris, *Highlands of Æthiopia*, iii. 171, 172, 322.
[6] Schweinfurth, *op. cit.* ii. 98.
[7] Bancroft, *op. cit.* iii. 129.

proclamation all get out of the way and bolt their doors; for any person seeing the king eat is put to death. A privileged few may be present, but they are bound to conceal their faces, or the king places a robe over his head. All that leaves his table is at once buried.[1] A crier proclaimed when the King of Cacongo was about to eat or drink, that the people might cover their faces or fall to the ground with down-turned eyes.[2] When the King of Canna was offered a glass of rum by Mr. Winwood Reade, he hid his face and the glass under a Turkish towel.[3] In Dahomey it is death to see the king eat; if he drinks in public, a curtain is held up to conceal him.[4] The King of Susa at meals is concealed by a curtain from his guests.[5] The King of the Monbuttoo always takes his meals in private, and no one may see the contents of his dish.[6] The King of Congo eats and drinks in secret. If a dog should enter the house while he is at table, it is killed. On one occasion the king's son having accidentally seen his father drinking was executed on the spot.[7] A Pongo chief never drinks in the presence of others without a screen to conceal him; on the Pongo coast it is believed that one is more liable to witchcraft when eating, drinking, or sleeping.[8] In Ashantee a man of consequence never drinks before his inferiors without hiding his face from them. The belief is that an enemy can then "impose a spell on the faculties" of the man who is drinking.[9] So in Tonga no one may see the king eat; therefore those present turn their backs upon him. Nor may

1 Bastian, *An der Loango Küste*, i. 220, 262, 263.

2 *Id. San Salvador*, 38.

3 W. Reade, *Savage Africa*, 184.

4 J. L. Wilson, *op. cit.* 202; Reade, *op. cit.* 53; Burton, *Dahomey*, i. 244.

5 Harris, *op. cit.* iii. 78.

6 Schweinfurth, *op. cit.* ii. 98.

7 Reade, *op. cit.* 359.

8 Wilson, *op. cit.* 308, 310.

9 Bowdich, *Cape Coast Castle to Ashanti*, 438.

one eat in his presence without averting the face. It is also forbidden to eat in the presence of a superior relation without turning the back.[1]

The basis of this preference for eating in solitude is the animal egoistic impulse; later it becomes altruistic, and also is combined, as we have seen this egoistic sensibility always combined, with general ideas about contact and transmission of properties. The modern small boy who eats his cake in a corner still shows the most primitive form of the custom.

The savage is extremely careful that what he eats and drinks shall be free from deleterious properties, inherent or acquired. Such properties are all those which, as we have seen, the savage attributes to material substances, and especially to dangerous persons, and are neither spiritual nor material but both, and can be imparted by all possible forms of material transmission. In this wide generalisation there would of course occur from time to time cases in which food possessed some harmful property, whether of poison or disease, and such cases corroborated the general precautions. The people of Kumaun use a special room for eating, into which nothing "unclean" may come. The cook has to put on clean clothes before cooking, and he is not allowed to touch any one after he has begun, nor to leave the room. No one is allowed to touch him when at work.[2] Maoris do not eat inside the house.[3] Bulgarians before drinking make the sign of the cross, to prevent the devil entering the body with the liquor.[4] Similarly, devout Russians have been observed to blow on the glass in order to neutralise "the Satanic opera-

[1] W. Mariner, *The Natives of the Tonga Islands*, ii. 235; Cook and King, *Voyage*, i. 232.

[2] *Panjab Notes and Queries*, iii. 2. 454.

[3] D'Urville, *op. cit.* ii. 411.

[4] Sinclair and Brophy, *A Residence in Bulgaria*, 14.

tion of spirituous liquors."[1] Amongst the Eskimo, when a new spring of water is found, it is usual for the oldest man present, failing an *angekok*, to drink first, in order to rid the water of any evil influence it may possess.[2] In Eastern Central Africa, when a chief has a beer-drinking, his priest or captain brings out the beer to the guests and tastes it to show that it is not poisoned.[3] So amongst the Damaras the chief must first taste the provisions before they are eaten by the rest of the assembly.[4] Amongst the Iddahs[5] the same custom is found, and amongst the Zulus it is not etiquette to offer beer without first tasting it; "it is meant to ensure the receiver against death in the pot;" while another is eating, it is wrong to spit.[6] Amongst the Krumen at a palm wine-drinking the goodwife of the house has to take the first and last draught herself, to show the guests that she has not been dealing in poison or witchcraft. This is called "taking off the fetish."[7] Amongst the Basutos, when food or drink is offered to a man, and he is not sure that it is not poisoned, he lets the host taste it first.[8] These customs are widely spread in Africa. In the Banks Islands on presenting food to a visitor the host first takes a bite himself to show that it is not charmed, or to take the risk upon himself.[9] In New Guinea it is a mark of friendship to offer water to a stranger. Before presenting it, the natives first drink themselves to prove that the water is not poisoned.[10] These cases show the idea that things new or strange possess a dangerous property.

The history of fasting forms a curious chapter in the

[1] Erman, *Siberia*, i. 415.
[2] Crantz, *op. cit.* i. 193.
[3] Macdonald, *Africana*, i. 191.
[4] C. J. Andersson, *Lake Ngami*, 222.
[5] Schon and Crowther, *Expedition up the Niger*, 82.
[6] Leslie, *op. cit.* 205.
[7] J. L. Wilson, *op. cit.* 124.
[8] *Zeitschrift für Ethnologie*, vi. 34.
[9] Codrington, *op. cit.* 204.
[10] Rosenberg, *Der Malayische Archipel*, 470.

development of the human soul. In origin it was a method used by primitive man to avoid the possibility of any injurious influence entering his body. The savage never fasts because he likes it, but simply to avoid danger. This painful process is not gone through unless for some very important reason; for instance, when a primitive crisis is at hand, when the food-supply is to be coaxed by magic, or the success of a hunt or a war to be secured, or a dangerous period of life to be passed through, such as puberty and mourning. In some of these cases the mere practice develops the further idea that fasting is useful as a training of the body and a discipline for the nerves. It is worth noting that the practice of fasting was referred to a primitive reason by the early Christians, namely, to prevent "evil spirits" entering the body.[1] The subject of taboos upon certain foods is a large one. The practice of forbidding certain kinds of food during a dangerous state is very widely spread; it includes cases of real dietetic science, embedded in fallacious instances based on analogy. Sometimes the choice is arbitrary, as it often is in an interesting extension of the custom, according to which an individual is throughout life, or for some particular period, forbidden a certain food. Thus, amongst the Bakalai, to every man some particular food is *roondah*; if he were to eat it, his wives would give birth to children resembling it.[2] Every man and woman in the Andaman Islands is prohibited all through life from eating some one or more fish or animal. It is generally one which in childhood was observed or imagined by the mother to occasion some functional derangement. When the child is old enough, the

[1] Mosheim, *Ecclesiastical History*, i. 116, 262.
[2] Du Chaillu, *op. cit.* 308; cf. Bosman, *Description of Guinea*, 400.

reason is explained, and, cause and effect being clearly demonstrated, the individual avoids it carefully.[1] The principle behind this custom is that of savage make-believe. If a particular food is taboo to a man, he believes that thereby his ordinary food will never hurt him. The practice correlates in principle with the arbitrary selection of fetishes and the like, and is connected with the beliefs and customs concerning external souls. The following cases are instructive in this connection; in Halmahera and Wetar sickness is often ascribed to eating forbidden foods.[2] Icthyosis and leprosy are regarded in Halmahera as due to eating forbidden food; and one may become a *suwanggi* by eating it. These *suwanggis* have the power of sorcery, and were often killed by the community for causing death.[3] Ordinary illness is ascribed in the Luang Sermata Islands to "bad winds" and bad food. Severe illnesses are ascribed to evil spirits.[4] Malay like modern European medicine is chiefly concerned with dieting.[5]

Further, the principles of primitive thought concerned with contact and material transmission find full development here, in all the forms of custom and belief relating to human relations and social taboo. Material contact leaves its impress for good or bad upon food, as upon everything else. Food that a man has touched is permeated by his properties, and accordingly can transmit these to others; it is also on the same principle a part of himself, and any injury done to it is believed to affect himself. The belief extends to any food, not that he has touched, but of the same kind as he usually

[1] Man, in *Journ. Anthrop. Inst.* xii. 354.

[2] Riedel, in *Zeitschrift für Ethnologie*, xvii. 83; and in *De sluik- en kroesharige rassen tusschen Selebes en Papua*, 452.

[3] *Id. l.c.* and 66. [4] *Id. op. cit.* 327. [5] Skeat, *op. cit.* 408.

eats. The connection of food with human attributes is well seen in the following example. The natives of the Mary River and Bunya-Bunya country have many idioms attributing the passions to the state of the stomach.[1] This is true of many languages, and in all ages men have more or less realised the fact, but early man realises this connection most keenly. It is natural that the nearer man is to his animal ancestors, the more his life should be guided by the chief process of animal life.

Food possesses the characteristics of that from which it is taken, and the savage avoids foods that are thus harmful, and prefers those that are thus nutritious. The Masai eat beef to make them strong, and a man will eat bullock's flesh for a whole day to get up courage for a battle.[2] We have seen how this obvious principle is extended to the eating of human flesh in order to acquire human courage and strength.

The method of injuring a man by magic use of remnants of his food is an extension of ideas of contact already described. In Tanna, as we saw, the disease-makers injure a man by burning his *nahak*, that is the refuse of his food, or any article that has been in close contact with his body. When a person is taken ill, he believes that it is occasioned by some one who is burning his *nahak*; and if he dies, his friends ascribe it to the disease-maker as having burnt the refuse to the end.[3]

In the next phase, that of involuntary transmission, the specific contagion of human influences is the object of precaution. Uncivilised man regards strangers with feelings of hostility and suspicion. These feelings extend to food that they have touched or tasted. Thus

[1] Curr, *op. cit.* iii. 191. [2] Thomson, *op. cit.* 264. [3] *Supra*, 126.

the Papuans of Humboldt Bay would not touch any food which their European visitors had previously tasted, nor even drink the water offered to them. This aversion was "due to superstitious ideas."[1] The Yule islanders refused to accept a share of anything which their visitors ate.[2] The black-fellows of Victoria regard as wholesome any food that is not poisonous or connected with superstitious beliefs, but they will not touch any food which has been partaken of by a stranger.[3] The Basutos were afraid to eat anything which a white man had touched.[4] The Poggi islanders would not touch the food offered them by Europeans until it had first been tasted by one of the ship's company.[5] This instance is a link with the last set of customs. Hence the Atiu islanders refused to eat with the missionaries,[6] and the Indians with the Prince of Wied.[7]

We have now arrived at the prohibition against eating with certain persons. In Tanna no food is accepted if offered with the bare hands, "as such contact might give the food a potency for evil."[8] In New Zealand one can be "bewitched" by eating or drinking from the calabash of an ill-wisher, or by smoking his pipe. Personal misfortunes are attributed to such indiscretions. When a man is sick, he is invariably questioned by the doctor, for example, whose pipe he smoked last.[9] In ancient India a Brahmin might not eat the food of an enemy or an ungrateful man, or that offered by an angry, sick, or intoxicated person.[10] In the Mulgrave Islands those who are not

[1] Rosenberg, *op. cit.* 478.

[2] D'Albertis, *op. cit.* i. 261.

[3] Dawson, *op. cit.* 18.

[4] Arbousset, *op. cit.* 149.

[5] Crisp, in *Asiatick Researches*, vi. 81.

[6] Gill, *Jottings from the Pacific*, 42.

[7] Waitz-Gerland, *op. cit.* iii. 166.

[8] Featherman, *op. cit.* ii. 76.

[9] Polack, *New Zealand*, i. 280, 265.

[10] Manu, iv. 213, 214, 207.

initiate ought never to drink from the same cup with sorcerers.[1] In Fiji persons who suspect others of plotting against them avoid eating in their presence.[2] The Fijians consider it objectionable, just as we do, for several persons to drink out of the same vessel.[3] No respectable Zulu would eat in the company of Amatongas, who are regarded as "evil-doers" (wizards).[4] In New Zealand no one dare eat the food of a "*tapued* person" (gentleman), "for this is equivalent to eating his sacredness." On one occasion a slave ate his chief's dinner by mistake; when told of what he had done he was seized with convulsions and cramp in the stomach, and died at sundown.[5] Similarly, if any one ate the Mikado's food, his mouth and throat would swell up and death would ensue.[6] Cadiack whalers are considered "unclean," and no one will eat out of the same dish with them, or even approach them, for that reason.[7] In Fiji the sick are credited with malignant properties; they are supposed to "pollute" objects which they touch, and food, by means of their saliva. Great care is always taken that no one touches the king's cup-bearer.[8] In Tahiti, all who were employed in embalming the dead were during the process carefully avoided by every one, as "the guilt of the crime for which the deceased had died was supposed in some degree to attach to such as touched the body. They did not feed themselves, lest the food, defiled by the touch of their polluted hands, should cause their own death, but were fed by others."[9] In New Zealand

[1] D'Urville, *op. cit.* ii. 408.
[2] Williams and Calvert, *Fiji*, i. 249.
[3] Wilkes, *op. cit.* iii. 349.
[4] Shooter, *op. cit.* 115.
[5] Shortland, *Maori Religion*, 26; *New Zealand*, by a Pakeha Maori, 114.
[6] D'Urville, *op. cit.* i. 386.
[7] Lisiansky, *op. cit.* 174.
[8] Featherman, *op. cit.* ii. 620; Wilkes, *op. cit.* iii. 115.
[9] Ellis, *Polynesian Researches*, iv. 388; so in Fiji, Meinicke, *op. cit.* iii. 40, Hawaii and Samoa, *id.* ii. 300, 276.

one who has touched a dead body may not use his hands to eat, but is either fed by others or picks up his food with his teeth from the ground or the food-basket. Those who feed such a person offer the food with outstretched arm, and are careful not to touch him.[1] In Samoa, while a dead body is in the house, no food may be eaten under the same roof; meals are taken outside or in another house. Those who attend upon the dead dare not handle their food, but are fed for some days by others. The penalty for breaking this rule is baldness and loss of teeth.[2] In Fiji any one who has touched a chief, living or dead, becomes *tabu*; he cannot handle food, but must be fed by others. Hence barbers are continually in this case.[3] In Tonga, when a man has touched a superior chief, or anything belonging to him, he may not feed himself with his own hands. Should he do so, he will infallibly swell up and die.[4] To take examples of another sort of contagion. In Burma one is defiled by sitting or eating with the "impure" caste of Sandalas.[5] The ancient Brahmin who ate the food of "outcasts" became thereby an "outcast" himself.[6] In modern India members of different castes will not eat food cooked in the same vessel; if a person of another caste touch a cooking vessel, it must be thrown away.[7] The food of a Fijian chief may not be carried by boys who have not been tattoed, lest the meat be rendered "unclean"; boys being "unclean" until then.[8] A New Zealand gentleman must eat apart from his friends in solitude.[9] The Tuitonga might not eat in the presence of older

[1] Brown, *New Zealand*, 11.
[2] Turner, *Samoa*, 145; *id. Nineteen Years in Polynesia*, 228.
[3] Erskine, *Western Pacific*, 254. [4] Mariner, *op. cit.* i. 150, ii. 80.
[5] D'Urville, *op. cit.* i. 173. [6] Manu, xi. 176, 181; Ward, *Hindoos*, ii. 149.
[7] Ward, *op. cit.* ii. 317. [8] D'Urville, *op. cit.* i. 166. [9] Yate, *op. cit.* 20.

members of his family.[1] The King of Loango from his birth may never eat with any one.[2] On the Loango coast, among numerous restrictions upon food, occurs a prohibition against eating in company with others.[3] Amongst the Alfoers of Celebes the priest who is responsible for the growth of the rice may not during his office eat or drink with any one, nor drink out of another's cup.[4] In Cambodia people will not eat with a priest.[5] In the Sandwich Islands no one could eat with the chief, who was "sacred."[6] In Tonga inferiors and superiors may not eat together.[7] In New Zealand a slave may not eat with his master, nor even eat of the same food or cook at the same fire.[8] In some parts of Polynesia a man will never eat with another out of the same basket.[9] It is extremely unusual for Nubians and the Niam-niam to take any meals in common.[10] This taboo is the main feature in certain systems of caste. In Tonga there are ranks and orders that can neither eat nor drink together.[11] In Uripiv (New Hebrides) the males are divided into ten "castes" corresponding to age in life. Promotion is marked by a change of name. The members of each "caste" mess together and may not eat with others. Unmarried mess-mates also sleep together.[12] In India "eating together is one of the grand tests of identity of caste." A Hindoo must take precautions "to insulate himself, as it were, during his meal, lest he be contaminated by the touch of some undetected sinner who may be present."[13] In Ceylon, under the Kandyan dynasty,

1 D'Urville, *op. cit.* ii. 77. 2 Bastian, *Loango-Küste*, i. 172. 3 *Id. l.c.*

4 *Mededeelingen van wege het Nederlandsch Zendeling-Genootschap*, xi. 126.

5 Aymonier, *op. cit.* 170. 6 Varigny, *op. cit.* 13. 7 D'Urville, *op. cit. l.c.*

8 Shortland, *Traditions and Superstitions of New Zealand*, 106.

9 Waitz-Gerland, *op. cit.* v. 54. 10 Schweinfurth, *op. cit.* 447.

11 Mariner, *op. cit.* ii. 236. 12 Somerville, in *Journ. Anthrop. Inst.* xxiii. 6, 7.

13 Mateer, *op. cit.* 331; Colebrooke, *op. cit.* vii. 277.

the most dreaded punishment for erring ladies was to hand them over to the low-caste Rodiyas. A Rodiya thereupon was ordered to put betel from his mouth into the mouth of the delinquent, after which her "degradation" was indelible. There were two lower castes than the Rodiyas, who were so despised that no human being would touch rice cooked in their houses.[1] The Black Jews of Loango are so despised that no one will eat with them.[2] The Santhals hate the Hindus, and will not receive food which comes from their hands.[3] The Paharias regard themselves as superior to the Keriahs, with whom they may neither eat nor drink.[4]

We next are met by familiar extensions of the principle of contagion. The prohibition against eating and drinking before the eyes of others is an outcome of that universal appreciation of the power of the human gaze which has reached its most superstitious development in the belief in the Evil Eye. The idea is still that of contagion, for facts show the belief that malignance and other properties can be conveyed by a look as certainly as by other methods of infection, and thus taint the food and drink of the individual who fears. The Oriental belief that food is rendered poisonous by the Evil Eye is a luminous instance. In Abyssinia, the doors are carefully barred before meals to exclude the Evil Eye, and a fire is lighted, otherwise "devils" will enter, and "there will be no blessing on the meat." The king always dines alone.[5] Amongst the Nubians no food is carried without being carefully covered, for fear of the Evil Eye. No one is ever seen

[1] Tennent, *op. cit.* ii. 189.
[2] Bastian, *op. cit.* i. 218.
[3] Rowney, *Wild Tribes of India*, 74.
[4] V. Ball, *Jungle Life in India*, 89.
[5] Harris, *op. cit.* iii. 171, 172, 322.

eating.[1] The Zafimanelo of Madagascar lock the doors before every meal, and no one ever sees them eat.[2] A Khol will leave off eating if a man's shadow passes across the dishes.[3]

It is clear that men believe human properties to be transmitted not only by contact with the food of others, but by eating with them or in their presence. The same idea lurks subconsciously in the modern mind; the objection against eating with "publicans and sinners" is still strong, and is based on the same "primitive" conception.

The altruistic development of these ideas is to be observed in such practices as the following. The Niam-niam are very particular at their meals, and when several are drinking together, they may be observed to wipe the rim of the cup before passing it on.[4] As always in connection with contact, the tendency is for any human emanation to be regarded as in itself undesirable, and with the growth of intellect and refinement such are, as *animal* characteristics, brought into the sphere of disgust, not only altruistic but individualistic also. Amongst the Natchez it was considered a great offence to drink out of the same cup or eat out of the same dish set apart for the chief.[5] It is forbidden in Wetar to eat or drink anything out of vessels used by the chiefs.[6] Young Bedouin boys show deference to their father by never presuming to eat out of the same dish, nor even in his presence.[7] The altruistic form is in principle, it will be observed, closely connected with the ideas of *ngadhungi*; to eat another's food is a real injury to him, in all the primitive sense

[1] Schweinfurth, *op. cit.* ii. 326.
[2] *Antananarivo Annual*, ii. 219.
[3] Rowney, *op. cit.* 65.
[4] Schweinfurth, *op. cit.* ii. 19.
[5] Featherman, *op. cit.* iii. 138.
[6] Riedel, *op. cit.* 455.
[7] Featherman, *op. cit.* v. 363.

of the word "real." In New Zealand to eat a man's food was a gross insult, it was equivalent to eating the man himself, or his "sacredness."[1]

In sexual as in social taboo generally these beliefs have had a remarkable influence. The widely spread rule of sexual taboo that men and women may not eat together, is, as are taboos of commensality generally, in origin a form of egoistic sensitiveness with regard to the most important vital function; sexual separation and sexual solidarity build upon this, and the general ideas of contact applied to sexual relations develop a superstitious fear that the contact, whether by contagion or infection, or otherwise, of food with the person, or influence of the female, transmits to the male the properties of woman, and, though this is not so much in evidence, food "infected" by males transmits to the female the properties of the male, and the rule becomes a complete taboo.

It is to be observed that the prohibition has several variations: for instance, women may not enter the cooking-house of the men, and men may not eat those kinds of food used by women, in some cases, by a natural extension, not even female animals.

To begin with some special circumstances—

In Ceram men during mourning may not eat the females of deer and certain other animals.[2] Amongst the Motu of New Guinea when a man is *helega*, for example after touching a dead body, he lives apart from his wife, and may not eat food that she has cooked.[3] A Yucatan "Captain" during his three years of office, might know no woman, nor might his food be served by women.[4] The cook of the King of Angoy was

[1] Shortland, *Maori Religion*, 26.

[2] Riedel, *op. cit.* 142.

[3] Lawes, in *Journ. Anthrop. Inst.* viii. 370.

[4] Bancroft, *op. cit.* ii. 741.

expected to keep himself pure, and might not even live with a wife.[1] Algonkin priests, who are ordained to a life of chastity, may not even eat food prepared by a married woman.[2] Buddhist monks in Burma may not eat food cooked by female hands; if a female offers rice, they may accept but not eat.[3] Individuals in a state of danger or solemn service, in other words "under taboo," have especial reasons to avoid female contagion.

The fact that the prohibition occurs at puberty serves to bring into relief the idea that danger from the other sex is apprehended at this period. Amongst the Kurnai of Gippsland a "novice" may not eat female animals; he becomes free of the forbidden food by degrees, in this way: an old man suddenly comes behind him and without warning smears the fat of the cooked animal over his face.[4] Amongst the Narrinyeri boys during the progress of "initiation," which is not complete until the beard has been pulled out three times, and each time has been allowed to grow to the length of two inches, are forbidden to eat any food which belongs to women. Everything that they possess or obtain becomes *narumbe*, sacred from the touch of women, a term also which is applied to themselves. They are forbidden to eat with women, "lest they grow ugly or become grey."[5] This belief is instructive, as showing how the superstitious fear of the other sex may exist side by side with a desire to please, or even give rise to means thereto.

The prohibition also applies to young men generally. The Dyaks of North-West Borneo forbid their young

[1] Bastian, *Loango-Küste*, i. 216.
[2] Bancroft, *op. cit.* iii. 212.
[3] Shway Yoe, *The Burman*, i. 136.
[4] *Journ. Anthrop. Inst.* xiv. 316.
[5] *Native Tribes of South Australia*, 17, 69.

men and warriors to eat vension, which is the food of women and old men, because it would make them as timid as deer.[1] In the tribes of Western Victoria boys are not allowed to eat any female quadruped. If they are caught eating a female opossum, for instance, they are severely punished; the reason given is that such food makes them peevish and discontented,[2] in other words, it gives them the failings which a black-fellow ascribes to the female sex. In the Andamans bachelors may only eat with the male sex, and spinsters with females.[3]

Amongst the Kurnai of Gippsland men may only eat the males of the animals which they use for food.[4] The Port Lincoln tribe observe· certain laws about animal food, the general principle of which is this: that the male of any animal should be eaten by grown-up men, the female by women, and the young animal by children only.[5]

In special circumstances, here as elsewhere, the intensified sexual property then acquired is believed to be transmissible by the agency of food. In Western Victoria a menstruous woman may not take any one's food or drink, and no one will touch food that has been touched by her, "because it will make them weak."[6] In Queensland menstruous women are "unclean," and no one will touch a dish which they have used.[7] Amongst the Maoris, if a man touched a menstruous woman, he would be *tapu*; if he had connection with her or ate food cooked by her, he would be "*tapu* an inch thick."[8] In the Aru Islands menstruous

[1] St. John, *op. cit.* i. 186, 206.

[2] Dawson, *op. cit.* 52.

[3] *Journ. Anthrop. Inst.* xi. 344.

[4] Fison and Howitt, *op. cit.* 197.

[5] *Native Tribes of South Australia*, 220

[6] Dawson, *op. cit.* ci. cii.

[7] Lumholtz, *op. cit.* 119.

[8] *Journ. Anthrop. Inst.* xix. 101.

women may not plant, cook, or prepare any food.[1] In Ceram-laut and Gorong, amongst the Samoyeds and Kalundas, wives at the *catamenia* may not prepare their husband's food.[2] At menstruation a Chippeway wife may not eat with her husband; she must cook her food at a separate fire, since any one using her fire will fall ill. The same rule is enforced at child-birth.[3] A Kaniagmut woman is "unclean" for some days both after delivery and menstruation; no one in either case may touch her, and she is fed with food at the end of a stick.[4] Amongst the Omahas and Ponkas women during the monthly periods may not eat with their husbands. These tribes have a belief that if one eats with a menstruous woman, the lips dry up, the blood turns black, and consumption is the final result. It is but fair to add that it is mainly children who believe this, the old people have no fear of the kind.[5] A Brahmin might not allow himself to be touched by a menstruous woman, or eat food offered by a woman.[6] Amongst the Vedahs of Travancore the wife at menstruation is secluded for five days, in a hut a quarter of a mile away, which is also used by her at child-birth. The next five days are passed in a second hut, half-way between the first and her house. On the ninth day her husband holds a feast, sprinkles his floor with wine, and invites his friends to a spread of rice and palm-wine. Until this evening he has not dared to eat anything but roots, for fear of being killed by the "devil." On the tenth day he must leave his house, to which he may not return until the women, his and her sister, have bathed his wife, escorted her home and eaten rice

[1] Riedel, *op. cit.* 178.
[2] *Id.* ii. 354.
[3] Ploss u. Bartels, *op. cit.* ii. 275.
[4] *Id. op. cit.* 209; Ploss u. Bartels, *op. cit.* i. 273.
[4] Dall, *op. cit.* 403; Bancroft, *op. cit.* i. 111.
[6] Manu, iv. 208, 211.

together. For four days after his return, moreover, he may not eat rice in his own house, nor have connection with his wife.[1]

In Fiji a wife when pregnant may not wait upon her husband.[2] In the Caroline Islands men may not eat with their wives when pregnant, though small boys are allowed to do so.[3] The Indians of Guiana believe that if a pregnant woman eat of game caught by hounds they will never be able to hunt again.[4] Amongst the tribes on the Amazon, if a pregnant woman eat any particular meat, it is believed that any animal partaking of the same will suffer; a domestic animal will die, a hound will be rendered incapable of hunting, and a man who eats such food will never again be able to shoot that particular animal.[5] Amongst the Chippeways a lying-in woman may not eat with her husband, and must cook her food at a separate fire;[6] a Kirgis woman when lying-in is "unclean" and may not give her husband his food.[7] In the islands Luang and Sermata the husband gives a feast after a birth, at which only women may be present. It is believed that any man tasting the food will be unlucky in all his undertakings.[8] Amongst the tribes of the Oxus valley the mother is "unclean" for seven days, and no one will eat from her hand, nor may she suckle her infant during that period.[9]

The examples of the prohibition in ordinary life are arranged geographically.

The Warua of Central Africa, when offered a drink, put up a cloth before the face while they swallow.

[1] Jagor, in *Zeitschrift für Ethnologie*, xi. 164.
[2] Williams, *op. cit.* i. 157.
[3] Ploss u. Bartels, *op. cit.* i. 514.
[4] im Thurn, *op. cit.* 233.
[5] Wallace, *The Amazon*, 501.
[6] Ploss u. Bartels, *op. cit.* ii. 353.
[7] *Id.* ii. 351.
[8] Riedel, *op. cit.* 326.
[9] Biddulph, *The Tribes of the Hindoo Koosh*, 81.

They will not allow any one to see them eat or drink, especially those of the opposite sex. "I could not," says Cameron, "make a man let a woman see him drink." Hence every person has his own fire, and every man and woman must cook for themselves.[1] On the Loango coast both bridegroom and bride must make a full confession of their sins at the marriage ceremony of *Lemba*; should either fail to do so, or keep anything back, they will fall ill when eating together as man and wife. Only such marriages as are performed in the presence of this fetish *Lemba* are legitimate; a negro dares not let any of his wives, except the one thus married, cook his food, or look after his wardrobe. This fetish also serves to keep the wives in order and to punish them for infidelity.[2] In Eastern Central Africa, when a wife has been guilty of unchastity, her husband will die if he taste any food that she has salted. As a consequence of this superstition, a wife is very liable to be accused of killing her husband. Accordingly, when a wife prepares her husband's food, she will often get a little girl to put the salt in.[3] Amongst the Braknas of West Africa husbands and wives do not eat together.[4] Fulah women may not eat with their husbands.[5] In Ashanti and Senegambia, amongst the Niam-niam and the Barea, the wife never eats with the husband.[6] Amongst the Beni-Amer a wife never eats in the presence of her husband.[7] Amongst the Krumen the chief wife only may eat with the husband.[8] In Eastern Central Africa each village has a separate mess for males and

[1] Cameron, in *Journ. Anthrop. Inst.* vi. 173.

[2] Bastian, *Loango Küste*, i. 170, 172.

[3] Macdonald, *op. cit.* i. 173.

[4] Girard-Teulon, *op. cit.* 107.

[5] Waitz-Gerland, *op. cit.* ii. 471.

[6] J. L. Wilson, *op. cit.* 182; W. Reade, *op. cit.* 453; Macdonald, *op. cit.* i. 227; Munzinger, *op. cit.* 526.

[7] *Id.* 325.

[8] Waitz-Gerland, *op. cit.* ii. 120.

females.[1] This prohibition is very general throughout Africa.

In Egypt the wives and female slaves are not allowed to eat with the master.[2] Amongst the Aeneze Arabs husband and wife do not eat together.[3] Amongst the Wahabees and Syrian Arabs the women may not eat with the male members of the family.[4] So with the Druses of Lebanon.[5] The Beni-Harith would not eat or drink at the hands of a woman, and "would rather have died of hunger than break the rule."[6] Herodotus states that Carian women did not eat with their husbands, nor would they address them as "husband."[7]

Amongst the Kurds husband and wife never eat together.[8] A Samoyed woman may not eat with men, much less with her husband, whose leavings form her meals.[9]

A Hindu wife never eats with her husband, "if his own wife were to touch the food he was about to eat, it would be rendered unfit for his use."[10] So in ancient India; to quote Manu, "let him not eat in the company of his wife."[11] A Brahmin might not eat food given by a woman, or by those "who are in all things ruled by women," nor might he eat the leavings of women.[12] In Travancore the women must eat after the men.[13] Amongst the Khonds the wife and children wait upon the master while he eats, then they may take their meal. Women may not eat hog's flesh, and may only

[1] Macdonald, *op. cit.* i. 151.
[2] Lane, *op. cit.* i. 236, 243.
[3] Burckhardt, *Notes on the Bedouins and Wahabys*, i. 64.
[4] Featherman, *op. cit.* v. 451, 393.
[5] Chasseaud, *op. cit.* 77.
[6] W. R. Smith, *Kinship and Marriage in Ancient Arabia*, 312.
[7] Herodotus, i. 146.
[8] Pinkerton, *op. cit.* ix. 15.
[9] Bastian, *Der Mensch*, iii. 295.
[10] Colebrooke, *op. cit.* 166.
[11] Manu, iv. 43.
[12] *Id.* xi. 153; iv. 217.
[13] Mateer, *op. cit.* 204; *id. The Land of Charity*, 65.

taste liquor at festivals.[1] The men and women of Kumaun eat separately.[2] Amongst the hill tribes near Rajmahal in Bengal the women are not allowed to eat with the men.[3] Amongst the Todas men and women may not eat together.[4] At a Santhal wedding the bride and bridegroom eat together after fasting all day; this is the first time she has ever eaten with a man.[5] In Cochin a wife never eats with her husband.[6] A Siamese wife prepares her husband's meals, but dines after him.[7] In the Maldive Islands husband and wife may not eat together.[8] The same rule is in force amongst the Khakyens.[9] In China by marriage a woman "only changes masters"; the wife neither eats with her husband nor with her male children; she waits upon them at table; she may not touch what her son leaves.[10] In Corea men and women have their meals separately, the women waiting on the men. "Family life is utterly unknown in Corea."[11]

Amongst the Indians of Guiana husbands and wives eat separately.[12] Macusi women eat after the men.[13] Amongst the Bororo women and children eat after the men, and finish their leavings.[14] Amongst the Araucanians only the chief wife may eat with her husband.[15] In ancient Mexico each person had a separate bowl for eating; the men ate first and by themselves, the women and children afterwards.[16] In Yucatan men and women

[1] Macpherson, *Memorials of Service in India*, 72.
[2] *Panjab Notes and Queries*, iii. 2. 454.
[3] T. Shaw, in *Asiatick Researches*, iv. 59.
[4] Marshall, *op. cit.* 82.
[5] E. T. Dalton, *Ethnology of Bengal*, 216.
[6] A. Bastian, *Allerlei aus Menschen- und Völkerkunde*, ii. 160.
[7] Pinkerton, *op. cit.* ix. 585.
[8] *Journ. Anthrop. Inst.* xvi. 168.
[9] Anderson, *op. cit.* 137.
[10] Huc, *L'empire chinois*, i. 268.
[11] *Journ. Anthrop. Inst.* xxiv. 306.
[12] im Thurn, *op. cit.* 256; Brett, *op. cit.* 23.
[13] *Id. l.c.*
[14] Von den Steinen, *op. cit.* 215.
[15] Waitz-Gerland, *op. cit.* iii. 516.
[16] L. H. Morgan, *Houses and House Life of the American Aborigines*, 101.

ate apart.[1] "So far as I have yet travelled," says Catlin, "in the Indian country, I have never yet seen an Indian woman eating with her husband. Men form the first group at the banquet, and women and children and dogs all come together at the next."[2] Amongst the Iroquois tribes the men ate first and by themselves, then the women and children took their meal alone. Of these people it has been said that the women "must approach their lords with reverence; they must regard them as most exalted beings, and are not permitted to eat in their presence."[3] Mandan women may not eat with the men.[4] So amongst the Abenaques, Seminoles, and Northern Indians.[5] The Seneca Indians relate of the changes in their customs resulting from the innovations of the whites, "that when the proposition that man and wife should eat together, which was so contrary to immemorial usage, was first determined in the affirmative, it was formally agreed that man and wife should sit down together at the same dish and eat with the same ladle, the man eating first and then the woman, and so alternately until the meal was finished."[6] Amongst the Natchez the husband used a respectful attitude towards his wife, and addressed her as if he were her slave; he did not eat with her.[7] An Eskimo wife "dares not eat with her husband."[8] Amongst the Indians of California husbands and wives eat separately; they may not even cook at the same fire.[9] Karalit and Kutchin women may not eat with men.[10]

[1] L. H. Morgan, *op. cit.* 103. [2] Catlin, *North American Indians*, i. 202.
[3] Morgan, *op. cit.* 99; Robertson, *History of America*, 178.
[4] Featherman, *op. cit.* iii. 297. [5] *Id.* iii. 94, 169; Hearne, *op. cit.* 90.
[6] Morgan, *op. cit.* 100. [7] Charlevoix, *Histoire de la Nouvelle France*, iii. 423.
[8] Waitz-Gerland, *op. cit.* iii. 308. [9] Bancroft, *op. cit.* i. 390.
[10] Featherman, *op. cit.* iii. 420, 384.

Amongst the extinct Tasmanians husband and wife ate separately.[1] The rule is general throughout Australia; the *gin* never eats till the man has finished, and then she eats his leavings.[2] In Victoria males and females have separate fires at which they cook their own food. Many of the best kinds of food are forbidden to women.[3] In Queensland also the husband reserved the best of the food for himself.[4] In Central Australia the men and women eat and camp separately.[5]

Amongst the Arfaks of New Guinea the men and women eat apart.[6] Amongst the Kayans and Punans of Borneo the men feed alone, attended on by the women.[7] Amongst the Battas of Sumatra husband and wife may not eat from the same dish.[8] In the Mentawey Islands the man eats alone in the house; the women are forbidden to use many kinds of food.[9] In the islands Wetar and Dama women may not eat with the men; in Romang husband and wife take their meals at the same time but separately.[10] Men and women may not eat together in Halmahera.[11]

In Melanesia generally, women may not eat with men.[12] In the Solomon Islands husband and wife do not eat together; she prepares his meal, and when he has finished she eats what he has left.[13] In the Banks Islands all the adult males belong to the men's club, *Suqe*, where they take their meals, while the women and children eat at home.[14] In Tanna women may not eat with men, they may not drink *kava*, nor share in

1 Featherman, *op. cit.* ii. 105.
2 Waitz-Gerland, *op. cit.* vi. 777.
3 Brough Smyth, *op. cit.* i. 234.
4 Lumholtz, *op. cit.* 161.
5 Spencer and Gillen, *op. cit.* 467, 469.
6 D'Albertis, *op. cit.* i. 218.
7 Hose, in *Journ. Anthrop. Inst.* xxiii. 160.
8 Ellis, *op. cit.* i. 117.
9 Rosenberg, *op. cit.* 196.
10 Riedel, *op. cit.* 458, 464.
11 *Id.* in *Zeitschrift für Ethnologie*, xvii. 59.
12 Waitz-Gerland, *op. cit.* vi. 676; Meinicke, *op. cit.* i. 67.
13 Guppy, *op. cit.* i. 41.
14 *Journ. Anthrop. Inst.* x. 237.

the *kava*-drinking feasts of the men.[1] In the New Hebrides generally, women always eat apart from the men.[2] In Uripiv "the most noticeable features of domestic life will be found in the curious segregation of the sexes and the superstitious dread of eating anything female. A few days after birth a killing of pigs takes place and the child is 'rated a man.' Henceforward he must cook his own meals at his own fire, and eat with men alone, otherwise death will mysteriously fall upon him. The fact of his being suckled, however, which often goes on for two years, is quite overlooked."[3] In Malekula men and women cook their meals separately, and even at separate fires, and all female animals, sows, and even hens and eggs are forbidden articles of diet. A native told Lieutenant Somerville that a mate of his had died from partaking of sow.[4] In New Caledonia women may not eat with the men.[5] In Fiji husband and wife may not eat together, nor brother and sister, nor the two sexes generally. Young men may not eat of food left by women. Boys, as being "unclean" until they have been tatooed, may not carry food to the chiefs, for their touch would render it "unclean."[6]

In Ponape the men take their meals in the clubhouse.[7] In Kusaie women may not eat with men owing to the *tabu*.[8] In Rarotonga the women ate apart from the men.[9] In the Hervey Islands husband and wife never eat together, and the first-born child, boy or girl, may not eat with any member of the family.[10] In Paumotu the women may not eat with

[1] Turner, *Nineteen Years in Polynesia*, 85.
[2] Meinicke, *op. cit.* i. 197.
[3] *Journ. Anthrop. Inst.* xxiii. 4.
[4] *Id.* 381.
[5] Meinicke, *op. cit.* i. 231.
[6] Williams, *op. cit.* i. 167, 136; D'Urville, *op. cit.* ii. 102.
[7] Waitz-Gerland, *op. cit.* v. 2. 72.
[8] Meinicke, *op. cit.* ii. 377.
[9] *Id.* ii. 143.
[10] Gill, *Life in the Southern Isles*, 94.

the men, and are not allowed to eat several kinds of food, such as large fish and turtles. These laws are enforced by the *tabu*.[1] So in Tubuai *tabu* forbids the women to eat with men, or to use as food turtles and pigs.[2] In the Marquesas Islands to each dwelling there is attached a special eating-house for the men, which the women are forbidden to enter.[3] In Nukahiva, according to another account, the rich have separate buildings for dining-rooms on particular occasions of feasting which women are not permitted to enter; so strict is the rule, that they dare not even pass near them. Women are forbidden *kava* and certain foods.[4] In Rurutu men and women do not eat together, "owing to superstitious fear; they believe that in such case the wife would be destroyed by a spirit."[5] In Bow Island the men threw the remains of their meals to their wives.[6] In Rotumah the men of the family eat first; when they have finished, the women and children begin their meal at a separate table.[7] In New Zealand, where every man eats by himself away from his friends, women and slaves may not eat with men. Men may not eat with their wives nor wives with their male children, "lest their *tapu* or sanctity should kill them."[8] In the Sandwich Islands the king's wives were not allowed to enter his eating-house.[9] In Hawaii the women were forbidden to eat in company with men, and even to enter the eating-room during meals. Three houses necessarily belonged to each family, the dwelling-house, a house for the

[1] Meinicke, *op. cit.* ii. 219. [2] *Id.* ii. 199. [3] *Id.* ii. 249.
[4] Lisiansky, *op. cit.* 87; Meinicke, *op. cit.* ii. 252, 247.
[5] Ellis, *op. cit.* iii. 97, 98. [6] Beechey, *op. cit.* i. 242.
[7] D'Urville, *op. cit.* ii. 440.
[8] Thomson, *The Story of New Zealand*, i. 60; Taylor, *op. cit.* i. 168.
[9] Kotzebue, *Voyage to the South Sea*, i. 305.

repasts of the men, and another for the meals of the women. The residence was common; the women's house was not closed against our sex, but a decorous man would not enter it. The eating-house of the men was tabooed to women. "We ourselves saw the corpse of a woman floating round our ship, who had been killed because she had entered the eating-house of her husband in a state of intoxication." The *raison d'être* of the two eating-houses belonging to each family was because the two sexes might not eat together. Women dared not be present at the meals of the men, on pain of death. Each sex had to dress their own victuals over a separate fire. The two sexes were not allowed to use the flesh of the same animal. Hog's flesh, turtle, several kinds of fruit, cocoa, bananas, etc., were prohibited to the women.[1] From another account of the Sandwich Islands we gather the following: women might not eat with men; their houses and their labours were distinct; their aliment was prepared separately. A female child from its birth until death was allowed no food that had touched the father's dish. "From childhood onwards no natural affections were inculcated; no social circle existed."[2] Ellis' account of the state of things in the Society and Sandwich Islands is as follows:—"The institutes of Oro and Tane inexorably require not only that the wife should not eat those kinds of foods of which the husband partook, but that she should not eat in the same place or prepare her food at the same fire. This restriction applied not only to the wife with regard to her husband, but to all individuals of the female sex, from their birth to

[1] Lisiansky, *op. cit.* 127, 126; Kotzebue, *op. cit.* iii. 249, i. 310; Meinicke, *op. cit.* ii. 300; H. T. Cheever, *Life in the Sandwich Islands*, 24.

[2] Jarvis, *History of the Hawaiian or Sandwich Islands*, 94, 95; Varigny, *op. cit.* 42.

their death. The children of each sex always ate apart. As soon as a boy was able to eat, a basket was provided for his use, and his food was kept distinct from that of the mother. The men were allowed to eat the flesh of the pig, of fowls, every variety of fish, cocoa-nuts, and bananas, and whatever was presented as an offering to the gods; these the females, on pain of death, were forbidden to touch, as it was supposed they would pollute them. The fires at which the men's food was cooked were also sacred, and were forbidden to be used by the females. The basket in which the provision was kept, and the house in which the men ate, were also sacred, and prohibited to the females under the same cruel penalty. Hence the inferior food for the wives and daughters was cooked at separate fires, deposited in distinct baskets, and eaten in lonely solitude by the females in little huts erected for the purpose." The whole custom was known as the *ai tabu* or "sacred eating."[1] Cook observed of the Sandwich islanders, that "in their domestic life, the women live almost entirely by themselves." This condition of family life was most noticeable in Tahiti. The Tahitians forbade men and women to eat together; they "had an aversion to holding any intercourse with each other at their meals, and they were so rigid in the observance of this custom that even brothers and sisters had their separate baskets of provisions, and generally sat some yards apart, when they ate, with their backs to each other, without exchanging a word."[2] To resume the previous account: "their domestic habits were unsocial and cheerless. This is probably to be attributed to the invidious distinction established by

[1] Ellis, *Polynesian Researches*, i. 116, 129, 263, iv. 386; *id. Tour in Hawaii*, 368.
[2] Cook and King, *op. cit.* iii. 130; Vancouver, *Voyage of Discovery*, i. 105, 139.

their superstitions, and enforced by *tabu* between the sexes. The father and mother, with their children, never, as one social happy band, surrounded the domestic hearth, or assembling under the grateful shade of the verdant grove, partook together, as a family, of the bounties of Providence. The nameless but delightful emotions experienced on such occasions were unknown to them, as well as all that we are accustomed to distinguish by the endearing appellation of domestic happiness. In sickness or pain, or whatever other circumstances the mother, the wife, the sister, or the daughter, might be brought into, *tabu* was never relaxed. The men, especially those who occasionally attended on the services of idol-worship in the temple, were considered *ra*, or sacred; while the female sex was considered *noa*, or common: the most offensive and frequent imprecations which the men were accustomed to use towards each other, referred also to this degraded condition of the females. 'Mayest thou become a bottle, to hold salt water for thy mother,' or 'mayest thou be baked as food for thy mother,' were imprecations they were accustomed to denounce upon each other."[1] Making due allowance for missionary prejudice, the action of sexual taboo in these islands had considerable results, and its meaning is shown in a marked fashion. King Kamehameha "broke" the *tabu* by eating with his wives.[2]

Cases of this taboo have even been found in modern Europe. At a Servian wedding the bride for the first and only time in her life eats with a man, and is served instead of serving. In Brandenburg it is believed that lovers and married people who eat from one plate or drink from one glass will come to dislike each other,

[1] Ellis, *Polynesian Researches*, i. 129.

[2] Varigny, *op. cit.* 42.

and in the district of Fahrland, near Potsdam, there is a prohibition, which is observed, against such persons biting the same piece of bread.[1]

It was suggested by Robertson Smith that the prohibition against husbands and wives eating together may have been due to the fact that by exogamy they were of different tribes, and therefore could not eat the same food. But on the present showing this is impossible. In later thought, this idea may occasionally have been developed, but that it was never original is shown not only by the present evidence but by the facts that the system of tribal, totemic, and "classificatory" foods is rare, while *sexual* taboo in eating is almost universal, and that the taboo is no less common between brothers and sisters, who are of the same tribe, and also, except in rare cases, of the same totem-clan or marriage-class.

[1] Reinsberg Düringsfeld, *Hochzeitsbuch*, 82, 217.

CHAPTER VIII

If contact of the two sexes is always potentially dangerous, owing to fear of the chief result of contact, contagion of properties, it is to be expected that to savage thought the dangers of contagion should be multiplied and deepened when the contact is of the most intimate kind possible. The savage regards intercourse commensal and sexual as the closest, and especially in marriage, of which state the sharing of *mensa* and *thorus* is the chief feature for ordinary thought. As commensality is regulated by this fear of contact, so is sexual intercourse. The ideas beneath each form of contact are the same. The supreme biological importance of the nutritive impulse, of which the sexual is an extension or complement, and the delicate mechanism of the organs of generation, have determined in the usual ratio man's psychological attitude towards this function. As all primitive psychological attitudes arise from what may be called physiological thought, the actual process of functions producing directly ideas concerning them, more or less reflex and subconscious, so as to be practically inherent in the human mind, so the depth of such ideas varies as the importance of the function. The impulse of sex is only less strong than that of hunger. Periodicity has assisted to make its psychological character less ordinary, and less of an everyday concern, and hence more shrouded in secrecy and more surrounded by mystery and fear. The instinct, as it may be truly called, for performing important functions in secret is of course due to anxiety concerning their unimpeded performance, and to fear of interruption. This principle can be traced right down to the lower animals. The savage is far more secretive in this function than is civilised man; what Riedel states of the Ceramese, is true of the generality of savage and barbarous peoples. In Ceram, he says, all natural functions, especially that of *coitus*, are performed in secret, by preference in the forest.[1] In Fiji, from motives of delicacy, "*rendezvous* between husband and wife are arranged in the depths of the forest, unknown to any but the two."[2] Bowdich stated that in Western Africa if a man cohabited with a woman without the house, or in the bush, they both became the slaves of the first person who discovered them, but could be redeemed by their families.[3] This less common rule presupposes more or less publicity in the forest. In the Aru Islands and Wetar intercourse is not performed in the house, but in the forest.[4] In Makisar all bodily functions are performed in secret, and exposure is reprehensible.[5] The savage is also more refined in language with regard to this subject than are most civilised men; thus in Ceram it is forbidden to speak of sexual matters in the presence of a third person;[6] and obscenity, that fungus-growth of civilisation through degeneration or wrong methods of education, is either unknown amongst savages or regarded as a heinous sin. Ethnology supplies many cases of apparent obscenity, but the expressions are not

[1] J. G. F. Riedel, *De sluik- en kroesharige rassen tusschen Selebes en Papua*, 96.
[2] Seeman, *op. cit.* 110, 191.
[3] Bowdich, *Mission from Cape Coast Castle to Ashantee*, 259.
[4] Riedel, *op. cit.* 250, 448. [5] *Id.* 406. [6] *Id.* 96.

obscene, they express a man's righteous and religious indignation, and have much the same force as "infidel" and "blasphemer" when used seriously.

Again, the phenomena of modesty in the female deepen this reserve. Dr. Ellis, who has given the best account of the origin of the feeling of modesty, points out the impulse in female animals and women "to guard the sexual centres against the undesired advances of the male. The naturally defensive attitude of the female is in contrast with the naturally aggressive attitude of the male in sexual relationships." This impulse for defence is carried on into the state of desire, and female animals are known to run after the male, and "then turn to flee, perhaps only submitting with much persuasion." There is the well-known case of a hind running away from a stag, but in a circle round him. "Modesty thus becomes an invitation."[1]

Sexual taboo has emphasised the ideas arising from this functional process, by filling them with a content of religious fear. As to the psychological attitude of the male sex, we often find, especially in European folklore, the fear of possible ligature or *impotentia conjugalis* at marriage, an anxiety coming straight from function and closely connected with the universal care, often passing into religious fear, about doing something for the first time, or something unusual or important. Witches are often supposed to be able to cause this, as in South Celebes.[2]

This feeling of egoistic sensibility, again, connects closely with the widely spread idea underlying contact, that injury may be caused by the ill-will or dangerous

[1] Havelock Ellis, *Studies in the Psychology of Sex*, ii. 29.

[2] B. F. Matthes, *Bijdragen tot de Ethnologie van Zuid-Celebes*, 97.

habit of another, either with or without intention, either by the means of sympathetic magic or of what may be called *sympathy*. This form of sympathetic magic to which I apply the term *ngadhungi*, is, as we have seen, a natural development of that simple idea of contagion which may be called sympathy, man using nature's "bacteriological" or "electrical" means for his own ends. As is the case with every physical function and organ, so against the organs of generation this method can be used. In Ceram difficult labour for woman, and in men, impotence, are caused by putting disease-transmitting articles where people may tread on them.[1] In Tanna aud Malekula "the closest secrecy is adopted with regard to the *penis*, not at all from a sense of decency, but to avoid *narak*, the sight even of that of another man being considered most dangerous. They therefore wrap it round with many yards of calico, winding and folding them until a preposterous bundle eighteen inches or two feet long is formed."[2] We have here the not infrequent converse of the "evil eye"; to see a thing is a method by which one may contract its contagious properties. Of the Arunta Messrs. Spencer and Gillen report, "as a general rule, women are not supposed to be able to exercise much magic except in regard to the sexual organs, but we have known of a woman being speared to death by the brother of her husband, who accused her of having killed the latter by means of a pointing stick. Women exercise peculiar powers in regard to the sexual organs. To bring on a painful affection in those of men, a woman will procure the spear-like seed of a long grass (*Inturkirra*), and having charmed it by singing some magic chant over it, she waits an oppor-

[1] Riedel, *op. cit.* 140.
[2] Somerville, in *Journ. Anthrop. Inst.* xxiv. 368.

tunity to point and throw it towards the man whom she desires to injure. Shortly after this has been done the man experiences pain, as if he had been stung by ants, his parts become swollen, and he at once attributes his sufferings to the magic influence of some woman who wishes to injure him. A woman may also charm a handful of dust which she collects while out digging up yams or gathering seeds, and having 'sung' it brings it into camp with her. She takes the opportunity of sprinkling it over a spot where the man whom she wishes to injure is likely to micturate. If he should do so at this spot he would experience a scalding sensation in the *urethra*, and afterwards suffer a great amount of pain. Women may also produce disease in men by 'singing' over and thus charming a finger, which is then inserted in the *vulva;* the man who subsequently has connection with her will become diseased and may lose his organs altogether, and so when a woman wishes to injure a man she will sometimes after thus 'poisoning' herself, seek an opportunity of soliciting him, though he be not her proper *Unawa*. Syphilitic disease amongst the Arunta is, as a matter of fact, very frequently attributed to this form of magic, for it must be remembered that the native can only understand disease of any form as due to evil magic, and he has to provide what appears to him to be a suitable form of magic to account for each form of disease."[1] The disease *Erkincha*, as we have noticed, is transmitted in the same way. The natives do not reason "from a strictly medical point of view; their idea in a case of this kind is that a man suffering from *Erkincha* conveys a magic evil influence which they call *Arungquiltha* to the women, and by this means it is

[1] Spencer and Gillen, *The Native Tribes of Central Australia*, 547, 548.

conveyed as a punishment to other men."[1] As in other forms of contact, so in this, the transmission of disease is included in the hylo-idealistic contagion of properties, though it is not the origin of these ideas. Similarly, amongst the Zulus, a man suspicious of his wife's fidelity gets "medicine" from a doctor, and takes it internally. By cohabiting with his wife he gives her the seed of disease, and any one cohabiting with her afterwards, acquires it, while she remains uninjured. They have also a "medicine" which can make a man sensitive to the existence of that state in a woman which can produce disease; it is rubbed into a scarification on the back of the left hand. If a woman whom he approaches is in this state, a spasmodic contraction attacks his fingers when he touches her, and he therefore abstains. "It is from dread of this 'disease' that a man will not marry a widow till she has had medical treatment to remove all possibilities of communicating it."[2] The "intention" is in this example well illustrated, being aimed at a third party, and leaving the intermediary free, and also being clearly a man's vengeance materialised and transmitted.

As has been pointed out, *ngadhungi* (*narak*) and beneficent transmission are exactly the same except in the character of the "intention," which is evil in the first case and good in the second, and love-charms proper, used to inspire love, are frequently based on this method. A man or woman in the Arunta and other tribes can charm another's love by "singing" a head-band, which is then given to the person to wear; a man can inspire a woman's love by "singing" the shell ornament he wears from his girdle. As they express

[1] Spencer and Gillen, *op. cit.* 412

[2] Callaway, *The Religious System of the Amazulu*, 287, 288.

the result, the woman sees "lightning" on it, and it makes "her inwards shake with emotion." The idealism of love and its physiological accompaniments are here put in a way worthy of any high culture. It is to be observed that this same method is used to cure sickness, the shell ornament being placed on the sick man's chest.[1] To inspire love, the people of Makisar place secret charms in the footprints of a man or a woman.[2] In the Kei Islands herbs mixed with women's hair and hung in a tree are used for this. The women arouse love in men by charming betel which they have themselves prepared.[3] Sympathetic charms are used by men and women in Buru to excite love. One takes some betel or tobacco, and after speaking a charm over it, places it in the betel-box. When the man or woman against whom the charm is directed makes use of this betel, he or she falls in love with the owner. The same effect is produced by muttering charms over the oil which the woman uses for her hair, or over a piece of hair one has got from a woman. The most potent method, however, is the burying of a piece of prepared ginger, with the muttering of one's desire, in some spot where the woman usually passes.[4] In Tenimber the men make considerable use of charms to engage the women's affections. To this end they place a mixture of roots and lime on some spot where the woman has urinated. It is believed that the woman after a short time will fall madly in love with the man. Young men are therefore forbidden to use lime.[5] In the Babar Islands when a quarrel occurs between lovers, the man avenges himself by keeping a piece of her hair, or some bit of betel she has thrown away. Afterwards, as a

[1] Spencer and Gillen, *op. cit.* 545.
[2] Riedel, *op. cit.* 414.
[3] *Id.* 223.
[4] *Id.* 11.
[5] *Id.* 302.

result, her children by another man will die. Lovers in these islands have full intimacy, but it must be kept secret, for there is a fine attaching. It is believed that men, if fined, are ungallant enough to make the woman ill and unlucky by curses.[1] Lovers in the Aru Islands give each other gifts, but never a lock of hair, for fear that if they quarrelled the one might make the other ill by burning it.[2] For love-charms Arunta women also "make and 'sing' special *okinchalanina* or fur-string necklets, which they place round the man's neck, or they may simply charm a food such as a witchetty-grub or lizard and give this to the man to eat." To promote desire, a man will give a woman to eat a part of the reproductive organs of a male opossum or kangaroo. In the case of a delicate woman, a husband tries to strengthen her by "singing" over such part of a male animal, which she then eats.[3] This instance shows the identity of such love-charms and the transmission of strength already described.

In the love-charms quoted, there are cases not only of *ngadhungi* but of transmission by ordinary contact. Leaving now this transmission of evil purpose and of love, we come to the general ideas of transmission of properties by ordinary contact. As one fears the malicious intention of an enemy which results in sickness or death by transmission of his malevolence, and welcomes or disdains, as the case may be, the feelings of love transmitted by material methods, so one fears or invites the involuntary transmission of another's qualities by contact. The lover is concerned with both sides of the taboo state in its beneficent aspect, he hopes to transmit his own love to his mistress and to receive hers by contact. But if, as is generally the case with

[1] Riedel, *op. cit.* 358, 370. [2] *Id.* 262. [3] Spencer and Gillen, *op. cit.* 548.

uncivilised man, the imperious instinct of love is crossed or conditioned by presuppositions concerning female character derived from the experience of ordinary life, the caution which he shares with the animals in the satisfaction of love will be accentuated by somewhat of fear of the contagion of female properties in the closest sort of contact. We shall see that the male sex, with an unanimity which is practically universal, ascribe to the female a relative inferiority in physical strength. This is a physiological idea arising straight from a sexual secondary difference which is practically universal. If savage man then fears that in ordinary association with women he may be infected with their relative weakness, and if the more civilised fear the moral "infection" of *effeminacy*, it is quite natural that in the closest form of contact this fear should be accentuated.

The conception is also based on what is the complement of the idea of female weakness, namely, the practically universal physiological belief that sexual intercourse is weakening. This is a conception that may be called instinctive, inasmuch as it arises straight from a peculiarity of the function. This peculiarity is the fact that sexual intercourse is followed by a temporary depression, resulting from increased blood-pressure. The idea, then, that contact with women entails weakness, thus arises in two ways which meet by a remarkable coincidence in the sexual act.

In further illustration we may note the idea, probably universal, and correlative with the above mentioned physiological conception, that strength resides in the male seminal fluid. It is an interesting case of effect put for cause. In ordinary human thought the seed is the strength, as much as the blood is the life. The folk-medicine of most countries, especially Europe, is full of cases where human *semen* is used to cure sickness. Primitive man most practically, it is to be noted, correlates weakness and sickness; and there are also numerous examples of *semen* being administered in order to produce strength. The idea is then carried on to the organs of generation, as has been already described. Zulus think the *testes* the seat of strength.[1]

Much indirect evidence from savage custom has already appeared showing the universal belief that sexual intercourse is enervating, a belief based on this double idea. The Seminoles believed that carnal connection with a woman exercised an enervating influence upon men and rendered them less fit for the duties of a warrior.[2] In Halmahera men must practice continence when at war, "otherwise they will lose their strength."[3] In South Africa a man when in bed must not touch his wife with his right hand; "if he did so, he would have no strength in war, and would surely be slain."[4]

The explanation of the rule, which forbids to warriors and hunters any sort of intercourse with women before and during their expeditions, may now be completed. The main feature of such rules is the injunction of continence, and the idea which prompts this is that while contact with women transmits female weakness, the retention of a secretion, in which strength is supposed to reside, ensures vigour and strength. A Congo belief is here instructive; when the *Chitomé* goes out to make his judicial circuit, criers "proclaim a fast of continence, the penalty for breaking which is death. The belief is that by such continence they preserve the life of their common father."[5] Similarly in the Kei

[1] *Journ. Anthrop. Inst.* xx. 116.
[2] Schoolcraft, *Indian Tribes*, v. 272.
[3] Riedel, in *Zeitschrift für Ethnologie*, xvii. 69.
[4] Macdonald, in *Journ. Anthrop. Inst.* xx. 140.
[5] W. Reade, *op. cit.* 362.

Islands men before going to war may have no intercourse with women, and those who remain behind must practice the same continence.[1] In New Caledonia, to abstain from carnal connection with women is considered a meritorious act, and is strictly observed on all solemn occasions, especially when going to war.[2] Strict chastity is observed by Malays in a stockade, else the bullets of the garrison will lose their power.[3] In Ceramlaut it is a sin not to cleanse the person after intercourse with a woman, when a man is about to go to war.[4] After killing his first man, the young Natchez warrior was required to abstain for six months from all sexual intercourse, and was prohibited from tasting meat.[5] A seven-days' taboo amongst the Malays, when fishing, is the scrupulous observance of chastity.[6] During the pilgrimage to Mecca which every Mussulman must perform once in his life, he has to abstain from all sexual intercourse.[7] The celibacy of warriors was a chief feature of Zulu and Fiji militarism. Tchaka based it on an existing custom and belief.[8] The Fijians had a custom identical with that of the ancient Thebans.[9] In practice, doubtless, an unmarried man may make a better soldier, precisely because there is no tie to render death more terrible.

Further, just as many detachable portions of the organism are regarded as parts of a man's soul, being filled with his life and character, and sometimes, for his safety, as external souls, so those secretions which have in fact the closest connection with life and strength might naturally be regarded in thought as having

[1] Riedel, *De sluik- en kroesharige rassen tusschen Selebes en Papua*, 223.
[2] Featherman, *op. cit.* ii. 92.
[3] Skeat, *Malay Magic*, 524.
[4] Riedel, *op. cit.* 168.
[5] Featherman, *op. cit.* iii. 146.
[6] Skeat, *op. cit.* 315.
[7] Burckhardt, *Travels in Arabia*, i. 163.
[8] Shooter, *op. cit.* 47.
[9] Williams, *op. cit.* i. 45; Polyaenus, ii. 5. 1.

inherent in them a considerable part of the life and soul, or sometimes as being identical therewith. The widely spread belief that the blood is the life is well known; it is also often regarded as containing the soul; soul, life, and strength are essentially identical in savage thought. We also find, not only the universal idea that the seed is the strength, but, as might be expected, also cases where the soul is actually believed to be contained in the organs of procreation. Thus, in the islands Leti, Moa, and Lakor, when a man is very ill, a ram is killed, and its genitals given him to eat. The people believe that "the principle of life resides in those parts."[1] Similarly, the Naudowessies believe that the father gives the child its soul, the mother its body only.[2] This is quite logical from the elementary notions of procreation. Now when we apply to these ideas the physiological fact that a temporary depression follows the sexual act, we may infer as probable a more or less constant physiological idea that in that act the man transmits some of his best strength, a part of his soul or life. We have had occasion to notice how primitive thought often anticipates modern scientific theory in some rough generalisation, and here is a conception on a par with other early conceptions, which anticipates somewhat the latest theories of the Germplasm.

In the next place, there is the preliminary part of the function, the perforation of the *hymen*. Here we have an instructive instance of the diffidence, anxiety, and caution with which the savage not only approaches things and acts unfamiliar or met with for the first time, but makes preparation for the due and proper performance of important functions, not by way of improving

[1] Riedel, *op. cit.* 393.

[2] Carver, *North America*, 378.

upon Nature, but of *making sure* of the working of Nature's mechanism. Deferring for a moment the latter consideration, we can estimate here the female attitude. There is in the female sex a universal physiological anxiety concerning this act. Savages cannot feel so much pain or so much pleasure as men of a more complex and highly organised brain, but their precautions against, and fear of, pain are far more elaborate and anxious. Like the higher animals, the savage is very diffident and timid by nature, except when a strong physical impulse is in full progress. Now we find that the savage uses more or less direct methods to avoid this preliminary act of handselling; the avoidance is due to a vague religious fear based on the ideas of sexual taboo, also to the anxiety about a difficulty and, doubtless, to consideration for the female. Thus in the Dieri and neighbouring tribes it is the universal custom when a girl reaches puberty to rupture the *hymen*.[1] In the Portland and Glenelg tribes this is done to the bride by an old woman; and sometimes white men are asked for this reason to deflower maidens.[2] The artificial rupture of the *hymen* is a very widely spread custom. In the practice we see clearly the double idea of ridding the function of such difficulty as is identified by the savage with a spiritual-material result, and of removing the first and therefore most virulent part of female contagion, as the West African "takes off the fetish" from a strange liquor by getting some one to "handsel" it.

Again, ignorance of the nature of female periodicity leads man to consider it as the flow of blood from a wound, naturally, or more usually, supernaturally produced. We must also bear in mind the connection

[1] *Journ. Anthrop. Inst.*, xxiv. 169. [2] Brough Smyth, *op. cit.* ii. 319.

often made between the menstrual flow and the blood shed at the perforation of the *hymen*. The two results appear so similar that man often infers more or less exact identity of cause.

An obvious inference was that the menstrual blood was caused by the bite of a supernatural animal, or by congress with such or with a supernatural human agent or evil spirit. The first of these is a fairly common idea. Certain Australian tribes believe that menstruation comes from dreaming that a bandicoot has scratched the parts.[1] In New Britain it is traced to the bite of a supernatural bird,[2] and in Portugal to that of a snake.[3] Messrs. Ploss and Bartels reproduce in illustrations wooden figures from New Guinea, one representing a crocodile biting a woman's *vulva*, another, a crocodile shaped like a snake emerging therefrom, and a third, a snake, in shape like the male organ, at the entrance of the *vagina*.[4] In Portugal, according to another account, it is believed that during menstruation women are "liable to be bitten by lizards, and to guard against this risk they wear drawers during this period."[5] In Abyssinia there is a belief that if the bride leaves her home in the interval between the betrothal and the marriage she will be bitten by a snake.[6] At the first menstruation of a Chiriguano girl old women run about the hut with sticks, "striking at the snake which has wounded her."[7] "In a modern Greek folk-tale the Fates predict that in her fifteenth year a princess must be careful not to let the sun shine on her, for if this were to happen she would be turned into a lizard."[8]

[1] *Journ. Anthrop. Inst.* xxiv. 177.
[2] Ploss u. Bartels, *Das Weib*[6], ii. 330, 334.
[3] *Id. l.c.*
[4] *Id. l.c.*
[5] H. Ellis, *op. cit.* ii. 237.
[6] M. Parkyns, *Life in Abyssinia*, ii. 41.
[7] *Lettres édifiantes et curieuses*, viii. 333.
[8] J. G. Frazer, *The Golden Bough*[2], iii. 220.

Some Australian tribes believe in a supernatural serpent which attacks women.[1] Macusi women at menstruation will not go in the forest, for fear of being loved by a snake.[2] In Rabbinical tradition the serpent is the symbol of sexual desire.[3] Amongst the Malays to dream of being bitten by a snake portends success in love.[4] The connection of the serpent with sexual matters is very familiar, especially in European folk-lore, and is found all over the world. The explanation has been several times hinted at and is obvious when one considers the likeness in shape of the serpent, lizard, eel, and similar animals, to the male organ of generation. It is worth noting that the curious phallic towers of Zimbabwe are surmounted by a bird's head.[5] And, as in primitive thought similar objects produce similar results, the dangerous effect of such supernatural organs is attributed to similar things, which may not therefore be touched or eaten by women at these dangerous times. Thus in New Guinea women are not allowed to eat eels, because a god once took the form of an eel to approach a woman who was bathing.[6] Young women in the Halifax Bay tribe are forbidden to eat the flesh of male animals and eels.[7] Amongst the Central Australians boys and girls may not before puberty eat large lizards, else they will acquire an abnormal craving for sexual intercourse.[8]

As to the second form of the belief, by the outward projection of the idea, the agent feared becomes an anthropomorphic spirit. Subconsciously the result is attributed to the male sex, but as the agent is invisible,

[1] Featherman, *op. cit.* ii. 175.
[2] Ploss u. Bartels, *op. cit.* ii. 334.
[3] Ellis, *l.c.*
[4] Clifford, *In Court and Kampong*, 189.
[5] T. Bent, in *Journ. Anthrop. Inst.* xxii. 125.
[6] Gill, *op. cit.* 279.
[7] Curr, *The Australian Race*, ii. 425.
[8] Spencer and Gillen, *op. cit.* 471, 472, 473.

the inference is naturally to a spiritualised man. Such is also the case with the widely spread belief in *incubi* and *succubi*, which is due to a similar inference from a common phenomenon of the early days of sexual life. The result is ascribed to a supernatural nocturnal visitor. Amongst the Yorubas erotic dreams are attributed to Elegbra, a god who, either as male or female, consorts sexually with men and women in their sleep.[1] In the particular question before us, we find a link between the serpent and a human agent in a common folk-tale motive. The old Sanskrit story tells of a beautiful girl who killed a cobra to get the jewel from its head. To avenge this, the king of the snakes assumed the form of a handsome youth, and after winning the girl's affections, married her. "At last the day came, and the nuptial ceremony was over, and the bridegroom went with his bride into the nuptial chamber. And he lifted her on to the marriage-bed, and called her by her name. And as she turned towards him, he approached her slowly, with a smile on his face. And she looked and saw issuing from his mouth and disappearing alternately, a long tongue, thin, forked, and quivering like that of a snake. And in the morning the musicians played to waken the bride and bridegroom. But the day went on, and they never came forth. Then the merchant, her father, and his friends, after waiting a long time, became alarmed, and went and broke the door, which was closed with a lock. And then they saw the bride lying dead on the bed, alone, and on her bosom were two small marks. And they saw no bridegroom. But a black cobra crept out of the bed, and disappeared through a hole in the wall."[2] In Siam evil spirits are believed to make "the wound"

[1] Ellis, *op. cit.* 67.

[2] *A Digit of the Moon*, 93, 94, 95.

which causes the monthly flow of blood.[1] The idea is further extended. In the Aru Islands the women fear the evil spirit *Boitai*, when traversing the forest, because he takes the semblance of their husbands, and has intercourse with them there, shown afterwards by bleeding from the *vagina*.[2] So in Kola and Kobroor the women avoid going alone in the forest, so as not to be approached by *sisi*, evil spirits, the result of which is the growth of stones in the *uterus* and subsequent death.[3] In the Babar Islands there are evil spirits in the shape of men who approach young women, in the form of their husbands, and make them pregnant. These are identified with the well-known *suwanggi*, who are actual persons versed in sorcery.[4] In the island of Wetar there is an evil spirit, named *Kluantelus*, who takes the form of a handsome man, and has intercourse with women; accordingly, women never go unaccompanied into the forest.[5] The Jews of the East believe that male spirits form alliances with women, while the female spirits "entangle in their cunning meshes of wedded love the young men of earth."[6] According to the Javanese the air is peopled by wandering *genii* of evil. Ghostly demons often disguise themselves in human form, and appear as counterfeit husbands to wives whom they mislead by their deceptive allurements.[7] In Nias the seducer is fined and the woman killed. A pregnant woman often asserts that she was ravished by a spirit, and she thus saves her life and that of her child.[8] The Malays suppose that *Pontianak* is the ghost of a woman dying in child-birth, which presents itself at midnight to men and emasculates

[1] Loubere, *l.c.*
[2] Riedel, *op. cit.* 252.
[3] *Id.* 271.
[4] *Id.* 340.
[5] *Id.* 439.
[6] Featherman, *op. cit.* v. 129.
[7] *Id.* ii. 396.
[8] *Id.* 356.

them.[1] The natives of Amboina and Uliase believe in evil spirits, male and female, who practise the following trick. When a man and a woman have made an assignation in the forest, one of these evil spirits is apt to take the shape and place of the man or the woman, and whoever has intercourse with such dies in a few days. These people also believe that *Pontianak*, who in these islands is feared by women in child-birth, steals away infants and the genital organs of men.[2] The correlation of evil spirits with human beings is here well illustrated.

To these ideas is partly due the common estimate of woman as a mysterious being who has communication with the world of spirits. The other factor in the belief is the hysteria which is more or less frequent in the sexual life of woman. Thus, in Buru hysterical prophetesses are believed to have had intercourse with evil spirits.[3] The idea further develops into the widely spread belief that women, especially about the time of puberty, have communication with gods, a belief emphasised by the common practice of secluding them at that time. This idea has been made much of by various systematised cults, and has resulted in many phenomena of religious *parthenogenesis*. In Cambodia it is sacrilege to abuse a young girl who is not of an age to marry. They are called the wives of *Prah En* (*Indra*). During the seclusion called "the shade" which is necessary at puberty, young girls are called the wives of *Rêa*, and it is a sin to abuse them. On leaving their retreat, they become the wives of men.[4]

Another agent sometimes connected with these phenomena of periodicity is the sun. Dr. Frazer has

[1] Featherman, *op. cit.* 434.
[2] *Id.* 9.
[3] Riedel, *op. cit.* 57, 58.
[4] Aymonier, *op. cit.* 192, 193.

given many examples of girls at puberty being forbidden to see the sun, or fire, in connection with the idea that the sun can cause impregnation, as in the familiar story of Danaë. He also points out that boys at puberty, mourners, warriors who have slain a foe, and other *tabu* persons may not look upon the sun or the fire. Associated with the fear is the belief that the *tabued* girl might *pollute* the sun, as Samoyed women can *pollute* the fire; *i.e.* make it dangerous from taboo qualities to others. This is the objective aspect of taboo. From the subjective aspect, the point of view of the person in danger, there is the belief that impregnation can be effected by the sun. Early thought speculated deeply on the connection of the sun with the fertility and growth of vegetable and animal life. Not only the gentle rain from heaven, but also the kindly rays of the warm sun were credited, not unscientifically, with the power of impregnating Mother Earth and her offspring. Inference from growth under the warm sun would naturally lead to the belief that women could thus be influenced by it. The moon also was sometimes credited with this power over women. Here we come to the interesting question how far early man had observed the rhythmical connection of female periodicity with the moon. That monthly periodicity belongs to women and moon alike could not fail to be marked, and there are indications that it was. Hence conceptions of an anthropomorphic kind concerning the connection of women with the moon. The "faithful witness in Heaven," by the way, is more often than not masculine in primitive thought. In both of these correlative ideas, as also in the case of fire, often identified more or less with the sun, as the earthly phenomenon of the heavenly idea, we have now to consider whether they connect with any functional peculiarity of women, especially at puberty. In the case of mourners and the like, the potential danger of fire, as a beneficent but somewhat dangerous essence, not to be trifled with, is enough reason for the taboo, and applies also to girls and boys at the beginning of the sexual life. There is, however, a further coincidence arising, as so often, from a function. A peculiarity of puberty which passes on into the phenomena of love, is sudden accession of bodily heat, by which the whole frame from time to time feels filled with fire. It is in ideas arising from this functional phenomenon that we are to find the ultimate explanation of this fear of the sun. In all these taboos at puberty, it is the dangerous results of association with the other sex that are guarded against, and so characteristic a symptom as accession of heat could not fail to be noticed and avoided as far as possible. The "patient," using the primitive connotation of this term, must keep *cool*. Parallel ideas from savage psychology bring this out. Anger, which is physiologically connected with an accession of heat, is often attributed by savages to possession by an evil spirit, as amongst the Battas.[1] More precisely there is a universal connection, seen in all languages, between love and heat. Malay physiology, for instance, states that love is made of fire.[2] We saw in a Greek folk-tale the connection between the sun at puberty and the lizard, a symbol of masculinity. A Central Australian myth of the origin of fire states that it came from the *penis* of a euro, which contained "very red fire."[3] Again, and the idea is natural enough in tropical countries, there is a frequent

[1] Junghuhn, *op. cit.* ii. 156.
[2] Featherman, *op. cit.* ii. 237.
[3] Spencer and Gillen, *op. cit.* 446.

connection made between heat and evil spirits. To keep cool is one of the points of savage comfort in a hot climate, a wish which naturally would pass into the spiritual life. In Ceram and Watubella a house which is filled with evil spirits is called a "warm" house;[1] and sickness is often identified with heat, and the patient is before all things to be made cool; while health and soundness are identified with coolness. For forty-four days after birth the Malay mother may not eat foods which have a heating effect on the blood, and the Malay infant is bathed with cold water every four hours "in order that it may be kept cool."[2] Especially fever is, of course, connected with heat. In the Wyingurri tribe of West Australia the sun is *Tchintu*. A stone of that name contains the heat of the sun, and is used to give a man fever by placing it where he will tread.[3] Here, as in so many cases before mentioned, there comes in the interesting question whether primitive man observed the connection of the temperature of the body with health and illness. As before, the case stands thus; man's unanalysed experience of temperature in sickness is included under an excessively wide generalisation, which has within it, though concealed in fallacy, a scientific truth, destined to emerge after a training in analysis and experiment.

This connection between illness, evil spirits, and heat is an adequate explanation of the rule whereby many persons in various kinds of danger may not see the sun or fire. *Pamali* (*tabu*) amongst the Hill Dyaks is imposed on all kinds of occasions. People subjected to it are not allowed to bathe, to touch fire, or follow ordinary occupations.[4] The heir to the throne of

[1] Riedel, *op. cit.* 141, 210.

[2] Skeat, *op. cit.* 343.

[3] Spencer and Gillen, *op. cit.* 541.

[4] Featherman, *op. cit.* ii. 278.

Bogota might not see the sun, nor converse with a woman.[1] When a Pima kills a man, he has to fast sixteen days, is cut off from all social intercourse, and may not look at a fire.[2]

Further, it is natural that on these ideas sexual intercourse should be especially forbidden at sexual crises, such as menstruation, pregnancy, and for some time after child-birth. Woman's subconscious physical fear of man here correlates with an instinct of physiological thought caused by the discomfort of the function, and for the male sex, his fear of female contagion is intensified by the presence of female "disease." It is not long since the medical world gave up the primitive idea that menstrual blood is deleterious. In the present connection this hylo-idealistic "disease" is identical with the property of the sexual taboo state; on these occasions woman is more of a woman than in ordinary circumstances, and the danger of contagion is accordingly intensified.

Such are the dangers connected with the sexual act in the mind of primitive man, and to remove the material contagion there was used, with more than the mere idea of cleanliness, a religious purification. The bath taken by a Cadiack bridegroom and bride after the wedding night, "for the purification of himself and his partner," is one instance of a universal practice.[3] The fear of transmission of female properties, here intensified, is also indirectly connected with female sexual secretions, such as menstrual blood, a special form of ceremonial "uncleanness." Moreover, when ideas of shame and disgust and, later, of religious purity, are brought in, the old undifferentiated spiritual-

[1] Waitz-Gerland, *op. cit.* iv. 359.
[2] Featherman, *op. cit.* iii. 240.
[3] Lisiansky, *op. cit.* 199.

material secretions, as they may be called, which combined contagion of female weakness, and imaginary disease and poison on the one hand, and on the other hand, of materialised physical fear of the male sex, in the *virus* which made contact dangerous, were split into specialised forms.

CHAPTER IX

These ideas concerning contact regulate in social taboo human relations generally, and in sexual taboo those of men and women. The sexual properties whose transmission renders contact dangerous or beneficent may now be recapitulated, and further proof given of their character and of the fact of their transmission. We have seen that where sympathy, desire, or love appears, contact between persons otherwise mutually dangerous becomes beneficent. Sympathy, aided by a common human impulse, which may be called allopathic, sometimes regards sexual difference as in itself efficacious to cure disease. For instance, the Australians employ the urine of the opposite sex as a cure for sickness. In very serious cases blood from a woman's sexual organs is given to a man, and his body is rubbed with it; or blood from a man is given to a woman.[1] From a similar idea comes a custom found in the Aru Islands, where a battle can be instantly stopped if a woman throws her girdle between the armies.[2] But apart from cases like these and the methods of contact employed in love-charms and marriage ceremonies, sexual contact is usually, on the principles of sexual taboo, regarded as deleterious. The Central Australians believe that to put a man's hair necklet or girdle near a woman would

[1] Eyre, *op. cit.* II. 300; Spencer and Gillen, *op. cit.* 464.
[2] Riedel, *op. cit.* 261.

be productive of serious evil to her. They believe that sterility may be brought about by a girl in her youth playfully or thoughtlessly tying on a man's hair waist-band. The latter so used, if only for a moment or two, has the effect of cramping her internal organs and making them incapable of the necessary expansion, and this is the most frequent explanation of sterility given by the natives.[1]

Owing to the monopoly of thought by the male sex it is rarely we hear of transmission of masculine properties to the female. It is more often a vague deleterious result that is thought of; for instance, Maori men may not eat with their wives, nor may male children eat with their mothers, "lest their *tapu*, or 'sanctity,' should kill them."[2] This male *tapu* is, of course, male characteristics, such as relative superiority of strength. The Miris will not allow their women to eat tiger's flesh, "lest it should make them too strong-minded."[3] We have noticed cases where men are not allowed to be present at lying-in, because their presence would hinder the birth. Another case is from Halmahera, where a pregnant woman is afraid to eat food left by her husband, for it would cause painful labour.[4] European folklore illustrates this masculine contagion, and the general idea that contact produces assimilation. In Hannover-Wendland and the Altmark, if a boy and girl are baptised in the same water, the boy becomes a woman-hunter, and the girl grows a beard. In Neumark if a girl is baptised in water used for a boy she will have a moustache. In Lower Saxony and Mecklenburg a boy must not be baptised in water which has been used for a girl, else he grows up beardless; while

[1] Spencer and Gillen, *op. cit.* 539, 52. [2] Taylor, *op. cit.* 168.
[3] Dalton, *op. cit.* 33. [4] Riedel, in *Zeitschrift für Ethnologie*, xvii. 78.

a girl if baptised in water used for a boy becomes mischievous like boys. In Scotland if Jeanie is baptised before Sandie, she grows a beard and Sandie is beardless.[1] Hessian lads think they can escape conscription by carrying a baby-girl's cap in their pocket.[2] Lastly, when females are of a masculine temperament they often assume male attire, an interesting practical method of assimilation.[3]

What, then, are the chief female properties the transmission of which is feared as deleterious? First of all, mere difference is regarded by the savage as dangerous, simply because it is unknown. In the second place, the difference is specialised as inferiority of physical strength and stature, relatively, that is, to the male standard. It is a universal conception amongst men of all stages of culture that woman is weaker than man. As a rule, man forgets the *relativity* of this characteristic, and regards woman as more or less absolutely weak. That this idea is practically inherent in human male nature, as a physiological inference of the simplest kind, is proved by its regular expression in the life and literature of all ages. The use and connotation of the word "effeminate" illustrates this well. This evidence taken with that of ethnology is overwhelming. Primitive man agrees with the most modern of the moderns, for instance, with a Nietzsche, who regards woman as a slight, dainty, and relatively feeble creature. The ethnological evidence for this masculine belief is very extensive.[4] General inferiority is sometimes found as a secondary result.

[1] Ploss, *Das Kind*, i. 217.

[2] A. Wuttke, *Deutsche Aberglaube*, 100.

[3] Masculine females assume male attire—Brooke, *Ten Years in Sarawak*, i. 131; *Journ. Anthrop. Inst.* xxiii. 7; G. A. Wilken, in *De Indische Gids* for 1881, 263; W. Reade, *op. cit.* 364; Bastian, *San Salvador*, 177 ff.; Giraud-Teulon, *op. cit.* 309 ff. (Amazons).

[4] Darwin, *Descent of Man*, 117, 597; Bastian, *Der Mensch in der Geschichte*, iii.

In the savage mind the belief has been corroborated by the fallacies that woman's periodic loss of blood marks enfeeblement—an idea which often correlates with the notion that woman is a chronic invalid, sickness and weakness being identified,—and that sexual intercourse is weakening.

In the next place is the relative timidity of women.[1]

292; H. Ellis, *Man and Woman*, 395; Tasmanians, Bonwick, *op. cit.* 10; Australians, Eyre, *op. cit.* ii. 207, *Journ. Anthrop. Inst.* xxi. 205, Lumholtz, *Among Cannibals*, 200, 163, *Native Tribes of South Australia*, 11, Waitz-Gerland, *op. cit.* vi. 774, 775, Letourneau, *Sociologie*, 169; Polynesians, D'Urville, *op. cit.* i. 520, Beechey, *op. cit.* i. 238, 241, Meinicke, *op. cit.* ii. 219, 198, Ellis, *Polynesian Researches*, iii. 199, 293, 294, 257; Fijians, Williams, *op. cit.* i. 156, 169, Wilkes, *op. cit.* iii. 332, Meinicke, *op. cit.* ii. 45, Waitz-Gerland, *op. cit.* vi. 627; New Caledonians, Meinicke, *op. cit.* i. 231, Garnier, *Océanie*, 186, 350, 354, Waitz-Gerland, *op. cit.* vi. 626, Anderson, *Fiji and New Caledonia*, 218, 232; New Hebrides, Meinicke, *op. cit.* i. 203, *Journ. Anthrop. Inst.* xxiii. 7; Queen Charlotte Islands, Meinicke, *op. cit.* i. 177; Solomon Islands, *id.* i. 166; Melanesia generally, *id.* i. 67, Parkinson, *Im Bismarck-Archipel*, 98, 99, Codrington, *op. cit.* 233, Powell, *Wanderings in a Wild Country*, 54; Papuans, Rosenberg, *op. cit.* 454, 532; Sumatra, Marsden, *op. cit.* 382, Junghuhn, *op. cit.* ii. 135, 81; Bali, *id.* ii. 359; Nias, *Tijdschrift voor Indische Taal-Land-en Volkenkunde*, xxxvi. 305; Sarawak, Brooke, *op. cit.* i. 101; Japan, Alcock, *The Capital of the Tycoon*, i. 265; Corea, Ploss u. Bartels, *op. cit.* ii. 434, Griffis, *op. cit.* 245; China, M. Huc, *L'empire chinois*, i. 268; India, *Missionary Records* (*India*), xviii. D'Urville, *op. cit.* i. 110, *Asiatick Researches*, iv. 95, *Histoire universelle des voyages*, xxxi. 352; Siam, *Pinkerton*, *op. cit.* ix. 379; Afghans, Letourneau, *op. cit.* 179; Samoyeds, Georgi, *op. cit.* 14, 15; Circassians, *Pinkerton*, *op. cit.* ix. 142; Russians, Ploss, *op. cit.* ii. 448; Ansayree, Featherman, *op. cit.* v. 495; Egyptians, Ploss, *op. cit.* ii. 455, Lane, *op. cit.* i. 252; Africa, Shooter, *op. cit.* 79, 80, 81, Waitz-Gerland, *op. cit.* ii. 387, 471, Ploss u. Bartels, *op. cit.* ii. 426, D. Macdonald, *Africana*, i. 137, 141, 35, C. New, *Life in Eastern Africa*, 359, Ploss, *Das Kind*, 442, Letourneau, *op. cit.* 172, P. B. Du Chaillu, *Equatorial Africa*, 52, 377, Harris, *Highlands of Ethiopia*, iii. 58, Proyart, *Loango*, 93, W. Bosman, *Description of Guinea*, 320, Bastian, *San Salvador*, 71, *Journ. Anthrop. Inst.* xiii. 465, xvi. 86, xxii. 118, 119, xxiv. 289, C. J. Andersson, *Lake Ngami*, 231; Madagascar, Waitz-Gerland, *op. cit.* ii. 438; Central and South America, Letourneau, *op. cit.* 175, Waitz-Gerland, *op. cit.* iii. 515, 308, 382, iv. 130, Brett, *op. cit.* 353, Bancroft, *op. cit.* iii. 694, Dobrizhoffer, *op. cit.* ii. 155; North America, Waitz-Gerland, *op. cit.* iii. 99, 101, Bancroft, *op. cit.* i. 511, Peter Jones, *History of the Ojebway Indians*, 60, Charlevoix, *Journal*, vi. 44, Powers, *op. cit.* 20, Sproat, *op. cit.* 91, Hearne, *op. cit.* 90, 310.

[1] The following are typical cases: Lumholtz, *op. cit.* 91; Featherman, *op. cit.* v. 495; Kotzebue, *Voyage to the South Sea*, ii. 56, *Asiatick Researches*, vi. 82; Garnier, *op. cit.* 328, 349; Coote, *op. cit.* 163, 164; Hearne, *op. cit.* 310; Waitz-Gerland, *op. cit.* vi. 775; Melville, *The Marquesas Islands*, 76; Wilkes, *op. cit.* iii. 232; K. von den Steinen, *op. cit.* 332; D'Albertis, *op. cit.* i. 15, 189, 200, 292, 318, 337, 342.

This characteristic and that of weakness are the complement of masculine courage and strength, and are connected with a physical subconscious fear of men. When associated with hysterical phenomena, timidity is merged in another conception of woman, as a "mysterious" person. The mystery is based on sexual differentiation, in particular on the sexual phenomena of menstruation and child-birth. As we have seen, this mystery is deepened by further ideas it creates, such as the ascription of taboo properties to woman, and the beliefs that woman has intercourse with the spiritual world at menstruation, and that she is more or less of a potential witch. The whole reasoning is clinched by the fact of a temporary depression, identified with loss of strength, following upon intercourse with this weak but mysterious creature, and the imperious demands of nature which enforce association with the female sex, inevitably cause a continuous repetition of sexual taboo and of the ideas which underlie it. These organic characteristics not only make woman peculiarly susceptible to religious influences, but have fitted her to be a useful medium for priestcraft, and often to hold the priestly authority herself. The priestess is a frequent feature of savage worship. Here is to be found the explanation of one set of cases of priests dressing as women. For example, amongst the Sea Dyaks some of the priests pretend to be women, or rather dress as such, and like to be treated as females.[1] Patagonian sorcerers, who are chosen from children who have St. Vitus' dance, wear women's clothes.[2] Amongst the Kodyaks there are men dressed as women, who are regarded as sorcerers and are much respected.[3]

[1] St. John, *op. cit.* i. 62.
[2] Bastian, *Der Mensch*, iii. 310.
[3] Waitz-Gerland, *op. cit.* iii. 313.

Doubtless the idea is to assume such emotional peculiarities of women as are useful to the priest. To the savage mind, the donning of another's dress is more than a token of the new position: it completes identity by communicating the qualities of the original owner. There is also the desire to command attention by eccentricity if not by mystery, for both of which ends change of sex is a time-honoured method.

It remains to add direct evidence for the belief, which is the chief factor in sexual taboo, that contact with women causes transmission of female characteristics, femininity, effeminacy, weakness, and timidity

In South Africa a man must not, when in bed, touch his wife with his right hand; "if he did so, he would have no strength in war, and would surely be slain." If a man touch a woman during menstruation, "his bones become soft, and in future he cannot take part in warfare or any other manly exercise." Stepping over another's person is highly improper; while if a *woman* steps over her husband's stick "he cannot aim or hit any one with it. If she steps over his *assegai*, it will never kill or even hit an enemy, and it is at once discarded and given to the boys to play and practise with."[1] The Galela and Tobelorese are continent during war, "so as not to lose their strength."[2] The Seminoles believed that "carnal connection with a woman exercised an enervating influence upon men, and rendered them less fit for the duties of the warrior."[3] In British Guiana cooking is the province of the women. On one occasion, when the men were compelled to bake some bread, they were only persuaded to do so

[1] J. E. Macdonald, in *Journ. Anthrop. Inst.* xx. 140, 119, 130.
[2] J. G. F. Riedel, in *Zeitschrift für Ethnologie*, xvii. 69.
[3] Schoolcraft, *op. cit.* v. 272.

with the utmost difficulty, and were ever after pointed at as old women.[1] North American Indians, both before and after war, refrain "on religious grounds" from women. Contact with females, some of them hold, "makes a warrior laughable, and injures his bravery for the future."[2] One of Hesiod's maxims is a prohibition against washing in water used by a woman.[3] In Homer, Odysseus fears lest he be "unmanned," and therefore susceptible to Circe's influence if he ascend her couch.[4] Assimilation to the female character from such connection is illustrated by a Cingalese myth.[5] In the Solomon Islands a man will never pass under a tree fallen across the path, for fear a woman may have stepped over it.[6] Amongst the Bongos stools are only used by women; the men avoid such seats as effeminate.[7] In Central Australia, during his period of initiation, a medicine-man must sleep with a fire between him and his wife; "if he did not do this his power would disappear for ever."[8] Amongst the Barea man and wife seldom share the same bed; the reason they give is "that the breath of the wife weakens her husband."[9] In Western Victoria a menstruous woman may not take any one's food or drink, and no one will touch food that she has handled, "because it will make them weak."[10] Among the Dyaks of North-West Borneo young men are forbidden to eat venison, which is the peculiar food of women and old men, "because it would render them as timid as deer."[11] A Zulu, newly married, dares not

[1] im Thurn, *op. cit.* 256.

[2] Waitz-Gerland, *op. cit.* iii. 158.

[3] Hesiod, *Works and Days*, 798.

[4] *Odyssey*, x. 301, 339-41.

[5] *Asiatick Researches*, vii. 439.

[6] Guppy, *op. cit.* i. 4.

[7] Schweinfurth, *op. cit.* i. 253.

[8] Spencer and Gillen, *op. cit.* 529.

[9] Munzinger, *op. cit.* 526.

[10] Dawson, *op. cit.* cii.

[11] St. John, *op. cit.* i. 186.

go out to battle, for fear he should be slain; should he do so and fall, the men say "the lap of that woman is unlucky."[1] A Fan so weak that he could hardly move about, was supposed to have become so by seeing the blood of a woman who had been killed. "The weak spirit of the woman had got into him."[2] Amongst the Damaras men may not see a lying-in woman, "else they will become weak and will be killed in battle."[3] In Ceram menstruous women may not approach the men, lest the latter should be wounded in battle.[4] In some South American tribes the presence of a woman just confined makes the weapons of the men weak.[5] The same belief obtains among the Tschuktsches, who accordingly remove all hunting and fishing implements from the house before a birth.[6] In the Booandik tribe if men see women's blood they will not be able to fight.[7] In the Encounter Bay tribe boys are told from infancy that if they see menstrual blood their strength will fail prematurely.[8] In the Wiraijuri tribe boys are reproved for playing with girls; the culprit is taken aside by an old man, who solemnly extracts from his legs some "strands of the woman's apron" which have got in.[9] Amongst the Omahas, if a boy plays with girls he is contemptuously dubbed "hermaphrodite."[10] In Brandenburg the peasants say that a baby boy must not be wrapped in an apron, else it will, when grown up, run after the girls. In Mecklenburg a new-born girl must be first kissed by the mother and a boy by the father, else the girl will grow whiskers and the

[1] Callaway, *op. cit.* 441, 443. [2] M. H. Kingsley, *Travels in West Africa*, 447.

[3] *South African Folklore Journal*, ii. 63.

[4] Riedel, *De sluik- en kroesharige rassen tusschen Selebes en Papua*, 139.

[5] Ploss u. Bartels, *op. cit.* ii. 26. [6] *Id. l.c.*

[7] J. Smith, *The Booandik Tribe*, 5. [8] *Native Tribes of South Australia*, 186.

[9] *Journ. Anthrop. Inst.* xiii. 448.

[10] J. O. Dorsey, in *Third Report of the Bureau of Ethnology*, 266.

boy's face be hairless.[1] The Khyoungthas have a legend of a man who reduced a king and his men to a condition of feebleness by persuading them to dress up as women and perform female duties. When they had thus been rendered effeminate, they were attacked and defeated without a blow. "That," say the Khyoungthas, "is why we are not so brave as formerly."[2] The advice given to Cyrus by Crœsus was identical with that of the Hillman, and the result was the same.[3] Contempt for female timidity has caused a curious custom amongst the Gallas; they amputate the *mammæ* of boys soon after birth, believing that no warrior can possibly be brave who possesses them, and that they should belong to women only.[4] From such ideas is derived the custom of degrading the cowardly, infirm, and conquered to the position of females. At the "initiation" of a Macquarrie boy the men stand over him with waddies, threatening instant death if he complains while the tooth is being knocked out. He is afterwards scarified: if he shows any sign of pain, three long yells announce the fact to the camp; he is then considered unworthy to be admitted to the rank of men, and is handed over to the women as a coward. Thenceforward he becomes the playmate and companion of children.[5] Amongst the Lhoosais, when a man is unable to do his work, whether through laziness, cowardice, or bodily incapacity, he is dressed in women's clothes and has to associate and work with the women.[6] Amongst the Pomo Indians of California, when a man becomes too

[1] Ploss, *Das Kind*, ii. 202, 205. [2] Lewin, *Wild Races of South-Eastern India*, 136.
[3] Herodotus, i. 155-57.
[4] Harris, *op. cit.* iii. 58. The cauterisation of the *mammæ* by Amazons is to be compared.
[5] G. F. Angas, *Savage Life and Scenes in Australia and New Zealand*, ii. 224.
[6] Lewin, *op. cit.* 255.

infirm for a warrior, he is made a menial and assists the squaws.[1] So in Cuba and Greenland, with the additional degradation of wearing female dress.[2] When the Delawares were denationalised by the Iroquois and prohibited from going out to war, they were, according to the Indian notion, "made women," and were henceforth to confine themselves to the pursuits appropriate to women.[3] The connection of lack of virility with the normal estimate of woman has also led to the remarkable custom of degrading impotent men and others to the position of females. Thus, amongst the Yukis and other tribes of California are to be seen men dressed as women, who are called *i-wa-musp*, man-woman. They appear to be destitute of desire and virility; they perform all the duties of women, and shirk all functions pertaining to men. Two reasons are given for the origin of this class, masturbation, or a wish to escape the responsibilities of manhood. There is a ceremony to initiate such men to their chosen life; the candidate is placed in a circle of fire, and a bow and "woman-stick" are offered to him, with a formal injunction to choose one or the other, and to abide by his choice for ever.[4] The Tsecats of Madagascar are impotents who dress as women.[5] The Higras of South India are natural eunuchs, or castrated in boyhood; they dress in women's clothes.[6] Impotent Kookies dress as women.[7] Herodotus and Hippocrates describe a class of impotent men amongst the ancient Scythians who were made to do women's work and to associate with women alone.[8]

[1] Powers, *op. cit.* 160.

[2] Bastian, *Der Mensch*, iii. 313, 314; *cf.* Waitz-Gerland, *op. cit.* iii. 472.

[3] L. H. Morgan, *The League of the Iroquois*, 16.

[4] Powers, *op. cit.* 132, 133.

[5] Bastian, *op. cit.* iii. 311.

[6] *Journ. Anthrop. Inst.* ii. 406.

[7] Lewin, *op. cit.* 280.

[8] Herodotus, i. 105, iv. 67; Hippocrates, i. 561.

With regard to the particular circumstances of menstruation and child-birth, the obvious *vehicle* of contagion is blood. But it is not the fear of woman's blood which is the primary cause of avoidance; this would not account, except by the most strained analogy, for most of the facts; nor is there any flux of blood during pregnancy, when woman is regularly *taboo*; woman's hair, nail-parings, and occupations can hardly be avoided from a fear of woman's blood; and there is also the female side of the question to be taken into account. It is necessary to note this, because an attempt has been made to build up for savage thought a shrine of mystery round woman, cemented with blood, and that not her own, but ordinary human blood.[1] The savage indeed regards blood, as he does flesh and other human substance, as containing the life, but sentimental ideas of the sacredness of blood in itself, as apart from its containing human or sexual properties, are not to be found in early thought; nor in early thought are there any such strong notions of the blood-tie of kindred, as is generally supposed. Blood is only one of many vehicles by which contact influences relation. Blood is freely used by savages to assuage thirst, as well as to produce strength. The prohibition against letting it fall on the ground has led to an erroneous idea of its "sacredness," and in most cases may be more simply explained. When slaying a hog for a feast, the Niasese plunge the knife into the heart, so as to lose as little blood as possible. Each person cooks his piece carefully, so as to retain the blood; some eat it raw.[2] Amongst the Karalits seal's blood is preserved

[1] As by E. Durkheim, "La prohibition de l'inceste et ses origines," in *L'Année Sociologique* for 1898.

[2] Featherman, *op. cit.* ii. 350.

in balls, and, to prevent the escape of the blood when an animal is killed, the wound is immediately closed up.[1] To savages who do not know the use of salt, blood is an excellent substitute. In the Central Australian tribes "blood may be given by young men to old men of any degree of relationship, and at any time, with a view to strengthening the latter." Again, blood is not infrequently used to assuage thirst and hunger; indeed, when under ordinary circumstances a black-fellow is badly in want of water, what he does is to open a vein in his arm and drink the blood.[2] Other Australian tribes "have no fear of blood or of the sight of it"; they drink it freely to acquire strength.[3] The Wachaga and Koos delight in drinking warm blood fresh from a slaughtered animal.[4] At the Dieri ceremony of *Wilyaru* blood drawn from men is poured on the novice's back "to infuse courage, and to show him that the sight of blood is nothing."[5] The latter reason is secondary. Woman's blood is feared or desired, just as are other parts of woman, because it is a part of woman and contains feminine properties.

The contagion of woman during the sexual crises of menstruation, pregnancy, child-birth, is simply intensified, because these are occasions when woman's peculiar characteristics are accentuated, these are feminine crises when a woman is most a woman. This is the only difference between contact then and contact in ordinary states, a difference of degree only.

We may now conclude the description of the ideas which have produced sexual taboo. We have traced

[1] Featherman, *op. cit.* iii. 420.
[2] Spencer and Gillen, *op. cit.* 461, 462.
[3] *Jour. Anthrop. Inst.* xxiv. 172-79.
[4] *Id.* xviii. 13; Rounsey, *op. cit.* 31.
[5] Howitt, in *Journ. Anthrop. Inst.* xx. 82.

its origin from sexual differentiation, difference of occupation, and a resulting solidarity in each sex; this biological material is then informed by religious ideas concerning human relations, which are regulated by contact. Thus the usual working motive in sexual taboo is that the properties of the one sex can be transmitted to the other by all methods of contact, transmission, or contagion, and by various vehicles. Animal-like, the savage fears weakness more than anything else. Two remarkable facts have emerged—first, that it is dangerous, and later, wrong, for men to have anything to do with women; intercourse commensal and sexual being especially dangerous because especially intimate, but there is a tendency against all living together; and secondly, that sexual intercourse, even when lawful morally and legally, is dangerous first, and later, sinful. To primitive thought all intercourse has one connotation of material danger, which later split into ideas of sins, such as incest and fornication, for any intercourse is the breaking of a personal taboo and a sexual taboo, and the material results of such breaking develop into moral sin.

Sexual taboo would seem to have had the useful results not only of assisting Nature's institution of the family and of producing the marriage system, by preventing licence both within and without the family limits, keeping men from promiscuity and incest, degradations which were never primitive — the early efforts of human religious thought being in the direction of assisting, not of checking, Nature—but also of emphasising the characteristic qualities of each sex by preventing a mixture of male and female temperaments through mutual influence and association, and, as the complement to this, of accentuating by segregation the charm each sex has for the other in love and married life, the charm of complementary difference of character. Man prefers womanliness in woman, and woman prefers manliness in man; sexual taboo has enhanced this natural preference.

Where sexual taboo is fully developed, the life of husband and wife is a sort of divorce *a mensa et thoro*, and the life of men and women is that of two divided castes. The segregation is naturally emphasised as between young persons of the opposite sex, most of all between those who, as living in the somewhat close contact of the family, are more strictly separated, both because parents prevent the dangerous results obviated by sexual taboo with all the more care since their own children are in danger, and because, subsequently, a feeling of duty in this regard is combined with the natural affection of brothers and sisters, which is due to early association. The biological basis of this separation is the universal practice by which boys go about with the father as soon as they are old enough, and the girls remain with the mother. This is the preparatory education of the savage child, beginning about the age of seven. Girls and boys till the age of seven or eight, and sometimes till puberty, are often classed as "children," with no distinction of sex, as amongst the Kurnai.[1] In Leti, Moa, and Lakor children are brought up together till about ten years old. The girls then begin to help the mother, and the boys go about with the father. So in the Babar Islands.[2] Amongst the Kaffirs, as amongst most peoples, boys and girls till seven or eight live with the mother. As soon as they are old enough, the boys are taken under the father's charge.[3]

[1] Fison and Howitt, *op. cit.* 189.

[2] Riedel, *op. cit.* 392. 355.

[3] Lichtenstein, *op. cit.* i. 260.

In Samoa the boys leave their mother's care at seven years of age, and come under the superintendence of their father and male relatives. They are now circumcised and receive a new name.[1] This case combines an "initiation" ceremony placed at a date earlier than usual. In Patagonia the sons begin to go about with the father at ten, and the girls with the mother at nine.[2] Amongst the Jaggas boys have to live together as soon as they can do without a mother's care.[3] Of some Australian tribes Mr. Curr reports that "from a very early age the boys begin to imitate their fathers, and the girls their mothers, in their everyday occupations. When the boy is four or five years of age the father will make him a miniature shield, spear, and *wommera*, with which the little fellow fights his compeers and annoys his mother and the dogs. About seven or eight years of age commences in earnest the course of education. At eight or ten the boy has to leave the hut of his father and sleep in one common to the young men and boys of the tribe."[4]

The following cases show how sexual taboo emphasises this. In the Society and Sandwich Islands "as soon as a boy was able to eat, his food was kept distinct from that of his mother, and brothers and sisters might not eat together from the earliest age."[5] In Uripiv boys from a few days after birth are supposed to eat with the male sex only, else "death would mysteriously fall upon them. The fact of suckling, however, is overlooked."[6] In Fiji brothers and sisters may not speak to each other, nor eat together. The boys sleep

[1] *Globus*, xlvii. 71.
[2] Musters, *op. cit.* 177.
[3] Krapf, *op. cit.* 245.
[4] Curr, *op. cit.* i. 71.
[5] Ellis, *Tour in Hawaii*, 368; *id. Polynesian Researches*, i. 263; Cook and King, *op. cit.* ii. 156.
[6] *Journ. Anthrop. Inst.* xxiii. 4.

in a separate room. The relationship between brothers and sisters is termed *ngane*, which means "one who shuns the other."[1] In some Australian tribes brother and sister are not allowed even to converse.[2] Amongst all the Indian tribes of California brothers and sisters scrupulously avoid living together.[3] In Melanesia there is a remarkable avoidance between a boy and his sisters and mother, beginning when he is first clothed, and in the case of the sister when she is first tatooed. He is also forbidden to go underneath the women's bed-place, just as a Melanesian chief thinks it a degradation to go where women may be above his head.[4] In Fiji, again, brothers and sisters may not converse, the boys' sleeping-room is separated from that of the girls, and boys may not eat with a female.[5] In New Caledonia brothers and sisters after having reached years of maturity are no longer permitted to entertain any social intercourse with each other; they are prohibited from keeping each other's company, even in the presence of a third person, and if they casually meet, they must instantly go out of the way, or, if that is impossible, the sister must throw herself on the ground with her face downwards. Yet, if a misfortune should befall one of them, they assist each other to the best of their ability through the medium of a common friend.[6] In Japan young princes are prohibited from all intercourse with the opposite sex. According to the moral code of the same country, "parents must teach their daughters to keep separate from the other sex. The old custom is: man and woman shall not sit on the same mat, nor put their clothing in the same place,

[1] Williams, *op. cit.* i. 136, 167.
[2] Powers, *op. cit.* 412.
[3] Featherman, *op. cit.* ii. 142.
[4] Codrington, *op. cit.* 232, 233.
[5] Williams, *op. cit.* i. 167; W. Coote, *Wanderings South and East*, 138.
[6] V. de Rochas, *Nouvelle Calédonie*, 239.

shall have different bathrooms, shall not give or take anything directly from hand to hand. On walking out, even in the case of families, the men must keep separate from their female relatives."[1] In the Hervey Islands the first-born son is forbidden to kiss his sister; "she may not cross his path when the wind which has passed over her is likely to touch his most sacred person."[2] Amongst the Nairs of Malabar a man honours his eldest sister; he may never stay in the same room with his other sisters, and his behaviour to them is most reserved.[3] In the Nanbúri caste of Travancore "women are guarded with more than Moslem jealousy; even brothers and sisters are separated at an early age."[4] In Tonga a chief pays the greatest respect to his eldest sister, and may never enter her house.[5] In Ceylon a father is forbidden to see his daughter at all after she has arrived at puberty, so also in the case of mother and son.[6] Amongst the Todas near relations of different sexes consider it a "pollution" if even their garments should touch, and a case is mentioned of a girl expressing horror when handled by her father.[7] A Corean girl is taught that the most disgraceful thing a woman can do is to allow herself to be seen or spoken to by any man outside her own family circle. After the age of eight, she is never allowed to enter the men's quarters of her own home. "The boys in the same way are told that it is unbecoming and undignified to enter the portion of the house set apart for females. The men and the women have their

[1] Siebold, *op. cit.* 208; Bird, *op. cit.* i. 323.
[2] Gill, *Life in the Southern Isles*, 46, 47, 9.
[3] Giraud-Teulon, *op. cit.* 153.
[4] Mateer, *Native Life in Travancore*, 144.
[5] Mariner, *op. cit.* ii. 156.
[6] *Trans. Ethnol. Soc.* iii. 71.
[7] H. Harkness, *Description of the Aboriginal Race inhabiting the Neilgherry Hills*, 72.

meals separately, the women waiting on their husbands. Thus family life as we have it is utterly unknown in Corea."[1]

With the approach of puberty, the sexual question appears which emphasises the separation, both natural and taboo, and at the ceremonies of initiation boys are formally taken away, as they have practically already been taken away, from the mother's sphere and female associations. The danger, now enhanced by a new instinct, produces the very common custom that from this time boys may not sleep even in the house or with the family. A common form of this custom is the institution of public buildings, which combine the features of a dormitory and a club, for the use of the young men. In Annam these are called *morongs*. The custom is found, for instance, amongst the Niam-niam and Bongos, the Dyaks, in the islands between Celebes and New Guinea, in New Guinea, Tonga, the Andaman Islands, South and West Africa, and amongst the Pueblos, in the New Hebrides, and Indo-China.[2]

The separation of the young outside the family is a fairly regular social rule. On Fraser's Island "a young man will not sit down on the same stool or box, or in fact anywhere where a young woman has been sitting at any time. They imagine that the young man would sicken and die. The shadow of young women must not pass over the sleeping-places of young men."[3] Among the Iroquois young men could have no inter-

[1] Griffis, *Corea*, 244; *Journ. Anthrop. Inst.* xxiv. 305, 306.

[2] Schweinfurth, *op. cit.* i. 303, ii. 21; Low, *op. cit.* 247; Riedel, *op. cit.* 12, 250, 287, 443; Gill, *op. cit.* 240; Parmer, *op. cit.* 47; *Journ. Anthrop. Inst.* xi. 137; Shooter, *op. cit.* 15; A. B. Ellis, *op. cit.* 97; Featherman, *op. cit.* iii. 230; *Journ. Anthrop. Inst.* xxiii. 273; Ball, *op. cit.* 645; and especially S. E. Peal, in *Journ. Anthrop. Inst.* xxii. 249.

[3] Curr, *op. cit.* iii. 145.

course with girls, nor even conversation;[1] and amongst most North American tribes, "the chastity of girls is carefully guarded."[2] "The separation of the immature youth of the two sexes is a feature strongly insisted upon in the social practice of all the North-Western American tribes."[3] Amongst the Northern Indians "girls are from the early age of eight or nine years prohibited by custom from joining in the most innocent amusements with children of the opposite sex. When sitting in their tents, or even when travelling, they are watched and guarded with such an unremitting attention as cannot be exceeded by the most rigid discipline of an English boarding-school."[4] Amongst the Omahas a girl may not speak to a man, except very near relations.[5] In Madagascar the tribes of the forest and East Coast have a higher morality than the Hovas, girls being scrupulously kept from any intercourse with the male sex until marriage.[6] Amongst the Greenlanders single persons of both sexes have rarely any connection; for instance, a maid would take it as an affront were a young fellow to offer her a pinch of snuff in company.[7] Eusofzye women consider it indecent to associate with the men.[8] In Loango a youth dare not speak to a girl except in her mother's presence.[9] Amongst the Hill Dyaks the young men are carefully separated from the girls.[10] In New South Wales unmarried youths and girls may not speak to each other.[11] In some Victorian tribes the unmarried adults of both sexes are kept care-

[1] Waitz-Gerland, *op. cit.* iii. 103. [2] *Id.* iii. 111.
[3] W. H. Dall, in *Third Report of the Bureau of Ethnology*, 81.
[4] Hearne, *op. cit.* 311.
[5] J. O. Dorsey, in *Third Report of the Bureau of Ethnology*, 270.
[6] Sibree, in *Journ. Anthrop. Inst.* ix. 43. [7] Crantz, *op. cit.* i. 145.
[8] Elphinstone, *Account of the Kingdom of Caubul*, i. 241, 243, 313.
[9] Pinkerton, *op. cit.* xvi. 568. [10] H. Low, *Sarawak*, 300.
[11] Brough Smyth, *op. cit.* ii. 318.

fully apart. Amongst the same people the seducer of an unmarried girl is beaten to death, and the girl is punished and sometimes killed.[1] In South Nias both the seducer and the girl are put to death.[2] In the Tenimber Islands (Timorlaut) it is taboo for a boy to touch a girl's breast or hand, and for her to touch his hair.[3] Amongst the Leh-tas of Burma boys and girls "when they may have occasion to pass each other, avert their gaze, so that they may not see each other's faces."[4] In Cambodia the girls are carefully secluded, and the reserve which they show is remarkable. "The stringency of custom prevents the intercourse of the young. Accordingly, the *rôle* of village Don Juan is scarcely possible."[5] In the Andaman Islands bachelors may only eat with men, spinsters with women.[6] In Tasmania "the young men and lads moved early from the camp in the morning so as not to interfere with female movements at rising. Unmarried men never wandered in the bush with women; if meeting a party of the other sex, native politeness required that they turned and went another way."[7] An Australian woman, in most tribes, is not allowed to converse or have any relations with any adult male save her husband. Even with a grown-up brother she is almost forbidden to exchange a word.[8] Here the proprietary jealousy of husbands is a factor in the rule; but the common Australian custom, as in the Central tribes, where no man as a general rule may go near the *Erlukwirra* ("women's camp") and no woman may approach the *Ungunja* ("men's camp"),[9] brings us

[1] Dawson, *op. cit.* ci.
[2] Rosenberg, *op. cit.* 167.
[3] Riedel, *op. cit.* 300.
[4] Fytche, *Burma*, i. 343.
[5] Aymonier, in *Cochinchine française*, vi. 191, 198.
[6] *Journ. Anthrop. Inst.* xii. 344.
[7] Bonwick, *op. cit.* 11.
[8] Curr, *op. cit.* i. 109.
[9] Spencer and Gillen, *op. cit.* 178, 467.

back to sexual taboo, and reminds us that this separation of the young is due to all the ideas of this taboo, and not to the fear of sexual intercourse only. Such rules as usual become further causes, and have perpetuated the separation of the sexes.

In the examples of separation of brother and sister, we have been really reviewing the process of preventing "incest," and in those of the separation of young persons generally, the process of preventing "promiscuity." Neither of these needed prevention, for neither was ever anything but the rarest exception in any stage of human culture, even the earliest; the former is prevented by the psychological difficulty with which love comes into play between persons either closely associated or strictly separated before the age of puberty, a difficulty enhanced by the ideas of sexual taboo, which are intensified in the closeness of the family circle, where practical as well as religious considerations cause parents to prevent any dangerous connection. We saw that in many cases, not merely is the intercourse of husband and wife not practised in the house, but even the performance of ordinary functions, such as eating, is prohibited there, as in New Zealand and the Sandwich Islands. Parents bring up their children by the same rule, which is, put briefly, that all close connection between the sexes is dangerous, and especially between those who are in close contact. Marriage of man and woman is theoretically a forbidden thing, both outside and inside the family circle. The very word "incest" originally meant simply "unchaste," connoting a merely general infringement of sexual taboo, such infringement being more reprehensible between those who are not likely to make it. As to the fictions of primitive "incest" and "promiscuity," both in popular tradition and scientific theories of primitive marriage, it is natural that marriage systems should be explained as intended to put a stop to a prevailing practice, by those who do not know how religion simply assists nature, but the explanation does not at all go to show that these practices ever existed.

Lastly, as will be discussed hereafter, it is the application of sexual taboo to brothers and sisters, who, because they are of opposite sexes, of the same generation, and are in close contact, and for no other reasons, are regarded as potentially marriageable, that is the foundation of exogamy and the marriage system.

CHAPTER X

WE have seen the complication of the eternal drama of sex, and now approach the *dénouement* as expressed in certain features of the ceremonies at puberty, and generally in love-practices and marriage ritual. The taboo is now to be broken.

The general removal of taboo takes many forms, some of which we have observed in passing. In all these forms alike the idea is to get rid of the material taboo substance, the "sacredness" or "uncleanness" with which the body has been, as it were, permeated and infected from contact of some sort with danger, religiously conceived, coming from spiritual or human agents, and, in human relations, especially from human agents sometimes spiritualised, sometimes conceived of abstractly, or embodied in concrete persons. As the dangers are, whether spiritual or material, conceived of materially, so the methods used to obviate or remove them are such as would be used in dealing with matter.

First, we may briefly refer to some of the commonest means of avoiding the dangers of taboo, used before these dangers have descended and in expectation of them. Persons in this state of expectation are already taboo, as we have seen, but no confusion need attach to the double meaning. Again, when a person is guarding himself against these dangers, their presence, potential or actual, causes other persons to avoid him, for fear of coming in for the same. So much being premised, we may instance the method of hiding from danger; thus sick people are frequently hidden so as to escape, if possible, from the evil influence.[1] People often change their house to avoid evil,[2] and it is a common practice after a death to burn the house down, or desert it.[3] When a man is sick, the Aru islanders fire off guns round the house, to drive away the evil spirits. If this fails, they take him to another house, to deceive them.[4] The Ceramese take a sick man to another house, to deceive evil spirits.[5] The Watubela natives remove a sick man from his house, "because it is a 'warm' house, or in order to deceive the evil spirits."[6] The latter is the object of this practice in the Kei Islands.[7] When a sick man is about to die, the Eskimo family gather up all their possessions, close up the hut, and seek another abode.[8] When death occurred amongst the Yumas, the site of the village was altered.[9]

Various forms of seclusion carry out the same idea. Taboo persons dwell in special huts, so as to protect themselves and to isolate themselves from others. A garb of woe is both appropriate to the feelings of the fearful soul and diverts the attention of evil. A sick Basuto sits under a rock, where, clothed with miserable rags, he eats the coarsest food; he never washes; and continually curses the person who has bewitched him.[10] A good instance of dressing in rags for the practical purpose of exciting pity in human hearts is the custom as used by defendants in ancient Rome.

[1] Bastian, *Allerlei*, i. 437.
[2] Riedel, *op. cit.* 265, 266, 267.
[3] A. B. Ellis, *op. cit.* 160; Spix, *op. cit.* ii. 251.
[4] Riedel, *op. cit.* 266.
[5] *Id.* 141.
[6] *Id.* 210.
[7] *Id.* 238.
[8] Featherman, *op. cit.* iii. 406.
[9] *Id.* iii. 192.
[10] Casalis, *op. cit.* 277.

Evil is again barred by drawing a line, or by making a barricade. Barriers of water or fire are often used. To drive away evil from the infant, the Timorlaut natives place it by the fire.[1] Next there is the use of protecting garments, and veils, the latter with special reference to the danger of being seen by or seeing the dreaded influence; there is also in this practice a desire not to infect others with the evil to which one is subject. Amongst the Wa-taveta pregnant women wear veils.[2] The veil is commonly worn by women at menstruation, as by other taboo persons, such as mourners. The King of Susa eats behind a screen.[3] The use of sacred umbrellas probably goes back to the same idea. Amongst the Dyaks an umbrella is placed over a sick person.[4] The common use of amulets to keep off evil needs no illustration. By the use of dummies one persuades the evil influence that one is dead already, or engages the attention of evil agents, while escape is being effected. The natives of Timorlaut cheat the evil agents, by using puppets to represent the sick.[5] The Burmese believe that the patient will recover if he is buried in effigy.[6] In Celebes the sick man is taken to another house and a dummy is left on his bed.[7] To prevent a dead mother taking her child, the Melanesians place a dummy in her arms.[8] A similar method is to pretend that the sick man is already dead; the friends hold a mock funeral with this object in East Central Africa.[9] To avoid sickness, the Babar natives set adrift dummies of themselves in a boat, wherein they also place bowls in which their sick

[1] Riedel, *op. cit.* 303.
[2] J. Thomson, *op. cit.* 61.
[3] Harris, *op. cit.* iii. 78.
[4] Brooke, *op. cit.* i. 95.
[5] Riedel, *op. cit.* 304.
[6] Shway Yoe, *op. cit.* ii. 138.
[7] N. Graafland, *De Minahassa*, i. 326.
[8] Codrington, *op. cit.* 275.
[9] Bastian, *op. cit.* i. 437; *Journ. Anthrop. Inst.* xxii. 114, 115.

friends have spat. They will also change houses to cure illness.[1]

Similar is the use of proxies or substitutes, to keep the danger from the person concerned. Once a year, a bull is killed by the Zulus on behalf of the king; the strength of the bull enters him, thereby prolonging his life and health.[2] In Tonga a human victim was slain to "avert the wrath of angry gods from the king."[3] Before the chief's son was circumcised, the Manyuema first tried the operation on a slave.[4]

Again, there is the common practice of giving up to the evil influence a part of one's self, in the large sense in which the savage conceives of such, a piece of one's hair, food, clothing, or the like; the idea being to sacrifice a part to preserve the whole, sometimes the whole man, at other times the whole of a particular organ or sense-process. In the Central provinces of India, when cholera is about, the priest takes a straw from each house and burns these. Chickens are also driven into the fire and burnt; the idea is that the straws and chickens are substitutes.[5] In Tonga people cut off a little finger to avert calamity. To propitiate the gods they would cut off a finger-joint, and holding up their hands confess "they had done wrong, but were sorry." Another account says that they would cut off a little finger on the occasion of illness, as a propitiatory offering to the gods.[6] This idea of sacrificing a part seems to be the meaning of cutting off a finger-joint or lock of hair at the grave of a dead person, or during mourning.[7] Connected with this is the no less logical

[1] Riedel, *op. cit.* 357.

[2] Farmer, *op. cit.* 53.

[3] Leslie, *op. cit.* 91.

[4] Ploss, *Das Kind*, i. 363.

[5] *Punjab Notes and Queries*, i. 418.

[6] Farmer, *op. cit.* 128; Mariner, *op. cit.* i. 454.

[7] Fiji, Wilkes, *op. cit.* iii. 100; Pimas, Comanches, Wichitas, Minnetarrees, Pimos, Blackfeet, Crows, and Sioux, *First Report of the Bureau of Ethnology*, 99 ff.;

method of making believe that one's soul is in some object, which is then put safely away, as an external soul.

Another most widely spread method is fasting, the idea of which is to avoid swallowing food which may be tainted by the dangerous influence—to prevent evil entering a man. Parallel to this is the method of continence, the object being to retain the source of strength within the body, for if it be allowed to leave the body, the individual will lose strength which he may need for the ghostly conflict, and also the ghostly enemy may use the person's strength thus detached from him to injure him by the method of *ngadhungi*.

Then in cases of actual taboo, where the person concerned is actually infected with danger, or probably has been, for the primitive mind makes no distinction in its wide generalisation, the commonest method of removing the contagion is "purification." The taboo essence, as if exuding from the pores, and clinging to the skin, like a contagious disease, is wiped off with water, the universal cleanser, or similar substances. After menstruation and child-birth, and sickness generally, the contagion is got rid of by a bath. In Shoa "defiled" men, who had eaten forbidden food, were sprinkled with water.[1] The contagion of death is removed in the same way, and so is the stain of sin from penitents.[2] At a later stage, the water used may be rendered more efficacious, by being itself "holy" or "medicinal." Or the patient is purified so as by fire, the other great cleanser, or by disinfectants of various sorts, smoke and incense, which are to fire as the offering

Tasmanians, Australians, Eyre, *op. cit.* ii. 343; Ellice Islands, Cooper, *Coral Islands*, ii. 256; New Caledonia, Anderson, *op. cit.* 220.

[1] Harris, *op. cit.* iii. 147.

[2] *First Report of the Bureau of Ethnology*, 123.

of incense is to a burnt sacrifice. The chair in which a Manchurian bride goes to the house of the bridegroom is "disinfected" with incense, to drive away evil spirits.[1] Or again it is taken off by a rougher method —wiped off with the hands, or a scraper of wood, a sacred strigil, as it were. The following is the description of a Navajo medicine-man's method: he pressed a bundle of stuff to different parts of the body, each time holding up this "receiver" to the smoke-hole, blowing with a quick puff, as if blowing away the evil influence drawn from the body.[2] After births and deaths "defilement" is taken off by the New Hebrideans thus: cocoa-nut milk is poured over the body, or a branch is drawn down body and limbs so as to sweep the substance away.[3] The Maoris remove *tapu* by water or by passing over the body a piece of wood, which is then buried.[4] Where the evil clings closer, it is beaten off. The method of beating is also used to drive out evil spirits, and there is a natural and easy confusion between the two ideas, as would be the obvious double inference from sickness, for instance. Infected clothes are removed and destroyed. The Navajo who has touched a dead body, takes his clothes off afterwards and washes himself before he mingles with the living.[5] The Cherokees flung their old clothes into the river, "supposing then their own impurities to be removed."[6] The Maori slave who took his clothes off before entering a sacred place which would have infected him with its "sanctity," was wiser in his generation.[7]

Again, the *virus* can be taken off and transferred by

[1] *Folklore*, i. 487.
[2] *Fifth Report of the Bureau of Ethnology*, 420.
[3] *Journ. Anthrop. Inst.* xxiii. 12.
[4] Yate, op. cit. 104, 137.
[5] *First Report of the Bureau of Ethnology*, 123.
[6] Frazer, op. cit.[2] iii. 74.
[7] Shortland, *Southern Districts of New Zealand*, 293.

contact to some one who is more or less always taboo, or is a *corpus vile*, in which case the savage infers that the *virus* leaves the original sufferer entirely. He infers this because he desires it; when he does not so desire, as in the case of a man's *mana*, the good quality that can be transferred, it passes, but not away. If a Maori chanced to touch any one's head, he received its "sacredness" by the contact, and had to rub his hands on fern-root, which was then eaten by the head of the family in the female line. Thus his hands became *noa* again.[1] The various Maori methods of "lifting" *tapu* are called *Whangaihan*. The Tongan method is interesting. If a man contracted *tabu* from touching a chief, he ceremonially touched the soles of the feet or a superior chief with his hands, and then washed himself. If a man ate food with *tabued* hands, he avoided dangerous results by putting the foot of a chief on his stomach. The idea is that by contact the *tabu* substance is transferred from the man's organs to the chief.[2] A *tapued* Maori would free himself from *tapu* by touching a child, and by taking food from its hands. The man was thus free, but the child was *tapu* for a day.[3] Of the Maoris it has been said that the "most marked peculiarities of their customs can be traced to the principle that food which has once touched a sacred object becomes itself sacred, and must not be eaten except by the sacred object."[4] Some of the previous cases show how food is used to remove taboo. In Fiji the taboo persons wash, and then wipe their hands on some animal, *e.g.* a pig. The latter thus becomes sacred to the chief, and they lose the *tabu*, and are free to work, to feed themselves, and to live with their

[1] Shortland, *op. cit.* 68.
[2] Mariner, *op. cit.* ii. 220, 82.
[3] Dieffenbach, *New Zealand*, ii. 105.
[4] Shortland, *op. cit.* 294.

wives. When a chief wishes to remove *tabu* from himself, he transfers it to a priest.[1] It is an important fact that where the ideas of contact underlying social taboo are most thoroughly worked out, as for instance, amongst the Maoris and Zulus, the connection of food plays an important part, not only in taboo but in its removal. The savage believes not only that what comes out of a man defiles him, but that what enters him does so also, and especially is this so with food. It is food that gives a man his life and strength, and that also may, by forming his very substance, transmit evil to him in the most certain way. By a natural analogy, the evil can best be removed from him by the use of food. Later we shall see how the taking of new food is connected with this. The connection of fasting and silence with taboo is well shown by some methods of removing it, which at the same time remove the obligation to abstinence and the ban of silence. The fast incumbent upon mourners is ended in the Nguria tribe by some one touching the lips of the mourner with meat. In this case, as in others, there is combined the idea of rendering the freedom to eat or speak, safe, by a rehearsal of the action.[2] The common ban of silence imposed in various ceremonies by the Central Australians is removed by touching the lips with food, or some sacred object.[3]

There is another important method—inoculation. The idea is earlier than Jenner and Pasteur; it is one of the oldest and most far-reaching conceptions of mankind. As with all primitive ideas, however, it must be remembered that it has a religious connotation, and is generalised round a much wider circle than even our

[1] Wilkes, *op. cit.* ii. 99, 100. [2] Curr, *op. cit.* i. 280.
[3] Spencer and Gillen, *op. cit.* 248, 381 ff.

metaphorical use of the word. As with other early theories, so with this, a successful positive instance ensures the general continuance of the method. When the savage inoculates for nearly every danger, as did the Zulus, there might well occur cases where, for instance, small-pox was thus successfully combated. In Abyssinia, when small-pox is raging, they take a boy and inoculate him, and with the lymph supplied by him every one is inoculated against the disease.[1] There is a curiously strong superstitious fear of lightning amongst the Zulus, doubtless the result of a peculiarity of their climate. A Zulu has explained, "it is this that causes fear in men; the dreaded thing comes from above and not from below. They are afraid of something that looks down upon all of us, not that it will really strike, but the fear arises from thinking that it is a thing above us; we cannot defend ourselves from it, as from a stone thrown by another." The somewhat incoherent statement would apply well enough to the more timid individuals in a civilised and scientific age. Now the Zulu theory is, that anything struck by lightning has in it the "power" of the lightning. The "doctors" make themselves proof against it by "inoculation," and are thus also brought into "sympathy" with electric forces, and know when it is going to thunder. To protect the people, the priests sometimes give orders that an ox struck by lightning must be eaten. After this preventive homœopathic dose they take emetics and wash.[2] Similarly, when a Zulu is about to cross a river full of crocodiles, he will chew some crocodile's excrement, and spatter it over his person, in the belief that this will protect him

[1] Harris, *op. cit.* ii. 159.
[2] Callaway, *op. cit.* 403, 380, 402.

against them.[1] The idea is clearly protection by assimilation through inoculation. In West Africa the blood of a slain enemy is drunk by all who have never killed an enemy before.[2] When Kaffirs have killed a lion, they rub their eyes with his skin before they look at his dead body.[3] The people of New Britain believe that after eating enemies they have slain they cannot be injured by the friends of the latter.[4] In South Africa warriors are inoculated before battle with a powder made from slain enemies. This is placed by the medicine-man in an incision on the forehead of each soldier, and gives him strength.[5] To avoid the evil effects of a stranger's eye who enters a house where an infant is, a Mentawey father will take off its head-covering and give it to the stranger, who after holding it a while returns it.[6] Amongst the Zulus, if a man wishes to obtain a favour from a chief or great man, or when he is accused of some crime and has to appear before the chief, he tries to get something belonging to the latter, and this he wears next his skin. So, if a man has an illness, caused, as he thinks, by some animal, the animal's flesh is administered to him.[7] The Malays regard the spines of a certain fish as poisonous, but believe that if the brain of the fish is applied to the wound it will act as a complete antidote to the poisonous principle.[8] This principle of the "hair of the dog that bit you" is inoculation after the event, the principle of homœopathy, assimilation to the object which causes injury. This extension brings out the identity of inoculation with other cases of assimilation by contact. The following examples, in which a sort

[1] Shooter, *op. cit.* 218.

[2] Bowdich, *op. cit.* 300.

[3] Arbousset, *op. cit.* 114.

[4] Powell, *op. cit.* 92.

[5] *Journ. Anthrop. Inst.* xx. 133.

[6] Rosenberg, *op. cit.* 198.

[7] Callaway, *op. cit.* 142.

[8] Skeat, *op. cit.* 309.

of "reverse inoculation" takes place, also show this clearly. Gipsy thieves in Servia put their own blood into the food of one who they suspect knows of their offence. They believe that this prevents him from betraying them, and makes him friendly.[1] Negro Indians believe that a dog will be faithful to his master if he gives it some bread soaked in his own sweat.[2] A Magyar maiden believes that if she rubs some of her blood in a young man's hair he will love her.[3] A Cherokee bridegroom, if jealous, will rub his saliva on the breast of his sleeping wife, to induce her to be faithful.[4]

There is often a difficulty about inoculation, viz., the procuring of *lymph*. Where this can be surmounted, however, many kinds of dangers and spiritual and material "diseases" are prevented from having their fullness of ill result by inoculating the patient against them. As is sometimes the case now, in connection with small-pox, so amongst savages inoculation is chiefly used, sometimes only used, when no other methods avail. The risk due to passing through even a reduced form of the particular danger is one that early man would not lightly undertake. As a rule, he takes no risks and undergoes no pains that he can help, and never except for some serious purpose. It is especially when one is, as it were, in an infected area from which one cannot escape, and among infected or dangerous persons with whom one must to some extent associate, that inoculation is seen by the savage, as by us, to be the best method of safety.

Inoculation is the infusion of diseased matter from a diseased person into a healthy person, who by contract-

[1] *Am Urquell*, iii. 64.

[2] Owen, *Old Rabbit*, 142.

[3] *Am Urquell*, iii. 269.

[4] *Seventh Report of the Bureau of Ethnology*, 380.

ing the disease in a very mild form, escapes the full effects which would result in the ordinary course of contraction. In other words, it is a form of contagion, it is the deadly method of Nature used against herself. It is the avoiding of the dangers of taboo by boldly courting them; taboo is minimised by breaking it. It will be obvious now, first, that the principle of inoculation is the same (differing only in intention) as that of involuntary contagion and of *ngadhangi*, which is only "contagion" developed. Comparing it with such typical cases as those in which one is involuntarily tainted or "inoculated," using the word to sharpen the point, with the dangerous qualities of another, we see its identity with all these ideas of contact. Secondly, it is identical with those love-charms and similar practices in which you take or receive a portion of the desired person, in order to receive into yourself his desirable properties, or transmit your own hate or love to another. Here are the passive and the active aspects of inoculation.

It is natural that such transmission should be especially effective when performed through the medium of food, for thereby the transmitted property is most surely taken into the system. Of this method in various forms we shall find illustration in ceremonies at puberty and marriage.

CHAPTER XI

THE last and most important method of breaking taboo remains to be described. In it the whole cycle of ideas of contact which underlie human relations generally and the relations of the sexes in particular, is completed, and thus the principles on which the ceremonies of marriage and the marriage system are based receive their full description.

Inoculation was the last method reviewed, and two forms of it were seen—inoculation of one person with the properties of another, and reverse inoculation, by which one person assimilates another to himself by inoculating him with himself. The method now to be described is simply mutual inoculation of two individuals with each other. A and B being mutually taboo, desire to remove the dangers of their relation; being destined to live together, or to perform some dangerous act together, or to be in more or less close and therefore potentially dangerous connection, their best method is, as we have seen, inoculation. A therefore inoculates himself against B by taking a part of B into his own system, and B does the same; but this is equivalent to reverse inoculation, for A has practically given B a part of himself, and B has done the same; the two methods here coincide. The results are those which belong to reciprocity; each has a part of the other in his keeping, and this part not only assimilates each to the other by transmission of properties, but is a pledge, deposit and hostage. Thus identity of interests is secured, and the possibility of mutual treachery or wrong is prevented, not only by the fact that injury done to B by A is equivalent to injury done by A to himself, but also by the fact that if B is wronged, he may work vengeance by injuring through his malicious properties or by the method of *ngadhungi* the part of A which he possesses; and not only this, but, theoretically at least, in such an event, the part of B possessed by A may punish A by the sympathy it still retains with B, its original owner. Each has "given himself away" to the other in a very real sense. Taboo against connection is broken by making the connection, just as Kamehameha broke the *tabu* by eating with his wives; and the result is simply union, in the most vital sense, effected by assimilation and passing into identification. But the ideas we have just described underlie all union of this kind, not only in early thought, but implicitly always; it is simply the psychological principle of union analysed into its component parts. The relation is the full development of contact, which it is unnecessary to trace again in detail. Of the various parts of one's self each and every one may be used. Hair, blood, garments, and names are common instances. The idea is also satisfied by each party partaking of the same thing, such as food and drink, flesh and blood, by smoking together, or by dividing a "token," familiar instances being the *σύμβολον* and split sixpence. In one of the most striking cases this is the umbilical cord of one party. This is often preserved, as has been seen, and is regarded as very sacred and as possessing part of the "life" of the original owner.

The Narrinyeri have the following custom. The remains of a child's umbilical cord are carefully preserved by the father in a bunch of feathers. The relic is called *kalduke*. This he will give to a man in another tribe who has children, by which act his child and the other man's children become *ngia ngiampe* to each other. The duties of this relation are that they may not touch or come near each other, nor speak to one another, and the usual object of the custom is that these children when grown may be entrusted with the barter of commodities between the two tribes. During such commercial transactions the *ngiampe* persons of course may not speak to each other, a third person does the talking. Moreover any two individuals may and often do enter this relation for a time, one cutting his own *kalduke* in two and each keeping half. They are *ngia ngiampe* as long as they each retain his piece. This relation is often imposed on two individuals to prevent them marrying.[1] The above is so typical an example, that I may be allowed to use the term *ngia ngiampe* hereafter to express this relation.

It is hardly necessary to give a multiplicity of examples which show each and every one of the possible vehicles of the mutual transmission; most of these have been mentioned already in cases of contact and of single inoculation. The latter practice, as the one-sided application of the principle, should be borne in mind when reviewing the following cases. First of all, lovers not merely symbolise their desire for union by this means, but really effect identification. In Wetar engaged couples exchange locks of hair, gifts, especially clothes that have been worn, in order to have the smell of the loved one near them. Lovers in Amboina ex-

[1] G. Taplin, in *Native Tribes of South Australia*, 32.

change hair, rings, and clothes they have worn. After their first meeting, a Timor-laut girl takes the girdle of the young man, in order to make him faithful to her. In Amboina lovers drink each other's blood; "it is a real sacrament."[1] Peasant lovers in France used to pledge their affections by spitting into each other's mouths.[2] The practice is most common between lovers, and as a marriage ceremony, effecting union, satisfying love, and producing the responsibilities of reciprocity.

The next most common uses are for hospitality and friendship, the making of alliances and covenants between man and man or tribe and tribe, the so-called "blood brotherhood"; also as a method of making peace, the compact being sealed in various ways, especially by eating together (just as now a bargain is sealed "over a drink"). Throughout the world the closest bond is produced by the act of hospitality, the sharing of one's bread and salt with the stranger within the gates. In the countless examples of this it is often quite naturally found that one side only is concerned (single inoculation), but practically the act, even when no commensality takes place, has all the effect of a reciprocal process. Thus, in the Mentawey Islands when a stranger enters the house, the father, by way of avoiding the ill effects of the stranger's eyes upon his child, takes from it its head-covering and gives it to the visitor, who after holding it a while returns it.[3] This case brings out well the fear and caution underlying acts of hospitality. Amongst the Koniagas visitors are presented with a cup of water, as a ceremonial act marking friendship.[4] In Java a superior pays to an inferior the highest compliment

[1] Riedel, *op. cit.* 447, 67, 300, 41.

[2] F. Liebrecht, *Gervasius von Tilbury*, 72.

[3] Rosenberg, *op. cit.* 138.

[4] Featherman, *op. cit.* III. 454.

if he offers him his half-chewed betel.[1] Amongst the Iroquois the regular act of courtesy towards any visitor was to present him with a dish of hominy. To neglect this was a breach of good manners.[2] In Sumatra the guest who pays a visit to his friend is presented with betel as a token of hospitality. This is an act of common politeness which can neither be omitted nor refused.[3]

The biological origin of the whole of the phenomena is shown by these cases. The Timorese salute each other by touching noses and drawing a deep breath.[4] When meeting friends and acquaintances, the Eskimo greet each other by rubbing noses together, and then they spit into their hands and mutually pass them over each other's face. When they wish to give assurance of mutual friendship they eat together, and mutually rub each other's breast, saying, *ilaga*, "let us be friends."[5] The biological origin is also clear when the method is the giving of food to a person, and the Greek fashion of drinking a health is a good type of these ideas. The fashion coincides naturally with the practice, illustrated above, of drinking first to show that the drink is not harmful. Such satisfaction of the senses, again, predisposes the consciousness to amity and goodwill; this is an innate human idea. The following illustrates it. Amongst the Knisteneaux the rite of smoking the *calumet* begins all public discussion. It dissipates all differences, and no one who entertains feelings of enmity towards another can smoke the pipe with him without being previously reconciled. No one is allowed to participate in the sacred rite who has not abstained from cohabiting with his wife for twenty-

[1] Featherman, *op. cit.* ii. 383. [2] *Id.* iii. 24. [3] *Id. op. cit.* ii. 303.
[4] *Id.* ii. 461. [5] *Id.* iii. 405.

four hours previously. Contracts solemnised by smoking the *calumet* are held to be inviolable.[1] The phrase of hospitality in the Society and Sandwich Islands is "let us eat together."[2] Amongst the North American Indians tobacco-smoking, and in the East Indies the chewing of *betel*, have naturally taken over all the ideas attached to food. The passing round of the *calumet* is the regular North American custom of making peace and alliances, and smoking together is a mark of hospitality and friendship. In principle, of course, the act itself produces these results. The Powhattans observed ceremonial forms in receiving a stranger or visitor. The most influential man brought the *calumet* or pipe of peace, lighted it, and having drawn a few puffs, he handed it to the stranger, who, if he were friendly disposed, accepted it; the pipe then went alternately from mouth to mouth until each one present had inhaled the smoke.[3] Amongst the Druses hospitality is one of the sacred duties whose implied obligations they never disregard or violate. No consideration of interest, no dread of power, can ever induce them to betray or deliver up to an enemy the stranger or fugitive with whom they have contracted the sacred engagement of "bread and salt."[4] Amongst the Bedouin Arabs, as is well known, a guest once received in the tent becomes "one of the family," and the duty of protecting him is sacred. All members of the tribe are also tacitly pledged for the security of his life and property. It is considered discourteous, if not an insult, to ride up to the front of a man's tent without stopping and eating his bread.[5] Amongst the tribes of the Nedjed it is customary to pour a cup of

[1] Featherman, *op. cit.* iii. 269.
[2] W. Ellis, *Tour in Hawaii*, 357.
[3] Featherman, *op. cit.* iii. 115.
[4] *Id.* v. 475.
[5] *Id.* v. 371.

melted butter on the head of the guest who partakes of the hospitality of the tent.[1]

Limbus who wish to form an alliance of "brotherhood" exchange ceremonially their scarves and some money, and smear each other's foreheads with rice paste.[2] The Kumis, when making a contract, kill a goat, and smear the head and feet of the parties with its blood.[3] The *Tindeko* ("blood brotherhood") is very common on the Upper Congo. The blood of the two parties is mingled and put on a leaf, which is then divided and eaten by the pair. "It is a form of cementing friendship and a guarantee of good faith, which is respected by the most unscrupulous; and it possesses a religious significance."[4] In the Kayan ceremony a drop of blood from each party is mixed with tobacco and smoked in a cigarette.[5] Amongst the Ardras drinking together forms a bond of friendship.[6] In Madagascar "brotherhood" is produced by the two parties drinking each other's blood, in which a piece of ginger is dipped. They then each drink a mixture from the same bowl, praying that it may turn into poison for him who fails to keep the oath.[7] The most indissoluble tie of friendship that can exist between one Dyak and another is called *sobat*, or the tie of "brotherhood." A vein is opened in the arm of each of the parties, and the blood is dropped into two cups. The two then exchange cups and drink each other's blood. Next, another cup, containing a mixture of the blood of both, is emptied in divided parts by each.[8]

The practice of exchanging names in order to seal friendship is universal throughout Polynesia and

[1] Featherman, *op. cit.* v. 372.
[2] H. H. Risley, *The Tribes and Castes of Bengal*, i. lviii.
[3] Lewin, *op. cit.* 228.
[4] *Journ. Anthrop. Inst.* xxiv. 292.
[5] *Id.* xxiii. 166.
[6] R. F. Burton, *Mission to Dahomey*, 245.
[7] D'Urville, *op. cit.* i. 81.
[8] Featherman, *op. cit.* ii. 264.

Melanesia.[1] The Australian natives form permanent ties of friendship and "brotherhood" by exchanging names.[2] For mutual protection and as a token of friendship the Vanikoros of the La Perouse Islands form ties of "brotherhood" with one another, and even with strangers whose favour they wish to secure. "To effect this the parties mutually exchange names; and each one first striking his own breast and calling himself by his friend's name, strikes next the breast of his comrade and gives him his own name. In confirmation of this indissoluble alliance, they mutually offer presents to each other."[3] Amongst the Chippeways, as with most North American Indians, the smoking together of the *calumet* confirmed alliance of friendship and treaties, and made the agreement so sacred that its violation would have had fatal consequences.[4] Amongst the Seminoles the drinking together of their favourite beverage, "the black drink," was the regular method of forming a tie of friendship.[5] Amongst the Dyoor mutual spitting is used as a salutation, a token of goodwill, a pledge of attachment, or oath of fidelity. It is the proper way to give solemnity to a league of friendship.[6] The same practice is used regularly by the Masai.[7] Amongst the Khamptis "exchange of clothes gives birth to or is a sign of amity; and by exchange of weapons even the most deadly enemies become fast friends, and if one falls in fight, it is the duty of the other to avenge him."[8] The Kingsmill islanders rub noses and exchange names as a mark of friendship.[9] The well-

[1] Ploss, *Das Kind*, i. 161.
[2] Featherman, *op. cit.* ii. 139.
[3] *Id.* ii. 95.
[4] *Id.* iii. 246.
[5] *Id.* iii. 172.
[6] Schweinfurth, *op. cit.* i. 205.
[7] Thomson, *op. cit.* 165, 166.
[8] Rowney, *op. cit.* 162.
[9] Wilkes, *op. cit.* iv. 51.

known *taio* system, in Tahiti, for instance, is a good example of this. When voyagers arrived, they were expected each to choose a *taio*; one exchanged names with him, and thus the two became protector and protégé, with "all things in common."[1] In the Marquesas friends are *tabu*.[2] The same principles underlie the giving and receiving of presents; this is in essence an exchange of one's self. In Buru the interchange of gifts is a regular method of making friendship,[3] as indeed it has been and still is all over the world, since Achilles and Diomed exchanged "gold for bronze." In Central Celebes the same bond of friendship is used.[4] In New Guinea the exchange of presents and of names with visitors makes the latter sacred and secure from harm.[5] The Dusuns of North Borneo exchange weapons to become sworn friends.[6] In Patagonia there is an elaborate etiquette amongst chiefs; one may not enter the *toldo* of another until presents have been exchanged.[7] A Timorese woman bestows the highest mark of attachment upon her lover, when she gives him the flower garland which adorns her hair, or the scarf pin from her bosom. A superior who wishes to show goodwill to a subordinate, presents him with a portion of the betel he has chewed, which the inferior then chews. Young girls send a dose of chewed betel wrapped in a banana leaf to the young men to whom they are favourably disposed, and receive a similar gift in exchange.[8] Friendship is made between villages in Leti, Moa, and Lakor by eating flesh and drinking blood together.[9] The following case resumes many

[1] Melville, *Omoo*, 154; D'Urville, *op. cit.* i. 527.

[2] Melville, *The Marquesas*, 155.

[3] Riedel, *op. cit.* 19.

[4] *Bijdragen tot de Indische Taal-Land-en Volkenkunde van Nederlandsch Indie*, xxxv. 5. i. 79.

[5] Gill, *op. cit.* 233.

[6] F. Hatton, *North Borneo*, 196.

[7] Musters, *op. cit.* 184.

[8] Featherman, *op. cit.* ii. 461.

[9] Riedel, *op. cit.* 395.

details, and is among many which prove the present explanation. In Timor-laut friendship is ceremonially sealed thus: the parties offer each other a present, and then take the *ravnoru kida* oath; a mixture of water, palm wine, and sea-water is prepared, in which a stone or a tooth is placed; the chief washes the hands of the two parties, and pricks a hand of each, letting the blood drop into the mixture. A prayer is offered to *Dudilaa*, as witness, that the one who breaks the oath may pass away like water, become weak like one who has drunk too much palm wine, or sink into the sea like a stone. The two then drink of the liquor, and the stone or the tooth is split in two to be kept by the parties as a testimony. Similar covenants between whole villages are sealed by eating together the flesh of a slave.[1]

In the next place, it is a common method of settling disputes, and of making peace, and in these cases we see clearly the fear of danger which underlies and induces the practice, as we have seen manslayers inoculate their dead foe with themselves, or themselves with the dead foe, to secure immunity from his friends or from his ghost. A case may be prefixed, which sums up much of the primitive conception. In Buru when a man has been detected in adultery, he has to pay a fine of a pig, with which a feast is prepared for the relatives of both parties. The guilty persons, however, before this can be partaken of, must "drink the oath." So in the same island the manslayer has to pay compensation, something for the head, something for the body, arms, legs, and so on, and also one or more pigs to make a family feast. At the feast he sits apart with a relative of the dead man, before a wooden bowl, in which are

[1] Riedel, *op. cit.* 284.

two plates of food. While eating, the pair exchange plates, and so the wrong is atoned for and peace is made.[1] Amongst the Barea, when "blood vengeance" is satisfied, there results (we may well suppose on the same principles) "a sort of relationship" between the murderer and the family of the murdered man.[2] The Arab manslayer kills a camel before the tent of his adversary (the avenger of blood), and the blood is supposed to wipe away that of the person slain (the original idea being that the camel is a gift and a substitute for the murderer's life); the flesh of the camel is immediately eaten by the friends of the parties.[3] In Amboina peace is made between villages by a feast.[4] In Buru, once more, when a family quarrel concerning a divorce has taken place, the ill-feeling is ended by a family feast. Before setting to, the father of the divorced woman puts on the shoulders of her late husband some clothes belonging to his (the father's) establishment; the husband simultaneously puts on the father a cloth which he has himself brought. Then the father and the husband exchange plates of food. "All this marks reconciliation, and will prevent any further quarrel."[5] Amongst the Tagalogs of the Philippines peace or an alliance of friendship was made by mingling blood and wine, and then drinking the mixture.[6] The Wakamba make peace by slaying an animal and eating its flesh together.[7] Oaths in the Watubella Islands are taken to terminate quarrels, or to make friendship. The "oath" is drunk. Peace is made after war by eating food mingled with the blood of the parties.[8] The people of Luang-Sermata make

[1] Riedel, *op. cit.* 18.
[2] Munzinger, *op. cit.* 502.
[3] Featherman, *op. cit.* v. 374.
[4] Riedel, *op. cit.* 52.
[5] *Id.* 23.
[6] Featherman, *op. cit.* ii. 473.
[7] Krapf, *op. cit.* 313.
[8] Riedel, *op. cit.* 198, 202.

peace by drinking together.[1] In the Babar Islands the blood of the two parties is mingled with liquor and drunk, both when peace is made between two villages and when two persons form a league of friendship, and also when a man and wife are divorced.[2] In the islands Leti, Moa, and Lakor, when a man has cursed another, the injury is put away by the two eating together at a feast made for the purpose.[3] Amongst the Kyans, if two enemies meet in a house, they will refuse to recognise each other, and a reconciliation can only take place after a fowl has been killed and a part of the blood has been sprinkled over them.[4] In forming alliances and making peace amongst the Battas the heart of a slain animal is divided into as many pieces as there are persons present, and eaten by all.[5] In New Caledonia, when two enemies become reconciled, they mutually cut each other's beard as a pledge that the hatred which they entertained for each other is extinct. The same ceremony is observed when two friends meet after a long absence.[6] The Nootka Indians ratified treaties by smoking the *calumet*. Safe conduct was guaranteed to ambassadors who carried the pipe of peace.[7] At peacemaking in Wetar the parties exchange presents and eat together. When a bond is made between two individuals or villages, the parties drink each other's blood as a mark of union. The members of such villages may not after this ceremony intermarry.[8] To make a bond of mutual assistance the Timor-laut natives kill a slave, and the two parties eat his flesh.[9] At making peace the Kei islanders ceremonially sever a *kalapa* leaf in two, and each party takes home half.[10]

[1] Riedel, *op. cit.* 124. [2] *Id.* 342. [3] *Id.* 379.
[4] Featherman, *op. cit.* ii. 281. [5] *Id.* ii. 333. [6] *Id.* ii. 85.
[7] *Id.* iii. 351. [8] Riedel, *op. cit.* 446, 447. [9] *Id.* 279. [10] *Id.* 234.

In Leti, Moa, and Lakor, at the making of peace, a stick is broken in two, and each party keeps a piece. In the ceremonial words uttered on the occasion, this phrase is used, "our women shall be sisters and our men brothers." Quarrels between individuals are settled by mutual kisses, and drinking together.[1] In the last few cases we have the "split token," the *kalduke*. The Ceramese habitually make alliance of friendship by exchanging presents, especially of food. Moreover, quarrels between two villages are settled, and peace made after war, in the following way. Gifts are exchanged, and a feast made in one village, to which members of the other are invited. The chiefs of both parties drop some of their own blood into a dish of food, in which swords and other weapons are dipped: This food they now alternately eat. (Here by the way is clearly seen the meaning of the primitive oath.) Then the other village celebrates a feast identical in details with the former, and thus the bond is sealed. Many villages have been through the ceremony. The ceremony is called *pela*, and "those who have taken part therein may not intermarry, but must help each other in war." A similar process is gone through by parties who are going "head-hunting" together.[2]

Another form of the relation of *ngia ngiampe* is the fairly frequent practice of lending or exchanging wives. A wife, in early thought, is a part of the man. Sometimes it is a case of hospitality, but always it is a very sacred act, and produces the religious results of this relation, as is shown by the Australian taboo between those who have exchanged their partners.[3] Hospitality, of course, is identical with *ngiampe* relations generally. I shall discuss the practice later, and there point out

[1] Riedel, *op. cit.* 389. [2] *Id.* 128, 129. [3] Eyre, *op. cit.* ii. 339.

one particular reason for it. Timorese who have made a pact of friendship in the usual way of *ngiampe*, may lend each other their wives.[1] In theory, of course, the lending will in its turn continue the *ngiampe* relation already begun, as it does in Australia. The Eskimo frequently offer their wives to strangers, and the women are not loath to perform this act of hospitality.[2] The Yumas, by way of hospitality, lent their wives to their guests.[3] A case which shows the principle of the custom is the following: in New South Wales when two tribesmen had quarrelled and wished to be reconciled, one would send his wife to the other, and a temporary exchange of partners was made.[4] The Northern Indians sometimes exchanged wives for a night. It was esteemed as one of the strongest ties of friendship. If either man died, the other was bound to support his children, a rule which was never broken.[5]

Very commonly this bond results when persons pass through the same ordeal or ceremony together. Thus amongst the Basutos the boys who have been "initiated" together, as also the girls, form a guild of friends.[6] Amongst Congo tribes the boys who are "initiated" together, practically form a "society"; "through after life there exists a bond of union between individuals who have been members of this strange fraternity."[7] The same thing is found in the case of Australian boys "initiated" together.[8] There, also, they are generally made "members of the totem," a sort of "mystical body," which is itself in effect a continuous *ngiampe* relation. There is also a similar bond

[1] Riedel, in *Deutsche Geographische Blätter*, x. 230.
[2] Featherman, *op. cit.* iii. 405.
[3] *Id.* iii. 189.
[4] Cameron, in *Journ. Anthrop. Inst.* xiv. 353.
[5] Hearne, *op. cit.* 129.
[6] *Zeitschrift für Ethnologie* for 1874, 37.
[7] *Journ. Anthrop. Inst.* xxiv. 289.
[8] Fison and Howitt, *op. cit.* 198.

between the operators and the boys they have operated upon.[1]

The chief result of the mutual act is the duty of mutual respect and mutual assistance. The primitive form of this twofold duty is a taboo against physical personal contact, combined with an obligation, for instance, to assist in war. In many cases, of course, circumstances render the assistance one-sided, becoming, for instance, protection. Amongst the Tacullis, or Carrier Indians, the cabin of the chief is a place of refuge, where the homicide is secure. He is also considered as being under the protection of the chief if he wears any article of his dress.[2] Amongst the Kabyles there is a universal institution called *anaya*, a kind of freemasonry, with all the inviolability of the protecting guardianship which it guarantees. It is a bond of union which makes all Kabyles brothers, and when once in possession of the well-known token or pledge of security, the stranger or fugitive may travel anywhere, and the passport will be recognised. A violation of the *anaya* would be regarded as a grievous insult, and give rise to an inveterate feud. The respect and consideration to which the *anaya* is entitled depend in a great measure on the reputation and character of the patron who confers the privilege. The *anaya* of a celebrated *marabout* is most extensive in its practical bearing and most certain in its conciliatory effects.[3] "Zaid-al-Khail refuses to slay the thief who has surreptitiously drunk from his father's milk-bowl the night before."[4] The protection is produced by eating "even the smallest portion of food belonging to the protector." A case is

[1] Spencer and Gillen, *op. cit.* 248; Eyre, *op. cit.* ii. 338, 339; *Journ. Anthrop. Inst.* xx. 84, 85.

[2] *Id.* v. 306.

[3] Featherman, *op. cit.* iii. 381.

[4] Robertson Smith, *op. cit.* 149, 150.

given by Burckhardt of an Arab proving that he had eaten of the same date with a member of the tribe.[1] A natural concomitant to the sacred duty of hospitality amongst the Bedouins is the no less important relation which exists between the protector and the protected (*dakheil* and *dakhal*), which involves mutual obligation religiously observed, and good faith fully guarded against all violations and shortcomings. To reproach a man with having broken his *dakheil* is to touch him on the most tender point of honour, for it constitutes the grossest insult in the social ethics of Arab manners. Various acts are employed to confer *dakheil*. Amongst the Shamars, if a man can seize a thread or string, one end of which is held by his enemy, he immediately becomes his *dakheil*. He acquires the privilege of *dakheil* if he only touches the covering of the tent, or even if he can hit it by throwing a weapon at it; and this right of claiming protection has been carried so far that by spitting upon a man one becomes his *dakheil*. Amongst the Arabs of Sinai, the *dakheil* is only considered effective if the fugitive has contrived to eat or sleep in the tent. If two enemies unexpectedly meet, and the *salam* passes between them, this is regarded as a signal of truce, and they will refrain from every hostile act, although the salutation may have been exchanged by mistake.[2] Another custom which exists among some Arabs, in particular the tribes of the Nedjed, is that of guardian, *wasy*. This institution, which makes a Bedouin who accepts the responsibility the special friend and protector of the family of an Arab even after the death of the latter, is principally designed for the security of minor children, women, and old men. The obligation of *wasy* and the claim of

[1] Burckhardt, *op. cit.* 186, 187.

[2] Featherman, *op. cit.* v. 372.

the protected are generally mutual, and descend by hereditary succession. Almost every Arab is a protector, and is in turn the protected. The means of effecting this is by the present of a camel.[1]

Further, it is clear that while it is this obligation of mutual assistance which is the object of forming this relation, yet the taboo against physical contact is an essential concomitant, which helps us to see the origin of the whole method. The reason for the resulting taboo is that A and B are become identical by transmission of personality, and therefore A avoids all physical contact with B, because it is through physical contact ultimately that all personal injury is effected, and by such contact he might injure himself in B; B on his side has the same feeling. The idea is well brought out in a Maori belief; if another person ate a man's food, he was regarded as "having eaten the man," and the insult was gross.[2] And so A avoids all physical contact with B, primarily for fear of injuring himself; he will not eat with B, lest he eat himself, nor touch B lest he injure himself by the harm inherent in contact. The feeling is deepened by the fact that it is mutual, and therefore each fears injuring the other, as well as himself, by physical contact. The breaking of the taboo of personal isolation has thus produced a fresh taboo of even greater force, yet still because egoism is its chief factor; in the original taboo one feared lest one should be injured by the contact of others, in this one fears lest one injure one's own self as well. The *kalduke* is identical with the *ngadhungi*.

That this is the origin of the taboo and also of the binding force of the *ngiampe* relation is shown by the

[1] Featherman, *op. cit.* v. 373.

[2] *Journ. Anthrop. Inst.* xix. 107.

following examples. The object of making men who are to go on an expedition drink each other's blood is said by the Central Australians to be the prevention of treachery.[1] In New South Wales when two tribesmen had quarrelled and wished to be reconciled, they made a temporary exchange of wives.[2] In Africa, when a wife is unfaithful, her husband will die if he eat food she has salted.[3] On the Loango coast bridegroom and bride are required to make a full confession of their sins at the marriage ceremony; should either fail to do so, or should keep anything back, they will fall ill when eating together as man and wife.[4] In Victoria friends exchange hair as a mark of affection. It is very unlucky to lose this; should one do so, he asks the other to cancel the exchange by returning his hair. If this were not done, the loser might die. So strong is this belief that persons in such circumstances have been known to fall into bad health, and sometimes actually die.[5] In the Moluccas a man going to war is at pains to make up any quarrel he may have, for fear the ill-wishes of his adversary may injure him in battle. Should a man have had an *affaire*, and have given up the woman, he goes to ask her forgiveness before setting out, and offers a present. If she will not be conciliated, he does not go on the expedition, for fear of the results.[6] Lovers in the Aru Islands give each other gifts. Hair, however, is not exchanged, for fear that in case of a quarrel the one may make the other ill by burning it.[7] When a lover is jilted in the Babar Islands, he will avenge this by hiding a piece of the girl's hair, or betel that she has used, in a tree. When she

1 Spencer and Gillen, *op. cit.*

2 *Journ. Anthrop. Inst.* xiv. 353.

3 Macdonald, *Africana*, i. 173.

4 Bastian, *Loango Küste*, i. 172.

5 Dawson, *op. cit.* 55.

6 Riedel, *De sluik- en kroesharige rassen tusschen Selebes en Papua*, 387.

7 *Id.* 262.

becomes a wife and mother, her children will then die.[1] In Brandenburg it is believed that lovers and married people who eat from one plate or drink from the same glass will come to dislike each other.[2] A similar fear was seen in the illustrations of the primitive oath.

Some typical instances of this resulting taboo are these. Between husbands who have lent each other their wives there is, in Australia, a taboo of a very stringent character, and in other parts of the world a duty enjoining the protection of the children of the lender after his death.[3] Amongst the Dieri boys may not speak to those who have operated upon them at "initiation" until a present has been given.[4] At the "initiation" ceremony of the Central Australians a taboo is set between the man who performs the operation and the boy who undergoes it. This is removed by the boy making him an offering of food. The final "initiation" ceremonies are ended by each initiate bringing an offering of food to his *abmoara* man who decorated him, and with whom there is up to now a taboo. It is called man's meat. At this ceremony also the old men are sprinkled with blood from the young men, sometimes into their mouths; the idea being to strengthen the older men at the expense of the younger. The removal of the taboo is thus: "the man receiving food sat down, and the young man brought it and put it before him. The old man took it up and held it, and then put it to the young man's mouth. Thus the ban of silence was removed." Previously the ban of approach may be removed by the *abmoara* rubbing him with red ochre.[5] Amongst

[1] Riedel, *De sluik- en kroesharige rassen tusschen Selebes en Papua*, 358.
[2] Reinsberg Düringsfeld, *op. cit.* 81.
[3] Eyre, *op. cit.* ii. 338, 339.
[4] Howitt, in *Journ. Anthrop. Inst.* xx. 84, 85.
[5] Spencer and Gillen, *op. cit.* 248, 381, 382, 383, 386.

the natives of the Murray River, those who have officiated at the initiation ceremony never afterwards mention the names of the boys, nor do the latter mention the names of those who have operated upon them. Also, if one gives food or anything else to another, it is either laid on the ground for him to take, or is given through a third person "in the gentlest and mildest manner possible, whereas to another native it would be jerked."[1] In serious cases of illness amongst the Central Australians, a woman's blood is given to a male patient and a man's to a woman. When the patient recovers, he or she may not speak to the person whose blood was given, nor may the latter speak to the convalescent, until a gift of food has been presented. Again, a woman "sings" a mixture of fat and red ochre, which she then rubs on the body of a sick man. On recovery he may not speak to her until he has "given her food."[2] Amongst the Munda Kols there is a relation of dutifulness between the child and the person who gives it its name.[3] Blood is regularly given by men of the Central Australian tribes to each other in order to produce strength; the man whose blood has been taken "becomes *tabu* to him until he releases him from the ban of silence by 'singing' over his mouth." Blood is drunk at meetings of reconciliation; and in connection with the giving of blood to a man to strengthen him, *e.g.* when he is going on an avenging expedition, there is the belief that "this partaking together of blood prevents the possibility of treachery."[4] Here we come back to the duty implied by the process, and the sanction which supports it; it is clearly seen also in the *pela* ceremony

[1] Eyre, *l.c.*
[2] Spencer and Gillen, *op. cit.* 464.
[3] Ploss, *Das Kind*, i. 163.
[4] Spencer and Gillen, *l.c.*

of the Ceramese, which produces the obligation of mutual assistance in war. The preparation of a young man for marriage in New Britain is identical with a sort of "initiation." He has to hide in the forest from all his female relatives for three, sometimes six, months. Should he happen to meet a female relative, "he does not run away from her, but keeps on his way until they meet, when he will step aside from the road, and hold out to her anything he may have in his possession. She takes it without a word, and they part. It now becomes the duty of the young man's friends to redeem for him that which he may have given to her." Until this pledge is redeemed, he is considered to be in disgrace and is much ashamed.[1] Chiefs in Patagonia will not enter each other's tents till presents have been exchanged.[2] For touching the head of a Maori chief whom he was treating for illness, Mr. Yate was asked to make a payment. He never administered a dose of medicine to a Maori without such a demand from the patient.[3] These are cases of the taboo of personal isolation which is implicit in all human relations. In the following case it is seen as self-respect, which is injured through the breaking of the taboo by an insult. Amongst the Zulus the term *unesisila* ("you have dirt") implies that you have done or said something, or some one has done or said something to you, which has "bespattered you with metaphorical dirt, in Scriptural phrase, 'has defiled you.'" The writer compares the expression, "his hands are not clean." To use this term to another is a gross insult. If a woman has received the worst possible insult a woman can, *omka ninazala*, which means "you will bear children to your

[1] *Journ. Anthrop. Inst.* xviii. 287.
[2] Musters, *op. cit.* 184.
[3] Yate, *op. cit.* 104, 105.

father-in-law," she makes a great to-do, and goes to the kraal of the offending person, and kills an animal belonging to him. This is eaten by old women or little children, but not by any one of marriageable age. "The beast has received into its substance the *insila* which has now left the woman who received the insult."[1]

The balance is set right by reparation, the receipt of a present being identical in principle with the taking of something from the other party. The various methods of breaking the taboo of personal isolation reproduce the state of taboo once more. The taboo is broken, and the breaking produces another taboo, which in its turn may be broken. This is inevitable from the principles which underlie the practice, and the fact also proves those principles. These cases naturally lead up to what may be called continuous *ngiampe*. A principle of contact is, once in contact always in contact; and this is actualised in permanent relations, *ngiampe* in theory, such as between friends and lovers, between husband and wife, parent and child, brother and sister.

When we remember the pregnant meaning which personal contact has in all its forms amongst primitive men, it becomes less difficult to realise the superlative importance of such a relation as this. It is, without doubt, in primitive thought, a bond of such transcendent strength and inviolability, owing to the sensitive individualism of early man, who practically regards every part of himself as sacred, that we may look in vain through history for a tie of equal power. Certainly no ordinary ancient or modern conception of the duties of kinship has such force, nor even modern principles of honour and similar moral ties; the primitive bond is the most binding Categorical Impera-

[1] Leslie, *op. cit.* 169, 174, 175.

tive invented by man, and in its origin and results alike, seems on a par with laws of nature; it is a kind of physical "identity in difference." The theory of Maine, that status precedes contract, and that contract is unknown in primitive culture, needs revision. His evidence applies to barbarism, not to savagery.

Further, the same idea, though not developed to its logical conclusion, though this is always ready to become actual instead of potential, runs through all ideas of contact, especially when consciously mutual. In eating together, the *kalduke* is the food; in sexual intercourse there is a similar conception. Sometimes the *kalduke* is split in two—and here we have the world-wide practice of dividing a "token"—of which each of the two parties keeps a piece. All who have anything in common, even a common aim or sympathy, are potentially in this relation, and the idea of *ngia ngiampe* is inherent in their reciprocal attitude. The thief and his partner, the confessor and his penitent, those who share the same dwelling, the same trade, those who are of the same sex or the same age, those who have the same totem, the same kindred, the same god[1]—all these are potentially bound by the same principle. The idea goes all round the circle of human relations, and is potentially existent wherever there is mutual connection. The more subtle sort is found where contact is continuous. To husband and wife, the *kalduke* is the marriage-bed, the living together, the child, born or unborn; this is illustrated by the phrase, common to many languages, which describes the child as a "pledge." True, it is often as a pledge of wifely chastity, but this is not merely an extension, but is the same idea

[1] In Fiji, when distant towns have the same gods, the inhabitants have the privilege of doing as they please in each others' town (Pritchard, *op. cit.* 364).

only half expressed. The fidelity of the wife is the chief attitude required of her by the *ngia ngiampe* relation. Between lovers, besides love-tokens, lovers' knots, and so-called charms and the like, the relation of *ngia ngiampe* underlies the kiss, the embrace, and any contact. Between friends also, the clasp of hands, the embrace, the savage rubbing of noses, show the principle. "Freemasonry" is an interesting case of an institution based on this.

These psycho-physical ideas continue into the psychical phenomena of emotion and cognition; they are here more subtle, but no less enduring, whatever the refinement of culture may be. In connection with the phenomena of ideation, we spoke of the memory-image of a man's foe impressed upon his brain; another instance would be the memory-image of a loved person. In both, and any similar cases, the memory-image is identical in kind, though necessarily less material in degree, with the *kalduke* of the Australian black-fellow. The image is the man's self in the keeping of another; in the one case it is an Erinys, the spiritual image of one who is hated and feared, in the other that of one who loves. In both cases it is a man's self transferred to another, and bringing with it all the ideas of hostage and pledge; and when the matter is reciprocal, there is the complex reciprocity which is seen in all mutual contact and personal relation. Again, the same applies, though necessarily the occurrence is sporadic, to the reflection of a person's image which he himself can see in the *retina* of the other. In the connection of love, this is a favourite commonplace of poetical and popular thought. "And she said: 'See, thy image is reflected a thousand times in these gems that reflect thee; yet look in my eyes, and thou shalt see thyself through their reflection in my heart.' Then the king looked into her eyes, and saw himself reflected in them like the sun in a deep lake. And he whispered in the shell of her ear: 'Thou hast robbed me of myself, give me back myself in thy form.'"[1] Again, in connection with the idea we saw reason to attribute to primitive man, namely, that all apparently abnormal or unusual states of emotion, such as sudden anger or ecstasy, or the surging of love, when close contact with another attends these states, as, for instance, in the case of love, both in popular language and in psychology there is recognised the idea that, if the emotional state is "transmitted," if, as we say, A is "infected" with B's enthusiasm or love, A is "inspired" with B, then B is transferred to him, and so we come to the *kalduke* again.

Lastly, the whole set of ideas is of course the psychological basis of union, physical and spiritual, and well shows the materialistic workings of the human brain. Mutual inoculation, *ngia ngiampe*, is union looked at from within. It should be noted also that the next category to that of union is identity, and it is interesting to trace in the thought and practice of mankind, as we may in these phenomena, both the recognition of this metaphysical truth and the attempt to realise it in human intercourse. As Aristophanes puts it of lovers in the *Symposium*: "Suppose Hephæstus with his instruments to come to the pair who are lying side by side, and say to them, 'What do you people want of one another?' they would be unable to explain. And suppose, further, that when he saw their perplexity, he said, 'Do you desire to be wholly one, always day and

[1] *A Digit of the Moon*, 117.

night to be in one another's company? for if this is what you desire, I am ready to melt you into one,' they would confess that this becoming one instead of two was their exact desire." And he visualises the whole psychology of love-practices and marriage-ceremonial in the *mythos*, worthy of the poet of the *Clouds*, in which the earliest man was a bisexual hermaphrodite being, "having a name corresponding to this double nature, which had once a real existence, but is now lost, and the name is only preserved as a term of reproach." . . . "The primeval man was round, his back and sides forming a circle; and he had four hands and four feet, one head with two faces, looking opposite ways, set on a round neck, and precisely alike. He could walk backwards or forwards, and could also roll over at a great rate, turning on his four hands and four feet like tumblers going over and over with their legs in the air; this was when he wanted to run fast." Primeval man became proud, and would have laid hands on the gods, and Aristophanes now gives his version of the Fall: "and Zeus said, 'Methinks I have a plan which will humble their pride and mend their manners; they shall continue to exist, but I will cut them in two, and then they will be diminished in strength and increased in numbers; this will have the advantage of making them more profitable to us. They shall walk upright on two legs, and if they continue insolent and will not be quiet, I will split them again, and they shall hop about on a single leg.' He spoke, and cut men in two, like a sorb-apple which is halved for pickling, or as you might divide an egg with a hair. After the division, the two parts of man, each desiring his other half, came together, and throwing their arms about one another, clung, and in their eagerness to grow into one were perishing from hunger without ever making an effort, because they did not like to do anything apart." "Human nature was originally one, and we were a whole, and the desire and pursuit of the whole is called Love."[1]

This reintroduction of a state of taboo, connoting mutual caution, respect and religious responsibility, has had a profound influence on the development of morality. In it we can see the religious nature of human relations, and the connection between morality and religion, in any sense of the latter term. It illustrates clearly the growth of the conception of responsibility to others, and marks the psychological process whereby altruism emerges from egoism, the two impulses being indeed but two sides of one idea, for man is both an individual and a social creature. As to the new taboo, the primitive form of the idea of mutual responsibility, the characteristics of the state are of course somewhat different from the original taboo of isolation; the dangers there were those arising from ignorance; these, now the original taboo has been removed by breaking it, a removal which forms union, a completion as it were of some magnetic circuit, or a double inoculation, these are the dangers which will result from breaking a bond which is as strong as death, for it is a bond made by giving one's own life in pawn, and thus they are the basis of duty.

When the mind has completed its inference of a superior power, this power is set up as the judge and upholder of such relations, and a friend may say to his friend or lover, as the token is exchanged, "Mizpah. The Lord watch between me and thee, when we are absent one from another." Taking another feature,

[1] Plato, *Symposium*, 190, 192 (Jowett's translation).

the primitive "oath" is first, the man's self, then his "substitute" or "pledge" in the "thing" administered, and later, the god who exacts vengeance on the perjured.

To return,—the brief statement that in the Marquesas "friends are *tabu*" gives the whole case in a nutshell. They are taboo to each other as the result of their intercourse, their contact, in fine, the *kalduke*. We can see the idea of the original taboo combined with the later one of mutual duty, in the taboo resulting in Australia between the men who perform the operation at puberty and the boys who undergo it. They have been in a peculiarly intimate relation, body and soul as it were have been exposed and made naked to each other's eyes, a dangerous service has been performed, and its results may be dire. Therefore, they may not speak to each other. The ban is removed by a present of food.[1] This act of union removes the original dangers but introduces a relation of sympathy and duty. We also saw that the *ngia ngiampe* of the Narrinyeri are taboo in that they may not speak, but their mutual responsibility is such that they are expressly made in order to conduct barter, their fairness has been, that is, rendered above suspicion. Exactly the same relation is induced between godparents and the like, and their *protégés*, as between the blackfellow and boy. The sponsors or "bridesmen" of a Beni-Amer bride have a peculiar relation with her. They may not speak to her for the rest of her life, but they are sworn to defend her and protect her, and actually do so when her husband's conduct requires it.[2] We observed above that the forming of alliances by eating together prevented the possibility of treachery on the part of either concerned. The ceremony is

[1] Spencer and Gillen, *op. cit.* 248.

[2] Munzinger, *op. cit.* 325.

often performed for this purpose only, just as is single inoculation. For a man will not betray his own flesh; just as duty is shown by not eating one's own totem or even looking at it.

These cases lead up to two results, most important for our present purpose. In the first place, I put it that, taking into account all the evidence, psychological and ethnological, concerning human relations, we have here the most important primitive conception of relationship. The biological tie is not so obvious as are those of physical contact, nor is the idea of "blood-kinship" at all an early conception. Those who hold that the "blood-covenant" is the original of which all these other cases are "deteriorations," are obliged to use the most forced analogies, and I do not think it necessary to point these out, for they are quite obvious. Nor is there, in any example quoted, any primary idea of making a man of the same kin; the idea is to identify two individuals, *quâ* individuals. Again, close daily contact is for the savage a more important tie than that of kinship, except in the case of parent, especially mother and child; blood-kinship is only one form of human relations, and that not the most patent. The tie or *kalduke* of having the same mother is the basis of the "maternal system," the tie or *kalduke* of physical close contact is the basis of all primitive kinship; as opposed to later ideas of "blood" the basis is this daily contact, which is a continuous *ngiampe* relation. To the savage mind blood is only one variety of human substance, though an important one. Enquirers often, it is to be noted, confuse the care taken of blood as being a part of an individual with the later idea of "blood" as a term for kinship. Lastly, all these cases of *ngiampe* may be in theory, as in practice they are, taken under the category of friendship, and friendship is a far stronger psychological tie than kinship of blood. I shall return to this conception of relationship later, and also to the next result. This is that very interesting detail in the Narrinyeri, Wetarese, and Ceramese customs. In the first of these persons are sometimes placed in the *ngia ngiampe* relation for the express purpose of preventing them from marrying. In the two latter cases, all who have been through the *pela* ceremony of eating together, such as accomplices in head-hunting, and members of two villages who have thus made peace, are bound to help each other in war, but may not intermarry. To these may be added the fact that "sponsorship" and "gossipry" in European custom are bars to marriage, both between the sponsors themselves and between them and the family, for a member of which they have been acting.

These facts supply the second part of the reason why brothers and sisters and those who live together may not marry. Before the sexual taboo is removed, that taboo prevents intercourse of all kinds, including marriage, between such persons; when it has been removed, either by a definite ceremony, as at "initiation," or by a recognition of continuous *ngia ngiampe* in living together, eating together, and the like, the resulting principles of this new relation also prevent intercourse, including marriage. The same fears which led up to and which enforce *ngia ngiampe*, now, in the form of duty, prevent what the original taboo prevented; and the prohibition, being superimposed on a continuous biological relation, becomes strengthened when the latter is fully recognised. Put shortly, the *ngiampe* relation prevents all physical contact, and marriage is a permanent form of physical contact.

More as to this hereafter; meanwhile I may note that the Narrinyeri, Wetarese, and Ceramese customs have not yet, so far as I am aware, been employed by the supporters of the theory that primitive kinship was welded by a conception of the "blood-tie," which in its legal pedantry is quite unprimitive. They would doubtless explain the rules of the Narrinyeri, Wetarese, and Ceramese as analogies from the "blood-covenant," but if so, why should there be a taboo preventing the two parties, when of the same sex, from speaking to each other or having any physical contact? Blood-relations do not usually send each other to Coventry. Why again should a "godfather" and a "godmother" not marry, though theoretically married? It is more scientific to argue for the development of the conception of blood-relationship and blood-covenant alike from the elementary ideas of human relations. The cause which prevents these people from marrying is identical with that which prevents others in the like relation both from betraying one another, and from having any physical contact, the relation of marriage being in primitive thought a dangerous one; and between those who are identified with each other by exchange of personality, no reciprocal act which may injure either through the other, and thus poison the connection, may be performed.

CHAPTER XII

A DIGRESSION, in which another application of the ideas of contact will be brought out, is necessary to throw further light on some particular features of the subject. The common practice of disguise is used to avoid both real and imaginary danger. Thus the New Caledonians, when about to murder a man, put on grotesque masks so as not to be recognised,[1] just as the highwayman of romance was wont to wear a black mask. In war the Tongans change their war-costume at every battle, by way of disguise.[2] Dr. Frazer has shown that mourning is disguise, being generally the reverse of ordinary wear.[3] Again, in Zanzibar parents paint the faces of their children to look like "little devils," so as to preserve them from "the evil eye."[4] For the same reason Persian parents would paint their children's faces black, and German parents put mud on their children's heads and dress them in mean clothes.[5] In Egypt the children who are most beloved are the worst clad. One may often see a fine lady walking in a magnificent dress, and by her side a boy or girl, her own child, its face smeared with dirt, and wearing clothes which look as if they had not been washed for months. The intention is to

[1] Anderson, *op. cit.* 222.
[2] Wilkes, *op. cit.* iii. 10.
[3] *Journ. Anthrop. Inst.* xv. 73, 98 ff.
[4] Ploss, *Das Kind*, i. 134.
[5] *Id. l.c.*

avoid "the evil eye."[1] The Chinese believe that certain evil spirits attempt to ruin the health of bright and promising children. To delude the spirit, they shave the child's head, and call him "little priest," treating him as a worthless child and of no more consequence than a despised Buddhist priest. They also use derogatory epithets and names, so as to make the evil spirits think that they care little about the child. Sometimes they have it adopted into another family, for the same reason.[2] A Javanese woman in the seventh month of pregnancy bathes and has cocoa-nut milk poured over her; also she has to change her dress seven times a day.[3]

An interesting form of disguise, which is found in early custom as well as in modern romance, is the wearing of the dress of the other sex; it is generally the male sex who adopt this disguise, and no doubt in many cases the same idea is present as that which leads to the wearing of rags and dirty clothes; evil influences are more likely to pass over the sex which, from the male point of view, is the less important. The ancient Lycians were ordered by their law to wear women's dress when they mourned a dead relative. Plutarch explains it as "by way of showing that mourning is effeminate, that it is womanly and weak to mourn. For women are more prone to mourning than are men, barbarians than Greeks, and inferior persons than superior. Among barbarians again, it is not the most manly races such as Kelts and Gauls, but Egyptians, Syrians, and Lydians who indulge most in mourning. The latter when mourning go into pits and will not

[1] Lane, *op. cit.* i. 60.
[2] Doolittle, *op. cit.* ii. 229.
[3] Featherman, *op. cit.* ii. 386.

look upon the sun."[1] When an Egyptian boy is circumcised, at the age of five or six, he parades the streets, dressed as a girl in female clothes and ornaments, borrowed from some lady. In front of him also a school friend walks, evidently taking his place as a "proxy," for he wears round his neck the boy's own writing-tablet. A woman sprinkles salt behind the boy to counteract "the evil eye"; this is doubtless the reason why he is dressed as a girl.[2] Possibly the story of Achilles in Scyros, living as a girl with the daughters of King Lycomedes, is connected with some such idea. Achilles also had his name changed, another method of disguise; Issa and Pyrrha being mentioned as the name taken. Similarly, to conceal the infant Dionysus from Hera, Zeus gave him to Hermes, who took him to Ino and Athamas with orders to nurse him as a girl.[3] In the Babar Islands a party of women bury the *placenta*. If the child is a boy, they wear male girdles, if a girl, female *sarongs*.[4] Here the idea is sympathy. When Zulus undertake the "black ox sacrifice" which produces black rain, the chief men put on the girdles of young girls.[5] The same idea is extended amongst the same people into a method of keeping off sickness from the cattle by changing their keepers, thus: when cattle disease is prevalent and expected, it is kept off by the *umkuba*, the custom of the girls herding the cattle for a day. All the girls and unmarried women rise early, dress themselves entirely in their brothers' clothes, and taking their brothers' knobkerries and sticks, open the cattle-pen and drive the cattle to pasture, returning at sunset.

[1] Plutarch, *Consolatio ad Apollonium*, 22; Valerius Maximus, xii. 6. 13.

[2] Lane, *op. cit.* i. 61, 62; ii. 279.

[3] Ptolemaeus, *Nov. Hist.* i.; Apollodorus, *Bibliotheca*, iii. 35; Nonnus, *Narrationes*, ii. 29.

[4] Riedel, *op. cit.* 354.

[5] Callaway, *op. cit.* 93.

No one of the opposite sex dares to go near them on this day, or speak to them.[1] Here the principle is, as it were, allopathic, change of sex is a method of changing the luck or averting bad luck.

Any sort of change or substitution may be used to escape danger. In Java the infant was carried about in the arms of female relatives until the navel was perfectly closed, and a stone cylinder dressed up as a baby took the place of the child in its basket cradle. When the child reached the age of seven months its feet were for the first time allowed to touch the ground, and to commemorate this a feast was given by the parents.[2] In Amboina, if a couple have lost several children, they will give the next to another woman to suckle.[3] Change of name is a common method of avoiding danger or of altering luck. A barren woman in Ceramlaut changes her name.[4] Amongst the Lopars every time the child fell ill the christening was repeated and the name changed.[5] Similarly amongst the Kingsmill islanders.[6] If a Malay child falls ill after receiving its name, it is temporarily adopted by another family who give it a different name.[7] In Nias a youth's name is changed at marriage, a girl's at puberty.[8] Tuscarora boys received a new name at puberty, and another when they became warriors.[9] The custom is very common throughout the world, and we may begin the next argument with this practice.

The savage boy receives a new name at puberty and gives up his old one, just as does the Catholic novice

[1] Carbutt, in *South African Folklore Journal*, ii. 12, 13.
[2] Featherman, *op. cit.* ii. 386, 387.
[3] Riedel, *op. cit.* 73.
[4] *Id.* 176.
[5] *Journ. Anthrop. Inst.* xxiv. 148.
[6] Wilken, *op. cit.* v. 102.
[7] Skeat, *op. cit.* 34.
[8] Featherman, *op. cit.* ii. 354.
[9] *Id.* iii. 128.

and the Catholic priest.[1] What is the idea behind the practice? It is part of a very widely spread human impulse to change one's personal identity, and the possibility of the change is more than half believed. As the infant at baptism was rescued from Satan, and became by the washing away of the "old Adam" a new creature, receiving a name as the symbol of its new life, as the warrior who has slain a foe takes his name to add to his own personality the properties of the owner, and sometimes to avoid reprisals by so doing, and as the novice turns his back on the old life and begins a new life, so there are occasions in every man's existence when he would gladly for various reasons become "another man," and in early society this was thought possible. These things that are changed to effect the transformation are parts of the man's life or soul, such as names and garments, and represent his whole being. Let us take some cases which prove this belief in change of personality. When a Central Australian is made a medicine-man, he is supposed to be killed by a spirit, who removes all his internal organs and supplies him with a new set. After this the man returns to life.[2] The Kaffir word used to express the initiation of a priest to his office, "means 'renewal,' and is the same that is used for the first appearance of the new moon, and for the putting forth of the grass and buds at the commencement of spring. By which it is evidently intended to intimate that the man's heart is renewed, that he has become an entirely different person from what he was before, seeing with different eyes and hearing with different ears."[3] The

[1] So the Yoruba novice at the end of his novitiate for the priesthood takes a new name, A. B. Ellis, *op. cit.* 97.

[2] Spencer and Gillen, *op. cit.* 523, 524.

[3] Maclean, *op. cit.* 79.

closing ceremony of the "initiation" of Kaffir boys is that they are chased to the river, where they wash off the white clay they have been smeared with during their separation; then everything connected with their stay is collected in the hut they have lived in, and the whole is burned. The boys are smeared with fat and red clay, and are given new *karosses*. They then depart, being careful not to look back upon the burning hut, lest some supernatural evil should befall them, and they therefore cover their heads.[1] After the initiation to manhood of Powhattan boys, it was pretended that a veil of oblivion had been cast over their past life. "Forgetting that they had been children, they entered by suffering and increased knowledge into their new career of manhood."[2] Amongst the Congo negroes boys and girls are "initiated" at puberty, each set of boys and each set of girls forming a sort of secret society, called *N'Kimba* and *Fua-Kongo*. The rite is commonly precipitated when it is supposed that the women are not bearing enough children. The person being "initiated" is supposed to die and rise again. At the end of the ceremonies the "initiates" take new names and pretend to have forgotten their former life; they do not even recognise their parents and friends.[3] In Corea, on the fourteenth day of the first month of the year, any one who is entering on a "critical year of his life," makes an effigy of straw, dresses it in his own clothes, and casts it on the road, and then feasts all night. Whatever happens to the cast-out image is supposed to happen to the man's former self, now gone into the past, and "Fate is believed to look upon the individual in new clothes as

[1] Maclean, *op. cit.* 99.
[2] Featherman, *op. cit.* iii. 116.
[3] *Journ. Anthrop. Inst.* xxiv. 289.

another man."[1] "At the end of the year all the men of certain Zulu tribes procure a strong emetic which they swallow. No special reason is given for the custom, except that it 'clears away all the evil humours of the body.'"[2] A Dyak will change his name after recovering from a severe illness, in the hope, as we may suppose, of thus getting rid of his former personality and its liability to disease.[3] Dr. Frazer has already pointed out that boys at "initiation" are often supposed to die and come to life again.[4]

As will be seen when "initiation" is discussed, "the old life" put away by the boy at puberty is that of women, the life of the nursery; and we may suppose that the ideas of sexual taboo fixed somewhat of the same belief upon the purification of infants, that is to say, the infant is baptized or purified from the taboo state in which child-birth left it and the mother, a state of ceremonial uncleanness arising from the breaking-up, as it were, of woman's organism, and the diffusion of her sexual properties.

Further, this desire to efface the past, to put off "the old man" and to put on the new, is very clearly brought out in those "festivals," generally annual and often coinciding with the beginning of the new year, celebrated by whole communities. Thus, in old Peru the people held an annual ceremony, the object of which was to banish all ills. They would shake their clothes, pass their hands over their faces and arms, as if in the act of washing. They bathed, exclaiming that their maladies should leave them. The Iroquois had

[1] Griffis, *op. cit.* 298. [2] *Journ. Anthrop. Inst.* xx. 132.
[3] St. John, *op. cit.* i. 73; *Journ. Anthrop. Inst.* xxiii. 165.
[4] Frazer, *The Golden Bough*[2], iii. 423.

an annual expulsion of evils, preceded by a general confession of sins.[1] Once a year the members of an Eskimo tribe assemble. The *angekok* offers up an invocation on behalf of the people for their happiness and prosperity during the coming year. Next day they form a circle round a vessel of water, and each member in turn eats a small piece of meat which he brings with him, wishing meanwhile for good things; then he dips a cup of water and drinks, thinking of his guardian divinity.[2] The Talmud Jews of Poland celebrate the New Year's festival on the first day of *Tisri*. On this day they believe that God sits in judgment over angels and men, to make a record of their deeds done during the last twelve months; their acts are weighed and scrutinised, the sentence is pronounced which is sealed on the great day of Atonement, and all are predestined for the coming year either unto life or death. Worshippers of both sexes are dressed in white burial-robes. In the evening they all go to a running stream, into which each one throws some crumbs of bread, that the water may carry away his sins. On the day preceding the day of Atonement, a cock is swung round the head of each male and a hen round the head of each female, and then killed and eaten as an expiatory offering to redeem the sinner from death.[3] The Cherokees had a new year's festival; one day was the general cleaning day; old clothes were burnt, the pots, pans, and other utensils were broken, the town and all the cabins were swept clean, and every kind of filth or dirt was banished out of sight. Even the remaining provisions were destroyed, and all fires were extinguished. The warriors after they had taken the war-medicine fasted for three days, and during this

[1] Frazer, *op. cit.*[2] iii. 72 *sq.* [2] Featherman, *op. cit.* iii. 407. [3] *Id.* v. 159.

period abstained from all sexual intercourse. Malefactors and exiles were pardoned. On the festival day the people dressed up in new apparel; new fire was lighted, and new corn cooked and eaten. In the evening music and dancing enlivened the proceedings. The festivities lasted three or four days. This was also the time for receiving and making visits, and friends from neighbouring villages interchanged courtesies and congratulated each other on having been favoured with a new lease of life for another year.[1]

In these examples of the common notion that a change of life best coincides with a new year, we see how the old personality is as far as possible cast away, and the new one put on with rejoicings. Certain "climacteric" seasons and biological crises in human life are also very natural periods for this impulse to show itself. One or two of these crises have been mentioned. In organised religions the practice is made the most of. At the monthly religious festivals in Bali, the priest distributes holy water to the worshippers.[2] Periodic feasts amongst totemic peoples, at which the totem is eaten, are similar in intention. Periodic "confession" in Catholic countries introduces a periodic "turning of a new leaf." After child-birth mother and child are purified, and dressed in new garments, after menstruation the woman is cleansed; mourners put away their sorrow by newness of life. The prominence of food and feasting in some of these examples is a fact liable to be overlooked, but of great importance. It is not merely the new corn and wine brought out and used for the first time at some of these annual Saturnalia that is to be noted, though this is a particularly instructive case, but the use of any

[1] Featherman, *op. cit.* III. 157. [2] *Id.* II. 410.

food, in these festivals and in others, at religious periods and biological crises, or even every day. The wine that "maketh glad the heart of man" and the "bread that strengthen's man's heart" are naturally, as is to be gathered from the previous account of food-customs, the best means of giving new life and strength. And in savage philosophy the laying-hold upon life and the preservation of strength, is the main duty of existence; it is so much more important to him than it is to us in an age where physical disabilities are so greatly reduced. We still use the phrase "to feel a new man" after a meal, and to the savage the phrase is more of a reality, and we may conclude that on certain occasions, when circumstances were suitable, primitive man did thus feel that his personal identity was more or less changed, as his natural force was renewed, by meat and drink. The Masai and the Wa-kwafi are the most practical beef-eaters in the world. A man will sit all day by a bullock gorging himself with its meat, in order to strengthen himself for battle.[1] During the "initiation" period the boys of many North American tribes, such as the Shawanese, besides observing dietary regulations, took a violent emetic at regular intervals.[2] This is a practical way of getting rid of one's original personal substance, and it has to be brought into connection with the common taboos upon various foods at and before puberty, removed when the boy is "initiate" and able to receive them. The intention of building up the lad's strength is expressly stated in many such cases. At the Seminole New Year festival, the "black drink" was drunk, and war-medicine taken. The latter was also taken, as it is in so many lands, before a battle, in order to inspire the warriors with strength and courage.[3]

[1] Thomson, op. cit. 264. [2] Featherman, op. cit. iii. 182. [3] Id. iii. 173.

This "black drink" is the Seminole national beverage, and its excellent qualities have helped to bring out in everyday practice the idea of beginning afresh and acquiring new life and strength. "The Seminoles drank every morning a kind of tea called 'the black drink,' a decoction of the leaves of the *Cassine* bush. It is slightly exhilarating, and the drinking of it was considered a solemn ceremonial act; it was supposed that it had a purifying effect upon their life, and effaced from their minds all the wrongs and injustice they had committed, that it possessed the power of imparting courage to the warrior and of rendering him invincible, and that it had a tendency of binding closer the ties of friendship."[1] Amongst the Zulus at the opening of the new year with the feast of first-fruits the men are "doctored" in order "to make them strong, healthy, and prosperous for the coming year."[2]

During and after sickness, again, the system is built up by new food. In Tasmania a sick man was given human blood to drink.[3] The Zulus give sick persons the gall of a he-goat.[4] Amongst the Dyaks sick persons are sprinkled with blood by the priest.[5] The Beni-Amer cure their sick by bathing them in the blood of a girl or of some animal. The blood of a goat is thus poured over a man's head and body.[6] Such cases often correlate with the idea of a substitute and with the common double idea, as in the Mithraic *taurobolium*, that blood both washes away sins and gives ghostly strength. On this principle the Zulus once a year kill a bull; "its strength is supposed to enter into the king, thereby prolonging his life and strength. In

1 Featherman, *op. cit.* iii. 171.
2 L. Grout, *Zulu Land*, 161.
3 Bonwick, *op. cit.* 89.
4 Callaway, *op. cit.* 368, 372.
5 Featherman, *op. cit.* ii. 283.
6 Munzinger, *op. cit.* 310.

some tribes a chief on his accession is washed in the blood of some near relative, who is put to death for the purpose."[1] In Tonga human victims were slain to deter angry gods from destroying the king.[2]

The universal desire for "representatives" and "substitutes," due partly to irresponsibility and partly to convenience, may be referred to here in a few examples. Amongst the Motu to ensure a good harvest some leading man becomes *helaga* (taboo).[3] In New Caledonia, when a great chief is ill, or when some great calamity befalls them, they select the best-looking girl, and stretching her out prostrate on the ground inflict on her a severe castigation, which is intended to act as a charm, in order to avert the impending evil.[4] In Shoa, to save the king's life, an animal is led round his bed and then slaughtered.[5] In Chrysee a straw man is burned as a substitute when one is ill.[6] The Arabian custom of killing a sheep at a birth is explained by them "as averting evil from the child by shedding blood on its behalf."[7] The Acaxées before taking the war-path select a maiden of the tribe, who secludes herself during the whole period of the campaign, speaking to no one, and eating nothing but a little parched corn without salt.[8] The practice is common with kings as the representatives of their people. Thus the Mikado had to sit on the throne for some hours every morning, with his crown on, motionless, so as to preserve peace and tranquillity in the empire.[9]

Again, "purification" is ended on all occasions by taking food, or otherwise assimilating new strength.

[1] Leslie, *op. cit.* 91; Shooter, *op. cit.* 216.
[2] Farmer, *op. cit.* 55.
[3] Chalmers, *op. cit.* 181.
[4] Featherman, *op. cit.* ii. 92.
[5] Harris, *op. cit.* iii. 385.
[6] A. R. Colquhoun, *Across Chrysê*, 384.
[7] W. R. Smith, *op. cit.* 153, 154.
[8] Bancroft, *op. cit.* i. 581.
[9] Kaempfer, *History of Japan*, i. 150.

The link between this and "washing off" the past, whether "contagion" or "sin," is seen in cases like this: sextons and mourners alike are "purified" amongst the Zulus from the "uncleanness" by being sprinkled with the gall of an animal sacrificed, or by drinking fresh milk.[1] After expelling all disease and ills, the Incas rubbed themselves with a paste of blood, to take away all weakness and infirmity.[2] The gall and the blood, of course, introduce new strength into the system.

New clothes form another method of starting afresh; a man feels more or less "new" when wearing a new dress, and this universal practice on great occasions of feasting, ceremonies, and marriage has this idea behind it. The link between washing, "purification," and new garments is made by such early toilet-practices as anointing the body with oil, fat, and paint. The "purification" of a Kaffir woman after child-birth is completed by smearing her with fat and red clay.[3] For her this is a renewal of "decent apparel."

We have thus traced the passage of disguise into change, and of change into newness of life; in the next place change passes into exchange, exchange of identity, with the same ideas behind the practice. The idea of a disguise is often latent in this, but seldom emerges, for it is fused with more important aims. It may be discerned in this account of the notorious Feast of Fools, an account which may be here placed first, as this exchanging of identity is most prominent in festivals of the Saturnalia type. "The priests were the principal actors; their faces were blacked, and they were dressed as clowns or women, and ate blood-

1 Shooter, *op. cit.* 241, 247.
2 Fraser, *op. cit.*[3] iii. 74.
3 Maclean, *op. cit.* 94.

puddings on the altar. Obscene songs were sung in the choir. Many other actors took part, both men and women, the men being disguised as women, and the women as men." This festival took place at Christmas. Similar practices were followed in the carnival on Shrove Tuesday, at which men dressed up as women and women as men.[1] The idea is also latent in an ancient Argive festival, the Ὑβριστικά, held every year, at which women dressed in men's garments, and men in women's robes and veils;[2] and also in many Saturnalian festivals, such as the Saturnalia of ancient Rome, at which slaves exchanged position and dress with their masters, and men with women. These cases are explained by the Zulu custom, according to which, to avert a cattle plague, the girls herd the cattle for a day. The idea is to change the luck by an exchange, which emphasises the interval thus placed between the old state and the new. So in New South Wales wives are exchanged, not only for reconciliation, but to escape some calamity.[3] The tribes on the Murray River practised temporary exchange of wives "in order to avert some great trouble which they fancied was coming; for instance, they heard once that a great sickness was coming down the Murray, and the cunning old men proposed to each other that they should exchange wives to ensure safety from it."[4] It is a simple method, but actually it has been interpreted as a proof of primitive "promiscuity." A detail used to corroborate the interpretation is that the old men thought it necessary to revert to "the old customs of the tribe"; but the old custom to which they returned was surely this

[1] Dulaure, *Des divinités génératrices*, xv. 315; Brand, *op. cit.* i. 36, 66.
[2] Plutarch, *Mulierum Virtutes*, 245 E.
[3] *Journ. Anthrop. Inst.* xiv. 353.
[4] Fison and Howitt, *op. cit.* 290.

temporary exchange of wives, not promiscuity. The suggestion proves too much. The sexual licence of the *Nanga* in Fiji was practised when any person fell ill.[1] The Kurnai, when alarmed at the appearance of an *Aurora Australis*, tried to send it away by magic, and also exchanged wives.[2] An Eskimo prescription for sickness is exchange of wives; if a child is ill, it changes its parents.[3]

The chief ideas in these ceremonial practices of exchange, whether of wives or other possessions, are, primarily, the wish for a preliminary interval before starting a new life, a sort of *vitai pausa* or artificial gulf between the old and the new, while there is implicit in the exchange an act of disguise; and secondarily, a desire for union with one's fellows, which is actually effected by exchange of identity. The latter, it will be noticed, is identical with union, and is the final principle of contact seen in the relation of *ngia ngiampe*. We saw that the "black drink" of the Seminoles has the property of uniting hearts, and the human expression of mutual friendliness by eating and drinking together has been fully described. This explains the characteristic feature in festivities of the type of the Saturnalia, held once a year as a rule, and conceived as a means of starting life afresh. The wild pranks and general misbehaviour often associated with these festivals are doubtless to a great extent the expression of rejoicing at putting away the troubles of the past, but there is a method in the madness, a psychological reason behind it. Restraints are indeed broken, but the breaking of them is, first, a break with the old life, and, secondly, a method of union, not merely the result of over-feeding

[1] *Journ. Anthrop. Inst.* xiv. 28.
[2] *Id.* xiii. 189.
[3] *Sixth Annual Report, Bureau of Ethnology*, 593.

and excessive drinking. Take the case of the so-called "promiscuous" intercourse often found on these occasions; it is exactly parallel to the exchange of wives we have already noticed. Each is the expression of a desire for union with one's fellows. The very fact that the lending of wives is frequent as an act of hospitality connects the principles together. Hospitality is a close form of union. Exchange of wives, of dress, of names, of positions, or of anything belonging to a man, alike produces union. This secondary result of the common practice of men and women dressing up in the garments of the other sex, followed in Alsace at vintage festivals,[1] and on many similar occasions elsewhere, is that the two sexes are united, just as they are united in theory and in practice in the so-called licence used on such occasions. As showing how assimilation in dress and the like is a form of the desire for union, the following case is instructive. At a dance of girls amongst the Rejangs several young men were observed to show excitement. At last they joined in the dance; and the postures they assumed were quite similar to those of the maidens. "It is on such occasions that marriage contracts are generally made."[2] This impulse towards assimilation is seen now when 'Arry and 'Arriet exchange hats. Similar methods of effecting union by contact are also brought back to one physiological impulse, by comparing with them the Eskimo method of salutation. They salute each other by licking each other's hands, and then drawing them over their own faces and bodies first, and afterwards over the face and body of the other.[3]

Again, all taboos are removed for a while to form an

[1] W. Mannhardt, *Der Baumkultus*, 314.
[2] Bickmore, *op. cit.* 496.
[3] Beechey, *op. cit.* i. 391.

interval between the old and the new, while the very act of breaking them produces the chief result aimed at, union, and this union is a Dionysiac form of the *ngia ngiampe* relation. Such union is effected by masters and slaves exchanging positions and attire, by men and women exchanging the garments of their sex, by eating together, by mutual feastings, by exchange of presents and of friendly visits, and the like. All these are methods of union, but they are no less exchanges of identity; all in fact are acts of the *ngiampe* type. Thus old wounds are healed, old quarrels patched up; the licence is simply a method of cementing union. New food and drink meanwhile renew man's strength, and food shared with others in feasts, or the flesh and blood of the totem or god sacramentally eaten, cement the union of one with another.

Man's desire for social union and harmony is very keen, and the fact that he has these ceremonial methods of producing it, as those others used to produce harmony and union between individuals, is one which tells strongly in favour of the view that, as man was perhaps not always gregarious, so in early society he had none of the solidarity of clan, tribe, or kin, which is often attributed to him. Why these anxious methods of welding together the body politic, if the "tie of blood" was instinctively so strong? Man's individualism, though diffident and shy of responsibility, was in primitive times by no means lost in socialism. Individual diffidence and the "desire for company," as it may be phrased, for the desire of children and of the average sensual man in every age is of the same nature as their primitive brother's desire, may be seen in what Ellis states of the Polynesians. "One of the reasons which they gave why so many slept in a house was their constant apprehension of evil spirits, which were supposed to wander about at night and grasp or strangle the objects of their displeasure, if found alone; great numbers passing the night under the same roof removed this fear and inspired confidence of security."[1] So the Nicobarese never bathe nor go to the burial-ground except in company, from superstitious fear.[2] The feeling has given rise to a common practice observed with "sacred" persons whose safety is either threatened or is important to the community. When the King of Boni in Celebes sits, all sit; when he rises, all rise; should he ride and fall from his horse, all must fall from their horses likewise; when he bathes, all the courtiers must bathe too.[3] The same custom is used in Fiji, and is known as *bale muri*.[4] In Abyssinia there are four officers called *Lika Mankuas*, who have to clothe themselves exactly like the king, so that the enemy may not be able to distinguish him. A Mr. Bell, an Englishman, once held this post.[5] In Uganda, if the king laughs, all the courtiers laugh, if he sneezes, all sneeze, and so on.[6] Amongst Kaffir tribes the "king has a sort of valets, who appear to wear his cast-off clothes; when he is sick, they are obliged to allow themselves to be wounded, that a portion of their blood may be introduced into the king's circulation, and a portion of his into theirs. They are usually killed at his death."[7] This case leads to those of "mock kings" and the like, who are often substitutes and proxies for the real monarch, as well as for the people, whose "pawns" they are. In the Yoruba country the king's eldest son

[1] Ellis, *Polynesian Researches*, i. 341.
[2] Featherman, *op. cit.* ii. 250.
[3] Mundy, *Narrative of Events in Borneo and Celebes*, i. 30.
[4] Williams, *op. cit.* i. 39.
[5] Krapf, *op. cit.* 454.
[6] Felkin, *op. cit.* 711. Athenaeus (249) and Strabo (xvii. 2, 3) give similar accounts of barbaric kings.
[7] Shooter, *op. cit.* 117.

governs jointly with him. He has to commit suicide when the king dies.[1] In connection with the fear of handselling, it is noteworthy that such persons are used to do acts for the first time, so as to remove the danger. Thus in the Hindoo Koosh the rajah begins the ploughing and sowing. The Todas employ the low-caste Curumbas to guide the first plough, sow the first seed, and reap the first sheaf.[2]

Let us now take some miscellaneous illustrations of these principles, occurring in these periodic festivals of renewal and of union, and on other occasions. During the winter season the Koniagas make and return visits; insults are forgiven and enemies reconciled by inviting each other to entertainments.[3] At the Saturnalia festival of the Mundaris the masters feast their labourers.[4] The Karalits celebrate an annual festival at the winter solstice. It is a time of general rejoicing, and is connected with the reappearance of the sun. Eating is the most conspicuous part of the entertainment. Frequently they lend their wives to each other.[5] There is some idea of securing an infant's safety in the practice, common throughout the Archipelago between Celebes and New Guinea, of giving a feast to a number of village children, when a child is born or receives its name.[6]

Amongst the Dieri and neighbouring tribes on occasions of making peace, covenants, and alliances, occasions, of course, which have in common with Saturnalia the intention of union, and also at tribal festivals generally, there is an exchange of wives all round and what is wrongly called "promiscuous"

[1] A. B. Ellis, *op. cit.* 167.

[2] Biddulph, *op. cit.* 106; Harkness, *op. cit.* 56.

[3] Featherman, *op. cit.* iii. 453.

[4] Dalton, *op. cit.* 196.

[5] Featherman, *op. cit.* iii. 432.

[6] Riedel, *op. cit.* 75.

sexual intercourse.[1] It is a sacred method of union as I have shown. The fact that jealousy is forbidden on these occasions, does not prove, as has been asserted, either that the custom is a return to previous communism, or that the Australian has no marital jealousy. If he has none, why forbid it? In the case of forming alliances the exchange is, of course, a factor in making the union, such contact sympathetically assists it. At the Saturnalia of the Hos "promiscuous" intercourse takes place.[2] The people of Leti, Moa, and Lakor hold an annual feast, at which free intercourse takes place.[3]

Amongst the Hawaiians "promiscuous" sexual intercourse takes place at the feast after a death.[4] In Mangaia, at the same feast, all exchange presents.[5] At the annual funeral feast on Nancowry Island, one of the Nicobars, numerous hogs are killed and eaten, and all the guests daub their faces with the blood.[6] The Battas celebrate a feast after a death, at which a number of animals are killed and eaten.[7] The Samoyeds kill a reindeer over the grave, the Arinzes a horse, and the mourners eat it there.[8] After a Chippeway funeral the "offering to the dead" is prepared, consisting of meat-soup or brandy, which is handed round to those present; while the portion reserved for a burnt-offering is thrown into the fire, and is supposed to have been accepted by the ghostly self of the departed.[9]

On such occasions there is to be seen the working of these principles; a desire for union among the survivors and a desire for new strength and life, both

[1] *Journ. Anthrop. Inst.* xxiv. 173. 163.

[2] Dalton, *op. cit.* 196.

[3] Riedel, *op. cit.* 373.

[4] Lisiansky, *op. cit.* 122.

[5] Gill, *op. cit.* 77.

[6] Featherman, *op. cit.* ii. 247.

[7] *Id.* ii. 329.

[8] Georgi, *op. cit.* 16, 31.

[9] Featherman, *op. cit.* iii. 251.

prompted by the sad example of the dead person; the two impulses are satisfied simultaneously by eating together, exchanging gifts, or similar acts of union, such as sexual intercourse. Again, as may be seen when the mourners eat the offerings of the dead, there is the further and most natural idea, retained by Catholicism in the feast of All Souls, of effecting union with the departed. This desire for the impossible is a psychological necessity in real mourning, and is well shown by such customs as that of widows in the Hervey Islands, who will wear the dress of their dead husbands. A widower may be seen walking about in a gown of his departed wife. "Instead of her shawl, a mother will wear on her back a pair of trousers belonging to a little son just laid in his grave."[1] Andamanese widows carry about the skulls of their dead husbands.[2] Red Indian mothers carry a doll, representing a dead child, and Australian women carry about the rotting remains of their dead husbands.[3] In Timorlaut as mourning the widow wears a piece of her dead husband's clothing in her hair; this is also done by widowers.[4] Communion with the dead is most exactly reached, and the identity of eating with a person and eating him most clearly shown, in the common Australian practice in which mourners drink the humours of the decaying corpse, or eat its flesh. The Kurnai anoint themselves with decomposed matter from the dead.[5] It is done in the Kingsmills "to remember him."[6] So in Timorlaut mourners smear themselves with the fluids of the corpse.[7] The Aru islanders drink them "to effect union with the dead man."

[1] Gill, *op. cit.* 78.

[2] Ploss u. Bartels, *op. cit.* ii. 500.

[3] Fison and Howitt, *op. cit.* 243.

[4] Riedel, *op. cit.* 307.

[5] Fison and Howitt, *op. cit.* 243.

[6] *Id. l.c.*

[7] Riedel, *op. cit.* 308.

Some is kept in order to injure enemies (by the contagion of death, we may well suppose).[1] This case resumes in itself all the principles of contact, and shows the fallacy of supposing such practices to be intended to keep "the life in the family." Of course, the idea correlates with the notion of getting a dead man's strength, as we have seen, but the impulse is individual. When Artemisia drank the ashes of Mausolus,[2] it was for love of him, and not to satisfy family pride. Here we once more reach the idea of receiving a man's properties by eating his flesh; and conversely in these mourning customs, there is sometimes to be seen a desire to avoid injury from the departed spirit, by inoculating oneself with him, an idea translated by many peoples into a fear that the ghost will be offended if he is not mourned for properly.

Another feature of these festivals is a practice which is very common in all early religious custom, and is a good illustration of that general habit of "make-believe," which is connected with sympathetic magic on the one hand, and on the other with primitive diffidence in action, and fear of close-quarters, an early stage in the growth of character which is not easily passed. At the Saturnalia of the Hos, sons and daughters revile their parents, and their parents revile them.[3] This method of showing the reality of the change of life by emphasising the interval between the new and the old may lead up to the feature we are to discuss. In Upper Egypt on the 10th of September of each year, there is a festival at which each town chooses a temporary lord, who is dressed up as a clown.[4]

[1] Riedel, op. cit. 267.

[2] A. Gellius, x. 18; V. Maximus, iv. 6, 5.

[3] Dalton, op. cit. 196.

[4] Klunzinger, *Bilder aus Ober-Aegypten*, 180.

In this, as in the case of most mock kings collected, there is a double idea. The mock king is a "proxy" for the people, he is their substitute, who bears their calamities away as a scapegoat; and he is reviled and mocked. He represents them, on the principles of substitution and make-believe; he takes away their troubles, on the same principles, and because of the desire for a periodic change of life and of personal identity. Why is he mocked and ill-treated? The actual word "mock," with its double meaning, preserves the answer. *They* deserve the reviling for their sins, but he as their proxy will receive it; it is a convenient method of substitution, of transference of responsibility. Moreover, by a natural confusion, he represents these evils, in particular those which admit of easy personification, such as diseases and the like; as such, he is to be scourged and mocked as they would gladly treat the actual evils. He is thus a proxy for two sets of persons.

The war-dance and similar sympathetic processes, which assist the real result by imitating it, show how the above mentioned idea is connected with sympathetic magic. These practices have a true psychological basis and subjective use; they resemble "rehearsals"; by previously going through the result, man ensures its successful issue, just as one runs over in his mind something he is about to do. In the Chippeway war-dance the warriors imitated the actions of surprising the enemy, of tomahawking, scalping, and drinking the blood of the foe.[1] In the Algonquin war-dance before an expedition each man in turn branished his tomahawk, and furiously struck the post round which they stood, in a manner as if he were killing a foe, whom

[1] Featherman, *op. cit.* iii. 256.

he then fictitiously scalped by a characteristic mimic action.[1] The Mandans before a buffalo hunt go through a dance imitating the various stages of the hunt. One man represents a buffalo, and he is slain in pantomime, skinned, and cut up.[2]

In some cases these fights, contests, and riotings are intended to drive away actual evil influences, in others the potentiality of evil is driven away, before it can become actualised; and this is naturally done on occasions when excessive joy by psychological law induces a fear of vague imminent danger, as seen in ideas of Nemesis. The practice is also followed to avenge some wrong, fancied or real, with a half serious, half "make-believe" feeling. Thus, in New Britain, when a boy and girl who are betrothed, are grown up, and part of the "price" has been paid, he builds a little house in the bush, and elopes with his bride. Her father sallies out with friends, apparently in anger, to kill the groom. They do not really wish to find him, but they burn the house. On their return they find the pair installed in their home.[3] Amongst the same people, when a widower marries, the female relatives of the dead wife assemble near his place. It is a day of liberty and fun with them. They take their husbands' or brothers' weapons, or any article of male attire they can find, and have the liberty of daubing with red paint any man they can catch. If a woman approaches a man he moves off. At a given signal they throw themselves on his house, fences, and property, and destroy as far as they can. The owner has no power to interfere. The custom is called *Varagut.* The only explanation they give is that "the women are angry on account of the first wife, they do not care to see the

[1] Featherman, *op. cit.* iii. 78. [2] *Id.* iii. 298. [3] Romilly, *op. cit.* 27.

labour of the first wife go to benefit the second."[1] Similarily at Fijian funerals, the women whip the men with long whips, and the men flip clay bullets at the women.[2] On the other side, savage "make-believe" is connected with diffidence, and with an interesting notion that the "intention" is everything. Amongst the Maoris a blow given by proxy is regarded as if it actually were dealt to the person intended, and is spoken of as such. A man, for instance, struck the ground close to his enemy, who was lying ill; Mr. Shortland on hearing an account of this was given to understand that the sick man had actually been thrashed.[3] A mourner in the Andaman Islands will shoot arrows into the jungle, evil spirits who cause death being supposed to dwell there; he also will pierce the ground with a spear all round the dead man, "hoping to inflict a mortal wound on an unseen enemy."[4] In Maori warfare a part of the stockade is called after a hostile chief and then fired at by the garrison. One often hears a chief complain that he has been shot at, when it was only his effigy.[5] South Australians when about to attack Europeans beat their weapons together, threw dust in the air, spat, etc., and made gestures of defiance.[6] All this kind of thing is well seen in the habits of children and of animals, and is due to fear of direct action. Now, in some of these annual festivals and on other occasions there are mock contests, which are explained by these ideas. We saw how parents and children revile each other at their Saturnalia; the same principle is behind the football match played at the annual festival in Shoa, first

[1] *Journ. Anthrop. Inst.* xxiv. 292.
[2] Wilken, *op. cit.* iii. 99.
[3] Shortland, *Southern Districts*, 21, 22.
[4] *Journ. Anthrop. Inst.* xi. 146.
[5] Shortland, *op. cit.* 26, 27.
[6] Eyre, *op. cit.* ii. 225.

between men, and then between women. The victorious side abuses the defeated, and riot and debauchery end the day.[1] After a successful fishing expedition Fijian women were seen to meet the returning men with dancing and songs and with a smart volley of bitter oranges, this the men returned by driving the women from the beach.[2] This simple case of delight expressed in recrimination is no custom, but a psychological result, quite common in human nature, which, however, is instructive here as illustrating the origin of customs which resemble it.

The same method is also used in primitive etiquette, which is based on fear and the taboo of personal isolation. When Krapf arrived at a Pemba village, the king was very friendly, but ordered his musketeers to fire a volley, "to expel evil spirits."[3] In Tonga presents are made to a new arrival, visitor, or native who has been away, but there is a curious proviso. The new-comers can be challenged by any one, and a sort of sham fight must take place. The visitors always get a thorough beating, but it is all done in a friendly way.[4] Mr. New was always received in the African villages he reached, with war-dances.[5] The Indians of the Yukon, on meeting Mr. Dall, advanced on him firing blank cartridge.[6] So amongst the Maoris mock fights were performed at all visits, reeds and rail-fencing being used instead of weapons.[7]

In savage as in other etiquette indirectness is universal. In East Africa a mistake in etiquette towards the chief is severely punished, and amongst the Waganda the offender may be slain on the spot. A man will

[1] Harris, *op. cit.* iii. 148.
[2] Williams, *op. cit.* i. 92.
[3] Krapf, *op. cit.* 269.
[4] Mariner, *op. cit.* 346.
[5] C. New, *Life in Eastern Africa*, 80, 301.
[6] Dall, *op. cit.* 93.
[7] Polack, *New Zealand*, i. 86, 87, ii. 170.

hardly address another directly as "you," nor will he use a direct negative if he can avoid it. The expressions are "the master knows," etc., and for a negative, "I will see if that happens."[1]

The "make-believe" method is often used in punishment. Amongst Australians and Tasmanians the offender against the customs was required to stand while spears were thrown at him, which he avoided as best he could by contortions of the body.[2] In the Milya-uppa tribe, when a man had given another some cause of complaint, custom required that he should allow his head to be struck by the individual offended, till blood came.[3] In some Australian tribes a culprit was provided with a shield, and "the prosecutors standing at a certain distance hurled spears at him. If he succeeded in warding off the weapons, he was discharged."[4] The Malays settle disputes between tribes thus; a certain number of combatants for each tribe beat each other with sticks till one or other cries enough, and the victors claim the right for which they contested.[5] The Fijian act of reparation to obtain forgiveness was called *soro*; it was the offering of a present in certain attitudes of humiliation.[6]

In many of the above-mentioned customs there is clearly brought out the subconscious feeling, so characteristic of the religious relations of man with man in primitive culture, that it is human persons who cause trouble and evil, human agencies that are to be punished or propitiated. In others the fiction of primitive "promiscuity" is exposed; others, again, illustrate the primitive conception of relationship.

[1] *Journ. Anthrop. Inst.* xxii. 119.
[2] *Id.* ii. 179.
[3] *Id.* ii. 429.
[4] Curr, *op. cit.* iii. 596.
[5] Featherman, *op. cit.* ii. 142.
[6] *Id.* ii. 214.

CHAPTER XIII

Sect. 1

At the beginning of the chain of culture appear one or two simple precautionary and educational measures applied to boys and girls on reaching the age of puberty, at our end of the chain are confirmation and a more or less lengthy period of education. In both of these. and in all intermediate stages and developments, the chief ideas behind the ceremonies of so-called "initiation" are concerned with the going-out of childhood and the entering-upon the state of manhood and womanhood. The putting-away of the old life of childhood and sexlessness, and the taking-up of the responsibilities, social and sexual, of the new, and also the education imparted, were often dramatised amongst early peoples by "sympathetic" processes. As noticed before, this kind of rehearsal was meant to ensure the proper performance of the duties represented in the mystery-play. We also find useful instruction given as to the duties of manhood and womanhood, the sexual relation and marriage; girls are entrusted with such feminine lore as the women possess, while the boys are entrusted with the tribal history and secrets by the old men, the repositories of power, and the real and responsible guardians of the State. The excellence not only of the military and political, but also of the moral instruction given at "initiation" has often been remarked.

Leaving this aspect of primitive confirmation, we proceed to examine the dangers spiritual and material, of the old life, which are cast aside, and of the new life, which are to be faced, to both of which the ceremonies at puberty have reference.

To take the case of girls first. There is nothing in the old life that is likely to be dangerous to her, for she will still find her best comfort and companionship with her mother and female friends, but she has to meet the dangers of the other sex, now that she is marriageable. These dangers we have already reviewed; there is the natural timidity, and subconscious physical fear of the male sex, deriving from the natural passivity and functional nervous characteristics of woman, and expressed in that coyness and shrinking, which are so potent a sexual charm; often, however, especially at marriage, and sometimes at child-birth, the latent fear comes out as direct fear of the male sex. We have seen how menstruation is regarded as the result of a supernatural act of violence or rupture of the *hymen*, and here too there is a functional timidity to be reckoned with, as also in the same act at marriage. All these functional ideas focus, as a rule subconsciously, into fear of the other sex, and consciously into vague fear of "spiritual" danger, all originally deriving from the psychological and physical change of the organism at puberty. On the other side, in the male view of female confirmation, there is the usual fear of a taboo state, emphasised here by the fact that it is *the* characteristic female condition, connoting loss of strength and transmitting weakness. In regard to male confirmation, the chief feature is that the old life with the women is given up, but the irony of nature insists that though the man may cast aside his life with women, he must soon return to it, in a more dangerous form. As for the casting-away of the life of the nursery, the Damaras reckon a man's age from his circumcision, not counting the previous years at all.[1] Amongst the Kurnai a part of the initiation is the following ceremony. The mothers stand in a line facing their sons, and each mother and son sprinkle each other with water; this signifies that they are no longer under their mothers' control.[2]

The dangers of this taboo state, that is, the disabilities of the old life and the responsibilities of the new, are neutralised by various means. Tests of endurance are gone through, fasting and purification; candidates are beaten, sometimes to increase their strength, at others to get rid of the dangerous substance of taboo; they are fumigated and purified, secluded and concealed.[3]

More precisely each sex is tabooed to the other, for it is against the dangers of sexual contact that the process is directed. So the maiden at puberty must not see males, or be seen by them, nor have any association with them whatever; first, for her safety, because it is the male sex in the abstract which causes her trouble and danger, and contagion from them is dangerous; secondly, for the safety of men, who by contagion of her accentuated femininity would be injured. In the same way, boys at puberty may not see nor have any association with females; first, for their own safety, because it is the female sex in the abstract which produces these dangers, and contact with

[1] *South African Folklore Journal*, I. 44.
[2] Fison and Howitt, *op. cit.* 197, 198.
[3] See Ploss, *Das Kind*, II. 424 ff.

them is dangerous, causing weakness and effeminacy; and secondly, we may infer that the girls are to be considered, and that when men are attaining their manhood some fear of manly contagion is present to the female mind, as it is at marriage. The Kurnai hold that sickness mutually results if women touch boys who are being initiated.[1] Kaffir girls at puberty are placed in a separate hut, and none but females are allowed to see them.[2] At the ceremony of excision of South Celebes girls no man may be present.[3] When a Cambodian girl enters "the shade," the rules she has to observe in "the shade" are: not to let herself be seen by a strange man; not to look at men, even furtively; not to bathe till night, lest any one should see her, nor alone, but accompanied by her sister. Many kinds of food also are forbidden her.[4] Loango girls at puberty are secluded in a hut in the forest, and no man may go near them. From the first day until they are given in marriage, they are called *nkumbi* (*hymen*). They are instructed in the duties of married life and motherhood.[5] Girls of New Britain, while in the "cages" where they are imprisoned from puberty to marriage, may not be seen by men; so with those of New Ireland. In both New Britain and New Ireland boys at initiation may not be seen by women.[6] The New Hebridean boy at puberty, when he is circumcised and receives a new name, may not see the face of woman.[7] Boys of the Irwin River and Murchison River tribes are separated from the women for several weeks after circumcision. A boy was once killed for being found in a woman's company.[8] In

[1] *Journ. Anthrop. Inst.* xiv. 306.
[2] Maclean, *op. cit.* 101.
[3] Matthes, *op. cit.* 71.
[4] Aymonier, *op. cit.* 193.
[5] Ploss, *op. cit.* ii. 439.
[6] Danks, in *Journ. Anthrop. Inst.* xviii. 284, 287.
[7] *Journ. Anthrop. Inst.* xxiii. 4.
[8] Curr, *op. cit.* i. 369.

New Caledonia no woman may see the boys while recovering from circumcision.[1] Amongst the Masai, Wakamba, Wanika, and Wakikuyu boys are circumcised in bands together; they are carefully kept from the girls and women.[2] Only men may be present at the circumcision of Mandingo boys.[3] At initiation Australian boys may not see women.[4] Ceramese boys at puberty may not be seen by women.[5] Special developments of this have been already noticed, such as the prohibition to look upon the sun or fire.

The boy's renunciation of the old life of the "nursery," woman's life, may be illustrated by the following cases. Boys amongst the Central Australians are called "children," as are girls, until the initiation, which begins between the ages of ten and twelve.[6] Swahili boys leave their mothers' care when circumcised at the age of seven.[7] Songo boys are initiated between the ages of eight to ten. Their mothers may not see them during this period; they are secluded in special huts.[8]

Frequently initiation is put earlier, and very often, as has been observed, the boy begins to go about with his father before the ceremony takes place. As a matter of convenience a boy has often to wait, but there is always to be borne in mind the distinction between the beginning of boyhood and of manhood. A Zuni boy is "initiated" any time after he is four years old. Previously he has been called "baby," now he receives a name. He has a "godfather," who breathes upon a wand, which he then extends to the child's mouth. The initiation is "mainly done by the

[1] Ploss, *op. cit.* i. 360. [2] *Id.* i. 362. [3] *Id.* i. 365.
[4] *Journ. Anthrop. Inst.* xxiv. 181, 183; Eyre, *op. cit.* ii. 333.
[5] Riedel, *op. cit.* 130. [6] Spencer and Gillen, *op. cit.* 215.
[7] Ploss, *op. cit.* i. 361. [8] *Id.* i. 364.

sponsors, and the boy must personally take the vows as soon as he is old enough."[1] Here we have a prototype of our baptism, and the distinction is made, as it often is where circumcision, for instance, takes place at five, six, or seven years of age, between reception into the ranks of boys and of men.

After initiation there is the almost universal rule that boys sleep and mess and live together, most often outside of the family dwelling. This we have already described.

The change of life is marked and assisted by various methods of altering identity, and it is important to notice that personal identity undergoes a very real transformation, physiological and psychical, at puberty. Wanika boys are smeared all over with white earth, so that they cannot be recognised. At the end of the initiation they wash.[2] The name being a universal mark of identity, and often conceived of, on the principles we have described, as a part of the organism, is thus changed at puberty. The new name—sometimes there has not been a previous one—is practically a new life. A Haida youth changes his name four times.[3] In Nias men take a new name at marriage.[4] The Aino receives a new name at puberty.[5] So with the Iroquois.[6] The extinct Tasmanians initiated their boys into the rights and duties of manhood with certain ceremonial forms. A secret name was whispered into the boys' ears at the conclusion of the ceremony.[7] In West and East Australia the boy's new name is whispered to him by the "sponsor."[8] In the Narrinyeri, Dieri, and Port Lincoln tribes boys

[1] *Fifth Report of the Bureau of Ethnology*, 553.
[2] Krapf, *op. cit.* 147.
[3] G. M. Dawson, *Geological Survey of Canada*, 131.
[4] Rosenberg, *op. cit.* 154.
[5] Ploss, *op. cit.* i. 160.
[6] Morgan, *Ancient Society*, 79.
[7] Featherman, *op. cit.* II. 105.
[8] Ploss, *op. cit.* ii. 417.

receive a new name at initiation.[1] So with the Basutos, Nufoers of New Guinea, the Samoyeds, South Americans, New Hebrideans, and the Indians of Nootka.[2] When a Japanese boy reached puberty, a "godfather" cut off his forelock and gave him a new name.[3] Girls in Nias and Sierra Leone receive a new name at puberty.[4] In the Andamans these names for girls are beautifully called "flower names."[5]

Again, there is here practised the common custom of sacrificing a part of the body, by way of ensuring the security of the rest and of assisting, by casting it away, the renunciation of the "old man." Mandan boys have the little finger cut off at puberty "as a sacrifice to their patron deity."[6] Aino boys have their hair cut at puberty;[7] the same is done to Warrau girls; Carib girls have it burnt off. Siamese girls and boys and Hindu boys have their hair cut.[8] The practice of knocking out one or more teeth at initiation has already been referred to. It probably is originally intended to secure the rest of the teeth, in especial reference to the adult's food which is now to be eaten. Sennar boys and girls have a tooth knocked out.[9] The Wakikuyu knock out both front teeth of the bottom row at puberty.[10] The Pepos of Formosa knocked out an eye-tooth of boys "to assist their breathing."[11] At the initiation of Macquarrie boys a tooth is knocked out; if the boy cries, the women taunt him for being a girl.[12] An Australian

[1] *Native Tribes of South Australia*, 51, 268, 224.

[2] Ploss, *op. cit.* ii. 423, 424, 445; *Journ. Anthrop. Inst.* xxiii. 5; R. Andree, *Ethnographische Parallelen*, i. 174.

[3] Ploss, *op. cit.* ii. 436.

[4] *Id. l.c.*; Featherman, *op. cit.* ii. 354.

[5] Man, in *Journ. Anthrop. Inst.* xii. 128.

[6] Featherman, *op. cit.* iii. 301; Ploss, *op. cit.* ii. 431.

[7] Ploss, *op. cit.* ii. 436.

[8] *Id.* ii. 435, 426.

[9] *Id.* ii. 437.

[10] *Id.* i. 306.

[11] *Id.* i. 306, ii. 424.

[12] *Id.* ii. 416.

boy, after having had two teeth knocked out, is told that no one may see him, nor must he see any one, "else his mouth will close up and he will die of hunger."[1] Here, and in the Formosan case, we may see a further reason for the practice, that is, to facilitate eating. Probably this is an essential part of the reason, as with the practice of filing the teeth at puberty, the East Indian parallel of the Australian custom.[2] In Ceram after the filing of the teeth all kinds of food are given to the child.[3] In the Goulbourn tribe, near Melbourne, two teeth are struck out and are given to the boy's mother, who places them on the highest bough of a young gum tree.[4] Here, lastly, we have a secondary result of the custom; the tooth, being a part of the personality, is instinct with the boy's life, and may be used as a sort of external soul.

As the initiation of boys removes them from the effeminate and weakening sphere of woman's life, so it also provides for a renewal of strength. The great ceremony of *Engwura* is supposed by the Central Australians to have the effect of strengthening all who pass through it. Shortly after the beginning of the performances, which sometimes last from September to January, the men are separated from the women until the end.[5] The boys are told during initiation that the ceremony will promote their growth to manhood, and they are also told by tribal fathers and elder brothers that in future they must not play with the women and girls, nor must they camp with them as hitherto. They have up to now gone out with the

[1] Ploss, *op. cit.* ii. 418.

[2] Riedel, *op. cit.* 228, 437; Skeat, *op. cit.* 359.

[3] Riedel, *op. cit.* 137.

[4] Ploss, *op. cit.* ii. 417.

[5] Spencer and Gillen, *op. cit.* 271-74.

women hunting for food, now they begin to accompany the men.[1]

We have seen how a man's strength can be transmitted to another by contact. This is the object of the following customs. The first ceremony of the initiation of boys in the Adelaide tribes is the covering them with blood drawn from a man's arm.[2] In Western and Eastern Australia the "sponsor" opens a vein in his arm, which the boy sucks, and the blood is also dripped upon the boy's back.[3] So in many other tribes of Australia, as the Dieri, men are bled and the blood is allowed to stream over the boy; "it gives him courage."[4] On the same principle the young Masai for some time after initiation, eats nothing but beef and drinks nothing but blood and milk. The initiate become the warriors, and the whole system is very like the training of young knights in mediæval Europe.[5]

"Man's meat" and the food of adults is naturally tabooed till maturity is reached. Andamanese boys and girls have a long list of foods they may not eat until initiated. The taboo on each food is taken off ceremonially. For instance, the "pig taboo" is taken off by pressing a pig on to the boy's body "in token of his becoming strong and brave." The "honey taboo" with girls is not removed till after the birth of the first child. The turtle "taboo" is thus removed; the chief boils turtle fat, and when cool pours it over the boy's head and body, and rubs it into him. He is then fed with turtle and nothing else for three days.[6]

The common rule of fasting at puberty is to prevent dangerous influences entering the system with food. It

[1] Spencer and Gillen, *op. cit.* 216. [2] Eyre, *op. cit.* ii. 333. [3] Ploss, *op. cit.* ii. 417.
[4] *Id.* ii. 421; *Journ. Anthrop. Inst.* xx. 82. [5] Thomson, *op. cit.* 187.
[6] Man, in *Journ. Anthrop. Inst.* xii. 134, 130.

also prepares for the reception of the new food. A frequent concomitant of fasting is the taboo against eating with other persons. Thus, during the initiation of Kaffir boys no one is allowed to eat with them.[1] Boys or girls at puberty must fast amongst the Guayquiris, Uaupés, Passés, Mandans, Andamanese, Tobas, Mataguayos, Chiriguanos, and Australians.[2]

Again, the ideas of sexual taboo regulate the diet; the most common prohibition is, of course, against eating with the other sex, for fear of contagion. The idea is extended thus. Women and children of the Powell's Creek tribe may not eat bandicoot, snake, or iguana;[3] the reason for the two former being doubtless that they are connected with the origin of menstruation. For boys, women's food, either what they have touched, or simply the species used for women's diet, is often tabooed, for feminine weakness would be transmitted by eating them. None but women and boys not grown up are allowed by the Dyaks to eat venison, the deer being a timid animal.[4] Amongst the Central Australians a boy not circumcised may not eat large lizards, nor may women ever do so, else they will have an abnormal craving for sexual intercourse.[5] In New South Wales a boy at initiation may not eat the emu, this being "the woman"; and he may not even look at a woman; and for some time must cover his mouth with his rug when a woman is near. The forbidden food is finally allowed to him, by giving him some to eat, or rubbing him with its fat.[6] This introduction to the forbidden food is a regular part of the ceremonies

[1] Maclean, *op. cit.* 98.

[2] Ploss, *op. cit.* ii. 429, 431, 427; Eyre, *op. cit.* ii. 293, 294.

[3] *Journ. Anthrop. Inst.* xxiv. 179.

[4] Low, *op. cit.* 266.

[5] Spencer and Gillen, *op. cit.* 471, 473.

[6] *Journ. Anthrop. Inst.* xiii. 455.

which end "initiation"; and it is to be observed how youths are inoculated against the dangers even of eating with women and of eating women's food.

Another method of emphasising the newness of life is that the boy receives an external soul in various forms, a tutelar divinity, or guardian angel; this is perhaps connected with the idea that the soul may escape in the act of union with women, as it is undoubtedly based on a psychological characteristic of puberty, that desire for the new and the strange, that romantic aspiration after ideals and guiding-stars, which is part of the blossoming of love, and has such an important connection with religion. It is here, indeed, that the psychological dependence of the religious faculty on the sexual first appears. Thus, the Iroquois boy fasted, until he dreamt of the spirit that was to be his good angel. The figure in which he appeared was tattooed upon the body of the boy, and rules were to be observed in order to obtain the favour and avoid the displeasure of the tutelar spirit.[1] The North Carolina boy at puberty looked for a tutelar spirit in his dreams. Anything that struck him particularly was chosen. He took his name from it.[2] The young Chippeway at puberty fasts and watches, in order to find his guardian *manitou*.[3] The Salish boy at puberty went into the forest, where he remained secluded, until some animal, bird or fish, appeared to him in a dream. This became his tutelary deity, and a claw, feather, or tooth of such was used as a protecting talisman.[4] In many of these cases there is found, as Dr. Frazer has pointed out,[5] the idea that the boy receives into himself the divine person. But this is a form of new life, and it thus correlates with

[1] Featherman, *op. cit.* iii. 42.
[2] Ploss, *op. cit.* ii. 431.
[3] Featherman, *op. cit.* iii. 260.
[4] *Id.* iii. 368.
[5] Frazer, *op. cit.*[2] iii. 422.

the idea of obtaining new life and strength by new food and similar methods. Thus, in the Arunta tribe, while circumcision is being performed, bullroarers are continuously sounded, so as to be easily heard by the women and children. By them it is supposed that the roaring is the voice of the great spirit *Twanyirika*, who has come to take the boy away. This spirit only appears when a boy is initiated. He enters his body after the operation, and leaves him after his seclusion. The same belief is found in most Australian tribes.[1] The Arunta explanation of impregnation is that an ancestor is re-incarnated in the form of a "spirit child," who enters a woman; when this takes place a *churinga* (a sacred object identical with the bullroarer used at initiation by most Australians) is found at the place. Each *churinga*—the tribe possesses a collection—is identified with an ancestor. Messrs. Spencer and Gillen infer that they are a modification of the common idea of the "external soul," by which the man's life is secured by being hidden away in a material object. The Kurnai identify the bullroarer used at initiation with a great ancestor, *Turndun*. When the old men reveal these objects to the boys, they say "we will show you your grandfather."[2] Considerable mystery is attached by the Arunta to their sacred objects, *churinga*, "a mystery which," say Messrs. Spencer and Gillen, "has probably had a large part of its origin in the desire of the men to impress the women of the tribe with an idea of the supremacy and superior power of the male sex." "The *churinga* is supposed to endow the possessor with courage and accuracy of aim, and also to deprive his opponent of these qualities. So firm is their belief in this that if two men were fighting

[1] Spencer and Gillen, *op. cit.* 246.

[2] Fison and Howitt, *op. cit.* 198.

and one of them knew that the other carried a *churinga* while he did not, he would certainly lose heart at once and without doubt be beaten."[1] Now amongst the Australians of the Arunta and neighbouring tribes, and the Yaroinga tribe, a man can charm a woman to love him, and a woman can do the same to a man, by making a noise with a bullroarer. The humming seems to be a sort of spiritual invitation; the belief, at least, is that the man or woman thus charmed, immediately comes to the person using the charm. This is actually a marriage ceremony.[2] We may suppose, then, that the use of the bullroarer at initiation is concerned with this new life in its sexual aspect, and that sexual strength for procreation is imparted by the ancestral spirits. The suggestion is corroborated by the Dieri custom and belief. A bullroarer is given to each boy at puberty. If a woman were to see it, the people would have no snakes or lizards. The boy on receiving it "becomes inspired by *Murauma*, who makes the noise, and it causes a supply of snakes."[3] The connection of the serpent and the male organ seems thus to explain the well-known initiation custom of the use of the bullroarer.

Initiation makes men and women, and prepares boys and girls for the responsibilities of contact with the other sex. The two quotations which follow illustrate this. In South Australia a stupid old man whom the natives have not deemed worthy "of receiving the honours of their ceremonies" was still called a boy.[4] In Australia universal law forbids a man to marry until after the ceremonies are performed by which the status

[1] Fison and Howitt, *op. cit.* 137, 130.
[2] *Id.* 541, 542, 545; W. E. Roth, *Aborigines of North-West Central Queensland*, 162.
[3] Howitt, in *Journ. Anthrop. Inst.* xx. 83.
[4] Eyre, *op. cit.* ii. 201.

of young men is reached.[1] Instruction in future duties is often imparted; thus Swahili girls at puberty are instructed in matters relating to sex.[2] Apache girls on arriving at a marriageable age were instructed by the chief in the duties and responsibilities of married life.[3]

But there are other methods of preparing each sex for their mutual relations. The artificial rupture of the *hymen* sometimes takes place in infancy, but generally at puberty.[4] The reason for this we have already given; the idea of a possible impediment is associated by the savage with certain physical peculiarities, such as the *hymen*. By removing this, both physical difficulties are removed, and the spiritual dangers that arise from the contemplation of the physical fact are also obviated. Fears of female contamination and of the performance for the first time of dangerous acts are also thus removed, and the material property of taboo which emanates from such is taken off by handselling. It is often combined, as in Australia, with a ceremonial act of intercourse which has the same object of preparing the woman for married life by removing imaginary dangers.[5]

Other peoples satisfy these fears by a "rehearsal" of the act, for the safety both of the male and of the female. At the puberty ceremonies performed on girls in Ceram no man may enter the house. One of the old women takes a leaf, and ceremonially perforates it with her finger, as a symbol of the perforation of the *hymen*. After the ceremony the girl has free liberty of intercourse with men; in some villages old men have access to her the same evening.[6] Amongst the Galelas

[1] Curr, *op. cit.* i. 106. [2] Ploss, *op. cit.* ii. 437. [3] Featherman, *op. cit.* iii. 190.

[4] *Journ. Anthrop. Inst.* xxiv. 168, 169 (Australian tribes).

[5] Spencer and Gillen, *op. cit.* 93 ff.; Ploss, *op. cit.* i. 376.

[6] Riedel, *op. cit.* 138.

and Tobelorese of Halmahera, boys are initiated at puberty in the festival *oi osi* (G.) *imalauhu* or *mahoiki* (T.). A number are brought into a large shed, in which are two tables, one for the men and one for the women, who must be separated while eating. An old man solemnly rubs a piece of wood, which makes water red, into a vessel of water, imitating while doing this, the act of *coitus*. This is done for each boy, whose name is called out. The red water represents the blood which results from the perforation of the *hymen*. The faces and bodies of the boys are smeared with this red water. Red is regarded as the colour of life and well-being. The boys then go to the woods, where they must expose themselves to the sun as much as possible.[1] The second feature of this Halmahera ceremony leads us to a further point. The religious importance of women's blood has been described by Dr. Frazer. The object of smearing the boys with the red water, symbolical of the blood shed at the perforation of the hymen, is to secure them from the harm, which the ideas treated of in this book explain, that may arise from sexual intercourse. The method is the familiar one of "inoculation." External application is a method of transmission, as we have seen, and sympathetic inoculation is a form of this. There is also to be observed the injunction that the boys must expose themselves to the sun. This fact taken in conjunction with the sun-taboo common at puberty, goes to show the origin of this idea, namely, that heat, natural or artificial, is a concomitant of sexual desire. The connection between fire and sex is also emphasised by the similarity in colour of fire and blood, and by the combination in one

[1] Riedel, in *Zeitschrift für Ethnologie*, xvii. 81, 82.

ceremony of painting the body red and exposure to the sun.

This "sympathetic" rehearsal is obviously intended to "initiate" the youths into the mystery of sexual union, and also to neutralise its dangers. I cannot see in the Halmahera custom any trace of a symbolical pretence of begetting them anew, as Dr. Frazer thinks is the meaning.[1]

The origin of circumcision has been already suggested. There is also often to be traced the idea that, by removing a part of the organism, dangerous and in danger as it is, these dangers are neutralised; this passes later into the notion that thus its "impurity" is removed, and the sexual act made less gross. A common practice, corresponding to circumcision of males, is the "excision" of girls at puberty, as amongst the Amakosa and Loanda tribes, the Masai and Wakuasi,[2] and the same idea is doubtless the origin of the practice.

There is next to be noticed in a remarkable set of customs a practice which also shows the object of these precautions; this is, in its simpler form, the introduction of the "initiate" to the opposite sex; in its completer form, there is sexual or other intercourse. The idea is of the same nature as that of "inoculation," as seen in the Halmahera custom, and is parallel to a "trial" of sexual relations. Now that the individual is prepared to meet the complementary sex, he must do so; for, however strong sexual taboo may be, men and women must meet, in marriage at least; and thus the two sexes make "trial" of each other, as if the preparation necessitated putting it to the test; and thereby each sex is practically "inoculated" against the other,

[1] Frazer, op. cit.[2] iii. 441.

[2] Ploss, op. cit. i. 384.

by being "inoculated" with each other, in view of the more permanent alliance of wedlock. We saw this practice followed in Australia after the ceremonial rupture of the *hymen*. So, immediately after circumcision, a Ceramese boy must have intercourse with some girl, it matters not with whom, "by way of curing the wound." This is continued till the blood ceases to flow.[1] In certain tribes of Central Africa both boys and girls after initiation must as soon as possible have intercourse, the belief being that if they do not they will die.[2] Narrinyeri boys during initiation after the preliminary rites had complete licence as regards unmarried females, not only such as they might lawfully marry, but even those of their own clan and totem.[3] After the seclusion of a Kaffir girl at puberty, she is allowed to cohabit with any one during a festal period which follows; and Kaffir boys after being circumcised are allowed to seize any unmarried women they please, and have connection with them.[4] A similar custom is found on the Congo.[5] The Muhammadan negroes of the Senegal are circumcised at fourteen. They are looked after for a month, during which time they walk about in a procession. "They may commit during this period any violence against girls, except rape and murder." After the month is up, they are men.[6] A Zulu girl at puberty goes through a ceremonial process. Secluded in a special hut, she is attended by twelve or fourteen girls. "No married man may come near the dwelling, and should any one do so he is beaten away by the girls, who attack him most viciously with sticks and stones. During her seclusion the neophyte must

[1] J. G. F. Riedel, *De sluik- en kroesharige rassen tusschen Selebes en Papua*, 139.

[2] Macdonald, *Africana*, i. 126.

[3] Howitt, in *Journ. Anthrop. Inst.* xii. 37.

[4] Maclean, *op. cit.* 102, 98.

[5] *Journ. Anthrop. Inst.* xxi. 100.

[6] Reade, *op. cit.* 451.

on no account see or address any man, married or unmarried." At the end of the period a number of girls and unmarried men have intercourse in the hut. After a further period of seclusion the girl bathes and is "clean," and after the perforation of the *hymen* by two old women, she is a woman.[1] After initiation to the warrior's set, *El-Moran*, the Masai young men associated freely with girls; in fact each *El-Moran* had a lady who went about with him, and the practice was very similar to that known in the Europe of Chivalry,—the girl, for instance, puts on the warrior's armour for him.[2]

The introduction to adults' food contains the same idea, and often is "inoculation" against contagion of women's food and eating with women. Before their initiation Halmaherese boys may not eat *pisang* or fowls. At the end of the initiation feast women give to the boys *pisang* and fowl's flesh to eat.[3] The idea was illustrated in connection with the removal of food-taboos at puberty.

The idea also assumes other forms in which we see both the savage impulse towards "make-believe," and the recognition that certain characteristics of puberty and puberty ceremonies alike have relation to sexual complementary function, a recognition developed, as so often by sexual taboo, into sexual antagonism. This sexual hostility appeared in some of the last few examples. Bamangwato girls at puberty go about in bands, and beat boys of their age with whips. The latter are not considered men until they have endured this ordeal without flinching. The girls also in their

[1] Macdonald, in *Journ. Anthrop. Inst.* xx. 117, 118.
[2] Thomson, *op. cit.* 187.
[3] J. G. F. Riedel, in *Zeitschrift für Ethnologie*, xvii. 82.

turn have to endure certain ill-usage from the boys.[1] This is also done by proxy. At the feast to celebrate the puberty of a Mura boy men and women beat each other with whips until the blood comes. It is an "act of love."[2] As often in such cases, especially when general licence takes place, the sympathy of others is shown in the most practical way. What is in effect the last phase of the *Engwura*, or final initiation ceremony of the Arunta, is a dance performed by young women, by way of invitation to men; and "at this period of the ceremonies a general interchange and also a lending of women takes place, and visiting natives are provided with temporary wives." This woman's dance goes on every night for two or three weeks.[3] Here we can see "sympathy" at work, and the union of society effected, not by "promiscuity," but by a sacred exchange, which assists the future union of the young people. This sexual sympathy passing into antagonism is sometimes fulfilled by one sex assuming the apparel of the other. Amongst the Basutos the initiation both of youths and girls at puberty was called *pollo*. It was not held at the same time for both sexes. The ceremony was incumbent upon every member of the community at the proper age. All who passed through it together, formed "a guild of friends." The candidates went out into the country—here we speak of the boys' *pollo*—and no woman dared come near them. Their food was prepared by the men in charge, who instructed them in male duties, and put them through tests of endurance. They were circumcised, and after the operation wore aprons for three months. The girls likewise were taken

[1] Ploss, *op. cit.* i. 381, 382.

[2] *Id.* ii. 427.

[3] Spencer and Gillen, *op. cit.* 381.

into the country, and were instructed by the women in female duties. They were smeared with ashes. No male might come near them. "The women folk acted like mad people during this time; they went about performing curious mummeries, wearing men's clothes, and carrying weapons, and were very saucy to men they met."[1] At the second initiation ceremony of the Arunta there are women who dance, carrying shields (the men's property); shields are never carried by women except on this occasion.[2]

Lastly, as the ceremonies of initiation prepare the two sexes for contact with each other, and are followed by introduction and intercourse, the practice is, so far, a preliminary marriage ceremony, in which a boy or girl is married to the other sex *in extenso*; more than this, however, is often the case, and "initiation" is actually marriage. Savage women, and to some extent men also, are marriageable and married at puberty, and the combination of ceremonies is a natural one. The ideas of sexual taboo, I take it, have caused the deferring of marriage to a later date. There are several examples which show the link between initiation ceremonies and marriage, which it is hardly necessary to quote. For instance Loanda girls eight days before marriage are excised by a medicine-man.[3] Amongst the Central Australian tribes the ceremony performed on girls at puberty is actually their marriage rite, though as Messrs. Spencer and Gillen point out, it serves as an initiation for the girls.[4] For the boys the initiation means more than this, but it also includes a reference to marriage; for instance after the first of

[1] Bodemann, in *Zeitschrift für Ethnologie* for 1874, 37 ff.
[2] Spencer and Gillen, *op. cit.* 220.
[3] Ploss, *op. cit.* i. 384.
[4] Spencer and Gillen, *op. cit.* 93.

the initiatory ceremonies the boy is painted by the man who is *Umbirna* to him, *i.e.* brother of the woman he may marry. Also the woman who will be the boy's mother-in-law, runs off with him, but the men bring him back again.[1] Amongst the Kamilaroi the novice is taken from the women by the men of that "clan" to which belong the women he may select his wife from. Each novice has a "guardian" of that clan.[2]

Sect. 2

In primitive society the young man and maiden are required to avoid each other from their engagement until marriage. This taboo is a repetition for two particular individuals of the taboo at puberty between the two sexes generally. The principle here also is to prevent all intercouse until the particular ceremonies which obviate the dangers of the new relation, mutual "contagion" between two particular persons, have been performed, and to prepare them for these and for the new state of life,—the taboo of avoidance being thought to be in itself some guarantee of future safety. The dangers are those of sexual taboo, here naturally emphasised, for the two sexes are now to meet; they coincide, as they are in origin connected, with that mutual diffidence arising from complementary sexual difference and accentuated at the awakening of love,—the shyness of sex. The young people are about to enter upon a critical state, that of living in more or less close contact with each other, and as that state derives its dangers from their reciprocal influence, a taboo is set between them until it is removed by the

[1] Spencer and Gillen, *op. cit.* 215, 443. [2] *Journ. Anthrop. Inst.* xxiv. 420.

ceremony which unites them while rendering them mutually innocuous.

The practice naturally coincides with the desire of parents to keep the couple waiting till arrangements are completed, and to prevent union until they are bound together, such premature union being thought especially dangerous, and in later culture sinful, while in all stages it leaves repudiation open to the man with consequent injury to the woman. Amongst the Nickol Bay natives girls promised in marriage are not allowed to speak to their future husbands, and are said to be *torka* to them.[1] So in the Newcastle tribe, when an old man promises a young friend that he shall have his wife after his death, the husband-expectant is forbidden to speak to his future wife or sit in a hut in which she is.[2] After betrothal in Nias, Borneo, and the Watubella Islands, no communication between the pair is allowed till the wedding.[3] In Buru, Ceram, and Luang Sermata, a youth when engaged may not go near his *fiancée*, look at her, or speak to her.[4] In Abyssinia during the time of betrothal, generally three or four months, the girl is strictly confined to the house. Intercourse with her friends is not interrupted, but she remains entirely invisible to the young man, who meanwhile frequently visits her father.[5] The lover in South Arabia sends his father or some near relative to ask for the lady's hand, and from the moment the proposal is accepted the girl can no longer go abroad unveiled, and she and her betrothed are no longer permitted to visit or to have any other personal relations with one another.[6] Amongst the Dorahs children are betrothed

[1] Curr, *op. cit.* i. 298.

[2] *Id.* i. 324.

[3] Rosenberg, *Het eiland Nias*, 38; Perelaer, *op. cit.* 50; Riedel, *De sluik- en kroesharige rassen tusschen Selebes en Papua*, 205.

[4] *Id.* 21, 134, 324.

[5] Featherman, *op. cit.* v. 604.

[6] *Id.* v. 421.

at an early age, and part of the "purchase-money" is paid then. Henceforth all intercourse between the two families is interrupted, and they are prohibited from speaking to one another, and the bride and bridegroom are not allowed to see each other, or even pronounce each other's name. Similarly amongst the Ayamboris of New Guinea.[1] Elsewhere in New Guinea betrothed persons may not see each other. Should they meet on the road, the girl must hide behind a tree until the young man has passed.[2] Amongst the Lampongs and Menangkabauers of Sumatra no communication is allowed between betrothal and marriage.[3] "The Malay *fiancée*, unlike her European sister, is at the utmost pains to keep out of her lover's way, and to attain this object she is said to be as watchful as a tiger."[4] The Wataveta bridegroom pays the "bride-price" in bullocks, sometimes by instalments. After one payment the bride is "sealed" to him. She is not allowed to go out of the house, and may on no account see a man, not even her betrothed. If the latter is poor, the engagement may last, as it often does in civilised races, for years.[5] Amongst the Jews of Morocco the pair never see each other from the engagement to the marriage.[6]

It is a curious fact, which will later be shown to have considerable importance, that the taboo between engaged couples reproduces the common taboo between a brother and sister; in other words, their state is a re-presentation of life in the family, where sister and brother are kept apart, and the "sanctity" of the home, in the primitive sense, is preserved by the mother on the principles of sexual taboo.

[1] Featherman, *op. cit.* ii. 33, 383.

[2] *Zeitschrift für Ethnologie*, viii. 180.

[3] Horst, in *De Indische Gids* (1880), 978; Van Hasselt, *Volksbeschrijving Midden-Sumatra's*, 275.

[4] Skeat, *op. cit.* 366.

[5] Thomson, *op. cit.* 61.

[6] Leared, *op. cit.* 34.

Lastly, these principles also supply the reason why betrothal is generally carried out by proxies, and why sometimes a man does not even woo his lady-love in person. Thus amongst the Kaffirs, when the suitor calls to make the acquaintance of the girl, the latter speaks to him through her brother, for she will not speak to him direct.[1] Amongst the Yao and allied tribes there is an institution which we might call "surety" or "god-parent." Every girl has a surety; and when her hand is sought in marriage it is this official who is approached and not her parents. He makes the necessary arrangements and sees what provision is to be made for her and her children, and also in the event of her being sent away without just cause, he interferes, and generally redresses her wrongs.[2] "Representatives" of the Malay suitor visit the girl's parents to perform the betrothal. After matters are arranged, one of these presents some *betel*, brought for the purpose, to the people of the house, saying "This is a pledge of your daughter's betrothal." The father replies: "Be it so, I accept it."[3] Sometimes the mothers perform this office; amongst the Iroquois the young girl was led by her mother to the bridegroom's lodge, and on entering she presented to her mother-in-law a few cakes of maize. The mother of the groom returned the compliment by offering some venison to the bride's mother. "This interchange of bread and meat gave final sanction to the marriage, and the young couple were now looked upon as man and wife."[4]

[1] Shooter, *op. cit.* 56.

[2] *Journ. Anthrop. Inst.* xxii. 118.

[3] Skeat, *op. cit.* 385.

[4] Featherman, *op. cit.* iii. 28.

CHAPTER XIV

FEW peoples, if any, of those known to us, are without some marriage ceremony. As to those who are said to possess none, it will generally be found that there is some act performed which is too slight or too practical to be marked by an observer as a "ceremony," but which when analysed turns out to be a real marriage rite. Two common modes of marriage amongst the Arunta and other Central Australian tribes illustrate this, and also go to prove the correctness of the view here put forward, that marriage rites of union are essentially identical with love-charms, and that other marriage rites coincide with precautions taken to lessen the dangers of contact between the sexes, not only in ordinary life, but at the critical stage of puberty. A man or woman in the Arunta tribe can charm a person of the other sex to love, by making music with a bull-roarer. If he or she soon comes to the musician, the marriage is thereby complete.[1] This method is a love-charm in the Yaroinga tribe.[2] The other method is the perforation of the *hymen*, at once an initiatory and a marriage ceremony.[3] In fact, the mere act of union is potentially a marriage ceremony of the sacramental kind, and as the ideas of contact develop directly from physiological functions, one may even credit the earliest

[1] Spencer and Gillen, *op. cit.* 541, 542.

[2] Roth, *op. cit.* 182.

[3] Spencer and Gillen, *op. cit.* 93 ff.

animistic men with some such vague conception before any ceremony became crystallised.

Marriage being the permanent living-together of a man and woman, what is the essence of a marriage ceremony? It is the "joining together" of a man and a woman, in the words of our English Service "for this cause shall a man leave his father and mother and shall be joined unto his wife; and they two shall be one flesh." At the other side of the world, amongst the Orang Benuas, these words are pronounced by an elder, when a marriage is solemnised: "Listen all ye that are present; those that were distant are now brought together; those that were separated are now united."[1] Marriage ceremonies in all stages of culture may be called religious with as much propriety as any ceremony whatever; but this religious character in most cases, and practically always except in the highest stages, concerns the human relations of the human pair. I have shown above how in primitive thought human relations contain the essentials of a religious character. I need not recapitulate here the principles of human relations as expressed in ideas of contact, or their application to relations between the two sexes. Before marriage, and in many cases also after marriage, the sexes are separated by these ideas of sexual taboo; at marriage, they are joined together by the same ideas, worked out, in the most important set of rites, to their logical conclusion in reciprocity of relations. Those who were separated are now joined together, those who were mutually taboo, now break the taboo. In the higher stages the ceremony lifts the union into the ideal plane, as, for instance, symbolising the mystic union of Christ and His Church; or, as in Brahmin

[1] Newbold, *British Settlements in Malacca*, ii. 407.

marriages, where the bridegroom says to the bride, "I am the sky, thou art the earth; come let us marry," words referring to "the two great parents of the Aryan race, as the Rig-Veda calls them, *Dyaushpitar* and *Prthivi matar*.[1] It is also unnecessary to recapitulate the various dangers which have been shown responsible for the taboo between the sexes and the various sexual properties of which the contagion is feared, all of which lead to the implicit idea that not only all contact of man and woman, but the state of marriage itself, is harmful and later, sinful, in fact theoretically forbidden. Hence the conception that marriage ceremonies "prevent" this danger and this sin. It is sufficient merely to state that the ceremonies of marriage are intended to neutralise these dangers and to make the union safe, prosperous, and happy. With this is connected the wish to bind the one to the other, so as to prevent, if possible, later repudiation. This, by the way, is exactly the idea held by the average man still. I may also point out here that the object of marriage ceremonies is not and never was, to join together the man or the woman, as the case may be, with "the life, or blood, or flesh of the *tribe*." There is no trace of this sentimental socialism in primitive society, though there are facts which look like it, no more than there is or ever was a community of wives; marriage is between individuals and is an individualistic act. The mere existence of the egoistic impulse, not to be casually identified with jealousy, is enough to discredit the suggestion; and the tendency of society from primitive animalism upwards has been from individualism to socialism. It is a perversion of history and of psychology as well, to make man more communistic the more

[1] Tylor, *Primitive Culture*,[3] i. 327.

primitive he is. There may be a few isolated cases in peoples whose tribal solidarity has become pronounced, where the later legal notion has arisen, but since in nearly all such cases, marriage is allowed within the tribe (exogamy nearly always sanctioning cousin-marriage), there can be no original intention of making tribe-fellows of two persons who are already tribe-fellows. Nor did any man ever yet marry a tribe, although in the humorous side of life, relatives are sometimes found to act as if he did; no man ever yet felt the tribal blood surge through his veins as he drank wine with his wife in the marriage ceremony. True, a new relationship is formed, a new member enters the family or tribe (rarely the latter), but this idea is secondary, and does not touch the marriage ceremony except in a few cases as referred to, in which it is very probable that the report is half inference, in any case it is a pseudo-scientific piece of myth-making, whether on the part of observer or native informant. The Church in her marriage service shows more insight than many ethnologists, when she repeats the words "for this cause shall a man leave his father and mother and shall be joined unto his wife, and they two shall be one flesh." The word "flesh," by the way, does not by any means refer to kinship or tribal union, as who should say in late human parlance "one blood." Even in the Hebrew the individual meaning is the primary one. This is also recognised by our Service; "So ought men to love their wives, as their own bodies. He that loveth his wife loveth himself, for no man ever yet hated his own flesh." Lastly, is it fear of the tribe that makes a maid veil her face before her intended husband, or a bridegroom dress up as a woman? The inadequacy of the theory is evident in every kind of marriage rite. We shall recur to this when discussing "group-marriage" and relationships.

Marriage ceremonies neutralise the dangers attaching to union between the sexes, in all the complex meaning of those dangers. The ritual may be divided into two classes, corresponding to the two divisions of ideas concerning contact, those namely that obviate or neutralise the dangers of taboo (1) by one or more of the simple methods, (2) by one or more of the double or complex methods, typified by *ngia ngiampe* or mutual inoculation. The first breaks taboo by removing or neutralising the taboo property, the second breaks taboo between two persons by breaking it, *i.e.* by assimilating the two persons, inoculating them with each other, the principle coinciding with that of union. Marriage sums up all the principles and practice of sexual taboo, as any close union between any two persons sums up those of social taboo, and in the details it will frequently be obvious how some ceremony answers to some taboo, as a positive to a negative.

Lastly, when we find only one or two sorts of ceremonies referring directly to sexual intercourse, while the others refer to ordinary contact, with special reference to eating together, and generally to the state of living together in contact, we need not refer marriage ceremonies generally to fear of danger from sexual intercourse alone, or from female periodicity; these take their place as parts of the whole, as they do in sexual taboo.

It is interesting to note the materialistic power attached to the marriage rite, as shown, for instance, in Burmah. It is believed in that country that when a wife dies in child-bed she becomes a maleficent demon. Accordingly, when a wife does die thus, the husband at once gets a divorce.[1] In Java if a man wishes to be divorced, the priest cuts the "marriage-cord" before witnesses, and this simple act severs the nuptial tie.[2] We may also note that with many peoples, and the fact is instructive, there is less ceremonial when a widow is married.[3] In cases where the "paternal system" is followed, there should on the tribal theory of marriage, be no ceremony at all when a widow is married, because she has already the life of the tribe flowing in her veins; but there is some ceremony. It is reduced precisely because she has been through the same thing before, and is therefore less in danger from men and less dangerous. She has been handselled.

For practical purposes, as is hardly necessary to premise, the complex fears of men and women are often subconscious, or are only expressed as a feeling of diffidence with regard to the novel proceedings, and also are not always focussed on the personality of either party with its inherent dangerous properties nor stimulated by conscious realisation of particular dangers. Potentially the consciousness has knowledge of all the principles, and cross-examination might elicit most, but actually the fears are vague, they are fears of vague strangeness and danger. We have, however, seen cases where the individual in marriage is consciously aware that it is his human partner who is to be feared, and others will occur as we proceed. Amongst the Mordvins, as the bridegroom's party sets out for the house of the bride, the "best man" marches thrice round the party with a drawn sword or scythe, imprecating curses upon ill-wishers. In Nizhegorod the "best man" walks thrice round the party, against the sun, holding an

[1] D'Urville, *op. cit.* i. 173. [2] Featherman, *op. cit.* ii. 383.

[3] Skeat, *op. cit.* 382; *Journ. Anthrop. Inst.* xxiv. 11; Lane, *op. cit.* i. 195.

eikon. Then he places himself in front of them, and scratches the ground with a knife, cursing evil spirits and evilly disposed persons.[1] In the county of Durham men with guns used to escort the bridal party to church. The guns were fired at intervals over the heads of the bride and bridesmaids. In Cleveland guns were fired over the heads of the newly married pair all the way from church.[2] In China it was supposed that when a new bride in her chair passed a certain place, evil spirits would approach and injure her, causing her to be ill; hence the figure of a great magician (a Taoist priest) riding a tiger, and brandishing a sword, was painted in front.[3] In Manchuria, when the bridal sedan-chair arrives at the bridegroom's house, the door is shut and crackers are fired to keep off "evil spirits."[4] Again, in South Arabia the bride goes in procession to the bridegroom's dwelling, her turban ornamented in front with a bouquet of garlic as a protection against the "evil eye."[5] In Manchuria the bride is taken in procession to the bridegroom's house. Two men run in front, each holding a red cloth, by which it is intended to ward off evil influences;[6] an excellent application of the man with the red flag. Also the sedan-chair in which she goes to the bridegroom's house is "disinfected" with incense, to drive away evil spirits, and in it is put a calendar containing names of idols who control the demoniacal hosts. Again, before a bride is taken out of her sedan-chair, on arriving at the bridegroom's house, he fires three arrows at the blinds.[7] Amongst the Bechuanas the bridegroom throws an arrow into the hut before he enters to take his bride.[8]

[1] *Folklore*, i. 445.

[2] W. Henderson, *Folklore of the Northern Counties*, 38.

[3] Doolittle, *op. cit.* i. 95.

[4] *Folklore*, i. 487.

[5] Featherman, *op. cit.* v. 422.

[6] *Folklore*, *l.c.*

[7] *Id. l.c.*

[8] *Journ. Anthrop. Inst.* xvi. 83.

So the Andamanese bridegroom when introduced to his bride has some arrows put in his hand.[1] Amongst the Bheels and Bheelalahs the groom touches the "marriage-shed" with a sword.[2] Thus is to be explained, and not as a survival of "marriage by capture," the old Roman custom, in which the bridegroom combed the bride's hair with a spear, the *cælibaris hasta*.[3]

The practice of throwing rice originated in the idea of giving food to the evil influences to induce them to be propitious and depart, but in many cases it seems to have developed into a sympathetic method of securing fertility, and on the other hand is regarded by some peoples as an inducement to the soul to stay. In Celebes, for instance, there is a belief that the bridegroom's soul is apt to fly away at marriage, and rice is therefore scattered over him to induce it to remain.[4] Flour and sweetmeats similarly in old Greek custom were poured over the new bridegroom.[5] Where, as often in folk-custom, such things are flung about among the onlookers, the idea was originally of the type first described. The nuts used thus at old Roman weddings are a well-known instance.[6]

A common class of preliminary ceremonial includes various kinds of lustration or purification, the inner meaning of which is to neutralise the mutual dangers of contact. Before the wedding the bridegroom in South Celebes bathes in holy water. The bride is also fumigated.[7] Shortly before the wedding day the Abyssinian girl has a thorough ablution and her diet is restricted.[8] When the Matabele bride arrives at the

[1] Featherman, *op. cit.* ii. 232.
[2] *Journ. Anthrop. Inst.* ix. 404.
[3] Festus, 44; Plutarch, *Quaestiones Romanae*, 87.
[4] Matthes, *op. cit.* 33.
[5] Scholiast on Aristophanes, *Plutus*, 768.
[6] Festus, 183.
[7] Matthes, *op. cit.* 21.
[8] Featherman, *op. cit.* v. 604.

bridegroom's house she pours water over him.[1] Purification by water forms "an integral part of Malay customs at birth, adolescence, marriage, sickness, death, and, in fact, at every critical period of the life of a Malay."[2] In all these it is called *tepong tawar*, which properly means "the neutralising rice-flour water, neutralising being used almost in a chemical sense, *i.e.* in the sense of 'sterilising' the active element of poisons, or of destroying the active potentialities of evil spirits." Amongst the Malays lustrations are continued by the newly married pair for three days. The first ceremonies at a wedding consist in fumigating the bride and groom with incense, and then smearing them with "neutralising paste" which averts "ill-luck."[3] Here the idea emerges into conscious realisation of the persons to be feared.

We saw that initiation practices are theoretically marriage ceremonies by which the individual is married in abstract to the other sex—that is, prepared for the dangers of intercourse. Naturally the two are often combined or show similarity of rite. Thus in British Guiana a young man before marriage undergoes an ordeal; his flesh is wounded, and he is sewn into a hammock full of fire-ants.[4] Amongst the Sakalavas and Betsileo the aspirant to a lady's hand has to be shot at with spears; he is expected to show cleverness and courage by avoiding them.[5] In Fiji girls are tattooed at puberty or immediately after marriage. During the process of healing they are *tabu siga*, "kept from the sun."[6] In connection with this, we have seen the meaning of the prohibition and may note that, as danger

[1] *Journ. Anthrop. Inst.* xxiii. 84.
[2] Skeat, *op. cit.* 77. 385. 376.
[3] Skeat, *op. cit.* 378.
[4] im Thurn, *op. cit.* 221.
[5] *Journ. Anthrop. Inst.* ix. 42.
[6] Williams, *op. cit.* i. 170.

is obviated by refraining from such exposure, in the same way as by abstinence at marriage, superstition and self-control alike being thus satisfied, so, when the individual is spiritually prepared, exposure or satisfaction becomes safe and even beneficial. After initiation Halmahera boys must expose themselves to the sun.[1] Similar was the custom amongst the Hindus, by which the bride had to look at the sun on the day before marriage.[2] In Central Asia the young pair greet the rising sun. Similarly amongst the Chacos.[3] The fertilising power of the sun is now useful and a blessing. We may compare our proverb, "Happy is the bride on whom the sun shines."

Weddings very commonly take place in the evening, or at night, a custom natural enough for its convenience and its obviation of dangers, such as that of the evil eye and those connected with human, and especially with female, shyness and timidity. Taken in connection with the last custom, we may without excess of fancifulness note the coincidence with nature's method of shrouding her processes of production in mystery and darkness, and of revealing their results in the light. Amongst the Santhals marriages take place at night, and the bride is conveyed to her husband in a basket.[4] In Morocco and the Babar Islands, amongst the Maoris, the Copts, and Polish Jews, to take a few cases, marriages are made after sunset or at night.[5] Amongst the ancient Romans the bridegroom had to go to his bride in the dark, a custom on which Plutarch speculates in his "Roman

[1] J. G. F. Riedel, in *Zeitschrift für Ethnologie*, xvii. 82.

[2] Frazer, *op. cit.*[2] iii. 222. [3] *Id. l.c.* [4] E. G. Man, *Sonthalia*, 98, 99.

[5] Leared, *op. cit.*; J. G. F. Riedel, *De sluik- en kroesharige rassen tusschen Selebes en Papua*, 350; Shortland, *op. cit.* 140; Featherman, *op. cit.* v. 509, 153.

Questions."[1] Amongst the Zulus it is against etiquette for the bridal party to enter the bridegroom's hut in the day-time.[2]

In the next place, we find various customs by which the young people hide, from vague evil, or from each other. In these customs, which pass into various sorts of seclusion, concealment, and veiling, the real meaning of such marriage ceremonial is often very clearly seen. Sexual shyness not only in woman but in man, is intensified at marriage, and forms a chief feature of the dangerous sexual properties mutually feared. When fully ceremonial, the idea takes on the meaning that satisfaction of these feelings will lead to their neutralisation, as in fact it does. The bridegroom in ancient Sparta supped on the wedding-night at the men's mess, and then visited his bride, leaving her before daybreak. This practice was continued, and sometimes children were born before the pair had ever seen each other's faces by day.[3] At weddings in the Babar Islands the bridegroom has to hunt for his bride in a darkened room. This lasts a good while if she is shy.[4] In South Africa the bridegroom may not see his bride till the whole of the marriage ceremonies have been performed.[5] In Persia a husband never sees his wife till he has consummated the marriage.[6] At marriages in South Arabia the bride and bridegroom have to sit immovable in the same position from noon till midnight, fasting, in separate rooms. The bride is attended by ladies, and the groom by men. They may not see each other till the night of the fourth day.[7] In Egypt the groom cannot see the face of his bride, even by a surreptitious glance, till she is in his absolute pos-

[1] Plutarch, *Q. R.* 65; Servius on Virgil, *Eclog.* viii. 29.
[2] Leslie, *op. cit.* 115.
[3] Plutarch, *Lycurgus*, xv. 48.
[4] Riedel, *op. cit.* 351.
[5] *Journ. Anthrop. Inst.* xix. 271.
[6] Chardin, in *Pinkerton*, ix. 154.
[7] Featherman, *op. cit.* v. 422.

session. Then comes the ceremony, which he performs, of uncovering her face.[1] In Egypt, of course, this has been accentuated by the seclusion and veiling of women. In Morocco, at the feast before the marriage, the bride and groom sit together on a sort of throne; all the time the poor bride's eyes are firmly closed, and she sits amid the revelry as immovable as a statue. On the next day is the marriage. She is conducted after dark to her future home, accompanied by a crowd with lanterns and candles. She is led with closed eyes along the street by two relatives, each holding one of her hands. "Such is the regard to propriety on this solemn occasion, that the bride's head is held in its proper position by a female relative who walks behind her." She wears a veil, and is not allowed to open her eyes until she is set on the bridal bed with a girl friend beside her.[2] Amongst the Zulus the bridal party proceeds to the house of the groom, having the bride hidden amongst them so that no one can see her. They stand facing the groom, while the bride sings a song. Her companions then suddenly break away, and she is discovered standing in the middle with a fringe of beads covering her face.[3] Amongst the people of Kumaun the husband sees his wife first after the joining of hands.[4] Amongst the Bedui of North-East Africa the bride is brought on the evening of the wedding-day by her girl friends to the groom's house. She is closely muffled up.[5] Amongst the Jews of Jerusalem the bride at the marriage ceremony stands under the nuptial canopy, her eyes being closed that she may not behold the face of her future husband

[1] Lane, *op. cit.* i 197.
[2] Leared, *op. cit.* 36, 38.
[3] Leslie, *op. cit.* 116.
[4] *Panjab Notes and Queries*, ii. 234.
[5] Munzinger, *op. cit.* 148.

before she reaches the bridal chamber.[1] In Melanesia the bride is carried to her new home on some one's back, wrapped in many mats, with palm-fans held about her face, "because she is supposed to be modest and shy."[2] Amongst the Damaras the groom cannot see his bride for four days after marriage. When a Damara woman is asked in marriage, she covers her face for a time with the flap of a head-dress made for this purpose.[3] At the Thlinkeet marriage ceremony the bride must look down and keep her head bowed all the time; during the wedding-day she remains hiding in a corner of the house, and the groom is forbidden to enter.[4] At a Yezedee marriage the bride is covered from head to foot with a thick veil, and when arrived at her new home she retires behind a curtain in the corner of a darkened room, where she remains for three days before her husband is permitted to see her.[5] In Corea the bride has to cover her face with her long sleeves when meeting the bridegroom at the wedding.[6] The Manchurian bride uncovers her face for the first time, when she descends from the nuptial couch.[7] As has already been shown, it is dangerous even to see dangerous persons. Sight is a method of contagion in primitive science, and the idea coincides with the psychological aversion to see dangerous things, and with sexual shyness and timidity. In the customs noticed we can distinguish the feeling that it is dangerous to the bride for her husband's eyes to be upon her, and the feeling of bashfulness in her which induces her neither to see him nor to be seen by him.

These ideas explain the origin of the bridal veil and

[1] Featherman, *op. cit.* v. 140.
[2] Codrington, *op. cit.* 242.
[3] *South African Folklore Journal*, i. 49; C. J. Andersson, *op. cit.* 225.
[4] Dall, *op. cit.* 415.
[5] Featherman, *op. cit.* v. 62.
[6] *Journ. Anthrop. Inst.* xxiv. 305.
[7] *Folklore*, i. 489.

similar concealments. Dobrizhoffer wrote of Abipone women as often hiding in the woods before marriage, many "seeming to dread the assaults of tigers less than the untried nuptials." When the bride was led to the groom's tent, eight girls held a carpet in front of her.[1] Amongst the Bedouins of Ethiopia the bride is concealed under a canopy carried by girls.[2] At Druse marriages the bride is hidden in a long red veil, which is removed by the groom in the bridal chamber.[3] The bridal veil is used, to take a few instances, in China, Burmah, Corea, Russia, Bulgaria, Manchuria, and Persia; in all these cases it conceals the face entirely.[4] Cases where a sacred umbrella is held over the head, as amongst the Chinese,[5] are connected with the sanctity of the head, the idea being to prevent evil coming down upon that sensitive part of the body. Thus when the King of Dahomey drank with Burton, a parasol was placed over him to prevent his being seen.[6]

Various methods of seclusion both from each other and from external danger, are illustrated by the following. In some Victorian tribes the young man, as soon as he had passed the ceremonies of initiation, was introduced to the bride, already assigned to him, to gaze at her, for he was forbidden to converse with her. She was then sent to her mother-in-law, who took care of her until the marriage had taken place, but the young man had no access to his future wife. At sunset the bride took her seat in front of her relatives and friends, being separated by a large fire from the bridegroom, who was seated in front of a group of his own friends.

[1] Dobrizhoffer, *op. cit.* ii. 208.

[2] Harris, *op. cit.* i. 287.

[3] Chasseaud, *op. cit.* 166.

[4] Doolittle, *op. cit.* i. 79; Anderson, *op. cit.* 141; Griffis, *op. cit.* 249; Ralston, *op. cit.* 280; Sinclair and Brophy, *op. cit.* 73; *Folklore*, i. 489.

[5] *Folklore*, i. 365.

[6] Burton, *op. cit.* i. 244.

He was then introduced by the groomsmen to the bride, who received him with downcast eyes and in perfect silence. After some feasting the pair were escorted to their future home, but they were still sequestered for two moons, sleeping on different sides of the fire and watched over by a female and a male guardian, who provided them with food. After this period the bride stayed with her parents for a fortnight and then went to her husband.[1] Amongst the Arabs of Mount Sinai the bride is required by decency to remain secluded in her tent for a fortnight, and the rule is that she may only leave it at night, so as not to be seen by men.[2] In certain South African tribes the girl is put in a hut alone. After some days she is taken to another hut, and then to her husband.[3] In New Britain the bride stays in the hut of her intended five days alone, while his relatives bring her food. Meanwhile he is in one of the hiding-places (known only to the men) in the forest, or hidden in tall grass.[4] In Port Moresby the groom sleeps with the bride, but must leave her before dawn, because "he is ashamed to be seen coming from his wife in daylight."[5] The Tipperah youth serves the bride's father for three years, during which time he uses her as a wife. But on the wedding-night he has to sleep with her surreptitiously; he leaves the house before dawn, and absents himself for four days.[6] Amongst the Nufoers the bride and groom may not meet each other alone till the fifth day, but even then only by night, and for four days more he must leave his wife's chamber before day.[7] Parallel to the New Britain custom is an extension of this idea, illustrated

[1] Featherman, *op. cit.* ii. 142. [2] *Id.* v. 368.
[3] D. Livingstone, *South Africa*, 412.
[4] R. Parkinson, *Im Bismarck-Archipel*, 98. [5] Chalmers, *op. cit.* 163.
[6] Lewin, *op. cit.* 203. [7] F. H. Guillemard, *The Cruise of the Marchesa*, ii. 287.

by the custom of Bedouin brides. At night the bride, before consummation of the marriage, runs away to the hills and hides. There her friends bring her food, while the husband looks for her. This is repeated the next night, and when he finds her he must consummate the marriage, and remain all night with her in the hills.[1] Conversely in Egypt on the day after marriage the man who carried the bridegroom upstairs takes him to an "entertainment" in the country, where they spend the whole day. This ceremony is called *el-hooroobeh*, "the flight." He returns in the evening.[2] In Corea after three days of marriage the young husband goes away for a time.[3] Again, both bride and groom are secluded within the house; for ten days in Luzon, during which no one may enter;[4] among the Minahassas for three days and nights in a dark room; amongst the Bedui for forty days.[5] It is said that amongst some of the Bedui, the wife may not leave the house for three years nor touch any work;[6] in Bulgaria they are shut up for a week, during which they may not go out nor receive visitors.[7] The newly wedded pair in the Aru Islands are shut up for four days, and are looked after by the bride's mother.[8] In Ceramlaut the young pair may not go out of the house for three days.[9] This applies often to the bride only, as amongst the Bedouins, where she stays in the tent for a fortnight.[10] In the Kingsmill Islands the house is screened with mats for ten days, and the bride may not go out.[11] For forty days after marriage the Javanese bride was secluded.[12] Amongst the Copts she may not go out, even to see her parents,

1 Burckhardt, *Bedouins and Wahabys*, i. 269. 2 Lane, *op. cit.* i. 214.
3 Griffis, *op. cit.* 251. 4 Featherman, *op. cit.* ii. 495. 5 *Id.* ii. 611.
6 Munzinger, *op. cit.* 148. 7 Sinclair and Brophy, *op. cit.* 73.
8 Riedel, *op. cit.* 262. 9 *Id.* 172. 10 Burckhardt, *op. cit.* i. 268.
11 Wilken, *op. cit.* v. 101. 12 Featherman, *op. cit.* ii. 384.

till the delivery of her first child, or until the end of a year.[1] Wataveta brides "are set apart for the first year as something almost too good for earth. They are dressed, adorned, physicked, and pampered in every way, almost like goddesses. They are screened from vulgar sight, exempted from all household duties, and prohibited from all social intercourse with all of the other sex except their husbands. They are never left alone, are accompanied by some one wherever they may wish to go, and are not permitted to exert themselves in the least; even in their short walks they creep at a snail's pace, least they should overstrain their muscles. Two of these celestial beings were permitted to visit me." They wore veils of iron chain, hanging to below the lips. "They honoured me only with their eyes; they did not let me hear the mellow harmony of their voices. They had to see and be seen, but not to be heard or spoken to. Brides are treated in this manner until they present their husbands with a son or daughter, or the hope of such a desired event has passed away. In the former case the goddess falls to the level of an ordinary housewife; in the other well for her if she be not despised or even discarded."[2] Here the practice passes into care for the unborn child and avoidance of risks on the part of the young wife. On the other hand, in Java again, neither bride nor groom may go out of the house, or perform any hard work, for forty days before the wedding.[3]

Behind these customs there is sexual shyness, and the ideas that association with women is improper as well as dangerous, leading to effeminacy, and that for women, association with men is improper; but, further, these

[1] Lane, *op. cit.* ii. 333.

[2] New, *op. cit.* 360, 361.

[3] Raffles, *History of Java*, i. 325.

ideas coincide with that solidarity of sex, which respects and sympathises with the sexual shyness of each party. Accordingly amongst the Bedui the bride spends the wedding-day with her girl friends and the bridegroom with young men.[1] At Watubella marriages the men take their place by the bridegroom, and the women by the bride.[2] The Babar bride is attended by women friends.[3] Amongst the Barbary Arabs the young wife is escorted to the *dowar* of her husband by all the women of the neighbourhood.[4] During the marriage feast of four days amongst the Damaras she may only sleep with the girls, behind her mother's house. He is not allowed to see his bride or even to enter the *werft*, during these four days, but stays somewhere behind it. When the pair go to his home, her mother and other women go with them to see her safely installed.[5] In Amboina the marriage takes place in the house of the young man's parents, but no men may be present. After a week a feast takes place at the house of the bride's parents, but at this only men may be present.[6]

Returning to the subject of disguise, used as a concealment from danger, "spiritual," personal, and sexual, vaguely conceived or clearly realised in a member of the other sex, we may note the practice of Muhammadans in the north-west provinces of India; for some days before marriage both bride and groom wear dirty clothes.[7] The common custom by which the bride's hair is shaven or a lock cut off is doubtless connected with the ideas which cause this practice in other taboo states. Something, some part of one, must be given up by way of propitiating evil influences, a

[1] Munzinger, *op. cit.* 147. [2] Riedel, *op. cit.* 205. [3] *Id.* 350.
[4] Featherman, *op. cit.* v. 53c. [5] *South African Folklore Journal*, i. 49.
[6] Riedel, *op. cit.* 69. [7] Crooke, in *Panjab Notes and Queries*, ii. 960.

part must be sacrificed for the whole. The idea is sometimes merged in the principle of change of identity, by supposing a part of the person to be instinct with the properties of the whole; in other cases it becomes later a sacrifice to some deity, as Greek brides cut off a lock of hair. In some of the Fiji Islands the bride cut off a long lock of her hair, in others all her hair was shaven off.[1] The head of a Kaffir bride was shaved.[2]

There are some interesting customs which show both the taboo character of bride and bridegroom and also an attempt at disguising them by fictitious change of identity. "The Malay wedding ceremony, even as carried out by the poorer classes, shows that the contracting parties are treated as royalty, that is to say, as sacred human beings, and if any further proof is required, in addition to the evidence which may be drawn from the general character of the ceremony, I may mention first the fact that the bride and bridegroom are actually called *Raja sari* (*i.e.* 'the sovereigns of a day'), and secondly, that it is a polite fiction that no command of theirs, during their one day of sovereignty, may be disobeyed."[3] During the first week of marriage the Syrian pair play at being king and queen; they sit on a throne, and the villagers sing songs.[4] Wetzstein conjectures that "the Song of Songs" is a collection of such.[5]

Somewhat similar is the idea underlying the habit of wearing finery or new clothes for a new or important event. On the same plane is the common custom of erecting a "marriage-bower," well known amongst

[1] Featherman, *op. cit.* ii. 203.
[2] Shooter, *op. cit.* 75.
[3] Skeat, *op. cit.* 388.
[4] *Zeitschrift für Ethnologie* for 1873, 270.
[5] S. R. Driver, *Introduction to the Literature of the Old Testament*, 452.

Hindu peoples, and once common in Spain.[1] For Abyssinian weddings a *dass* or bower of green branches is erected in the courtyard. Here bride and groom sit in state on opposite sides, each surrounded by friends.[2]

Next comes the very interesting custom of substituting a mock bride for the real one. Thus, amongst the Beni-Amer the groom and his friends are often mocked when they come to take the bride, her people substituting a false bride for the true one. The substitute is carefully disguised and allows herself to be taken, and at last when the procession is well outside the village, she reveals herself and runs back laughing. This may be done more than once.[3] Amongst the Saxons of Transsylvania the bride is concealed with two married women behind a curtain, on the evening of the wedding-day, and the husband has to guess which is his wife; all three try to mislead him.[4] This kind of thing is common in European folk-custom. Amongst the Moksha an old woman dressed up as a bride dances before the company.[5] Amongst the Esthonians the bride's brother dresses up in woman's clothes, and personates the bride. In Brittany the substitutes are first a little girl, then the mistress of the house, and lastly the grandmother. In Poland an old woman, in Polonia a bearded man personate the bride.[6]

Bride or groom is sometimes attended by one or more persons dressed up to resemble him or her. These persons are intended to be duplicates, and the idea is "safety in numbers," combined with similarity of costume, much as the sacred shield of Roman worship was kept safe by being placed amongst a number of fac-

[1] Th. Moore, *Marriage Customs*, 56.
[2] Featherman, *op. cit.* v. 604, 605.
[3] Munzinger, *op. cit.* 324.
[4] Gerard, *The Land beyond the Forest*, i. 185.
[5] *Folklore*, i. 446.
[6] *Folklore*, ix. 147.

similes. The *bale muri* of Fiji has the same origin. The modern Egyptian bridegroom walks between two friends dressed exactly like himself.[1] Amongst the Abyssinians, when a princess is married, she is accompanied in the procession by her sister, dressed exactly like herself.[2]

The very natural practice of being accompanied on these, as on other important occasions, by a friend of one's own sex, has crystallised into the institution of groomsmen, bridesmaids, and the like. They resemble generally persons like the Roman *advocati*, who were witnesses to character and general supporters of a litigant. In marriage ceremonial their original function is sympathy and assistance in a trying ordeal more or less fraught with "spiritual" danger, but sometimes their duty becomes more specialised. At Egyptian weddings the bride is attended by several girls who cluster round her under the same canopy.[3] We may compare the Zulu custom of surrounding the bride with a throng of maidens. At Malay weddings the bride is attended by one or more girl-companions, and the bridegroom by two pages.[4] During the first few days after a wedding the South Celebes bride is attended by eight girls, and also is accompanied by a lady of her own age, who is dressed exactly like her. The bridegroom is also accompanied by a young man of his own age, dressed like himself.[5] The Abyssinian bridegroom is attended by six to twelve bridesmen, called *arkees*, "to whom particular functions are assigned and extraordinary privileges are allowed." Boys of the same social class unite together and form a kind of society, binding themselves to act as *arkees* for each other. At

[1] Lane, *op. cit.* i. 212.
[2] Harris, *op. cit.* ii. 225.
[3] Lane, *op. cit.* i. 217, 200.
[4] Skeat, *op. cit.* 375.
[5] Matthes, *op. cit.* 29.

the marriage ceremony they pledge themselves to fulfil towards the bride the part of "brethren"; they wait on her, and furnish her with meat should she hunger, and with milk should she thirst. During the first few weeks of marriage the *arkees* sleep in the bridal chamber and supply the pair with anything they may want in the night; and one *arkee* keeps constant watch during this period over the bride.[1] In these examples is well seen the way in which the women stand by the bride and the men by the groom, a fact which indicates the real origin of marriage ceremonies. The last case shows a chivalrous perversion of sympathy. Again, in Russia on the wedding-night a man called a *klyetnik* was appointed to watch round the bridal chamber.[2] Similarly in ancient Greece one of the bridegroom's friends was called θυρωρός; he used to stand at the door and prevent the women assisting the bride when she screamed.[3] The hardy suggestion which has been made, that our "best man" was originally the strongest of the bridegroom's friends who assisted him in capturing the bride from the foreign tribe is well refuted by this as by all the evidence. It is sex, not the tribe, that is concerned.

It is a very general custom that as many preliminaries as possible, including the proposal of marriage and the arrangement of the contract, should be performed not by the bride and bridegroom-elect, but by friends or sponsors. The reason is obvious after what has been said. Thus, in Egypt the marriage contract is performed between the bridegroom and the bride's deputy (*wekeel*). These two join hands which are ceremonially covered with a cloth.[4] We thus arrive at proxies in the marriage rite. Amongst the Karens it is

[1] Featherman, *op. cit.* v. 606.

[2] Ralston, *Songs of the Russian People*, 281.

[3] Pollux, *Onomasticon*, iii. 42.

[4] Lane, *op. cit.* i. 200.

the sponsors of the pair who offer the cup to each other, drinking out of which forms the ceremony.[1] In Persia marriage by proxy is the rule, and the groom never sees his wife till he has consummated the marriage.[2] An interesting parallel is found in Cingalese custom. An astrologer has to decide if the horoscopes of the suitor and the girl suit each other. Once when the bridegroom's horoscope was not suitable, he produced that of his infant brother, which was satisfactory. This child personated the groom and was married to the bride.[3] The bride and bridegroom in South Celebes have each a "representative," *doëta;* if the bride's representative is a man, that of the groom is a woman, and *vice versâ*. The South Celebes bride does not appear at the wedding. She is represented by her deputy, and is herself secluded in an inner room. After the ceremony, at which the bride is not present, the bridegroom may not see her yet, but goes home, leaving his sword as his representative. After being separated from his bride for three days, he returns to take his sword; he gets it back by giving a present.[4] A link with other customs is the following. At the weddings of Creek Indians the bridegroom ceremonially stuck a reed into the ground, and the bride did the same, placing her reed close to his. They then each took the other's reed, and by this act became man and wife.[5]

The interesting custom by which one of the pair, or both, are married to trees, is a good instance of the primitive fashion of "make-believe," by which an effigy does duty for a person, all risks thus being obviated. Amongst the Mundas, after a mimic fight for the

[1] Mcmahon, *The Karens of the Golden Chersonese*, 322.

[2] Pinkerton, *op. cit.* ix. 154.

[3] Forbes, *Eleven Years in Ceylon*, i. 328.

[4] Matthes, *op. cit.* 22, 27, 29, 30.

[5] Featherman, *op. cit.* iii. 160.

bride, the pair are anointed with turmeric and wedded to two trees, the bride to a *mahwa*, the groom to a mango, or both to mangoes. They touch the tree with *sindur*, clasp it, and then are tied to it. Subsequently he touches her forehead with *sindur*.[1] This case brings out the point, that the mock ceremony is intended to ensure the harmlessness or success of the real ceremony. Amongst the Kumis the bridegroom is first married to a mango tree. He embraces it, and is tied to it with thread, and he daubs it with red lead. The bride also is wedded to a mango. She is brought to her home in a basket, and the groom is carried thither on a platform supported by men.[2] It is a Hindu custom, when misfortune in marriage is foretold by the astrologers, for the person concerned to be first married to an earthen vessel.[3] Again, the Hindus consider it dangerous to be a man's third wife; accordingly in such a case the bridegroom is betrothed first to a tree, which is supposed to die in the woman's stead.[4] Another account states that when a Hindu takes a third wife, he is married first to a tree, "to avoid the danger of being married for the third time."[5] These last three examples throw light on the practice in Bengal, and the two last show that the danger is mutual. In the so-called "child-marriage" of the Nayars of Travancore, a sword may represent the bridegroom.[6] At Malay marriages the ceremony is actually performed with the bridegroom alone. The priest says to him, "I wed you, A, to B, daughter of C, for a portion of two *bharas*."[7] This instance may serve to show the marriage rite developing into a civil act.

[1] Dalton, *op. cit.* 194.
[2] *Id.* 319.
[3] *Journal of the Asiatic Society of Bengal*, liii. i. 100.
[4] Ward, *op. cit.* i. 134, ii. 247.
[5] *Panjab Notes and Queries*, ii. 252.
[6] *Journ. Anthrop. Inst.* xii. 293.
[7] Skeat, *op. cit.* 382.

The next class of marriage ceremonies includes various kinds of abstinence. Bride and bridegroom must maintain silence for a certain period. This is a common taboo upon persons passing through a critical period, and the principle behind it is a natural impulse of egoistic sensibility, a sort of recognition of the importance of the occasion, combined with more or less of spiritual fear, either of general danger or, in this case, danger from each other. It is dangerous to speak to dangerous persons, and the principle here combines with sexual shyness. Some such practice is doubtless responsible for the Greek name of the wedding-night, *νὺξ μυστική*. The bride and groom amongst the Andamanese are introduced to each other, after sitting apart in silence for some time. They then remain silent until the evening. Often the pair pass several days after marriage without exchanging a single word, and even avoid looking at one another. "One might suppose they had had a serious quarrel."[1] In Corea the bride is expected to keep absolute silence on the wedding-day and in the nuptial chamber.[2]

Again, they must keep awake, for the same reasons of sexual taboo. In New Guinea after the ceremony bride and groom sit up all night. If sleep threatens they are at once aroused; the belief being that by remaining awake they will have a happy life. This goes on for four nights. Not until the fifth day may they meet each other alone, but even then only by night, and for four days more the husband must leave his wife's chamber before daybreak.[3] Amongst the Sumatrans the pair sit up all night in state.[4] After the marriage ceremony of the Dorahs the guests pass the

[1] Man, in *Journ. Anthrop. Inst.* xii. 138.
[2] Griffis, *op. cit.* 247.
[3] Guillemard, *op. cit.* ii. 287.
[4] Marsden, *op. cit.* 269.

night in feasting; the young couple take no part, and are not allowed to go to sleep for one moment, because it is supposed that this nightly vigil can alone secure their future happiness.[1] The young pair in Borneo may not go to sleep, "else evil spirits would make them ill."[2]

The pair frequently are obliged to fast, with the object of preventing evil influences entering the system by means of food. Thus amongst the Wa-teita the bride and groom are shut up for three days without food.[3] The young Macusi bridegroom-elect fasts from meat for some time before marriage.[4] Amongst the Thlinkeets they are required to fast for two days, "in order to ensure domestic concord and happiness." At the expiration of that time they are allowed to partake of a little food, when a second fast of two days is added, after which they are allowed to come together for the first time.[5] Here is seen the curious association between commensal and sexual intercourse, which derives from the biological connection between the nutritive and sexual impulses, and is often expressed in physiological thought.

A very frequent rule is that the consummation of the marriage is deferred for a time. This points to the dangers already reviewed of this close physical connection, in which, as in eating together, the ideas of sexual taboo are concentrated, and illustrates a principle which runs through all these practices of abstinence, as from sleep and eating, and is seen in all similar taboos, that a temporary self-denial of a dangerous satisfaction will obviate the risks of its ordinary fulfilment. There is also later developed in this rule the idea that sexual

[1] Featherman, op. cit. ii. 32.
[2] Perelaer, op. cit. 53.
[3] J. Thomson, op. cit. 57.
[4] im Thurn, op. cit. 222.
[5] Bancroft, op. cit. i. 111.

intercourse, as such, is improper. The Chinese practice of putting a charm-sword, made of "cash," on the bridal bed, illustrates the danger of this union.[1] Amongst the Narrinyeri it is "a point of decency for the couple not to sleep close to each other for the first two or three nights; on the third or fourth night the man and his wife sleep together under the same rug."[2]

The result is often attained by placing a person between the pair, as Sigurd placed his sword between himself and Brynhild. For three nights after a wedding in the Kei Islands, an old woman sleeps between the pair, sometimes a child is used for this.[3] In Luzon the pair sleep on the first night with a space of two ells between them, in which lies a boy, six or eight years old.[4] Elsewhere certain persons are deputed to keep them apart. The Southern Slav bridegroom has a *djever*, "bride-carrier," who sleeps during the first night beside the bride, the bridegroom not being allowed to sleep with her for two nights.[5] After the mock flight and pursuit in the bridal chamber, the South Celebes couple are attended during the night by women called "bridesmothers," who prevent all intimacy between them.[6] In Achin the young couple may not come together for seven nights, and they are kept awake by old women.[7] In the Babar Islands the pair during the first few nights sleep in the same room, but the bride sleeps with some female relatives and the bridegroom with some male relatives.[8] In Endeh for four nights old women sit up with the pair to prevent them from approaching each other.[9] Amongst the

[1] Doolittle, *op. cit.* ii. 313.
[2] Curr, *op. cit.* ii. 245.
[3] Riedel, *op. cit.* 236.
[4] Blumentritt, *Ethnographie der Philippinen*, 38.
[5] F. S. Krauss, *Sitte u. Brauch der Südslaven*, 608.
[6] Matthes, *op. cit.* 35.
[7] Kruijt, *Atjeh en de Atjehers*, 193.
[8] Riedel, *op. cit.* 351.
[9] *Tijdschrift voor Indische Taal- Land- en Volkenkunde*, xxiv. 525.

Nahuas in the feasting, drinking, and dancing, the bride and groom took no part; they now had four days' fasting and penance, in the strict retirement of their own room, where they were closely guarded by old women. On no account might they leave the room. The time was to be passed in prayer; "and on no account were they to allow their passions to get the better of them or indulge in carnal intercourse."[1] Amongst the Mayas the pair had to remain quite still, until the fire burnt out, and not until then could they consummate the marriage.[2] The Thlinkeet bridegroom could not claim his marital rights until four weeks after marriage.[3] Amongst the Nootkas no intercourse may take place between the pair for ten days.[4] In the Frazer Island tribe of Queensland they do not come together for nearly two months after marriage.[5] In Persia the husband does not consummate the marriage for several days.[6] Amongst the Dyaks the pair may not come together for two or three nights and days. The groom feasts with his friends, the bride is with her mother and female relatives.[7] Amongst the Soendanese the bridegroom has no access to his bride for four days. She will not look at him or speak to him.[8] Amongst the Madoerese the marriage is not consummated till the third night.[9] Amongst the Nufoers this takes place on the fifth day; on the first night they are set back to back, so as not to see each other. This is repeated each night. When he leaves her each of these mornings, they must not see each other, "a sign of her maiden shame."[10] Amongst the Tengger of Java the

[1] Bancroft, *op. cit.* ii. 261.

[2] *Id.* ii. 676.

[3] *Id. op. cit.* i. 111.

[4] *Id.* i. 198.

[5] Brough Smyth, *op. cit.* i. 84.

[6] Pinkerton, *op. cit.* ix. 154.

[7] Perelaer, *op. cit.* 53.

[8] Ritter, *Java*, 29.

[9] Veth, *Java*, i. 635.

[10] Van Hasselt, in *Zeitschrift für Ethnologie*, viii. 181 ff.

marriage is not consummated for five days after the wedding.[1] In Egypt it is customary for husbands to deny themselves their conjugal rights during the first week after marriage with a virgin bride.[2] In the last case we see the consideration produced by the actual intensity of maidenly feelings, which is the usual psychological phenomenon at the first union; sexual taboo regards this as an especial property of woman, and combines with it the other idea that first contact with a virgin is more dangerous than with other women. This latter point is clearly brought out in the next group of customs.

Before proceeding to these, we may notice an excellent example of the way in which these principles develop religious abstinence as a meritorious act. There is a story in the Syriac *Judas Thomas's Acts* of a bride and a bridegroom who were converted by an apparition of the Lord in the bridal chamber, and passed the night in continence. Next morning the king, the bride's father, came in and found them sitting, the one opposite the other; and the face of the bride was uncovered, and the bridegroom was very cheerful. "The mother of the bride saith to her: 'Why art thou sitting thus and art not ashamed, but art as if, lo! thou wert married a long time and for many a day?'" And her father too said, "Is it thy great love for thy husband that prevents thee from even veiling thyself?" And the bride answered and said, "Truly, my father, I am in great love, and am praying to my Lord that I may continue in this love which I have experienced this night. I am not veiled because the veil of corruption is taken from me, and I am not ashamed because the deed of shame has been removed far from me."[3]

[1] Featherman, *op. cit.* iii. 399.

[2] Lane, *op. cit.* ii. 273.

[3] Wright, *Apocryphal Acts*, ii. 156 ff. For the idea that union in marriage is sinful, see *id.* ii. 122, 155, 191, 223, 233, 234.

Sexual intercourse, summing up as it does in primitive thought all the dangers of sexual taboo, especially the danger of weakness and effeminacy, produced by contagion from women and by loss of strength (both of body and soul) on the part of the man by emission, is rendered more safe by certain ceremonies, the meaning of which is very obvious, though enquirers have curiously missed it. These ceremonies are not to be confused with the so-called *jus primæ noctis*, which has occurred sporadically in history, though mis-termed. That practice is simply a barbarous assertion of despotic authority of the patriarchal sort, appearing for instance in feudal or similar stages of society. With it these customs have nothing to do.

This marriage ceremony consists in perforation of the *hymen* by some appointed person other than the husband; it is most common in the lowest stages of culture, especially in Australia. Tribes which have this rite are commonly said to practise no marriage ceremony. This statement is of course erroneous; to primitive thought this ceremony is a very real marriage rite. The best examples come from the Arunta and connected tribes of Central Australia, and have been well described by Messrs. Spencer and Gillen.[1] The ceremony, rude and practical as it may seem, is nevertheless sacred and even religious, as is shown by the facts that the natives regard it as a ceremony, and that the operators are painted with charcoal, a sacred custom followed in magical rites, and especially when an avenging party is being sent out. The tribes of Central Australia who have this ceremony are the Arunta, Ilpirra, Kaitish, Warramunga, Iliaura, Waagai, Bingonguia, Walpari, and Luritcha. When a girl

[1] Spencer and Gillen, *op. cit.* 93 ff.

arrives at puberty she is, owing to the convenient classificatory system, already marked out as the potential wife of the men of the proper complementary division, and has been, or is then, allotted to a particular suitor. The ceremony is performed by persons who vary according to the tribe; sometimes it is done by a sister; the important point is that the prospective husband never undertakes it. The *hymen* is artificially perforated, and then the assisting men have access (ceremonial, be it observed) to the girl in a stated order, and in some tribes it is men of a division which has no intermarriage with the girl's division, who have this access. The object of the custom is clearly to remove the danger of sexual intercourse for the husband, and perhaps also for the wife, by a ceremonial previous rehearsal of it. The danger partly coincides, as we have seen, with the apparent physical impediment to intercourse. The act is in two parts, perforation and intercourse. The men who have access do not possess the right as an "expiation" for individual marriage, or anything like it; it is a religious act, and altruistic at that; it is not done as a reminder that they, as "communal" or "group-husbands," have really as much right to the woman as her husband has; the mere fact that men of forbidden groups sometimes have access proves this. It is simply a removal of the danger by proxy, and the rite may be classed with other proxy-marriages. The next point to be observed has been already referred to, namely, that here "initiation" and marriage are one.[1] This economy shows that "initiation" ceremonies of this kind are marriages to the other sex in abstract, and is itself due to the convenience of the classification, which

[1] Spencer and Gillen, *op. cit.* 93.

decides what persons are marriageable to each other. Amongst the Wataveta the bridegroom seizes his bride by force; in this he is aided by four friends, who have access to her during the five days' festivities of the wedding.[1] Amongst the Wa-teita she hides, and the groom with four friends catch her. The four friends have intercourse with her.[2] This last fact has been used as a proof of primitive promiscuity and the like. It is nothing of the kind. Comparing it with the Central Australian custom, we see in it the same service, which is the last act of subjugation as it were, the last detail in the preparation of the bride for her husband. It may, and to some extent doubtless does, develop into a kind of reward given on the part of the husband to the friends who have assisted him, but such a development is quite secondary. The Kurnai suitor was assisted by some friends, who had intercourse with the bride.[3] This religious service is often performed by such persons in Australian tribes. An important preliminary of marriage amongst the Masai is the performance of this operation on the girl.[4] This defloration is performed by the father of the bride amongst the Sakais, Battas, and Alfoers of Celebes.[5] In the Philippines there were certain men whose profession it was to deflower brides, in case the *hymen* had not been ruptured in childhood by an old woman who was sometimes employed for this.[6] The defloration of the bride was amongst some Eskimo tribes entrusted to the *angekok*, or priest.[7] The idea sometimes develops later into a belief that the contact of a holy person renders marital contact safe, or will ensure fertility.

[1] *Journ. Anthrop. Inst.* xxi. 365.
[2] J. Thomson, *op. cit.* 51.
[3] Fison and Howitt, *op. cit.* 202.
[4] J. Thomson, *op. cit.* 258.
[5] Ploss u. Bartels, *op. cit.* ii. 490.
[6] Featherman, *op. cit.* ii. 474.
[7] *Id.* iii. 406.

In childless families the Karalits often invite the *angekok* to have connection with the wife.[1]

There is next a large class of marriage customs which in the first place bring out very clearly sexual solidarity; the women, as it were, make marriage an opportunity for showing their mutual sympathy with each other as women, and they take the side of the bride in her bashfulness or resistance, as if the occasion were a test case between the two sexes, as indeed it is. We have seen the same sort of thing in connection with birth, and have noticed how the women cling together at marriage till the last moment. These phenomena also show how marriage ceremonies have inherent in them, as binding the pair together, or neutralising each other's dangerous influence, the intention and power to make their life harmonious and sympathetic. In the second place, these customs are one of the best guides to the ideas of sexual taboo in their relation to marriage ritual. We here see one of the chief factors of sexual taboo, woman's shyness, timidity, and modesty, accentuated by the physiological sensibility which resists physical subjugation, chiefly in connection with the act of intercourse, but appearing more or less throughout all the proceedings. It is an instance of the taboo of personal isolation. The phenomena all lead up, by the way, to the correct understanding of so-called "marriage by capture." There is also to be noted the diffidence characteristic of both sexes upon entering a new and strange state, a diffidence psychologically identical with that produced on other similar and taboo occasions.

Hence the common practice of carrying bride or groom or both; amongst the Kumis the groom is carried to the bride's house on men's shoulders.[2] In

[1] Featherman, *op. cit.* iii. 432.

[2] Dalton, *op. cit.* 319.

Egypt it is considered right that the groom as well as the bride should exhibit some bashfulness, and a friend therefore carries him up to the *hareem*.[1] In Honduras and amongst the Miaos the bride was conveyed to her husband on a man's shoulders.[2] In Guatemala and Salvador the pair were carried by their friends to their new house, and shut in a room.[3] The Nahua bride was borne upon a litter or on the back of a brideswoman or sponsor.[4] In civilised societies a brougham is used on what is really the same principle, an especial arrangement for an especial occasion, in which convenience combines with ceremonial. There is no survival, in these cases, of "marriage by capture," though they sometimes of course coincide with the desire to checkmate female resistance, as they have been found to coincide with a prevention of results from bashfulness, both these feelings being part of the foundations of taboo. The innate tendency to what may be called polar or complementary opposition between the sexes is well brought out in a Kurnai practice. If the men were backward in marrying, the girls would kill some of the *yeerung*, the birds that were the sex-totems of the men. This led to a fight with sticks between the two sexes. Next day the young men killed some *djeetgun*, the sex-totems of the women; a second fight was the result. The ultimate issue was a marriage or two.[5] Fighting makes friends sometimes amongst savages as amongst modern boys. At betrothal amongst the Kamchadales when the man takes hold of the girl, the married women ceremonially beat him.[6] Amongst the Mos-

[1] Lane, *op. cit.* i. 214.
[2] Bancroft, *op. cit.* i. 730; Colquhoun, *Across Chrysê*, 383.
[3] Bancroft, *op. cit.* i. 703.
[4] *Id.* ii. 255.
[5] Fison and Howitt, *op. cit.* 201.
[6] Georgi, *op. cit.* 83.

quitos the bridegroom has to charge into a circle of women who surround the bride; "he shoulders her like a sack and trots off for the mystic circle (of men), into which the women may not enter, and reaches it, urged on by the frantic cries of the women, before the crowd can rescue her."[1] This may be called "capture," but it is capture from the female sex. The Makuana suitor has to throw the girl in a wrestling bout in order to secure her hand. Also the father and mother give him a few ceremonial blows with a stick, "as if to assure themselves that he sincerely loves their daughter."[2] In Sumatra the bride is not surrendered to her husband immediately after the marriage ceremony of the joining of hands, for custom requires that the young girl should show at least a feigned reluctance to sacrifice her virginity, and in this resistance she is aided by the old matron who is her ceremonial attendant and was the messenger sent by the bridegroom with his proposal of marriage. The bride sits in state all night for two or three nights, carefully guarded.[3] The Wakamba groom, after paying the bride-price, has to carry off the bride by force, the parents not surrendering her without a struggle.[4]

Of the same origin is the common practice of abusive language at weddings. Amongst the Kaffirs the bride insults the groom, showing thereby that the moment of her submission has not yet come.[5] In the Punjab it is a general custom for the relatives of the bride to hurl abusive epithets at the bridegroom.[6] This has actually been supposed to be a relic of "marriage by capture"! The *Fescennina locutio* is a case

[1] Bancroft, *op. cit.* i. 733.
[2] Featherman, *op. cit.* ii. 306.
[3] Shoeter, *op. cit.* 71.
[4] Arbousset, *op. cit.* 249.
[5] Krapf, *op. cit.* 354.
[6] *Panjab Notes and Queries*, ii. 976.

in point. In many instances, of course, as in European folk-custom, the abuse is directed against the "evil eye" and possible external danger to the young couple.

We have noticed the impulse in animals and mankind to guard the sexual centres against the undesired advances of the male. "This is carried on into desire, and female animals are known to run after the male and then turn to flee, perhaps only submitting with much persuasion. Modesty thus becomes an invitation. The naturally defensive attitude of the female is in contrast with the naturally aggressive attitude of the male in sexual relationships."[1] Such maiden coyness or physiological shrinking, as has been explained before, is accentuated at marriage, especially in connection with the act of union. Amongst the Bedouins the bride cries loudly while the marriage is being consummated.[2] In Sumatra when the young couple are left together, custom demands that she shall defend herself; the struggle often lasts some days.[3] "Husbands have told me of brides who sob and tremble with fright on the wedding-night, the hysteria being sometimes alarming. E, aged twenty-five, refused her husband for six weeks after marriage, exhibiting the greatest fear of his approach. Ignorance of the nature of the sexual connection is often the cause of exaggerated alarm. In Jersey I used to hear of a bride who ran to the window and screamed 'murder' on the wedding-night."[4] Now in primitive thought this characteristic has to be neutralised, and it is done by a ceremonial use of force, which is half real and half make-believe. General cases of force used in connubial "capture," so called, will illustrate this, as of course the violence there used has the same meaning, though

[1] H. Ellis, *op. cit.* ii. 29.

[2] Burckhardt, *op. cit.* i. 166.

[3] D'Urville, *op. cit.* i. 184.

[4] H. Ellis, *op. cit.* ii. 25.

generalised. Returning to more general developments of bashfulness and timidity as against the other sex, leading up to acts of mock half-real violence, we find that at Kaffir weddings, the "principal idea seems to be to show the great unwillingness of the girl to be transformed into a wife." After the reception of the bride's party, the bride creeps up to the bridegroom's wives, if he has any, or his mother, and says she has come to stay and hopes they will be good to her, otherwise she will go back to the father, mother, and relatives who were so loath to part with her. They reply that they do not know—they are not sure—they will see how she behaves herself, and so on. She then pretends to run away, but a female relative of the groom brings her back. In the evening she runs about the *kraal* with a following of girls crying after her. She is supposed to be running back to her old home, and the girls are supposed to be preventing her. Next day she *hlonipas* (hides) from the male sex, but in the afternoon she comes out with some girls, and commences the ceremony of *hlanibeesa* (literally, "washing"). She takes water and throws it about the men.[1] The neutralising of evil influences from the other sex by the use of water is seen in the last detail. The various stages of the following ceremonial show well how it is the maiden who is to be conciliated. In Fiji the first act of wooing, to obtain the girl's consent, was called "mutual attachment." The next step was "nursing"; the girl was conducted to the bridegroom's house. As she wept copious tears at being torn from the parental home, the friends of the groom endeavoured to assuage her sorrow by offering presents. This was called "the drying of tears." The next step was the "warming," and con-

[1] Leslie, *op. cit.* 196, 117, 118.

sisted in the sending of food to the bride by the bridegroom. For the next step, the groom and his friends arrived and the girl served them with food she had prepared, and she and the bridegroom ate together. This was known as "the bathing," for before it the bride bathed in the sea.[1] Cases of "connubial capture" have nothing whatever to do, it need hardly be observed, with so-called "marriage by capture." Among the Karens the candidate for a maiden's hand has to escalade her cabin, and is expected to overthrow a strong man placed for her defence.[2] The stock description of Australian marriage, for instance at Botany Bay, that the man knocks the woman down with a club, and carries her off, is exaggerated.[3] An Australian girl, when made over to her husband, goes to his hut with reluctance, and when that feeling does not occur, it is the fashion to assume it, and occasionally the husband uses violence and compels his wife to enter his camp, "a circumstance," adds Mr. Curr, who knew the natives well, "which has been much burlesqued by some writers."[4] Aelian states of the Sacae that the bridegroom had to do battle with his intended, and naïvely adds, "they do not go so far as to kill each other."[5] Amongst the Tunguzes and Kamchadales a marriage is not definitely "arranged and concluded until the suitor has got the better of his beloved by force, and has torn her clothes.[6] The Makuana suitor has to wrestle with his bride.[7] Amongst the Samoyeds the groom has to take his wife by force, because she resists strenuously.[8] In Greenland two old women are sent to negotiate with the parents of the girl. The latter, on hearing the

[1] Williams, *op. cit.* i. 169, 170.
[2] J. Bowring, *Siam*, ii. 45.
[3] As by Bastian, *Der Mensch*, iii. 292.
[4] Curr, *op. cit.* i. 110.
[5] Aelian, xii, 38.
[6] Erman, *op. cit.* ii. 442.
[7] Arbousset, *op. cit.* 240.
[8] Georgi, *op. cit.* 13.

proposal, runs out of doors, tearing her hair; for single women "affect bashfulness and aversion to any proposal of marriage, though their betrothed are well assured of acquiescence." Sometimes they swoon, or run off to some deserted spot. Women go in search of the refractory maiden, and drag her forcibly to the suitor's house, where she sits for some days disconsolate and refuses nourishment. When friendly exhortation is unavailing, she is compelled by force and even blows to receive her husband.[1] At the ceremony of uncovering the face of an Egyptian bride, the groom has to give her a present of money therefor, and she does not allow the uncovering without some reluctance, if not violent resistance, in order to show her maiden modesty. He then sees her face for the first time.[2] Marriages amongst the Nestorians are solemnised in church an hour after midnight. Standing before the altar in separate groups, each surrounded by their respective friends, the bride refuses to join hands with the bridegroom, and some degree of force is necessary to accomplish the object.[3] When asked in marriage the Karalit maiden feigns the greatest bashfulness. Sometimes her resistance is of a serious nature; she often escapes and hides in the mountains. The two matrons who negotiated the betrothal for the bridegroom go out to find her, and drag her to the house of the suitor. Here she remains for days in a sullen and dejected mood, with dishevelled hair, and refusing to eat. She is sometimes compelled by blows to accept her new position.[4] Amongst the Thlinkeets the bridegroom gives valuable presents to the father of the bride. On the wedding-day the guests sing and dance, in order to induce the

[1] Cranz, *op. cit.* i. 146.
[2] Lane, *op. cit.* i. 214.
[3] Featherman, *op. cit.* v. 75.
[4] Featherman, iii. 434.

bride to leave her hiding-place in the corner of the room. She at last comes forth, and with a downcast countenance takes her seat by the side of the bridegroom.[1] Amongst the Eastern Tinnés the woman who is asked in marriage affects an unwillingness to change her condition; but the suitor takes hold of the hair of his betrothed and drags her out of her father's dwelling.[2] K. O. Müller explains the form of "capture" in ancient Sparta more correctly than do ethnologists; "it indicates," he says, "that a girl could not surrender her freedom and virgin purity unless compelled by the violence of the stronger sex."[3] In ancient Rome at plebeian marriages the groom and his friends invaded the house and carried off the bride with feigned violence from her mother's lap.[4] The Khonds hold a feast at the bride's house. Far in the night "the principals in the scene are raised by an uncle of each upon his shoulder and borne through the dance. The burdens are suddenly exchanged, and the uncle of the youth disappears with the bride. The assembly divides into two parties; the friends of the bride endeavour to arrest, those of the bridegroom to cover her flight, and men, women, and children mingle in mock conflict." "I saw a man bearing away upon his back something enveloped in an ample covering of scarlet cloth; he was surrounded by twenty or thirty young fellows, and by them protected from the desperate attacks made upon him by a party of young women. The man was just married, and the burden was his blooming bride, whom he was conveying to his own village. Her youthful friends, as it appears is the custom, were seeking to regain possession of her, and hurled stones and bamboos

[1] Featherman, iii. 390.

[2] *Id.* iii. 248.

[3] K. O. Müller, *The Dorians*, IV. iv. 2.

[4] Appuleius, *Metamorphoses*, iv.

at the head of the devoted bridegroom until he reached the confines of his own village. Then the tables were turned and the bride was fairly won; and off her young friends scampered, screaming and laughing, but not relaxing their speed till they reached their own village."[1] The Kalmuck bridegroom, when the "price" is fixed, goes with some friends to carry off the bride. "A sham resistance is always made by the people of her camp, in spite of which she fails not to be borne away on a richly caparisoned horse, with loud shouts and *feux de joie*."[2] A century ago in Wales, "on the morning of the wedding-day the groom with his friends demanded the bride. Her friends gave a positive refusal, upon which a mock scuffle ensued. The bride, mounted beside her nearest kinsman, is carried off and is pursued by the groom and his friends with loud shouts. When they have fatigued themselves and their horses, he is suffered to overtake his bride, and leads her away in triumph."[3] The Fuegian suitor, as soon as he is able to maintain a wife, obtains her relatives' consent, and does work for them. Then he watches for an opportunity to carry her off. If she is unwilling, she hides in the woods until her admirer is tired of looking, but this seldom happens.[4] The Aeneze groom, soon after sunset, goes to a tent pitched for him at a distance from the camp; there he shuts himself up and awaits the arrival of the bride. The bashful girl meanwhile runs from the tent of one friend to another till she is caught at last, and conducted in triumph by a few women to the bridegroom's tent; he receives her at the entrance, and forces her into it.[5] Amongst the

[1] Macpherson, *Repor*[illegible] *n the Khonds*, 55; Campbell, *Personal Narrative of Service in Khondistan*, 44. [illegible] De Hell, *Travels in the Steppes of the Caspian Sea*, 259

[3] Kames, *Sketches of* [illegible] *story of Man*, i. 449.

[4] Fitzroy, *Voyage of the* [illegible] *enture and Beagle*, ii. 182. [5] Burckhardt, *op. cit.* i. 107.

Bedouins of Sinai the bride is met in the evening by the groom and two of his young friends, and carried off by force to her father's tent. "She defends herself with stones, and often inflicts wounds on the young men, even though she does not dislike her lover, for according to custom the more she struggles, bites, kicks, cries, and strikes, the more she is applauded ever after by her own companions." There follows the throwing over her of the *abba*, or man's cloak, and a formal announcement of the name of the husband. Then she is dressed in bridal attire, and, still struggling, is led two or three times round and finally into the groom's tent. The resistance is continued to the last.[1] In New Zealand "even where all were agreeable, it was the custom for the groom to go with a party and appear to take her away by force, her friends yielding her up after a feigned struggle."[2] The Baca custom is this: "A young man first tells some of his friends that he admires a certain girl, and after a stated period he speaks to her and says he would like to *twala*, *i.e.* carry her off. If she is agreeable to this *twala*, he carries her off by stealth to his parents' village." On the third day she is returned to her father's house with the dowry cattle.[3] Some of the following cases are of the same class as the practice of hiding already noted. On an appointed day the Ayetas send the prospective bride to the forest to hide herself. If she is favourably inclined to the match, she takes care that her place of concealment shall be easily discovered. If she is found by the groom before sunset, and is brought back to her parents, the marriage is completed.[4] Amongst the Hos after three days of marriage, the bride has to leave her husband, and he

[1] Burckhardt, *op. cit.* i. 263, 264.

[2] Taylor, *op. cit.* 163.

[3] *Journ. Anthrop. Inst.* xx. 138.

[4] Sherman, *op. cit.* ii. 33.

has to carry her home again, while she strenuously resists, kicking, screaming, and biting. "It should be done as if there were no shamming about it."[1] Amongst the Orang-Benuas of Malacca the bride runs away into the forest during the wedding ceremonies; the groom chases her, and if he falls or returns unsuccessful, "he is met with the jeers and merriment of the whole party, and the match is declared off. It generally happens though, that the lady contrives to stumble over the root of some tree friendly to Venus, and falls (fortuitously of course) into the outstretched arms of her pursuer."[2] In the Mezeyne tribe of the Sinai peninsula the girl after betrothal is furnished with provisions by her female friends, and is encouraged to run away and fly to the mountains. If the bridegroom succeeds in finding her retreat, he is bound to consummate the marriage on the spot, and pass the night in the open country. He brings her home, but she repeatedly escapes and only consents to live in her husband's tent after she is far advanced in pregnancy. After remaining with her family about a year, she rejoins her husband, though she may not be expecting a child.[3] Amongst the Digger Indians of California, after the parents' consent to the marriage has been obtained, the girl leaves the paternal home and conceals herself, and if the suitor succeeds in finding her twice out of three times, he is entitled to claim her as his own.[4] The same kind of thing is sometimes seen on the part of the bridegroom, sexual bashfulness not always being confined to the female sex. It is the Egyptian custom that the bridegroom as well as the bride should exhit [illegible] ashfulness; and he is carried up

[1] Bell, *op. cit.* 479.

[2] Newbold, *British Settlements in Malacca*, ii. 407.

[3] Burckhardt, *op. cit.* i. 2

[4] Featherman, *op. cit.* iii. 212.

to the *hareem* by a friend.[1] In the Andamans the bride sits among the matrons, and the groom among the bachelors. The chief approaches him in order to lead him to the bride, but he assumes a modest demeanour and simulates reluctance to move; after encouragement he allows himself to be led slowly, sometimes he is dragged, up to the girl, who, if young, displays much modesty, weeping and hiding her face; her female attendants straighten her legs, and the groom is then made to sit on her thighs, and thus they are married.[2] Amongst the Kaffirs the groom, no less than the bride, runs away, but is brought back by the women.[3] In the above cases we have seen the maiden "captured," if the term be kept, but from herself, from her innocent, shy, and timid personality, by a rough but half-kind method of violence, which has the effect of obviating her bashfulness by conquering it, and of neutralising its results, which, being part of the basis of sexual taboo and a peculiar property of the female sex, are dangerous to men, by a make-believe or sympathetic process.

In some of the following examples we see the bride "captured" and taken away from her *sex* also, who, by psychological necessity, take her part, as previous examples have shown. Ceremonial or mock fights here naturally signify both the sexual opposition and the need of force to ensure the safety of the union. Amongst the Bedouins of South Arabia the bridegroom and his young friends go to the dwelling of the bride's father to demand the lady. They are gravely informed that she has fled to unknown parts. They then proceed to search, and find a cavern guarded by a troop of young girls, and on approaching it y are met with a shower of stones. They endeavou , storm the place,

[1] Lane, *op. cit.* i. 214. [2] *Journ. Anthrop. Inst.* xii . [3] Shooter, *op. cit.* 76.

and in the end the young women take to flight, leaving the bride to the assailants. The bridegroom enters the cavern and takes possession of his bride, and after a short time they come out together, the bride having her face veiled in the manner of married women.[1] At a Druse wedding the bride, closely veiled, is conducted in solemn procession to the house of the bridegroom. Modesty, whether real or feigned, on the part of the bride requires that the moving column should proceed but slowly, to indicate to her future husband that she is not over-anxious to enter upon the duties of the married state, and a halt is made at short intervals, when the weary march is enlivened by songs and the exhibition of the sword-dance. On passing the threshold of the bridegroom's house, the bride sticks firmly to the door-post a lump of yeast. At this moment her intended husband is standing on the housetop exactly above the door, holding a drawn sword over her head, "emblematical of the absolute authority which he is to exercise over her."[2] The inference which ends this account may give the modern explanation of the custom, but does not reach its original meaning. The detail is parallel to those cases, previously mentioned, where a weapon is presented or thrown. At the marriage of sheikhs amongst the Druses the bride and her party on their way to the bridegroom's home are met by a party representing the bridegroom. A mock fight takes place, in which the bridegroom's party is generally driven back, and after a vigorous resistance the bride forces her way in, and is safely lodged in the *hareem*. When t[illegible] bridegroom is about to enter, she throws a massive [illegible] of muslin and gold over her head, covering her face, [illegible]ck, and shoulders, and reaching to

[1] Featherman, *op. cit.* [illegible] 2.

[2] *Id.* v. 480.

the waist. The noise of footsteps is then heard, and the bridegroom enters, lifts her veil, and after a hurried glance at her, replaces it and retires. While the groom sits in state, his brother returns thanks for congratulations in his stead.[1] Amongst the Dorahs of New Guinea the bride is conducted by her female relatives to the house of the bridegroom, where she places herself behind a mat-screen so as not to be seen by the men. Here the dowry of the bride is given to the groom's parents. She is then led back to her own house, where she awaits the arrival of the bridegroom. When he makes his appearance with his friends, he finds the door shut against him, and it is only at the earnest remonstrance of the father of the young woman that the portals of the nuptial chamber are opened.[2] When the Malay bridegroom arrives at the bride's house, there is a mimic conflict for the person of the bride. In some cases a rope or piece of red cloth is stretched across the path to bar the progress of the bridegroom's party, and a stout resistance is made till the groom pays a fine. He enters the house amid volleys of rice, and fights his way to the reception room.[3] After the three days' separation which follows the South Celebes wedding, the bridegroom, on coming to claim his bride, finds the house barricaded, and the inmates fire muskets. Entrance is allowed after a payment. Later on he enters the bridal chamber, where the bride sits on the bed concealed by curtains, and when he is about to open the curtains, he is resisted by the women who are in attendance on the bride. When this difficulty is surmounte :he bride pretends to run away; however, she stays : the ceremony in which one sews the pair toge by their clothes.

[1] Featherman, *op. cit.* v. 481. [2] *Id.* ii. 31 [3] Skeat, *op. cit.* 381.

This is followed by the ceremony of placing one garment, a *sarong*, over the pair, who are then considered united. The rite is called *ridjala-sampoe*, "catching the bride with a *sarong* as with a fishing-net."[1] It is a curious coincidence that, while the bridegroom is on his way to the bride's home, his escort *fish* the air for evil spirits with nets.[2] Further, when the pair are released from the *sarong* which is about them both, the bride pretends to run away again; she is followed by the bridegroom, and pushes him off with her fan. The next night and for two nights more the running away is repeated with variations. The whole business is ended by a final ceremony called "reconciliation."[3] In small towns and villages of modern Egypt the bridegroom visits the mosque, and meanwhile the bride and her party take possession of his house. He is conducted home in procession by his friends, who carry lighted torches, and perform sham fights. When he reaches his dwelling the women are summarily turned out, and he is ushered in as it were by main force. Here a lighted lamp reveals to him the face of his bride, which he pretends never to have seen before.[4] In Soemba a sham fight takes place between the men who act for the bridegroom and the female relatives of the bride, until the former manage to seize her.[5] Amongst the Mundas and Oraons there is a mimic fight for the bride.[6] Such mock fights and "captures" are very common in the peasant-customs at marriage throughout Europe.[7] Amongst the Saxons of Transsylvania, a crowd of

[1] Matthes, *op. cit.* 31, 33.

[2] *Id.* 31.

[3] *Id.* 35, 37, 42.

[4] Featherman, *op. cit.* v. 563, 564.

[5] *Verhandelingen van het* [...]*en. Genootschap van Kunsten en Wetenschappen*, xxxvi. 53.

[6] Dalton, *op. cit.* 194, 253.

[7] Reinsberg-Düringsfeld, *Hochzeitsbuch*, *passim*.

masked figures attempt to separate the newly wed pair. If they succeed, the bridegroom has to win her back by a fight or a ransom; it is a bad omen if they are separated.[1] This is a good example, as showing how force on the part of the husband is in all these customs intended to make the union secure.

There are a few cases where destiny is propitiated by a retreat after the ceremony. This coincides with the natural desire to escape from a more or less trying ordeal. In some cases the escape is to one's old home. On the night of the third day after a Malay wedding there is a very curious ceremony. The relatives of the groom assemble and make a bonfire of rubbish under the house of the newly married couple. Such a smoke is raised that presently the bridegroom comes down, ostensibly to see what is the matter, but as soon as he appears he is seized and carried off bodily to his own parents' house. These proceedings are known as "the stealing of the bridegroom." Next day he is escorted back in a grand procession. On his arrival the pair are sprinkled with water to avert ill-luck, and with holy water to bring good luck.[2] The day after marriage the Egyptian bridegroom is taken into the country, by the man who carried him up to the *hareem*; this is called "the flight."[3] Amongst the Wa-teita, after the three days' fast and seclusion which follow marriage, the bride is conveyed to her old home again by a procession of girls.[4] Amongst the Larkas she runs home after three days and tel[ls] her parents she is not happy. The groom has to [co]me and take her back by force.[5] Other cases [hav]e been mentioned incidentally.

[1] Gerard, *op. cit.* i. 186. [2] [illegible], *op. cit.* 385, 386.
[3] Lane, *op. cit.* i. 214. [4] J. Thomso[n], *op.* [illegible]. [5] Rowney, *op. cit.* 67.

There is a curious custom, with one or two variations, which is found occasionally. It is the custom of drubbing the newly wedded pair, or "ragging their rooms." It is not an "expiation" for marriage, but is induced by that common human feeling which prompted the superstitious Greek to throw away something of value so as to avoid *Nemesis*. It is a sort of sacrifice to propitiate destiny, combined with the idea that people who have been thus rendered more or less destitute will be passed over by jealous powers of evil. It is done by the Maoris, who swoop down upon the dwelling of the newly wed couple, and plunder and destroy their goods. The practice is also followed on all great occasions as a mark of respect. It is instructive to note that it is performed when one has broken *tapu* (as, by the way, a married pair have broken sexual taboo), and when one has had an accident.[1] Another account states, "as soon as the marriage is consummated, the nearest relatives of both attack the hut, rob it, and give the pair a sound thrashing. This ceremony is also performed on the occasion of misfortune happening to a person."[2] The same idea is to be seen in the common practice of breaking something at a wedding, such as a piece of crockery, as amongst the Saxons of Transsylvania, who still say it is to keep off misfortune.[3] It is the Dyak custom, when two tribes make peace, for each in turn to invade and plunder each other's land. It is done ceremo lly.[4] This half-real revenge is intended to satis ne's feelings, in accordance with the savage instin e habit of make-believe. This sacrifice of prope has become a regular thing

[1] Yate, *op. cit.* 86, 97. 237.
[2] Polack, *op. cit.* i. 141.
[3] Gerard, *op. cit.* ii. 35.
[4] Brooke, *op. cit.* i. 368.

amongst the Haidahs, who make a *potlatch* on every possible occasion, the system being in fact a sort of stock-exchange gamble and settling up.[1] Cases such as the following, which are often misunderstood, are explained in the same way: when a Kurnai girl elopes (the recognised method of getting married), she is beaten by her relatives, not as a punishment, but "simply to follow an ancestral custom," which, it may be added, is not "expiation for marriage."[2] The idea of the parents is, by a make-believe beating, with somewhat of reality in it, to relieve their parental feelings.

Few theories of primitive society have had such vogue as that of Marriage by Capture, yet few theories have been built on such slender foundations. The tinge of romance belonging to the hypothesis has no doubt had something to do with its popularity. Its general unscientific nature, however, has been demonstrated by Mr. Fison and Dr. Westermarck; it remained to examine the types of formal and connubial "capture." The explanation of these forms as not being survivals, as not indeed having anything to do with "marriage by capture" proper, but arising in a natural way from normal human feelings, destroys what was the chief support of the old theory of "capture." The theory, then, that mankind in general, or even any particular section of mankind, ever in normal circumstances were accustomed to obtain their wives by capture from other tribes, may be regarded as exploded. There ha[s] been, of course, and still are, sporadic cases of cap[ture] of wives from hostile tribes or others, but such c[ases do n]ot prove a rule. A useful illustration may be dr[awn] from Australian custom. It has often been asser[ted] that marriage by

[1] G. M. Dawson, *op. cit.* 126, 127.

[2] [Fison] and Howitt, *op. cit.* 259.

capture is a common practice amongst the natives. Messrs. Spencer and Gillen note this, and point out that it is of the rarest occurrence amongst the Central Australians, and that when it does occur, it arises out of an expedition of vengeance against a hostile tribe.[1] Mr. Curr also states that it is very rare throughout the continent.[2] The capture of women is naturally an attendant circumstance of invasion. Further, the "marriage by capture" so often attributed to the Australians simply amounts to this, that the woman to be married, according to peaceful tribal custom and classificatory arrangement, is sometimes forcibly taken by the bridegroom for obvious reasons, as we have seen, or, as in all ages happens, elopement take place. In Ceram, for instance, we are told that "marriage by capture (*sic*) takes place usually when the girl's parents are opposed to the match."[3] When carefully examined, most of the old examples adduced as instances of marriage by capture turn out to be either mere inferences of such, or cases of connubial and formal capture, or, as the last case and many of McLennan's examples, elopements.

"Capture" proper, that is, hostile capture from another tribe, has never been, and could never be, a mode of marriage, it is only a method of obtaining a wife. These two have often been confused. Connubial and formal capture are very widely spread, but are never survivals of real capture. The former is often found as matter of fact proceeding to secure the person of t wife, and sometimes occurs side by side with forma pture. In fact, formal capture far from being itsel survival, either of connubial or of hostile capture, i ie ceremonial mode of which con-

[1] Spencer and Gillen, *op* [2] Curr, *op. cit.* i. 108. [3] Riedel, *op. cit.* 133.

nubial capture is the non-ceremonial; each is a living reality, the one being material and the other ideal, the one practical and the other ceremonial. If, as Prof. Tylor holds with McLennan, formal capture is a survival of real capture (hostile or connubial), there ought to be no cases of formal capture in the maternal stage. But there are such. The people of New Britain who reckon genealogy by female descent have marriage by "formal capture."[1] Again, what precise bearing, we may ask, on this question have cases where the bridegroom is captured? Such a practice (formal) is followed by the Garos, a maternal people.[2] Is this a record of the passage from a paternal to a maternal system? For Prof. Tylor regards "capture" as being the way by which "paternal" households gradually superseded "maternal."[3] The young bridegroom certainly is often under this, perhaps more often than under the paternal system, more or less looked after by his parents-in-law, but it is because of paternal and maternal feelings, not because of the maternal system. But there is no evidence that the maternal system was ever general or always preceded the paternal system; such evidence as the common practice of a man living with his bride's parents for a short time, before setting up house for himself, proving nothing except that they wish to look after their daughter's welfare until a child is born, and to see that permanence is thereby assured to the tie; or in many cases that it is a convenient arrangement until the pair get a hous[e] As to capture setting on foot paternal institutions, [we] may here see another way in which misconception [m]ay arise as to the maternal system. This is, after [all,] except in rare cases, simply a method of genealog[y, a]nd has nothing

[1] *Journ. Anthrop. Inst.* xviii. 294 ff. [2] Rowney, op. [illegible] [3] *J.A.I.* xviii. 260.

to do with the husband's authority in the family; yet, under any system, and in any age, sexual difference makes the wife the housekeeper with some control within the house, while the husband is guardian of the family and has general control. This is well seen in those Australian tribes which have the maternal system, but the husband is master and guardian of the family, and has a taboo with his mother-in-law. I mention the last detail, because that has been adduced as a proof of marriage by capture, the mother it is supposed being so indignant at the heartless "capture" of her daughter that she will not even speak to her son-in-law. Of course such cases may have occurred.

Lastly, exogamy is by no means a result of real or any sort of capture. To attempt to show that it is would be as hardy as to try, with McLennan, to prove the practice of capture as resulting from infanticide of female children. Capture cannot be proved universal enough to have given rise to so widely spread a system as exogamy; also the real meaning of the term exogamy is often misunderstood.

It is now perhaps evident that it is not the tribe from which the bride is abducted, nor, primarily, her family and kindred, but her *sex*. A second class of cases are those where woman's sexual characters of timidity, bashfulness, and passivity are sympathetically overcome by make-believe representation of male characteristic ion. A third class combines these two, and pote lly, they may always merge in each other. Connu l capture and formal capture are identical, but th atter is on the spiritual plane.

The ceremoi to be next mentioned form a link between neutrali ceremonies and those which actually and materially unite the man and woman. The principle behind them is that of inoculation. That principle has been described, and its use to lessen sexual danger has been seen in the account of initiatory rites. Being one-sided only, it is useful for marriage in abstract or *in extenso*, as initiation may be called, but is naturally not common as a sacramental method of marrying two individuals. As the initiatory practice is in essence identical with love-charms of similar character, so is this marriage ceremony. A case which shows the identity of principle is from Morocco. On the evening before the marriage, the "*henna* night," the bridegroom visits the bride. He applies *henna* to her hands, and removes a ring from her finger and a bracelet from her arm, and wears the one or the other until the nuptials are finally celebrated.[1] He thus assimilates himself to her, and brings himself into communion with her, satisfying his instincts of love and his subconscious fear of union at the same time. The example is also instructive as being on the way to become a double inoculation in the fact that he applies something to her. The common Indian practice of *sindur*, by which the groom touches the bride with red ochre, sugar and water, and the like, is inoculation of her with himself. The Bheel ceremony in which the bride does this as well, shows inoculation become mutual.[2]

There are some interesting cases in which the principle of inoculation is expressed by one or other of the pair wearing the dress of the oppos sex. It is inoculation and assimilation effected by aring the same kind of clothes as the loved and aded person, and is paralleled by many cases in wh a lover wears a bracelet or some article of clothi of his mistress.

[1] Leared, *op. cit.* 35, 36.

[2] *J. Anthrop. Inst.* ix. 402.

Thomson says of Masai weddings: "Strangest of all, and strikingly indicative of the fact that he had exchanged the spear for the distaff, the bridegroom had actually to wear the garment of a *ditto* (girl) for one month; just imagine what fun it would be in this staid and dignified country of ours, if a young man had to spend his honeymoon in a cast-off suit of his wife's maiden clothes."[1] In ancient Cos, according to Plutarch, the bridegroom was dressed in women's clothes when he received his bride.[2] The story of Heracles and Omphale may have some similar origin. Plutarch connects the custom and the myth; but in the old fashion makes the myth the origin of the custom. On the other hand, in ancient Argos there was a law, that brides "should wear beards when they slept with their husbands."[3] The Spartan bride was clothed in a man's cloak and shoes, and put on her bed in the darkness by her bridesmaid, to wait for the entrance of the groom.[4] It may be noted that there are some cases in European custom, as in Wales, where the bride is disguised in men's clothes.[5] The chief point in these is the disguise, and in origin the European customs may be nothing more.

We now reach the ceremonies which, more than any others, unite the man and woman. The principle of their action is double or mutual "inoculation," which renders the union innocuous on either side. Having already fully described this method of *ngia ngiampe*, we need here only eat that it is the completion of ideas of contact. N ual inoculation is, when looked at from the other le, union; each of the two parties

[1] Thomson, *op. cit.* 25
[2] Plutarch, *Quaestiones Graecae*, 58.
[3] *Id. Mulierum Virtutes* [illegible] E, F.
[4] *Id. Lycurgus*, xv. 48.
[5] [illegible]*oure*, *Marriage Customs*, 37.

gives to the other a part of himself, and receives from the other a part of him; this part, on the principles of contact, may be, as it is in love-charms, a lock of hair, a piece of clothing, food that has been touched or not, blood, and the like. This effects union by assimilating the one to the other, so as to produce somewhat of identity of substance. When the act is done simultaneously, its sacramental character is intensified. The union thus effected has, in accordance with the ideas behind it, a most binding force, each party as having given part of himself into the other's keeping is thereby bound, and as having received part of the other has thereby a hold over the other; and the act is the materialised expression of a desire for union, identical in principle with physical contact, especially with contact in love. It sums up and recapitulates the whole cycle of conceptions as to human relations, which are latent in human nature.

First we find the very general ceremony of joining hands and the like. Here mere mutual contact fulfils the union. It is a ceremonial pre-representation of the actual union in marriage, assisting that union by making it safe and by making it previously, and as it were objectively. In Fiji the chief marriage ceremony is the joining of hands, as it is amongst the Algonquins, Egyptians, and many another people, including ourselves.[1] At Abyssinian weddings the bride and groom crook their little fingers together under a cloth which is held over them.[2] The Puttooas the thumbs of the pair together.[3] The Egyptian ide and groom stand face to face, grasp each othe right hands and press the thumbs together, a hanc rchief being put

[1] Wilkes, *op. cit.* iii. 91; Featherman, *op. cit.* iii Lane, *op. cit.* i. 200.
[2] Featherman, *op. cit.* v. 606. Rowney, *op. cit.* 93.

over the clasped hands.[1] A curious example of the close connection the pair sometimes have with their attendant sponsors, combined with ideas of sexual solidarity, is from the Bondei. The bride and groom hold hands, each takes his and her *kungwi* by the hand, each *kungwi* holds the hand of a child, the male *kungwi* that of a boy, and the female that of a girl.[2]

In Nias, again, mutual contact is expressed in another way. The chief marriage ceremony is the pressing together of the heads of the young pair.[3] The Andamanese marriage ceremony is this: the bridegroom is made to sit down on the bride's legs, which are, sometimes forcibly, straightened out for the purpose.[4] The pressing together of two things is an obvious method of union and of inoculation; and the marriage ceremony is curiously paralleled by the Andamanese method of making a boy at initiation "free" of a forbidden food, pig, for instance. A pig is pressed down upon him, and brought into contact with most of his person.[5]

Another method of joining the pair together is by throwing a garment over them to cover them both; the same method has been noticed as applied to the joining of hands. At marriage amongst the Jews of Jerusalem a white cassock is thrown over the pair, "to indicate that they now belong to one another." All present exclaim, "May it be a good sign!"[6] The same is done by the Hovas.[7] In Tahiti the pair were enveloped in a cloth.[8] So in the south-east of Borneo, North [illegible]s, and amongst the Battas of Sumatra.[9]

1 Lane, *op. cit.* i. 200.
2 Featherman, *op. cit.* [illegible] 54.
3 Dale, in *Journ. Anthrop. Inst.* xxv. 199.
4 *Journ. Anthrop. Inst.* xii. 137.
5 *Id.* 135.
6 Featherman, *op. cit.* v. 140.
7 *Journ. Anthrop. Inst.* [illegible] 1.
8 W. Ellis, *Polynesian Researches*, i. 117.
9 *Ausland* for 1885, 78 [illegible] Sundermann, in *Allgemein. Missions-Zeitschrift*, xi. 443; van der Tuuk, *Bataksch Woordenboek*, s.v. [illegible]

One would expect to find cases of double "inoculation" by means of dress, each wearing the dress of the other sex. In European folk-custom there are several traces of this, bride and groom exchanging head-dresses and the like.[1] After betrothal the Ainu boy and girl wear each other's clothes.[2] This method of union is a common phenomenon in love-practice, and when a modern 'Arry and 'Arriet exchange hats, the fact is no coincidence, but is due to the same principle inherent in the human consciousness. To the same order of ideas belongs an Andamanese custom. "They address young married people in a strange way, calling the husband by the name of the wife."[3]

The commonest of all marriage ceremonies of union is eating and drinking together. This mutual inoculation by food is the strongest of all ties of the *ngia ngiampe* sort, and breaks the most important of sexual taboos, that against eating together. Eating food together produces identity of substance, of flesh, and thereby introduces the mutual responsibility resulting from eating what is part of the other, and giving the other part of oneself to eat; each has the other in pledge, and each is in pawn to the other; any ill-feeling later, or sin, will produce bad results between the pair. The closest union is produced with the closest of responsibilities. Its binding force has been already traced to its origin, as is shown by the Loango custom, that bride and groom must make a full confession of their sins at the marriage ceremony, else they will fall ill when eating together.[4] The practice is of course identical with those we have surveyed in connection with hospitality, the sharing of "bread and

[1] Reinsberg-Düringsfeld, *op. cit. passim.*

[2] Batchelor, *The Ainu*, 142.

[3] *Journ. Anthrop. Inst.* xii. 129.

[4] Bastian, *Loango Küste*, i. 172.

salt," a large class of love-charms, and acts of *ngiampe*. It goes back to the animal expression of sympathy by contact and by a gift of food. The practice has nothing to do originally with transferring the groom or the bride to the other's kin ; food produces flesh, and flesh is connected with blood, but the "tie of blood" is an inference not very prominent in early thought, the tie of eating together is recognised earlier both in practice and in theory. The bride and groom become "one flesh," but this is union of two individuals only ; it is only late in culture, and then but rarely, that kinship assumes such superiority over individualism. For instance, the exogamous Melanesians say that the wife never becomes one of her husband's "clan," but is "at the door," "half-way across."[1] The pair are brought into a close relation, but not relationship, although in primitive thought the latter is a relation. The theory that the "blood covenant" and the similar marriage ceremony are intended to cause the blood of the tribe to flow in the veins of the new member, is based on late legal fictions. Exchange of blood is commoner between lovers than as a marriage ceremony, and lovers are not likely to think of tribal union ; the act in Amboina, for instance, is regarded as a real sacrament of affection.[2] Also, on the theory relatives by marriage should not marry as they do. Again, are all the cases where husbands and wives do not eat together to be explained by the fact that, owing to exogamy, they are of different tribes? Robertson Smith made a further suggestion that it was because they were of different totems and therefore had different systems of forbidden food;[3] but the latter system is rarely applied to marriage. This theory of tribal communion

[1] *Journ. Anthrop. Inst.* x. 3-4. [2] Riedel, *op. cit.* 41. [3] *Op. cit.* 312.

involves too many inconsistencies, and we need some explanation more in accordance with human nature, and with primitive thought. Well, as to this sex-taboo and marriage ceremony alike, exogamy rarely implies that the husband and wife are of different tribes. They more often than not are of different families only, and often cousins. Again, brothers and sisters are often forbidden to eat together. They are actually of the same family, of the same totem, and of the same tribe. What does the taboo imply but sex? Lastly, it has been overlooked that in most cases one person only is added to the tribe, namely, the new wife or the new husband. This being so, it should not be necessary, if the idea is simply to make that person a member of the tribe, for more to be done than that he or she only should eat some tribal food or drink some tribal blood; but in most cases the other party also eats and drinks — why? To cause the tribal blood of the stranger's tribe to flow in his or her veins? This seems supererogatory. It may be said, the idea is to knit the two tribes together, but that is another story. Here I will only observe that primarily it does nothing of the kind, and that the theory breaks down before such cases as the following, in which the ceremony has for its sole object this knitting together of two tribes. The ceremonial communion, by which two tribes or villages in Ceram and Wetar form alliance, is intended to join them together for mutual help in war.[1] It will be allowed that such covenants form as important a bond, for treachery is thereby neutralised, as that made by an intermarriage. Now, after this ceremony, it is expressly forbidden for them to intermarry. Here we may remember that married

[1] Riedel, *op. cit.* 123, 129, 446, 447.

couples do not always live together as such, but, as has been shown, often do not eat together. On the present theory, this apparent contradiction, and the curious result of the Ceramese and Wetarese tribal covenants both receive a satisfactory explanation.

The offering of a gift of food, which is part of the biological basis of the custom, is often used as a proposal of marriage. In Halmahera and Borneo a proposal is made by offering *betel* to the girl. She shows her acceptance by receiving it.[1] In Samoa the suitor offers her a basket of bread-fruit; or he asks her parents for her hand. If they are friendly and eat with him, his addresses are sure to be favourably received.[2] Here is seen the ordinary use of the method as a test of friendliness. At the betrothal ceremony of the Yezedees the sheikh delivers to the bridegroom a loaf of consecrated bread, half of which is eaten by each of the betrothed.[3] The very common practice of a love-gift thus passes into a proposal of marriage, and in the last case it is seen in the process of becoming a marriage rite. This marriage rite may indeed be described as a crystallisation of the love-charm of exchange of food.

At marriage there are some interesting variations. In the Duke of York Islands a cocoanut is broken over the heads of the pair, and its milk poured over them.[4] Amongst the Barbary Arabs the parents of the groom present the young wife on her arrival with milk and honey.[5] An gst the Koosa Kaffirs the relatives of the groom ha milk to the bride, reminding her that it is from t cows which belong to the bride-

[1] Riedel in *Zeitschrift für Ethnologie*, xvii. 75; St. John, *op. cit.* i. 54, 161.

[2] Wilkes, *op. cit.* ii. 138.

[3] Featherman, *op. cit.* v. 62.

[4] *Journ. Anthrop. Inst.* xviii. 290.

[5] Featherman, *op. cit.* v. 530.

groom. Of this milk she may not drink while the bridegroom is her suitor only, but now she is to drink it, and from this moment the union is indissolubly concluded. The people shout, "She drinks the milk! She hath drunk the milk!"[1] This case, of course, is one-sided "inoculation"; the bride eats the bridegroom's food, that is, she eats his *substance* in both senses of the word. In the next two cases, sexual shyness has played its part. At weddings in Ceram-laut the bride does not appear, being hidden in her chamber; the bridegroom eats with her people.[2] In Amboina an old woman puts "food of the house" (the wedding being in the bridegroom's dwelling) in the bride's mouth.[3] The South Celebes bridegroom is offered the *betel*-box of his bride, from which he takes some *betel*.[4] In Ceram the bride eats a male opossum, and the bridegroom a female of the same animal.[5]

A Servian bride ate with her husband on the wedding-day, the first and last occasion in her life on which she ate with a man.[6] Niam-niam women never eat with men, but at the marriage ceremony they eat with their husbands.[7] At Hova marriages the pair eat together, and then a *lamba* is thrown round them both.[8] The joining of hands is used in the Malaccas, where it is followed by eating together;[9] so in Nias and Timor, and amongst the Orang-Sakai of Perak.[10] Amongst the Topantunuasu of Celebes the pair are placed on one mat, and the bridegroom places his

[1] Lichtenstein, *op. cit.* i. 262.

[2] Riedel, *De sluik- en kroesharige rassen tusschen Selebes en Papua*, 172.

[3] *Id.* 70. [4] Matthes, *op. cit.* 30. [5] Riedel, *op. cit.* 133.

[6] Reinsberg-Düringsfeld, *op. cit.* 81. [7] Schweinfurth, *op. cit.* ii. 28.

[8] *Journ. Anthrop. Inst.* ix. 41. [9] *Journal of the Indian Archipelago*, i. 338.

[10] Rosenberg, *op. cit.* 38; Müller, *Reizen en onderzoekingen in den Indischen Archipel*, ii. 258; *Journ. Ind. Archipelago*, iv. 431.

right leg on the left leg of the bride. They then eat rice together.[1] Santhal couples fast on the wedding-day, but after the *sindur dan* they eat together. This is the first and last time she eats with a man.[2] In the Kei Islands, the young couple eat together and exchange *betel*; this forms the wedding ceremony. In Ceram after these words are repeated by an elder, "what the husband wishes the wife must wish, and what the wife wishes the husband must also wish, and let them not forget their parents," the couple eat together. The young couple in Timorlaut eat together out of one dish at the wedding. When the Babar bridegroom has found his bride, after the search in the dark, his friend places their heads together, and then the pair eat together out of the same dish.[3] The Batta bride and groom sit together and eat rice from the same dish.[4] So in Rao, "as a token of friendship."[5] Eating together is the marriage ceremony in Palembang, Tebing-Tinggi, and Ranau, and amongst the Orang-Mantra; in Borneo we have the same ceremony, sometimes varied by smoking the same cigarette.[6] In Mindanao and Celebes there is the same ceremony of marriage, and also in Bali, Flores, and the Sawu Islands.[7] In many of the above cases *betel* is chewed together by the pair. In New Guinea the rite is common.[8] The Navajo couple ate maize-pudding

[1] *Bijd. T.L.V.K. Ned. Ind.* iii. 5. 1. 90.

[2] Dalton, *op. cit.* 216.

[3] Riedel, *op. cit.* 236, 133, 301, 351.

[4] *Tijdschrift voor Nederlandsch Indie*, i. 346, ii. 179.

[5] *Tijdschrift voor Indische Taal-Land en Volkenkunde*, xxvii. 578.

[6] Pritorius, in *De Indische Bij.* i. 429; *Tijdschrift voor Nederlandsch Indie* (1873). x. 295; Forbes, *Eastern Archipelago*, 219; *Tijdschrift voor Indische Taal-Land en Volkenkunde*, x. 428; St. John, *op. cit.* 50, 51.

[7] *Tijdschrift voor Nederlandsch Indië* (1840), i. 122; *Tijdschrift voor Indische Taal-Land en Volkenkunde*, xviii. 383; *Globus*, xliii. 60; Graafland, *De Minahasa*, i. 319; Veth, *Java*, i. 634; Riedel, in *Revue Coloniale Internationale* (1885), i. 308, (1886). i. 70.

[8] Rosenberg, *Der Malayische Archipel*, 455.

from the same plate.[1] In Russia and Scandinavia the pair used to drink from the same cup; so in Brazil and Japan.[2] Amongst the Ghonds and Korkus the garments of the pair are tied together, and they interchange things and eat together.[3] At Dorah weddings the oldest man present joins the right hands of the young couple, reminding them of their mutual duties and expressing his best wishes. A pot filled with sago-mush is then placed before them, of which they serve to each other three mouthfuls in alternate succession.[4] In the Kingsmill Islands the pair sit on a new mat, and the priest presses their foreheads together, and sprinkles their faces with water. They then eat together some fish and bread-fruit.[5] At Dyak marriages the bride and groom eat together, and are sprinkled with rice.[6] In the Manuahiki Islands the priest gave the man a cocoanut to drink and he, after sipping the milk, gave it to the woman and she drank.[7] In Fiji the marriage ceremony was the eating by the pair out of the same dish.[8] In Madagascar bride and groom eat together, and thus become man and wife. It is "apparently a symbol of the future unity of their interests."[9] At a wedding in the Philippines the young couple were required to eat from the same plate and drink from the same cup.[10] At a Malay wedding friends put in the hands of bride and bridegroom handfuls of rice, and with this the two feed each other simultaneously.[11] Amongst the Larkas rice and meat are offered to her, "by partaking of which she becomes of her husband's

[1] Waitz-Gerland, *op. cit.* iii. 105.
[2] Westermarck, *History of Human Marriage*, 419.
[3] Forsyth, *The Highlands of Central India*, 149.
[4] Featherman, *op. cit.* ii. 32.
[5] Featherman, *op. cit.* ii. 266.
[6] Williams and Calvert, *op. cit.* i. 170.
[7] Wilkes, *op. cit.* v. 101.
[8] Turner, *Samoa*, 276.
[9] Sibree, *op. cit.* 195.
[10] Featherman, *op. cit.* ii. 474.
[11] Skeat, *op. cit.* 383.

caste" (*sic*). Later, a cup of beer is given to each, these are mingled and the pair drink; this "completes the marriage."[1] At marriages in Java the groom offers the bride some rice which they eat together out of the same dish, or the pair take *betel* out of the same box, "to indicate their union."[2] In the valleys of the Hindoo Koosh the marriage ceremony is that the pair eat together a cake of bread.[3] In Ceylon the pair have their little fingers tied together. They then eat out of the same dish, "to show they are now of equal rank" (*sic*).[4] In Mangaia the marriage ceremony was that bride and groom ate together;[5] so amongst the Sarae.[6] The Khyoungtha bride and groom are tied together, and fed by the priest with rice, each receiving seven alternate helpings.[7] Amongst the Chukmas the pair are tied together and in that position they feed each other, the best man and bridesmaid guiding their hands.[8] In Dardistan the pair eat together, this being the marriage ceremony.[9] Eating together is a common marriage custom amongst European peasants. In Germany the pair eat off the same plate.[10] In ancient Rome at marriage by *confarreatio*, the bride and groom ate together *panis farreus*, in the presence of the *Flamen Dialis* and *Pontifex Maximus*.[11] In South Slavonia the bride eats half an apple and gives the other half to the bridegroom.[12] If we can isolate the folk-lore element in the story of Eve's apple, it seems most probable that some such love-practice or marriage rite as this is behind it. There is an unmistakable reference to sexual

[1] Rowney, *op. cit.* 67.
[2] Featherman, *op. cit.* ii. 355.
[3] Biddulph, *op. cit.* 79.
[4] Forbes, *op. cit.* i. 331.
[5] Gill, *Life in the Southern Isles*, 63.
[6] Munzinger, *op. cit.* 384.
[7] Lewin, *op. cit.* 129.
[8] *Id.* 177.
[9] G. W. Leitner, in *Asiatic Quarterly Review*, v. 153.
[10] A. Wuttke, *Der deutsche Volksaberglaube*, 560.
[11] Gaius, i. 108 ff.
[12] Krauss, *op. cit.* 276, 459.

relations in the story, the serpent being the zoomorphic presentment of virility, which, as has been noticed, is a widely spread way of explaining certain sexual phenomena. Further, there is the knowledge of evil as distinguished from the state of innocence, a fact curiously paralleled by the psychological analysis of the result of the *ngia ngiampe* relation, of which eating together it the most typical form. The symbolism of the apple, as found in Greek and Latin folk-lore, is of course later.

Drinking wine is no substitute for or survival of drinking blood; each has the same effect, but wine is primarily liquid nourishment. The taking together of the Communion is in Catholic countries an essential part of the marriage ceremony. It is so in the English Church, according to the rubric. Some examples of drinking together have been already noticed. In the island Romang the pair drink together out of one cup; this is the wedding ceremony.[1] At marriages in Morocco the priest hands to the couple a glass of wine after blessing it, and each drink of it. The glass is then smashed on the ground by the groom, "with a covert meaning that he wishes they may never be parted until the glass again becomes perfect."[2] The idea is originally to prevent others making magic use of the vessel to the harm of those who have drunk, and, later, to prevent any undoing of the rite. At the marriage ceremony of Polish Jews the Rabbi hands a goblet of wine, over which he pronounces a blessing, to the pair, who sip each in turn of the wine.[3] Amongst the Hos, Lepchas, and Tipperahs, the bride and groom drink beer together out of the same cup.[4] In China

[1] Riedel, *De sluik- en kroesharige rassen tusschen Selebes en Papua*, 460.

[2] Leared, *op. cit.* 37.

[3] Featherman, *op. cit.* v. 154.

[4] Dalton, *op. cit.* 193; Risley, *op. cit.* ii. 8; Lewin, *op. cit.* 202.

and Corea they drink wine out of two cups which are tied together by red thread.[1] Amongst the Nestorians the final act of the marriage ceremonial is the taking of the Communion together.[2]

Various national narcotics, sedatives, and the like, are used in the same practice, as has been seen already. The Aru bride is carried to the wedding, and the ceremony is the partaking together of *betel*.[3] The Sibuyou bride and bridegroom sit side by side on two crowbars; their heads are knocked together, and they then put *betel* in each other's mouth. Previously to the last rite, the priest waves a pair of fowls above their heads. After the exchange of *betel*, the fowls are killed, and from the appearance of the blood the priest predicts the future fortunes of the newly wedded pair. The Balans at marriage chew *betel* together. The Sintahs rub the chest, forehead, and hands of the pair with a paste of saffron, gold-dust, and fowls' blood. Lastly, a string of beads is bound round the wrist of each of the pair.[4] Amongst the Minahasses of Celebes the young couple sit side by side, and, *betel* being placed in the hand of each, they exchange it and chew it. They are thus legally married.[5] In the Natchez wedding ceremony the pair ate together out of the same dish. Afterwards the bridegroom smoked the *calumet* and "wafted the first fumes towards the parents of his wife, and then towards his own parents in token of the alliance."[6]

Drinking each other's blood has no real pre-eminence in early custom over other means of assimilation; blood is simply a part of one's self. Where the practice is

[1] Doolittle, *op. cit.* i. 86; Griffis, *op. cit.* 249.
[2] Featherman, *op. cit.* v. 75.
[3] Riedel, *op. cit.* 262.
[4] Featherman, *op. cit.* ii. 267.
[5] *Id.* ii. 64.
[6] *Id.* iii. 139.

followed, it is not relationship that is the result, but relation,—of *ngia ngiampe*, just as is effected by food and other vehicles of contact. It is rather a rare custom, far more rare than the "blood covenant," and a corollary of the blood covenant between two tribes was actually found to be that they may not intermarry. This was explained in the account of *ngia ngiampe*. It is in fact commoner as used by lovers than as a marriage ceremony, and lovers are the last persons to think of tribal union. In Amboina lovers drink each other's blood, mixed with food, "to show their close attachment," and the custom is said to have a sacramental binding force.[1] This practice of lovers is very common in Europe and elsewhere.[2]

At marriages amongst the Wukas the young couple mutually make a slight cut in their foreheads sufficiently deep to let the blood flow, and the other members of both families follow their example. "This binds together all the relatives on both sides in the closest fraternal alliance."[3] A common variation is anointing with blood. Amongst the Bengal tribes the marriage ceremony is the *sindur dan*, in which the groom marks the bride's forehead with red lead. Red lead is possibly, but not certainly, a substitute for blood.[4] The Birhor ceremony is that bride and groom smear each other with blood drawn from their little fingers.[5] The Kewat ceremony of marriage is the *sindur dan*, after which blood is drawn from the hands of bride and groom and mingled with food which is then eaten by the pair. Similarly amongst the Rajpoots.[6]

The same principles of relation, of *ngia ngiampe*,

[1] Riedel, *op. cit.* 41.

[2] Ploss u. Bartels, *Das Weib*, ii. 442 ff.

[3] Featherman, *op. cit.* ii. 32.

[4] Dalton, *op. cit.* 160, 216, 252, 273, 321.

[5] *Id.* 220.

[6] Risley, *op. cit.* i. 456; ii. 189.

more subconscious indeed, but still inherent and always liable to pass from potentiality to actuality, are behind the practice of feasting at weddings. We have found this kind of thing in connection with Saturnalia festivals. So at marriage the friends of both feel somewhat bound together by the union of the pair, and expression is given to this by eating and drinking together. Here indeed the new member is united to the family, so far as sharing in a feast effects this. Just as two men nowadays are more or less brought into friendly union by taking wine together or "having a drink," and members of societies are united in closer sympathy by a dinner or a feast, so the husband and wife are joined together by communion, and to some extent also their friends by mutual feasting. These happen to be different families, but rarely different tribes; their union, however, is not primarily a fiction of blood-kinship, but a more general relation of friendliness, as persons who have the same interests and a mutual acquaintance in the happy bride or bridegroom, but, originally, as persons who eat together. The connection of feasting with the importance of food is shown at Huron weddings, where there was a feast of every kind of game, including fish, and meat for dogs.[1] As to other expressions of joy and good feeling, we may say of wedding dances what an old Motu-Motu man said to Mr. Chalmers: "No drums are beaten uselessly, there are no dances that are merely useless."[2]

The same ideas are behind the common practice of gifts from bride to groom and from groom to bride, and between the friends and relatives of the pair; just as they are behind the identical practices of love-gifts and gifts from man to man. A gift means far more

[1] Featherman, *op. cit.* iii. 56.

[2] Chalmers, *op. cit.* 181.

to primitive man than it does to us; it is part of himself. A Patagonian chief is prevented by custom from entering the tent of another till presents have been exchanged.[1] This case shows the principles of *ngia ngiampe*. Amongst the Khakyens there seems to be little more of marriage ceremonial than interchange of presents, this is essential, and really seems to constitute marriage.[2] The importance of gifts in this connection is shown by the Kaffir custom that the bride may not eat food from the bridegroom's *kraal* until the "presents" have duly arrived.[3] The marriage gifts in South Celebes between bride and groom are very numerous and most of them are variously symbolical of marriage, amongst them are ginger-roots which have grown together.[4] In Japan the sending of presents to the bride by the groom is one of the most important parts of the marriage ceremony. When done, the contract is complete, and neither party can draw back.[5] It is not, as Dr. Westermarck thinks,[6] a relic of a previous custom of marriage by purchase; the latter is, on the contrary, a development from this.

The explanation of bride-gifts is really the explanation of what is mis-called "marriage by purchase." In many peoples, of course, as commercial instincts ripen, and daughters are found to have their price, the old idea fades into the "light of common day," and buying and selling become connected with marrying and giving in marriage. But originally it was not so. The so-called bride-price was originally of the same class as the *kalduke*, a pledge, a part of one's self, given to another and received from him. Buying and selling

[1] Musters, *op. cit.* 184.

[2] Anderson, *op. cit.* 30.

[3] Shooter, *op. cit.* 54.

[4] Matthes, *op. cit.* 13-18, 22-26, 25.

[5] *Transactions of the Asiatic Society of Japan*, xiii. 120.

[6] *Op. cit.* 395.

with primitive peoples have not the same sordid connotation as they now have. The principle involved is more personal, more religious; there is less of price and more of value, more of the pledge than of profit and loss. As showing something of the early idea of payments and purchase, the following case is useful. When two villages in the New Hebrides make peace, the offending village is mulcted in a sum of pigs. There is, however, a sham fight, in which the village which has to pay the pigs is defeated, thus giving a pretext for the payment.[1]

In the Banks Islands, when all the "purchase-money" for the bride has been paid, the women come forward and refuse to let the bride go until a further sum is put down.[2] The *harta*, or bride-price, amongst the Minahasses of Celebes "should not be considered as a price, it has rather the nature of a compensation paid to the bride's family for the loss of one of its working and child-producing members."[3] Amongst the Todas and Osages the marriage contract "resembles, but is not, an act of barter." The Osage bride is stripped of all her clothes and ornaments, which become the property of the groom's mother; but she receives in exchange a new suit equally valuable. The ceremonies are concluded by a family feast;[4] much as amongst the Chippeways, whose weddings were ended by a feast at which presents were exchanged between the bridegroom and the relatives of the bride.[5] As to the bride-price amongst the Kaffirs a good observer states, "the transaction is not a mere purchase. The cattle paid for the bride are divided amongst the male

[1] *Journ. Anthrop. Inst.* xxiii. 17.

[2] Codrington, *op. cit.* 237.

[3] Hickson, *A Naturalist in North Celebes*, 282.

[4] Marshall, *op. cit.* 211; Featherman, *op. cit.* iii. 308.

[5] Featherman, *op. cit.* iii. 249.

relations, and are considered by the law to be held in trust for the benefit of herself and children, should she be left a widow. She can accordingly legally demand assistance from any of those who have partaken of her dowry."[1] At Kaffir betrothals a goat is killed at the *kraal* of the suitor, or if he has no goat, a present of beads is made to the girl. Until the one or the other is done, she may not eat at the *kraal*, where she remains a few days. Besides the cattle he has to "pay" for his wife, he must give a cow to the bride's mother; this is called *ukutu*, referring to the thongs made from an ox-hide, and hung round the bride during infancy. This ox is thus "repaid" by the groom. Again, there is "the ox of the girl" to be slain at the marriage; this is given by the bride's father to the groom. It is also called "the ox which has a surplus," and represents these ideas: (1) it stands for the value of the girl, (2) it gives an assurance to the recipient that the spirit of the father—*I-hloze*—will not after his death come to disturb the place where his daughter lives, and (3) that his girl will bear many children. On arriving at the bridegroom's *kraal* after sunset, she gives him a present of beads, but does not speak; she receives also a present from him which she hands to her brother. Next day, the friends of the bride go to the *kraal* to demand from the bridegroom the ox called *um-golistwa*. The groom says he has no ox, and is thereupon informed that the bride will be taken away. After remaining concealed for a time, he now tries to run away, but is prevented by a company of women, a smile on his face showing that his efforts are merely formal. The *um-golistwa* is now brought and given to the bride's friends. The father of the bride delivers a lecture to the groom, on

[1] Maclean, *op. cit.* 53; *Journ. Anthrop. Inst.* xix. 270.

the duty of behaving well to her, and warns him of the impropriety of beating his wife. Then the slaughter of "the ox of the girl" takes place; this is the "fixing point of the ceremony," previously the bride could be removed.[1] This account brings out clearly the religious importance of "bride-gifts," and is instructive as showing the identity of the "purchase-money" with these. It is to be noted lastly that there underlies the practice an idea that the "ox of the girl" is a substitute for her, and the ox of the bridegroom a substitute for him, securing safety, both religious and practical, to both parties.[2] There is also to be noted the sexual shyness on the part of the bridegroom, as shown by the formal attempt to escape.

To conclude this sketch of marriage ceremonies, it is to be observed that the reason why marriage ritual is often excluded from religion proper by enquirers, and why much of it is apparently secular, is precisely the fact that the subconscious fear of the one sex towards the other is here so liable to emerge into consciousness, when a man and a woman stand face to face. Much of religion begins with, as it returns to, human personalities.

[1] Shooter, *op. cit.* 54, 71, 72.

[2] The Damara custom may be compared; a special part of the ox sacrificed at a wedding may only be eaten by young girls. With the fat therefrom the bridesmaids deck the hair of the bride.—*South African Folklore Journal*, i. 49.

CHAPTER XV

HUSBAND and wife are thus in the relation of *ngia ngiampe*, emphasised by its being a sexual form; they have been brought into that relation by a special ceremony of union, and remain in it both as a result of that ceremony, of which permanence of union is not the least important object, and as a result of living together, which is itself a potential mode of *ngia ngiampe*. This continuous contact introduces once more all the original dangers of sexual taboo, as it were in spite of the act of *ngia ngiampe*; in other words, the factors of contact which produce the taboo remain, after the taboo is broken by union, so as to give that union its sanction or binding force. The resulting taboo, that of responsibility, is thus emphasised by the original ideas of contact. We saw how this new taboo of responsibility arises, and that it is the psychological basis of altruism; of this and of the original sexual taboos between husband and wife, which also now recur, not inconsistently, as a result of the *ngia ngiampe* relation, it is unnecessary to quote instances, but a few illustrations will be given to show how the mutual responsibility of married persons is based on the original ideas of contact. The duty resulting is primarily between husband and wife, then between parents and children, and between the children themselves, secondarily between either of the married pair and those brought by the marriage into relation with each. Many details, such as the following, show how conscious application of the ideas of contact supplement such biological relations. A Zulu mother, when about to leave her baby for a few minutes, will squeeze her milk over its hands, breast, and back, or spit on it, "as a protective charm" to ensure its safety during her absence.[1] Amongst the Maoris if the mother's breasts give no milk, she and her husband are kept apart for a night, to allow the *karakia* (incantation), which has been employed as cure, to take effect.[2] In Luang Sermata, if a woman's children have died while being suckled, the next born is given to other people to be nursed.[3] Amongst the people of the Loango Coast the bridegroom and the bride before the marriage ceremony have to confess their sins to the priest; if they fail to do so, or if either keep back anything, evil and misfortune "will result when they eat together."[4] This example is an excellent illustration of all these ideas. In South-East Africa a guilty wife may be forgiven but the husband cannot live with her till a third party has been with her. If a guilty woman were to put salt in her husband's food, and he were to eat it, he would surely die, therefore many women ask a little girl to put in the salt.[5] We see here and in the following how the adhesive substance of guilt which may injure the wronged party is prevented from acting, by the use of an intermediary. After divorce an Egyptian husband cannot legally take his wife again, till she has been married and divorced by another man. They employ a poor, ugly, or blind man for this,

[1] Leslie, *op. cit.* 147.

[2] Shortland, *Maori Religion*, 30.

[3] Riedel, *op. cit.* 327.

[4] Bastian, *Loango Küste*, i. 170, 172.

[5] *Journ. Anthrop. Inst.* xxii. 110.

called *moostakhhill*. Many rich Turks keep a special black slave for this purpose, generally one who has not reached puberty.[1] Amongst the Samoyeds, if birth is difficult, one suspects the woman of adultery.[2] Amongst the Druses, if a wife leave her husband's abode without an injunction to return, this is equivalent to divorce. However willing both are to unite, they cannot come together till she has first been married to a third party, who must then divorce her; after this she can return.[3] Again, when a Chiquito man fell ill, they used to kill the wife thinking her to be the cause of his sickness, and imagining when she was removed that he would recover.[4] Amongst the Krumen when a wife dies, the husband is believed to have caused her death by "witchcraft."[5] In Congo tribes widows and widowers are similarly accused.[6] In Madagascar the widow is reviled and informed that it is her fault that her *Vintana* (fate) has been stronger than that of her husband, and that she "is virtually the cause of his death."[7] When a Zulu woman has lost her husband and is married by a brother or other man, the spirit of her late husband follows her continually. If she is pregnant and the spirit comes to her, she falls ill and miscarries. By placing in an ant-heap some spittle, collected in her mouth while dreaming of him, the ghost is laid.[8] In China it is believed that when members of a family are sick one after the other, there is a mysterious and injurious influence existing between, for example, husband and wife, or father and son.[9] In Samoa, when one was sick, the priest assembled all the

[1] Lane, *op. cit.* i. 228.
[2] Georgi, *op. cit.* 14.
[3] Chasseaud, *op. cit.* 186.
[4] Dobrizhoffer, *op. cit.* ii. 264.
[5] J. L. Wilson, *op. cit.* 115.
[6] Waitz-Gerland, *op. cit.* ii. 120.
[7] *Journ. Anthrop. Inst.* ix. 45.
[8] Callaway, *op. cit.* 161.
[9] Doolittle, *op. cit.* i. 143.

family round the sick-bed, and made them confess their sins. "The requisition was always implicitly obeyed, and each one confessed everything he or she had ever at any time done. Whether it were theft, adultery, seduction, lying, or invoking a curse upon the sick person, however long concealed, all was openly and with solemn contrition confessed."[1] Here is evident the idea of danger inherent in all contact, emphasised by the very closeness of the relation, in spite of the friendliness of a united life; it is to be compared with the Loango rule that husband and wife must confess their sins, else they will be injured by eating together. Amongst the Samoyeds at a Shaman's performances, his wife "as an unclean thing, must keep out of the way."[2] In New Guinea when a man is taboo he lives apart from his wife, and his food is cooked by his sister.[3]

The same ideas are somewhat differently expressed in the following. In Timor-laut a married man's hair may not be cut, else his wife will die.[4] A Sarawak man will put himself under *pamali* to cure a sick child.[5] The conduct of one connected by contact reacts upon the other, when either is absent. No water may be boiled inside a Mahlemut house while the deer-hunt continues.[6] If a Hottentot goes out hunting, his wife kindles a fire. "She may not do anything else but watch the fire and keep it alive. If the fire should be extinguished, the husband will not be lucky." She may throw water about instead; if she gets tired, her servant must do it. If neglected, the same result follows.[7] When absent on a journey Acaxée men refrained from

[1] Pritchard, *op. cit.* 147.
[2] *Journ. Anthrop. Inst.* xxiv. 141.
[3] *Journ. Anthrop. Inst.* viii. 370.
[4] Riedel, *op. cit.* 292.
[5] Low, *op. cit.* 402.
[6] Dall, *op. cit.* 147.
[7] Hahn, *op. cit.* 77.

using salt; they said: "Perhaps our wives are not behaving well in our homes and we shall die."[1] Amongst the Kaffirs, should a man's wife, while he is on a journey, anoint herself with the oil or fat in daily use, she will not only suffer herself but bring calamity upon her husband; should she dream during his absence, she must offer a private gift for herself and her absent lord.[2] When a Malay is at war, his pillows and sleeping-mat at home are kept rolled up. If any one else were to use them, the "absent warrior's courage would fail, and disaster would befall him." His wife and children may not have their hair cut during his absence.[3] Not only was the traveller obliged, according to the Nahua superstition, to abstain from baths during his absence, but even his family during the same period, while allowed to bathe the body, might not wash the head or face oftener than once in eighty days.[4] In East Central Africa while a woman's husband is absent on an expedition, she goes without anointing her head or washing her face; she must not bathe, she scarcely washes her arms. She must not cut her hair; her oil-vessel (*chisasi*) is kept full of oil till his return, and may be hung up in the house, or kept by the side of her bed.[5] In time of war, amongst the Tshi-speaking peoples, the wives of the men who are with the army paint themselves white, and decorate themselves with beads and charms, and make a daily procession through the town, invoking the protection of the gods for their absent husbands. "This ceremony is called *Mohbor-meh*, a word compounded of *mohbor*, 'pity,' and *meh*, 'me,' and which may be freely translated, 'Have mercy upon

[1] Bancroft, *op. cit.* i. 581.
[2] *Journ. Anthrop. Inst.* xx. 116.
[3] Skeat, *op. cit.* 524.
[4] Bancroft, *op. cit.* ii. 392.
[5] Macdonald, *Africana*, i. 81.

us!' Besides the daily procession, *Mohbor-meh* women, painted white from head to foot, dance publicly in the streets, uttering howls and shrieks, leaping and gesticulating, and brandishing knives and swords. On the day upon which a battle is expected to take place they run to and fro with guns, or sticks roughly carved to represent guns, and pierce green *paw-paws* with knives, in imitation of the foemen's heads. This ceremony is generally performed in a complete state of nudity, and frequently some of the principal women appear with two hen's eggs fastened above the *pudenda*. Any man, except the aged and infirm, who may be discovered in the town or village, is at once assailed with torrents of abuse, and charged with cowardice, taunted with want of manliness, assaulted with sticks, and driven out of the town. *Mohbor-meh* women appear to be regarded in some respects as female warriors, who guard the town in the absence of the men."[1] The impersonation of the male sex is doubtless intended to complete identification, and so make sympathetic action more certain. In the Babar Islands, when the men are at war, the women must fast and abstain from sexual intercourse.[2] In Timor-laut, when a ship is at sea, the girls of the village are bound to sing and dance daily on the beach, by way of bringing the men back speedily.[3]

In other connections there are instructive cases like the following. The foreskin removed at the circumcision of an Arunta boy is swallowed by the younger brother of the initiate; the idea is that it will strengthen him, and make him grow tall and strong. The blood is rubbed over his elder sisters, and they

[1] A. B. Ellis, *The Tshi-speaking Peoples of the West Coast of Africa*, 226, 227.

[2] Riedel, *op. cit.* 341.

[3] *Id.* 290.

cut locks of his hair.[1] Here there is doubtless the intention of strengthening those with whom one is in a responsible relation, and perhaps the contact thus intensified helps to intensify the particular taboo of sex here involved. In the Central Australian tribes an important right and duty is the giving and receiving of hair. It is often given in return for a favour; and the principle behind the custom has been already described. A man's chief supply comes from his mother-in-law; he also gets hair from his son-in-law and brother-in-law.[2]

Marriage being an act of danger is on these principles tabooed between certain persons. As we saw in Ceram marriage between different tribes is allowed, and even between "upper and lower classes," the only restriction is that villages which have performed the *pela* ceremony of eating together sacramentally, which necessitates alliance in war, may not intermarry.[3] The principle is well illustrated by this: in the islands Leti, Moa, and Lakor, *Dera* and *Luli* are the protecting deities of the village, the former is male, the latter female. They are the spirits of the founders of the village, and their lineal descendants are employed as go-betweens, *muani riesre* and *puata riesre*, between these gods and the villagers, procuring, for instance, help in sickness for the latter. If the *muani riesre* dies, his sister's son succeeds him; the *puata riesre* is succeeded by her sister or daughter. Both man and woman have equal privileges, but they may never marry.[4]

Cases have already been cited to show how a dangerous service produces a taboo of the *ngia ngiampe*

[1] Spencer and Gillen, *op. cit.* 251.
[2] *Id.* 465.
[3] Riedel, *op. cit.* 134.
[4] Riedel, *op. cit.* 375.

species. The taboo between the operators and those operated upon in puberty ceremonies, is identical with the common taboos between men who have exchanged wives, between sponsors and god-children, and between a married person and the assistant in the act, and in each case it is one of duty and responsibility. The last-mentioned custom may be well illustrated from the Beni-Amer. When a wife quarrels with her husband and seems inexorable, one of her bridesmen is called in. She cannot resist this intervention; "for between the bride and the companions of the groom there exists an eternal friendship, which never fails, though they may not see each other."[1] The duty of natural affection similarly renders a brother and sister in New Caledonia most ready to help each other though they are taboo to each other,[2] and generally between husbands and wives the same result is regular, both for psychology and for religious custom.

The general principle that persons closely connected by contact must avoid dangerous contact, which would lead to personal as well as mutual harm, is illustrated by totemic customs. The Bakalai believe that if a man ate his totem, the women would miscarry, or give birth to animals of the totem kind.[3] The Omahas think that eating the totem, which is forbidden food, will cause sickness to the man's wife and children.[4] Here, as so often, a man's conduct affects his intimates, through the continuous contact he has with them.

The same conception of danger combined with intimacy appears very clearly in a Central Australian belief. A man is obliged to supply his wife's relatives with a certain amount of food; but he is always cautious

[1] Munzinger, *op. cit.* 325.
[2] De Rochas, *op. cit.* 239.
[3] Du Chaillu, *op. cit.* 309.
[4] James, *Expedition to the Rocky Mountains*, ii. 50.

that these people should never see him eating, "else their smell would get into the food and make him ill."[1] The results of contact generally, of dangerous services and dangerous relations, are all taboos of the same order.

Accordingly, we may decide that in primitive society, as now, individualism still shows itself above any connection of marriage or relationship. Owing to the taboo of personal isolation and egoism, all society, as such, is dangerous. The ties of intermarriage and of blood-kinship are special cases of *ngiampe*, and in early society they have not superseded this general conception of relationship.

There is perhaps no savage custom, if we except the Couvade, which has so increased the gaiety of civilised nations as the common taboo between a man and his mother-in-law. Amongst early peoples, this custom forms a real part of the marriage system, and is a result of the *ngia ngiampe* relation of marriage. The taboo is also found between wives and their fathers-in-law, and, though far less commonly, between other relations by marriage, as between the husband and his sisters-in-law, the wife and her brothers-in-law, and in a few cases irrespective of sex, but by far the commonest form is the mutual avoidance of husband and wife's mother. The mother-in-law almost assumes the *rôle* of a supernatural person. A Zulu swears by his mother-in-law.[2] When we examine complete accounts of the custom, it is clear that the prohibition is one of extraordinary strength and conceals no ordinary meaning. It also becomes evident that the relation is one of the *ngia ngiampe* sort, that it is a particularly intense expression of the ideas of sexual taboo, and that the feelings con-

[1] Spencer and Gillen, *op. cit.* 469.

[2] Shooter, *op. cit.* 101.

cerned are religious in their character, the sentiment connected with the breaking of the rule being one of religious horror.

In many cases the avoidance begins, naturally enough, with betrothal, as amongst the Bondei.[1] In the tribes of New South Wales there is a taboo between a man and the mother of his promised wife, but not so pronounced as it is after marriage.[2] In some Victorian tribes the girl's mother and aunts may not look at the suitor nor speak to him from betrothal till death. When they speak in each other's presence they have to use a "turn-tongue." He may never mention his mother-in-law's name.[3] Some typical examples follow, in which various ideas of contact occur, and the connection with sexual taboo is seen. The Zulu system of *uku-hlonipa* is a network of sexual taboos; of this particular case the following account is given. "This is a very singular custom, and in its nature and tendencies presents insuperable difficulties to the introduction of civilised habits into the domestic circle, and especially to the exercise of those kindly offices which Christianity inculcates. By this strange custom, a daughter-in-law is required to *hlonipa* her father-in-law, and all her husband's male relations in the ascending line, that is, to be cut off from all intercourse with them. She is not allowed to pronounce their names even mentally. Hence this custom has given rise to an almost distinct language among the women. The son-in-law is placed under certain restrictions towards his mother-in-law. He cannot enjoy her society, or remain in the same hut with her, nor can he pronounce her name. The daughter-in-law must to a certain extent *hlonipa* her mother-in-law

[1] *Journ. Anthrop. Inst.* xxv. 198. [2] *Op. cit.* xiv. 353. [3] Dawson, *op. cit.* 29.

also."[1] Another account states that the husband must not speak to, look at, or eat with his mother-in-law, and neither husband nor wife may utter the names of each other's relatives. "This is *hlonipa*. When a mother-in-law meets her son-in-law, she will not speak to him, she will hide her head and the breasts that suckled his wife. If she meets him on the road, where she cannot turn away, and where she has no covering, she will tie a piece of grass round her head as a sign that she *hlonipas*. All correspondence has to be carried on between third parties. . . . A woman does not mention her father-in-law, and she hides from her son-in-law. She says it is not right that he should see the breasts which suckled his wife."[2] Amongst the Fijians "a free flow of the affections between members of the same family is prevented by the strict observance of national or religious customs, imposing a most unnatural restraint. Brothers and sisters, husbands and wives, fathers and sons-in-law, mothers and daughters-in-law, brothers and sisters-in-law are thus severally forbidden to speak to each other or to eat from the same dish."[3] This account is not very explicit, but is important as connecting these customs with the taboos between husbands and wives, and brothers and sisters. Amongst the Sarae and Barea the mother-in-law conceals herself from her son-in-law.[4] Amongst the Arawaks the son-in-law might not see the face of his mother-in-law, and if they lived in the same house, they were obliged to keep on opposite sides of a partition.[5] Mr. Curr, speaking of the mutual avoidance of son-in-law and mother-in-law, "a singular and widely

[1] Maclean, *op. cit.* 95, 96.

[2] Leslie, *op. cit.* 102, 141.

[3] Williams, *op. cit.* i. 136.

[4] Munzinger, *op. cit.* 388, 526.

[5] Tylor, *Early History of Mankind*, 285.

spread custom in Australia," says, "when a girl has been promised to a man in marriage, or when he is married, the man and the mother of his wife or betrothed scrupulously avoid each other's presence. Should the mother-in-law require to pass even within a hundred yards of her son-in-law, she covers herself, if the tribe wears clothes, from head to foot with her cloak. Also they never exchange words together except in cases of necessity. I have often noticed the awkward occurrences to which this custom leads, but I could not get the blacks satisfactorily to explain its design. Nevertheless the object of the practice seems to lie on the surface."[1] It was criminal for a son-in-law and mother-in-law to look at one another, in the tribes of the Mary River and Bunya-Bunya country.[2] On Fraser's Island "the mother-in-law must not look upon her son-in-law at any time: they believe that if she did he would go mad, and would go and live in the bush like a wild man."[3] Amongst the Banyai a man must sit with his knees bent in the presence of his mother-in-law, and may not put out his feet towards her.[4] In Central Celebes the son-in-law may not speak to his mother-in-law privately.[5] Amongst the Omahas and Hidatsas a man does not speak to his wife's mother.[6] The prohibition of intercourse of the slightest sort between a man and his mother-in-law is practically universal throughout Australia. The taboo between a man and his father-in-law is there probably rare. Mr. Howitt asserts that it does not exist.[7] Amongst the North American Indians, however, it seems fairly

[1] Curr, *op. cit.* i. 97.

[2] *Id.* iii. 163.

[3] *Id.* iii. 145.

[4] Livingstone, *op. cit.* 622.

[5] *Bijdragen tot de Taal Land- en Volkenkunde Nederlandsch Indie*, xxxv. 5. 1. 91.

[6] J. O. Dorsey, in *Third Report of the Bureau of Ethnology*, 262; Featherman, *op. cit.* iii. 329.

[7] *Journ. Anthrop. Inst.* xii. 503.

common, though not so common as the ordinary form.

Amongst the Bondei the prospective bridegroom does not eat with his betrothed after betrothal, nor with his father-in-law or mother-in-law, nor does the girl with him or his parents. At the wedding ceremony the pair eat together, and the groom eats with his father-in-law, but neither then nor on any occasion may he eat with his mother-in-law.[1] In Amboina the son-in-law may not eat with the mother-in-law;[2] so also in Buru;[3] in Halmahera the son-in-law when in his wife's house may not eat out of vessels used by her parents, and the same prohibition applies to her when in his.[4] A Congo proverb runs: "My mother-in-law is angry with me, but what do I care? We do not eat from the same dish."[5]

In Ceram the son-in-law may not come near his mother-in-law. She may not utter his name, nor he hers. He calls her "mother."[6] This prohibition against uttering each other's name is found in the Torres Straits, amongst the Sioux and Omahas, the Kaffirs, in Buru, the Aru Islands, the Kei Islands, and Wetar.[7] In the Banks Islands a man will not name his wife's father, but will sit with him and converse; as to his wife's mother, he will not come near her, nor mention her name; he and she avoid each other, though if necessary they will talk at a distance. No person can be induced to mention his own name.[8] This mutual taboo on names is a real duty, the utter-

[1] *Journ. Anthrop. Inst.* xxv. 200. [2] Riedel, *op. cit.* 43. [3] *Id.* 23.
[4] *Id.* in *Zeitschrift für Ethnologie*, xvii. 69. [5] *Journ. Anthrop. Inst.* xxiv. 296.
[6] Riedel, *De sluik- en kroesharige rassen tusschen Selebes en Papua*, 102.
[7] *Journ. Anthrop. Inst.* xix. 338; Schoolcraft, *op. cit.* ii. 196; Harmon, *Travels in Interior of North America*, 341; Leslie, *op. cit.* 172; Riedel, *op. cit.* 5, 263, 236, 445. [8] Coote, *op. cit.* 138.

ance of another's name being equivalent to putting him in danger. Accordingly, in Amboina, the son-in-law calls his mother-in-law "mother." People are never called by their names.[1] In Ceram the son-in-law may not mention his mother-in-law's name, and he therefore calls her "mother."[2] In Wetar the son-in-law calls his mother-in-law "mother," and father-in-law "father."[3] The same titles are used by the Kaffirs. Amongst the latter people the wife is called "daughter of so-and-so."[4] Similar results are found where the common prohibition occurs against husband and wife mentioning each other's name. In Buru the father-in-law of *Jadet* is called "father of *Jadet*."[5] In the Aru Islands the son-in-law calls his mother-in-law, his wife's name being *Madamar*, "mother of *Madamar*," and his father-in-law "father of *Madamar*."[6]

Where the classificatory system is well developed, the taboo is extended to persons who potentially may or might have come into this relation. Thus, in the Urabunna tribe the mother of a man's wife is called his "*nowillie* (equivalent to father's sister), and any woman of that relationship is *mura* to him and he to her, and they must not speak to one another."[7]

Three explanations have been attempted. The first is that of Mr. Fison,[8] and has been suggested by others. It is that the rule is due to a fear of intercourse which is unlawful, though theoretically allowed on some classificatory systems. This seems to be corroborated by such traditions as that of the Gaboon natives, who say the rule was founded "because of an incest,"[9] and by a few recorded cases, due to special circumstances, in

[1] Riedel, op. cit. 43.
[2] Id. 102.
[3] Id. 448.
[4] Leslie, op. cit. 172, 173.
[5] Riedel, op. cit. 5.
[6] Riedel, op. cit. 263.
[7] Spencer and Gillen, op. cit. 61.
[8] Fison and Howitt, op. cit. 103.
[9] Bowdich, op. cit. 437.

which a man has married mother and daughter at once. This explanation also is one most likely to occur to explorers, who have personal knowledge of savages; for there is no doubt at all that the horror felt by the savage at infringement of the taboo between himself and his mother-in-law is of the same character as that inspired by the idea of incest, among savage and civilised peoples alike, a *horror religiosus* rather than *naturalis*. But against this explanation, it is enough to point out the antecedent improbability of any man, not to mention a savage, ever falling in love with a woman old enough to be his mother or mother-in-law, and the improbability of so many peoples concurring in being afraid of this, while there is a general preference amongst savages for marriage within the same generation. Moreover, technically such connection is not incest, except in the four-class system. What truth there is in the theory is this, that the practical man is apt to focus sexual taboo upon sexual intercourse, and, while theoretically the mother-in-law is marriageable in many systems (and so there would be no "incest" except in so far as the idea of incest in primitive thought was not differentiated from any sexual connection, all such being theoretically dangerous), yet, this general intercourse being feared may be referred to in this special way. Still the question remains, why should this be so feared?

The second explanation is that of Sir J. Lubbock, who traced it to "marriage by capture."[1] "When the capture was a reality, the indignation of the parents would also be real; when it became a mere symbol, the parental anger would be symbolised also, and would be continued even after its origin was forgotten." This

[1] *Origin of Civilisation*, 114.

theory has been assisted by one or two mistaken accounts of explorers; but, in the first place, "marriage by capture" was never more than a rare sporadic result; in the second place, the preponderance of sex is overlooked. Why should the "indignation" be so generally expressed by the mother only? Thirdly, no fact ever remained as a symbol or ceremony without some real psychological impulse to inspire it.

The third explanation is that of Prof. E. B. Tylor, who thinks that the custom is simply the familiar one of "cutting," and is due to the idea that the husband for instance, when coming to live with his wife's parents, is regarded as an outsider, not one of the family, and is therefore "not recognised." This is altered, however, when the first child is born. Now, having contributed to the formation of a new member of the family, he is recognised at last and the taboo is over.[1] Prof. Tylor, indeed, shows some probability that the custom by which the husband is "cut" is causally connected with the practice according to which the husband resides with his wife's family. This, however, would go without saying, as would the converse also, precisely because the person chiefly concerned is a stranger, and is one amongst many. The explanation is simply a restatement of the problem. He adds, however, that there are no cases of avoidance between the wife and the husband's family, where the husband lives with the wife's family. But there are such cases, as in Ceram;[2] though such are naturally uncommon, precisely because only one member of the husband's family is on the spot. Mr. Howitt also, while asserting that there is a taboo throughout most of Australia between a man and his mother-in-law, denies that there

[1] *Journ. Anthrop. Inst.* xviii. 246 ff.

[2] Riedel, *op. cit.* 102.

is a taboo between a man and his father-in-law.[1] Why should the cutting fall to the mother? Prof. Tylor does not take into account the preponderance of sex in these customs. In each and every case the prohibition is focussed on the husband and the mother-in-law, or, more rarely, on the wife and the father-in-law, though it may include various relations of either sex. Again, though it is, so far, "cutting" and non-recognition, yet such terms fail to explain the religious horror with which the rule is connected, nor does there seem to be any warrant for such an extraordinary intensity of family exclusiveness. Moreover, such cases as the following are in principle quite opposed to "cutting." In Central Celebes a man may not speak *privately* to his mother-in-law.[2] When typical cases are examined the feeling behind the custom is widely different from that behind the practice of "cutting" a person, whether a non-relative or otherwise; also the avoidance is mutual in the generality of cases. Still less does this explanation explain the no less intense horror found between a man and his mother-in-law amongst peoples where the wife resides from the first at her husband's home; on his theory, this would be a survival from the practice in the maternal stage, but such survival shows too much life, and the hypothesis that the maternal system always preceded the paternal is itself untenable. The taboo ceases in a few cases when a child is born; what usually happens is, that the pair who live with the wife's parents set up a house for themselves when a child is born, the birth of a child being a common signal that the union is to be perma-

1 *Journ. Anthrop. Inst.* xii. 503.

2 Riedel, in *Bijdragen tot de Taal- Land- en Volkenkunde van Nederlandsch Indie,* xxxv. 5. 1. 91.

nent, in other words, that the marriage is complete; as we shall see, there is reason for the cessation, but it is not that the man is now become a member of the family.

It is clear that the custom cannot be explained by ordinary modern conceptions either of incest or of family exclusiveness. The custom is, in fact, part of the great system of ideas which has produced both the marriage system with its various bars, and the solidarity of the family. On the face of it the taboo in typical cases seems analogous to the phenomena of sexual taboo. This has been indicated by its connection with engagement taboos. Amongst the Zulus the mother-in-law taboo is but one detail of an intricate system of social and sexual taboo, the latter predominating. We have seen that the ideas underlying sexual taboo have produced amongst other things mutual avoidance between engaged couples, and between the married man and his wife. If a man avoids his own wife so carefully, why in the name of probability should he avoid or be avoided by his mother-in-law as well, if the reason be either fear of incest or social non-recognition? It seems to be causally connected with a man's avoidance of his own wife. Now when we rid our minds of associations, it becomes relevant to ask, why should she be called the man's *mother* at all? It is at least strange, in spite of the suffix "in-law." The theoretical primitive form of the family in its bi-sexual character was, as we have seen, separation of man and wife, except when the needs of love require satisfaction, and separation of the boys and girls as soon as puberty drew near. The young boy went about with his father as soon as possible, and at puberty was formally weaned from association with the nursery and its feminine atmosphere, and his life became masculine. He no longer was to live in the house where, as he might remember, he was so early separated from his sisters, a separation naturally ascribed to the mother, being an older person, with authority, of the same sex as the girls in her care. The sex so dangerous to man, because of those qualities which spoil a man, was taboo to him—for a season. Soon, however, the inevitable came—love drove him to the dangerous sex, and he must needs obey. Similar was the case of the primitive girl, in regard to the sex dangerous to her. The taboo has to be broken, the two tabooed persons must be joined together. In other words, the young man has to enter once more that feminine sphere from which he was so early taken away; he has to live with a woman again, no longer in the innocent ignorance of childhood, but with full knowledge of the dangers and responsibilities of the union. His female comrade is not now his sister, as in the old days, but his wife; and in the ages before the importance of blood-kinship, when living together or any close contact was the obvious bond, there was no hard conventional distinction between women of the same age. Poetry and popular language preserve this vagueness; the lover in the Song of Songs cries "My sister, my spouse," and the savage lover uses the same phrase. As showing the re-entrance into the feminine sphere, an initiation custom may be cited. At a certain stage of the proceedings of initiation amongst the Arunta, the boy's prospective mother-in-law runs off with the boy, but the men fetch him back.[1] Again, the new female companion of our hero also has a mother, who is not indeed his own mother, but the mother of his partner or *quasi*-sister, as who should say "mother-in-law." The analogy between the two

[1] Spencer and Gillen, *op. cit.* 443.

states is complete. This new life with a new woman whose mother is in a position, as mother, to guard her daughter and see to her new son's behaviour, is a reproduction of the old life, when his mother-in-blood regulated the household and separated the children. It is the same picture with higher lights and deeper shadows. He again lives under one roof with that dangerous creature, a woman, but in the new relation of wife; he again has a mother controlling to some extent the new relation which is a new version of the old, but she is a mother-in-law. His attitude towards the wife, when love is not upon him, will be what it was to his sister, but he now knows the reason, and his attitude towards the mother-in-law will be what it was to his mother, but the connotation of that term has altered. She might rather be called his "spiritual mother," his "mother-in-religion," if we may pervert the meaning such terms would have now. All the religious principles of sexual taboo inform the relation, and between husband and wife there is a taboo pregnant with religious meaning, the more so in proportion to the closeness of the sexual tie, closer than that between brother and sister. The relation between the husband and his wife's mother is also full of religious meaning; it is to begin with an embarrassing one, for she is neither his mother, though of that age, nor his sister, nor his wife, though a woman. Yet she is his "mother" in a religious sense. As he, from sexual taboo, *ngiampe* duty, and inequality of age, would avoid all physical intimacy with his own mother, so does he *à fortiori* avoid it with his mother-in-law. For the taboo is enhanced, and here Prof. Tylor's theory has some truth, by the fact that the woman is not the man's real mother, and is to that extent less familiar, as is also the case with his wife in relation to himself.

When the practical aspect of the relation is considered, the mother-in-law is responsible for her daughter's safety, and oversees the husband's behaviour, but in primitive custom this also renders his attitude towards her one of religious respect; in the case of taboo between the wife and her father-in-law, the same applies, and the attitude is strengthened by her religious fear of the male sex. There are many facts which show the practical side of this relation, the natural anxiety of the mother concerning her daughter's welfare, and here the preponderance of sex in these customs and the causal connection with residence are explained. This anxiety concentrates upon child-birth, and is often concerned with the prevention of repudiation on the part of the husband, a question settled by the birth of a child. Amongst the Damaras, when the pair go to their home, the bride's mother and other women go with her to see her safely installed.[1] Identity of sex increases affection between mother and daughter; and here there is naturally some indignation at the loss of a loved daughter. Abipone mothers "could hardly bear to part with their daughters."[2] In modern Egypt a man prefers that his mother-in-law should live with him to protect his wife's honour, and consequently his own. The mother-in-law is called "protector."[3] Mr. Yate gives the following statement as to a Maori Christian wedding. The bride's mother came to him and told him she was pleased that her daughter was going to be married to Pahan, but "that she must be angry about it with her mouth." On returning with the bridegroom

[1] *South African Folklore Journal*, i. 49. [2] Dobrizhoffer, *op. cit.* ii. 208.

[3] Lane, *op. cit.* i. 219.

and bride the procession was met by her. "She began to assail us all furiously. She put on a most terrific countenance, threw her garments about, and tore her hair like a fury; then said to me: 'Ah, you white missionary, you are worse than the devil; you first make a slave lad your son by redeeming him from his master, and then marry him to my daughter. I will tear your eyes out!' The old woman, suiting the action to the word, feigned a snatch at my face, at the same time saying in an undertone, that it was 'all mouth,' and that she did not mean what she said."[1] In the case of a young married pair in Cambodia, neither of whom have been married before, it is believed that when the wife is *enceinte* for the first time, the husband is able to take from her by magic the unborn babe. Accordingly "the parents of the bride never trust their son-in-law, and will not let the young couple go out of their sight."[2]

There is another element already hinted at, which enters the question. It will be found that the mother-in-law taboo tends to disappear when the taboos between husband and wife are intensified, and *vice versâ*. The other element is this; as sexual taboo must be kept up for safety, all the more so because of close union and especially until a child is born, for the pair are continuously breaking the rule and all their conduct affects the child, a substitute to receive the onus of taboo is useful, and the best substitute is the mother-in-law; if the husband avoids her, his relations with his wife will be secure, and if the mother-in-law avoids him, her daughter's safety will be secured likewise. This idea coincides with filial and maternal duty, and is a good instance of savage make-believe in shifting responsi-

[1] Yate, *op. cit.* 97. [2] Aymonier, *op. cit.* 187.

bility. The embarrassing relation of a mother who is no mother assists in the formation of the conception. Again, the principles of contact find here their full development; the wife is the link between the mother-in-law and the husband, she belongs to and is a part of each, she is the *kalduke* as well as the "mediator" between them, and this important form of connection produces the most intensified responsibility, and taboos the two parties. The *ngia ngiampe* relation is shown by the Central Australian custom, according to which a mother-in-law and son-in-law are bound to supply each other with hair and game,[1] and by the necessary result in all cases of the taboo that a third party is the medium of communication, as in the Torres Straits, and amongst the Omahas,[2] the wife being the intermediary for conversation and communication.

This explanation finds a parallel and a proof in what is the same thing in modern society. The avoidance by a man of his mother-in-law is a well-known feature of *bourgeois* manners, and is a frequent subject of humorous anecdote. The Germans have the proverbial phrases "Schwiegermutter—Teufelsunterfutter," "Schwiegermutter—Tigermutter," and English has the expression "mother-in-law and daughter-in-law are a tempest and a hailstorm." In the practical sphere, the taboo still obtains in civilisation. The reason underlying both the primitive and the civilised form of this phenomenon is the same, though the religious meaning has evaporated from the latter. The modern husband resents her interference, to which he half-consciously knows she has a right, as being of the

[1] Spencer and Gillen, *op. cit.* 26, 40, 465.

[2] *Journ. Anthrop. Inst.*, xix. 338; *Third Report of the Bureau of Ethnology*, 262.

same sex as his wife, an older woman and her mother; and she does not quite trust him, in her anxiety for her daughter's welfare. Both now and then the mother-in-law is avoided, precisely because she is the mother-in-law.

CHAPTER XVI

No general account of customs and beliefs concerning child-birth is here attempted; some of the more important have been referred to, and one or two others will be discussed. As a dangerous crisis child-birth is attended by evil influences; as a sexual crisis these, as we have seen, are sexual. Direct attribution of the danger to the agency of the opposite sex often appears, while conversely that sex especially fears the contagion of femininity at a crisis when the female organism is, as it were, broken up. Men, and even the husband, are prohibited from being present, as in the Marianne Islands, Wetar, New Caledonia, amongst the Zulus, Damaras, and Dyaks.[1] In the Aru Islands and Amboina, the reason is given that the presence of men would hinder the birth.[2] Similar reference to the origin of these taboos in sexual ideas is seen in such beliefs as that of the Aleuts, who suppose that difficult labour is due to misconduct on the wife's part, a belief that sometimes causes domestic discord.[3] In Samoa all the pains of child-birth are imputed to the fault of the husband.[4] This idea of mutual responsibility between persons in close contact is illustrated by a Maori practice. If the mother's breasts give no milk, both

[1] D'Urville, *op. cit.* ii. 484; Riedel, *De sluik- en kroesharige rassen tusschen Selebes en Papua*, 449; Garnier, *op. cit.* 183; Shooter, *op. cit.* 88; *South African Folklore Journal*, ii. 62; Low, *op. cit.* 307.

[2] Riedel, *op. cit.* 263, 73.

[3] Featherman, *op. cit.* iii. 467.

[4] Globus, xlvii. 70.

husband and wife are sprinkled ceremonially with water, and kept apart to allow the charm to have its effect.[1]

The Saturnalia practices already referred to, occur at child-birth and with the same meaning. Thus in Abyssinia after a birth the women rush out into the courtyard singing and shouting, and if a man dares to approach them, he is invariably caught and retained captive until he purchases his freedom with a ransom in money or beer.[2] In Fiji at the feast to celebrate a birth the men paint on each other's bodies the tattoo marks used by women.[3] This is the same in principle as wearing the dress of the other sex.

The customs and beliefs relating to the birth of twins are both numerous and interesting. Here I will merely point out that the chief idea behind such superstitions is that not only is the occurrence abnormal, but one of the infants is the offspring of a spirit or god. Twins are very sacred amongst the Damaras, all present at the feast are called "twins," and afterwards form a sort of guild.[4] Amongst the Yorubas the god Elegbra, who is a patron of Love, is also the tutelar god of twins. One of twins is always called after him. This god is supposed to consort with men and women during sleep, and so fulfils the function of the *incubus* and *succubus*.[5] The twin children of Amphitryon are a case in point. Many peoples on the other hand kill one of twin infants.

The most interesting practice in connection with child-birth is the curious custom to which Prof. Tylor has given the name of *Couvade*. In its perfect form

[1] Shortland, *Maori Religion*, 30.

[2] Featherman, *op. cit.* v. 607.

[3] Williams, *op. cit.* i. 175.

[4] *South African Folklore Journal*, ii. 107.

[5] A. B. Ellis, *The Yoruba-speaking Peoples of the Slave Coast of West Africa*, 80, 67.

the husband takes to his bed and pretends to be lying-in, while the wife goes about her usual employments as soon as may be after delivery. Some connect it with the world-wide belief that the conduct of the mother before and also after birth affects the child. The Hottentots believe that if a pregnant woman eats lion's or leopard's flesh, the child will have the characteristics of those animals.[1] In European folklore the belief occurs that if a pregnant woman walks over a grave her child will die;[2] in Transsylvania, if one throws a flower in her face, the child will have a mole on that part of its face.[3]

Further, it is quite natural in view of the closeness of the tie, which, as *ngia ngiampe*, is regulated by contact, that the conduct of the father also should affect the welfare of the child. The biological tie is enforced by the ideas of contact. In the Andamans a pregnant woman abstains from pork, turtle, honey, iguana, and *paradoxurus*, and after a while her husband also abstains from the last two foods, believing that the embryo would suffer if he ate them.[4] Similarly amongst the Coroados, Puris, and Coropos.[5] Amongst the Californian Indians the old women washed the child as soon as born, and "although the husband did not affect the sufferings of labour, his conduct was supposed in some measure to affect the unborn child, and he was consequently laid under certain restrictions, such as not being allowed to leave the house or eat fish and meat."[6] At Suan the husband shuts himself up for some days after the birth of his first child, and will eat nothing.[7] During the forty-four days of "unclean-

[1] Hahn, *op. cit.* 88.
[2] Panzer, *op. cit.* 262.
[3] Gerard, *op. cit.* i. 191.
[4] *Journ. Anthrop. Inst.* xii. 355.
[5] Spix, *Ethnographie Süd-Amerikas*, ii. 247.
[6] Bancroft, *op. cit.* i. 412.
[7] Chalmers, *op. cit.* 265.

ness," taboos are imposed on the Malay husband as well as on his wife. He may not, *e.g.* shave his head; may not hurt or kill anything.[1] Amongst the Piojés both father and mother fast for three days after the birth.[2] The Niasese wife and husband both refrain from certain foods before the birth.[3] In Greenland, if the husband works just before the birth, the child will die.[4] Amongst the Dyaks the number of foods forbidden to the pregnant woman is increased during the last month; and even the father of the expected child is put under the same restrictions; neither may light a fire, nor approach one, else the child will be born spotted; they may not eat fruit, else the child will have stomach-ache; they may not make holes in wood, else it will be born blind, nor dive under water, else the child will be suffocated in the womb and be still-born.[5] This kind of thing is common in New Guinea.[6] Amongst the Indians of Guiana the father abstains from certain kinds of animal food. If he eats the flesh of a *water-haas*, which has protruding teeth, the child will have the same; if he eats the spotted *labba*, the child will have spots. Mr. im Thurn says, "there is some idea that if the father eats strong food, washes, smokes, handles weapons, it would have the same result as if the babe did so."[7]

Couvade proper is combined with these practices by the last-mentioned people. "The woman works as usual up to a few hours before birth; she goes to the forest with some women, and there the birth takes place. In a few hours she is up and at work, and suffers little. As soon as the child is born, the father

[1] Skeat, *op. cit.* 345.
[2] Ploss, *Das Kind*, i. 36.
[3] *Journ. Anthrop. Inst.* viii. 222.
[4] *Id.* i. 35.
[5] Perelaer, *op. cit.* 38, 39.
[6] Chalmers, *op. cit.* 165.
[7] *Journ. Anthrop. Inst.* xix. 462; im Thurn, *The Indians of British Guiana*, 218.

takes to his hammock, and abstains from work, from meat, and all food but weak gruel of *cassava* meal, from smoking, from washing himself, and above all from touching weapons of any sort, and is nursed and cared for by all the women of the place. He may not scratch himself with his finger-nails, but may use a splinter of cokerite palm. This goes on for days, sometimes weeks."[1] Amongst the Digger Indians, when the wife is about to be delivered, the husband plays the invalid; he stretches himself on his couch, grunts and groans as if oppressed with pain, and is attended to and nursed for several days.[2] Amongst the Dyaks the family is interdicted (*pomali*) for eight days; and during this time the husband plays the invalid. He is fed on rice and salt, that the infant's stomach may not swell, and is required to keep out of the sun, and abstain from bathing.[3] Amongst the Passés he paints himself black, and stays in his hammock fasting, until the navel-string of the child has fallen off.[4] In Zardandan, and amongst the Ainus, Miris, and Miaos, the Lagunero and Ahomama, the Caribs, and in Martinique, Surinam, Guiana, Brazil, amongst the Jivaros, Mundurucus, Macusis, Arawaks, and Arecunas, and in Wanga, Malabar, and the Nicobars, the father lies-in after the birth.[5] In Celebes and California he lies-in and is attended by his wife.[6] Amongst the Erukala-Vandhu of Southern India "directly the woman feels the birth-pangs, she informs her husband, who immediately takes some of her clothes, puts them on, places on his forehead the mark which the women usually place on theirs, retires into a dark room, where there is

[1] im. Thurn, *The Indians of British Guiana*, 217.

[2] Featherman, *op. cit.* iii. 213.

[3] *Id.* ii. 268.

[4] Martius, *Ethnographie Süd-Amerikas*, i. 511.

[5] H. Ling Roth, in *Journ. Anthrop. Inst.* xxii. 228 ff.

[6] *Id. l.c.*

only a very dim lamp, and lies down on the bed, covering himself up with a long cloth. When the child is born, it is washed and placed on the cot beside the father, *assafoetida*, jaggery, and other articles are then given, not to the mother but to the father. During the days of ceremonial uncleanness, the man is treated as the other Hindus treat their women on such occasions. He is not allowed to leave his bed, but has everything needful brought to him."[1]

Two explanations of the practice have been suggested, one by Bachofen, supported by Prof. Tylor; and the other by Prof. Tylor, which he afterwards abandoned for the former. Bachofen "takes it to belong to the turning-point of society when the tie of parentage, till then recognised in maternity, was extended to take in paternity, this being done by the fiction of representing the father as a second mother. He compares the Couvade with the symbolic pretences of birth which in the classical world were performed as rites of adoption. To his significant examples may be added the fact that among certain tribes the Couvade is the legal form by which the father recognises a child as his."[2] In other words, it is a piece of symbolism whereby the father asserts his paternity, and accordingly his rights as a father, as against the maternal system of descent and inheritance. Prof. Tylor finds it most frequent in what he calls the maternal-paternal stage, represented by peoples with whom the husband lives for a year with the wife's family, and then removes. As a record of the change from a maternal to a paternal system, and a means whereby that change was effected, it should not, as he points out, occur in the purely maternal

[1] J. Taylor, in *Indian Antiquary*, May 1874, p. 151.
[2] E. B. Tylor, in *Journ. Anthrop. Inst.* xviii. 256.

stage. According to his tables it does not, but, as Mr. Ling Roth has shown, cases of the Couvade are actually found in the maternal stage; viz. amongst the Arawaks and Melanesians, both of whom have maternal descent. Further, the custom would be too much of a legal fiction if it meant all this originally; and early man has not, as may easily be shown, any such lawyer-like love of formality in matters of descent and inheritance; like the animals, he attaches himself to those with whom he happens to be born; and as to inheritance, there is nothing to inherit. Doubtless in certain cases, as amongst the Mundurucus, the Couvade may have come to be used as a method whereby the father recognises the child as his; but this, besides being secondary, is not the same thing as a legal fiction asserting the father's rights as against the maternal system. It is rather a case of paternal pride. It would be expected that a people should themselves be aware of the fact, if assertion of paternal rights as against maternal were the object of the custom, the maternal system and counter-assertions being so obvious, but no tribe actually holds this meaning of the Couvade.

The second explanation, proposed and later abandoned by Prof. Tylor, may be also given in his words. He laid stress on the "magical-sympathetic nature of a large class of Couvade rites as implying a physical bond between parent and child: thus, an Abipone would not take snuff lest his sneezing might hurt his new-born baby, and a Carib father must abstain from eating sea-cow lest his infant should get little round eyes like it. This motive, which is explicitly or implicitly recognised by the savages themselves, certainly forms part of the explanation of the Couvade. It is, however, secondary, being due to the connection considered as subsisting between parent and child, so that these sympathetic prohibitions may be interpreted as originally practised by the mother only, and afterwards adopted by the father." This explanation covers more facts than does the other; it is also more scientific than the other, in its application of primitive psychology rather than later legalism to a primitive custom. But it does not apply at all to Couvade proper.

Each of these explanations, however, like many another explanation of marriage customs and systems on legal lines, really errs in not taking into account the woman's side of the question. They show a sympathy with the father and with the child, but forget the mother, and are thus a modern document illustrating the history of woman's treatment by man.

On examining the facts, we can distinguish two classes of Couvade customs, which often combine, but are essentially distinct. We have first a very widely spread group of customs, in which the father, as well as the mother, must avoid certain acts and certain things for fear of injuring the unborn or new-born child. These have been illustrated, and show a result of the *ngia ngiampe* relation. They are a good example of the principles of contact underlying human relations and relationships. Things and persons that have been or are in contact of any sort, or between whom there is any tie of contact or connection, retain the connection in a material form, and either party can thereby sympathetically influence the other. As Mr. Ling Roth points out, there are cases where the child affects the father.[1] On Bachofen's theory, this would be an assertion of paternity by the child; but on the principles of *ngiampe* it is natural enough. The child's substance

[1] H. Ling Roth, in *Journ. Anthrop. Inst.* xxi. 234.

is part of the father and the mother alike, both in biological fact and in primitive inference from this and from the principles of contact, and parental affection and responsibility apply the principles of contact, which are the material basis of affection and responsibility, in order to ensure the child's welfare. All such connection being potentially of the *ngiampe* species, the sympathy is a result of that relation, and shows the material nature of the bond. Similar phenomena have already been noted, such as the conduct of women when their husbands are absent. Thus, in South East Africa, if a man's wife while he is on a journey anoints herself with the oil or fat in daily use, she will not only suffer herself but bring calamity upon her husband.[1] On the same principle in Paraguay, when a child is ill, all its relatives fast, abstaining from such foods as are supposed to be injurious to the child.[2] In the East Indies it is a common thing for a father to become *helaga*, *i.e.* put himself under taboo, in order to cure a sick child.[3] When a Thlinkeet medicine-man is about to give an exhibition, his relatives who form the chorus must fast and take emetics previously.[4] At the circumcision of a Madagascar boy both the parents fast, and also the nurse and those who prepare the boy's food.[5]

The dangers of contact which underlie the relation, as between husband and wife, assist towards the husband's duty. When a Kaffir woman is pregnant, he should not bathe "because he will quickly be carried away by water."[6] When a Guatemala wife was barren, she confessed her sins; if that had no effect, her husband also confessed, and his cloak was laid on his wife.[7]

[1] *Journ. Anthrop. Inst.* xxii. 116.

[2] St. John, *op. cit.* i. 175.

[3] Ploss, *Das Kind*, i. 150.

[4] Dall, *op. cit.* 426.

[5] W. Ellis, *Madagascar*, i. 187.

[6] Callaway, *op. cit.* 443.

[7] Bancroft, *op. cit.* ii. 678.

Here the connection we are speaking of is almost developed into Couvade. So in a case of difficult labour, which was believed due to some breaking of *tapu*, the Maori husband plunged in the river, while the priest pronounced a charm.[1] By extension of the *ngiampe* relation we get a case like that of the Chiriguanos, with whom not only the father but the other children lie-in and fast at the birth.[2] Such an example does not fit with Bachofen's theory, for on that theory the children would be claiming paternity.

Any connection with residence that may remain after distinguishing true and false Couvade, is due to the cause behind that residence. In real Couvade the husband lies-in; the simulation by the father of the mother's part is obviously the essence of the custom. If we examine the phenomena of Couvade proper, and apply to them the principles of primitive religion, we have but to explain why the father should pretend to be a mother, or, for this is apt to be ignored, though it inheres in the definition of Couvade and is its explanation, why does he pretend to be his wife? Any account of birth-customs, or of the religious ideas connected with this important event, will show sufficient reason. Birth is an occasion of religious peril, witness the evil spirits and evil influences which ever lie in wait to injure both child and mother; and who so proper a person to defend mother and child from them as the father and husband? He does do so in many ways, as in the island Serua, where the husband prays when his wife is confined;[3] or in the Philippines, where he walks round the house all night fighting the demons with a drawn sword.[4] The Miaos recognise the husband's

[1] Shortland, *Maori Religion and Superstition*, 30.
[2] *Globus*, xlviii. 35.
[3] Riedel, *op. cit.* 468.
[4] Bowring, *The Philippines*, 120.

duty, when they explain that the husband's going to bed for forty days is on the principle that he should bear the same hardships as his wife.[1] In the other set of cases, the most prominent feature is the sympathy between father and child, but in Couvade proper the chief feature is the taking over by the father of the personality of the mother. He defends mother and infant, by pretending to be the mother. The idea is the familiar one of substitution; if he pretends to be ill, and if his wife makes no fuss, but goes about her work quietly, the evil influences and agencies may possibly be deceived and think that the pretended mother is their real victim. They do not know that the poor invalid is a strong and healthy man, and the natural guardian and protector of the family besides. The result is a happy issue from the peril,—the husband has done his duty. A case which is decisive is that of the Erukala-Vandhu, already noted. As soon as birth approaches, the husband puts his wife's clothes upon himself, and makes the woman's mark on his forehead and lies-in. He is treated as the mother during the whole period of "uncleanness."[2] A German peasant woman, in the same way, will wear her husband's coat, "in order to delude the evil spirits who are liable to attack her" from the time of birth till the "churching."[3]

As has been shown already, sympathy expressed by contact is always tending to pass into substitution and exchange of identity. This is notably the case in Couvade, where no doubt in most cases of the husband's lying-in, the idea is sympathy only, and though it is not always extended to its logical conclusion as amongst

[1] Colquhoun, *Across Chrysê*, 335. [2] *Indian Antiquary* (1874), 151.
[3] Ploss, *Das Kind*, i. 123.

the Erukala-Vandhu, yet subconsciously and potentially the final form is there.

A remarkable instance of the Saturnalia customs referred to as practised at birth, shows this sympathy practised by another than the husband, and may be compared with the cases where the children also lie-in. The matrons of certain East Central African tribes sing and dance to celebrate the approeching birth; one of them pretends, by dressing up for the part, to be a woman with child.[1] Such a case seems to dispose of the legal explanation of the Couvade, for the Couvade here is performed by a woman. When the *Mohbor-meh* women of the Tshi peoples dress up as men, and pretend to be their soldier-husbands, we see the same principle which is behind the Couvade.

Many cases show not complete substitution, but the idea that the father's influence helps the mother by contact, effected in various ways. Often there is but a slight step needed to make the substitution complete. In the Watubella Islands, if the wife's delivery is difficult, some of her hushand's clothes are put under her.[2] The father's personality thus transmitted by his clothes assists the mother. In primitive thought, as has been shown, dress contains the properties of the wearer, as the mantle of Elijah contained his virtue, and thus imparts to others the health, strength, and power of resistance belonging to the owner. In Central Australia, when the labour is difficult, a man takes the husband's hair-girdle, and ties it round the woman's breasts; if after a time the child is not yet born, the husband walks once or twice slowly past the *Erlukwirra* (women's camp) to induce the unborn child to follow

[1] D. Macdonald, *Africana*, i. 129.

[2] Riedel, *op. cit.* 207.

him.[1] In Lechrain a mother before the churching has taken place puts on her husband's hat when she goes out, "to prevent evil happening to her."[2] In Brandenburg on a similar principle of contact, if a woman is anxious about her husband, he burns a piece of his stocking and rubs the ashes on her, before his departure. The idea, as the peasants say, is that then she will not be afraid.[3]

The child is often protected in this way by the garments of either parent. After the birth of a Chinese baby its father's trousers are hung up in the room, "so that all evil influences may enter into them instead of into the child."[4] In Thüringen the child is protected against evil spirits by hanging a man's shirt before the window, or a woman's dress in front of the door.[5] In Hungary and South Germany the father's smock is laid upon the child to protect it against fairies.[6] In Königsberg it brings luck to the child to wrap it in his father's smock; also, to prevent its being carried off by the evil *Drud* before baptism the mother puts on it her clothes.[7] Amongst the Basutos, if a child vomits, the medicine man cuts a piece from the father's *setsiba* garment, and binds it on the child. This helps towards a cure.[8] In Silesia a sick child is wrapped in the mother's bridal apron, to make it well; a Bohemian mother ties a piece of her dress on a sick child.[9] In Bern a child is wrapped in its father's shirt to make him strong.[10] Ideas of sexual taboo influence this custom sometimes, as in a German custom of wrapping a boy in his father's smock after birth, to bring him luck, but never in his mother's.[11]

[1] Spencer and Gillen, *op. cit.* 467.
[2] Ploss, *op. cit.* i. 254.
[3] *Id.* i. 30.
[4] Doolittle, *op. cit.* i. 122.
[5] Ploss, *op. cit.* i. 123.
[6] *Id. l.c.*
[7] *Id. l.c.*
[8] Gritzner, in *Zeitschrift für Ethnologie* for 1877, p. 78.
[9] Ploss, *op. cit.* ii. 217, 221.
[10] *Id.* i. 62.
[11] *Id.* ii. 40.

Is Couvade intended, as anthropologists assert, to preserve the infant only? It may be so, but when we consider the man who dresses up as his wife, and cases where the protection of the wife is explicit, and when we remember also that the savage is a better man than he is generally painted, and has a real altruism and marital responsibility, we may give him credit for the intention to protect his wife no less than his child.

A custom parallel to those in which father and mother, or both, take the child under their protection by putting part of themselves in contact with it, is the common practice whereby the parents assume the name of the child. Thus, amongst the Babar islanders, who have the maternal system of descent, the parents change their names at the birth of the first child, thus, *Rahajana umlee*, father, and *Rahajana rile*, mother, of *Rahajana*.[1] In Wetar the parents are called after the name of the first child—"father of A B," "mother of A B"—"because they are now become more important than the barren and unmarried."[2] Parents in the Aru Islands take the name of their first child, thus, *Kamis aema*, father, and *Kamis djina*, mother, of *Kamis*.[3] In Leti, Moa and Lakor, and the Kei Islands, the parents are called by the name of the first child, "father of A B," "mother of A B."[4] Forty days after the birth of a child in Java its head was shaved, and the name was given and announced by the father, who, and the mother, henceforth bore the name of their son.[5] In Buru, Ceram, and Ceramlaut, the parents are called "as a title of respect" by the name of the oldest child.[6] In Halmahera the parents change their names thus at

[1] Riedel, *op. cit.* 353. [2] *Id.* 450. [3] *Id.* 260.
[4] *Id.* 392, 238. [5] Veth, *Java*, i. 642. [6] Riedel, *op. cit.* 5, 137, 152.

the birth of their first child.[1] Both parents take the name of the first child in Celebes, Sumatra, and amongst the Patagonians.[2] The Dyaks are very fond of children. Parents sink their own names on the birth of the first child, and are called by its name with the prefixes *Pa* and *Ma*. "It illustrates their family pride." Should the eldest child be dead or lost, they are called after the next surviving one. Thus, Pa-Jaguen was called Pa-Belal till his daughter Jaguen was restored from slavery by the assistance of the Rajah of Sarawak.[3] In some Australian tribes, "numerical names are given to children in the order of birth, the suffix showing sex. Thus the first child, if a boy, is called *Kertameru*, if a girl, *Kertanya*; the second child in the same way is called *Warritya*, or *Warriarto*. Soon afterwards another name is added from some plant, animal, or insect. This name continues until after marriage and the birth of the first child, when the father and mother take the name of the child, with the affix *binna* or *spinna* (adult) for the father, *ngangki* (female) for the mother; thus, Kadli being the child's name, the father is called Kadlispinna, the mother Kadlingangki. The names of both father and mother are thus changed at the birth of every child."[4] Amongst the Bechuanas "the parents take the name of the child." "Our eldest boy," says Livingstone, "being named Robert, Mrs. Livingstone was after his birth always addressed as Ma-Robert, instead of Mary, her Christian name."[5]

Prof. Tylor explains it thus;[6] the husband is "treated as a stranger till his child, being born a member of the family, gives him a status as father

[1] Riedel, in *Zeitschrift für Ethnologie*, xvii. 80.
[2] G. A. Wilken, in *De Indische Gids* (1881), p. 284; Musters, *op. cit.* 177.
[3] Low, *op. cit.* 197; Perelaer, *op. cit.* 42.
[4] Eyre, *op. cit.* ii. 324, 325.
[5] Livingstone, *South Africa*, 126.
[6] *Op. cit.* 249.

of a member of the family," whereupon he ceases to be "cut." But if the father in the same way as Prof. Tylor suggests concerning the Couvade, borrowed the idea from the mother, it is hardly likely that the mother originally practised the custom for a quite different reason. If she did it for the same reason, that is, to assert her maternity, this ought to presuppose a previous paternal system, and if she continued to do it for the same reason, the result is a strange competition. Prof. Tylor's explanation fails to take into account the fact that in almost every case, even, as amongst the Babar islanders, in maternal systems, the mother also takes the child's name. Again, why, as amongst the Mayas, should the father call himself by the name of his son, and the mother call herself by the name of her daughter? the son being *Ek*, and the daughter being *Can*, the father was named "father of Ek," and the mother "mother of Can."[1] This example shows what is not uncommon, an attempt to supersede relationship by sex.

There is, without doubt, in the practice a sort of assertion both of paternity and maternity, but not as against the opposing system. This assertion is, as the savage himself has explained, a paternal and maternal expression of pride, just as in the highest stages of civilisation, a man or woman who has a distinguished son likes to be referred to as the "father or mother of so-and-so." Amongst the Thlinkeets, if a son acquire a reputation, the father will drop his own name and call himself "father of N or M."[2] In Madagascar parents sometimes assume the name of their children, especially should they rise to distinction in the public service, as *Raini Mahay*, father of Mahay, *Raini*

[1] Bancroft, *op. cit.* ii. 680.

[2] Featherman, *op. cit.* iii. 391.

Maka, father of Maka."[1] The Malagasy have the regular custom also; both parents take the name of the eldest child, *Raini Soa*, father of Soa, *Réni Soa*, mother of Soa.[2] But when we take into consideration the religious importance of the name in primitive thought, we may confidently infer that this feeling of pride is only secondary, and is combined with the more vital reason, namely, that the parents, father and mother alike, take the child under their protection by taking its name, that vital part of him as it is supposed to be, thus protecting him from those who might take this name in vain or work worse mischief against it, and by significantly calling themselves father and mother of the child, profess in the most material way their responsibility for it, and their relation to it. The practice is an instance of *ngia ngiampe*, but naturally one-sided and not a mutual exchange, for the child is an "infant" still. The method is exactly half of that common form of *ngiampe*, which consists in mutual exchange of names to effect identity and mutual responsibility between two persons. Further, this taking over of the child's personality or part of his soul, so as practically to form a religious surname for the parents, renders them in a real sense the child's "spiritual" parents and protectors, as they are already its biological guardians. They are now its godparents also. There is another result however. As the child on the principles of relation is the pledge, the *kalduke* between father and mother, this simultaneous adoption by the pair of its name, renews, as between themselves, the relation of *ngia ngiampe* which has been performed at marriage, and which is also inherent in their continuous

[1] Ellis, *History of Madagascar*, i. 154.

[2] Sibree, *Madagascar and its People*, 198, 199.

living together. If we may say so, the act confirms their "spiritual" wedlock, and is a sort of re-marriage. This is natural enough when we consider the fact that the birth of the first child (and it is usually the name of the first child only that is thus assumed) in savage custom seals finally the marriage alliance, as it is indeed a signal of permanence in the tie and psychologically binds the pair together in the joy that a man is born into the world. This is corroborated by such facts as the Zulu practice. The wife in Zululand is not designated a wife until she has borne a child.[1] The idea is seen from another side in the not unfrequent custom that the husband does not gain incontrolled possession of his bride until she has become a mother. Amongst the Nubians the husband is not till then allowed by custom to build a separate house for himself.[2] So amongst the Knisteneaux the husband lives with his wife's parents until the first child is born. "The birth gives full sanction to the marriage, and the wife henceforth calls him by the honorary title of 'father of her child.'"[3] The Chippeway bridegroom lives with his father-in-law until the first child is born.[4] This is part of the explanation of the common practice whereby the husband lives till then with his wife's parents. As this custom is not part of a matriarchal system, so the assumption of the name is no assertion against such, it is simply the completion of the marriage. There are also found actual instances of this potential renewal of marriage at the first birth. Amongst the Todas it is not uncommon for the pair to separate until a second marriage ceremony has taken place. "When it is apparent that they are likely to

[1] Shooter, *op. cit.* 74.
[2] Featherman, *op. cit.* v. 260.
[3] *Id.* iii. 261.
[4] *Id.* iii. 248.

have a family, this second ceremony ensues. In most respects this corresponds with the preceding one"; the husband ties another *tali* round the neck of his bride. "It is seldom that disunion takes place after this."[1] Just before lying-in the South Celebes wife is practically married again to her husband, she and he being ceremonially covered with one garment, as they were at marriage.[2] The idea here is to secure safety to the woman by reasserting the mutual responsibility of the pair, as in Couvade, and is a very natural practice now that the trinity of father, mother, and child is about to be actualised. A case already cited shows the principle of *ngiampe* between husband and wife in connection with names, combined with the *ngiampe* relation between parent and child. The Andamanese call a young husband by his wife's name; when she is pregnant, he is called by her name with the name of the child prefixed (it is a common practice in early races to name the child before birth), and now the wife also has the child's name prefixed to her own.[3]

The custom is also found rarely at puberty. Amongst the Alfoers when a boy named, for instance, *Taleamie*, arrives at puberty, his father, named *Sapialeh*, now calls himself Sapialeh-Taleamie-amay; when his second son reaches puberty he adds his name also, thus, Sapialeh-Taleamie-Karapupuleh-amay.[4] The custom thus merges in the practice of changing the name at puberty. It also is found in marriage. Thus in Buru the father-in-law of Jadet, for instance, is called "father of Jadet."[5] The mother-in-law, as we have seen, commonly makes a *ngiampe* relation with the son-in-law.

[1] Harkness, op. cit. 116.

[2] Matthes, op. cit. 51.

[3] Man, in *Journ. Anthrop. Inst.* xii. 129.

[4] Ploss, *Das Kind*, ii. 424.

[5] Riedel, *De sluik- en kroesharige rassen tusschen Selebes en Papua*, 5.

Here we come back again to sexual taboo as between husband and wife. The practice naturally coincides sometimes with the taboo on the names of husband and wife. In savage custom, as we have seen, rarely is any one addressed by his real name, to do so is to place such an one in danger, it is a wrong done to his personality. Responsibility between husband and wife emphasises this rule. Thus amongst the Barea and Beni-Amer the wife may not utter her husband's name.[1] Perak women in talking of their husbands use a periphrasis which means "house and house-ladder," and is tantamount to saying "my household" instead of "my husband."[2] Amongst the Tuyangs a man will speak of his wife as "my dull thorn," or "the thorn in my ribs," or "the mean one of the inner room."[3] The idea is not so much contempt as a desire to protect her personality. Amongst the natives of the New Hebrides a woman after marriage is called "wife of so-and-so," a practice common everywhere, and identical in principle with the modern European custom.[4] The custom of calling the parent "father" or "mother of the child" is a convenient way of avoiding the use of the personal name, both generally and as between husband and wife. Amongst the Zulus there is the rule in connection with *hlonipa*, that all females related to the girl's family may never call her husband by name, but "father of so-and-so"; if there are no children they call him *umkwenyana*. "They think it not respectful to call him by his name, and so with all young persons to old ones." The son-in-law will not call his mother-in-law by name, but simply *mother*, and the wife is called "so-and-so of so-and-so," "child of her father." A woman must not

[1] Munzinger, *op. cit.* 526, 325.
[2] Colquhoun, *op. cit.* 250.
[3] Skeat, *op. cit.* 369.
[4] *Journ. Anthrop. Inst.* xxiii. 7.

call her husband by name, either to him or of him, but "father of so-and-so."[1] Amongst the Zulus the child often has its name given before birth, "probably because it is not considered etiquette for the people of the bridegroom's *kraal* to speak to or of the bride by her own name," and she is therefore frequently known as "the mother of so-and-so," before the marriage has taken place, although women more correctly take the name or surname of their father on marriage, *e.g.* a woman whose father's name is *Jiba* is *Oka-Jiba*—"she of *Jiba*," *i.e.* daughter of Jiba. If a woman is known as "mother of *Nobatagati*," her first child will receive that name if it be a girl; if a boy, the masculine form, *Matagati*, will be used.[2]

As has been already noted, the parents protect the child by taking its name into their keeping. The ideas so prevalent as to the importance of the name and the dangers that may threaten it may be referred to once more. The Dyaks alter the name of a sick child to deceive the evil spirits.[3] The Tonquinese give children horrid names to frighten away evil spirits.[4] Amongst the Cingalese the name of the child never transpires; it is known to the father and astrologer alone. The father gives it by whispering it in the child's ear. At puberty it receives a new name.[5] In Abyssinia one's baptismal name is concealed to prevent evil spirits from injuring one thereby.[6] The name of a child is never mentioned in Guiana, "because those who know the name would thus have the child in their power."[7] The Pulayers of Malabar dare not even

[1] Leslie, *op. cit.* 173; Callaway, *op. cit.* 316.

[2] *South African Folklore Journal*, ii. 15.

[3] St. John, *op. cit.* i. 197.

[4] Bastian, *Kambodja*, 386.

[5] Forbes, *Eleven Years in Ceylon*, i. 326.

[6] M. Parkyns, *Life in Abyssinia*, 301.

[7] im Thurn, *op. cit.* 220.

call their children "children," but term them "monkeys."[1]

The name-giving is therefore naturally regarded as an important business. It is practically always a religious act, as it gives the child a personality, a soul. Sexual taboo here finds a place, as in Luang Sermata and Ceram, where the father names the boys and the mother the girls.[2] In Hawaii a son, when hardly weaned, took the father's name, and the mother was no longer allowed to eat with the child or touch its food.[3] The importance of the ceremony is brought out in the Narrinyeri belief that it is unlucky to name a child before it can walk,[4] in the custom of giving up the name when a person bearing it dies, and in the Egyptian method of giving the name. The *Kadi* sucks a sweetmeat, and lets it trickle into the child's mouth. He thus "gives the name out of his mouth,"[5] a practical method of showing the material nature of the name in early thought.

The giving of a name, as of anything else, also produces no less than the taking of a name, the *ngiampe* relation; the gift is, as such, a real part of one's self. Thus the Koosas have the custom of giving a man a new name, which no one knows but he who gives it. It is regarded as a very great honour.[6] Amongst the Munda-kols a relative or friend gives the child its name, and between the two there is throughout their lives a "relation of dutifulness."[7] The already subsisting *ngiampe* relation between parent and child is thus emphasised when the parent gives it a name, as it

[1] Ploss, *op. cit.* i. 168.
[2] Riedel, *op. cit.* 327, 135.
[3] D'Urville, *op. cit.* i. 475.
[4] Featherman, *op. cit.* ii. 145.
[5] Ploss, *op. cit.* i. 164.
[6] Lichtenstein, *op. cit.* i. 258. Compare *Revelation*, ii. 17, xix. 12.
[7] Ploss, *op. cit.* i. 163.

is when he takes it. In European folklore there is a common belief, natural as a result of ideas of contact, that the characteristics of the person who gives the child its name, or of those who bear the same name, or of godparents generally, affect the child.[1] There is a Sioux custom called "the transfer of character"; a brave and good man breathes into the infant's mouth.[2] Lastly, the idea that the name is an external soul may be illustrated from the Todas. From fear of the "evil eye," an infant may not be seen by any one except its parents until it receives a name. Then at last it may be shown to outsiders;[3] the idea being that it is rendered secure by having a double personality, part of which can be easily concealed or withheld.

The ceremonial "uncleanness" attaching to the mother is one of the most universal results of sexual taboo. The separation between husband and wife after a birth is often prolonged until the child is weaned, the idea being that milk, as a female secretion, is a specially dangerous vehicle for transmission of her effeminate properties. Hence the infant from contact with the mother is also "unclean," that is, "dangerous," in the taboo sense, no less than it is in danger. To this idea is due the practice, which is fairly common, of taking boys away from the mother as soon as possible. The interest taken by all women in a birth, as well as in a baby, and the diffidence found in the male sex concerning the same, arise straight from sexual differentiation; the next development of this is the common psychological phenomenon that women both resent indifference as to the event, and for a time express diffidence, a sort of fear of causing disgust, in connection with the

[1] Ploss, *op. cit.* i. 159, ii. 226.
[2] *Eleventh Rep. Bur. Ethn.* 482.
[3] Harkness, *op. cit.* 99.

first showing of the child to the father. Amongst the Northern Indians the mother is "unclean" for five weeks after birth, and remains in a separate hut. No male may approach her, not even her husband; if he were to see mother and child, it is feared that "he might take a dislike to the latter."[1] The recognition of the child by the father follows as a matter of course upon such a principle. Conversely in Egypt the father dares not see his child till the seventh day, "for fear he might injure it unwillingly by a look."[2] The Kurnai infant is first taken to the father's brother, and then to the father.[3] The object is doubtless to make the former a go-between, and so to facilitate the natural course of paternal emotion. Amongst the Basutos the father is separated from mother and child for four days. He is introduced to them thus: the medicine-man performs a ceremony called "the helping, or the absolution of the man and wife." If this is not done, the husband will swell up, or, if he goes to his wife, he will die. The *lepheko*, a log four or six feet long, which is laid in front of the door when any one is sick, is brought, and she is set on it, and the husband put opposite her so that their legs touch. The medicine-man then rubs them all over with a preparation of roots and fat. Healing water is also drunk first by the husband and then by the wife.[4] The name and nature of this ceremony well show the ideas of taboo behind it, and also point to the inference that it is another renewal of the marriage tie, similar to the South Celebes custom.

The ideas of sexual taboo are responsible for such

[1] Hearne, *op. cit.* 93. Cf. Crooke, *op. cit.* i. 277.

[2] Ploss, *Das Kind*, i. 132.

[3] Fison and Howitt, *op. cit.* 204.

[4] Grützner, in *Zeitschrift für Ethnologie* for 1877, p. 78.

customs as this of the Zulus. The first-born and second-born sons cannot inherit, "because," say the Zulus in a vague way, "they are the sons of the womb."[1] This is an interesting detail in the history of primogeniture.

As to the taboo on the infant, the Roti belief that the first hair of a child is not his own, and unless cut off will make him weak, is explainable ultimately as being due to connection with the mother.[2] All the contagious matter, however, is removed from mother and child by the usual purification ceremonies. The churching of women is a development of this. In Malay ceremonial "lustration is generally accomplished either by means of fire or of water." "Infants are purified by fumigation, and women after child-birth are half-roasted over the purificatory fire."[3]

The principles of responsibility in *ngia ngiampe* have in this connection an interesting result. For instance in Wetar the parents may not name their child, "for it would thus be liable to illness."[4] Such parental anxiety for the child's safety, combined with the primitive impulse to shift responsibility as the best way of meeting it, is the ultimate *raison d'être* of godparents. The principle is similar to that of the relation of parents-in-law. In primitive thought both sets of persons are religious representatives. The godparents are proxies for the real parents, and as such render the responsibilities of the latter easier. Similar relations are those formed between the operators and the boys operated upon at initiation ceremonies, and between the bridesmen and the bride, and the taboo there resulting

1 Arbousset and Daumas, *op. cit.* 149.

2 *Tijdschrift voor Neerlandsch-Indië*, iii. 635.

3 Skeat, *op. cit.* 77.

4 Riedel, *op. cit.* 449.

is often paralleled by a taboo between godparents and children. Amongst the Haidas at the ceremony of naming the child a sister of the father's holds it and becomes its godmother.[1] At the circumcision of a Hova boy the parent or other person who holds it, and also the operator, are called *rani jaza*, "father of a child." A woman also acts as mother on the occasion, and is called "mother of a child." "They are a kind of godfather and godmother."[2] Godparents are found amongst the Mayas, Caribs, and Japanese.[3] Their representation of the parents is shown in European folklore, as in Thüringen, where they receive each a half of the christening cake.[4] In Altmark bread and cheese are given to the godparents, who divide it between themselves.[5] All over Europe it is the practice for them to give each other presents.[6] Their responsibilities are illustrated by the German notion that they must be chosen carefully, because all their qualities, especially moral, pass to the child. In Voigtland and Franconia the godfather must be careful to wash, else the child will be unclean in habits. In the Erzgebirg he may not carry a knife, for fear the child may develop suicidal mania. Godparents must fast, that the child may not be greedy.[7] The taboos are illustrated by the prohibition regular in Europe, that godparents may not marry either their godchildren or each other.

Lastly, there is an interesting case of that method of securing safety by spreading one's identity over a number of similar persons, which has been illustrated in connection with Saturnalia. Union, as was seen, is a

[1] G. M. Dawson, *op. cit.* 131.
[2] *Journ. Anthrop. Inst.* ix. 40.
[3] Ploss, *op. cit.* i. 151, 293, 291.
[4] *Id.* i. 232.
[5] *Id.* i. 234.
[6] *Id.* i. 241
[7] *Id.* i. 159; ii. 226.

result of this. In the Kei Islands after the name-giving the parents entertain all the children of the village.[1] After the infant has been bathed the parents in Ceram-laut feast some children of the village.[2] Shortly after a birth in Amboina three to five children are brought into the chamber and there feasted.[3] The reason behind these customs is shown by the following cases. In Amboina, if a child does not thrive, the parents gave a feast to the children of the village; these latter are supposed to give presents to the sick child.[4] In other words a *ngiampe* relation is established. The next cases show the principle of securing safety by substitution. Soon after a birth the Watubella mother bathes in the sea, accompanied by eight or ten children out of the village. If she is too weak to go, another woman takes her place. On the way these children have to shout continually, "in order to divert the attention of the evil spirits from the child."[5] The Thlinkeets hold festivals "in honour of children." Slaves to the number of the children for whom the celebration is made receive their liberty. The operation of boring the ears of the children is performed on this occasion.[6]

[1] Riedel, *op. cit.* 238.
[2] *Id.* 174.
[3] *Id.* 73.
[4] *Id.* 73.
[5] *Id.* 207.
[6] Dall, *op. cit.* 413.

CHAPTER XVII

The study of the marriage system has been blocked, owing to the neglect of students to use primitive data of custom and thought for the explanation of rules invented by primitive man. By using modern or relatively late conceptions of relationship, generally legal in character, and by ignoring the significant series of facts which show the primitive relations of men and women, and on which, rather than on later legal ideas, primitive marriage and primitive relationship rest, they have explained the origin of marriage ceremonies and the marriage system on legal lines, and have thus been led to attribute to early man such monstrosities of improbability, as the general practice of female infanticide and of marriage by capture, promiscuity of wives, "group-marriage," and general incest. Moreover, they have been compelled on their theory to explain certain ceremonial acts, the religious character of which is obvious, as being legal fictions. The reconstruction, however, of primitive society cannot be effected with "bricks of law," but only with bricks of human nature mortared by religion.

In order to explain the origin of the marriage system, *i.e.* the relation of marriage to relationship, we must first penetrate to the ideas which underlie human relations generally, and sexual relations in particular. This has been done; and as a result we have worked out the primitive conception of marriage and its responsibilities, and the origin of the marriage ceremonies and practices which arise from that conception. Secondly, we must reach the ideas behind the primitive conception of relationship. This also has been done. Relationship comes from relation, and the primitive conception of relationship is identical with the primitive conception of human relations. As Messrs. Spencer and Gillen remark of Australian relationship, we must, in order to understand it, first disabuse our minds of the modern conception of kinship.

The chief characteristic of the primitive marriage system, as is well known, is exogamy. But it is no less the characteristic of all marriage systems in every age. For what is exogamy? It is often strangely misunderstood; but obviously the one invariable antecedent in all exogamous systems, indeed in all marriage systems, is the probibition of marriage "within the house." This prohibition is the essence of exogamy and of all bars to marriage. I have shown how sexual taboo produces a religious separation of children in the home; originally based on the sexual difference which leads the father to take the boys about with him, while the mother takes the girls, it is afterwards enforced by the principles of sexual taboo, and its extension by the use of relationships produces the various forms of exogamy. Robertson Smith set the question in the right direction when he said, "whatever is the origin of bars to marriage, they certainly are early associated with the feeling that it is indecent for housemates to intermarry."[1] If we apply to the word "indecent" the connotation of sexual taboo, which gave rise amongst other things to the especial meaning of this word, and

[1] W. Robertson Smith, *Kinship and Marriage in Early Arabia*, 170.

if we understand by "housemates" those upon whom sexual taboo concentrates, we have explained exogamy.

It is unscientific to have recourse to an hypothesis of primitive incest or promiscuity. The frequent myths which seem to countenance the suggestion are easily explained by the ideas of sexual taboo, which attach potential "sin" to any sexual relation. All the facts are distinctly opposed to any probability that incest or promiscuity was ever really practised at all. I shall return to this point when discussing "group-marriage."

On the other hand, Dr. Westermarck's explanation of the prohibition against the marriage of near kin is equally mistaken. He supposes that there is a general human "instinct" against inbreeding, resulting from the survival of those peoples who have avoided it, inbreeding being assumed to be deleterious. In the first place, this presupposes in some remote period a general use of the very practice which elsewhere he argues was never general. In the next place, though many attempts have been made, it has never yet been rendered even probable that inbreeding, as such, is deleterious to the race. Evidence drawn from animals in domesticity, or from civilised peoples, proves nothing with regard to primitive man, the conditions being so entirely different. The utmost that can be shown by such evidence is, that inbreeding perpetuates or reproduces congenital taints. This result is important enough, but it was other considerations that led man to avoid "incest," not inbreeding, for the latter has rarely been avoided at all. The well-known statistics of Professor G. H. Darwin really left the question undecided. Dr. Westermarck considers that they proved the injurious results, while most enquirers consider that they proved the contrary. A satisfactory statistical proof requires a higher percentage than this, little short in fact of a hundred thousand to one. On the other hand, there is at least one case of a people living more or less in a state of nature, who actually seem to be physically benefited by inbreeding, viz. certain Fijian stocks, with whom first cousins are required to marry. Mr. Basil Thomson has shown that these Fijians are considerably the superiors in all the usual physical tests, of those who forbid cousin-marriage.[1] Mr. Curr states that the Australian natives he knew were well aware that the aim of the marriage system was to prevent the union of nearly related individuals; but he could not discover on what ground consanguineous marriages were held to be objectionable.[2] As to disadvantages of inbreeding, the Australians whom he knew were quite ignorant.[3] Certain South American tribes give no other reason for avoidance of marriage between near relatives except "shame."[4] Huth gives much evidence to show that there is no innate horror of incest in man.[5] The peasants of the Government of Archangel say that marriages between blood-relations are "blessed with a rapid increase of children."[6]

Again, in nearly all the exogamous systems known, that is, in the common type of two exogamous classes, and also in the less common type of two exogamous classes each split into two sub-classes, it is necessitated by the system that first cousins, when children of a brother and sister, may marry, and where the system is, as is generally the case, rigidly followed, are expected to marry. This, however, is no more a proof of primitive inbreeding and incest, than is the Archangel notion.

[1] *Journ. Anthrop. Inst.* xxiv. 383 ff.
[2] Curr, *op. cit.* i. 112.
[3] *Id.* i. 236.
[4] Westermarck, *op. cit.* 315, 320.
[5] A. H. Huth, *The Marriage of Near Kin* 10-24.
[6] *Fil[illegible]*, i. 464.

If then there is an "instinct" against inbreeding, it stultifies itself in a very curious way. Also the evidence which Dr. Westermarck cites necessarily concerns cousin-marriage chiefly, and yet he is forced to come back to an "instinct" against marriage between housemates, though cousins are rarely such. It would be more correct to say that there is an "instinct" *for* inbreeding, which is checked by human religious ideas. He does not make allowance, in connection with the prohibition between housemates, for the common prohibition of marriage between first cousins (when children of two brothers or of two sisters), who do not live together, and between totemic tribe-fellows, for instance, who have never seen each other; nor does he explain the common fact that persons entirely unrelated, though living together, may marry (the "instinct" against inbreeding would here show the wonderful insight that "instinct" was once supposed to possess), or the more common fact that persons entirely unrelated who live together may not marry (here the "instinct" would seem to have been easily duped).

There is also the remarkable fact, as has been seen, that to no little extent brothers and sisters, mothers and sons, fathers and daughters, do *not* live together. This is a result of sexual taboo, and is originally a part of the cause why such marriage is avoided, and not a result of the avoidance of incest.

Lastly, it is not scientific to use the term "instinct" of this kind of thing. Instinct proper is only concerned with immediate processes of function; it is physiological thought, and has nothing in its content except response of function to environment. Instinct possesses neither tradition nor prophecy.

The present hypothesis gives the reason why brothers

and sisters in some cases do not live together, which reason is also the chief factor in producing what is really a complex feeling, the subconscious or conscious "aversion" to love and marriage, first, between those who are in continuous contact, and secondly, between those who are not. In the simple form of the aversion we have seen the intensification of sexual taboo in the closeness of the family circle, where no dangerous acts may be performed, such as eating in some cases, to the extent that parents prevent brothers and sisters from eating together, speaking together, or having any ordinary physical relations. These prohibitions are an accentuated form of the taboo of personal isolation, inherent in human relations. They of course include the dangerous act of marriage. They are not due originally to a fear of incest, as such, but to the fear of sexual contagion of properties, of which the idea of incest is one particular result. Practically all sexual relations, and not merely intercourse, are "incest" for primitive man, in his sense of the word—the breaking of a taboo instituted to prevent the dangerous results of physical contact between persons who are, *quâ* sexual, mutually dangerous; and it would be easy to show that, psychologically, the belief in the injurious results of inbreeding is of religious origin, and parallel to the belief that sickness is due to sin or violation of taboo.

As showing that sexual intercourse is not the chief or only relation that is feared, it is to be observed that amongst several peoples illicit connections between the young before they are of age to marry are allowed, though illicit marriage is strictly forbidden. Licence before marriage is very common in the East Indies.[1] It

[1] G. A. Wilken, in *Bijdragen tot de Taal-, Land- en Volkenkunde van Nederlandsch Indië*, xxxviii. 3, 438 ff.

is allowed between members of "classes" that may not intermarry in some Australian tribes, of the Lower Murray, Lower Darling, and perhaps the Port Lincoln and Kunandaburi tribes,[1] but it is probable that these Australian cases, if all the facts were known, would bear another explanation. Here, as in marriage itself, it is the living together, the permanent contact, the sharing of life at bed and board, together with the procreation of children, that are the important things.

The other factor in the simple form of the prohibition is a psychological result of sexual solidarity and sexual taboo. The bringing-up of children in this manner produces what is a psychological impossibility of sexual love between brothers and sisters. Separation before the sexual instinct shows itself, has in effect set the consciousness outwards by the time puberty arrives, and then, when the sexual instinct has appeared, it is biassed towards realisation out of the "house," and this is what actually occurs; for out of the house the prohibition is not so stringent nor so carefully enforced, while love is produced by chance meetings with acquaintances. This coincides with the psychological fact that love's awakening turns the mind away from what is familiar and known towards what is strange and romantic.

We may now pass to cases where the children are not strictly separated. Here, when living together becomes a sentiment, we have reached the complex form of the prohibition. It is the relation of *ngia ngiampe* once more. Living together, especially where commensality is allowed, forms one of the closest bonds of mutual respect and duty. Originally the feeling of

[1] J. G. Frazer, *Totemism*, 59; Brough Smyth, *op. cit.* i. 37; *Native Tribes of South Australia*, 222.

duty is one of reciprocal caution, if not of fear, for each person has part of the other in his or her keeping; but this conception soon merges into that of mutual responsibility, and between the parties concerned any dangerous relation such as marriage is out of the question. It is not convenient, it is improper, it is an offence against the harmony of the house for such dangerous relations to occur, and parents prevent such occurrences. The case is identical with that of eating together. As we have seen, such dangerous functions are often not permitted in the house or family circle at all, where in the confined space and personal proximity their dangerousness would be intensified. Moreover, it is natural that parents should apply their own experience for the advantage of their children. They know, if not the responsibilities, at least the superstitious dangers attaching to any relations between the sexes, and in particular, accustomed as they are to refer all mutual disagreements, perils of the soul and body alike, in sexual and other crises, to their own reciprocal action and mutually dangerous relations, that is, to the principles of mutual contact (*ngia ngiampe*), they will naturally prevent any repetition of such between their children.

In this question we see fully developed once more the primitive ideas of contact in relation, and, in particular, how physical relations of any sort, including that of marriage, are tabooed, first between persons different enough or distant enough to be spiritually or physically dangerous; and secondly, between persons near enough and closely enough connected to be mutually responsible, that is, potentially dangerous in a more complex way, to each other. In the former, danger is intensified, in the latter, duty.

Of the former, the typical result is the Ceramese and Wetarese practice of forbidding marriage between members of villages who have made a military alliance by the *pela* ceremony, the nature of the ceremony preventing treachery, while it brings them into the second class of persons; of the latter the prohibition of marriage between brothers and sisters is the typical result.

In the former, again, there is implied the impulse to endogamy, as seen in the constant marriage of cousins, in the latter the impulse to exogamy, which, in its lowest terms, is the avoidance of marriage between brothers and sisters.

Lastly, at puberty the separation between brothers and sisters is stereotyped, both by natural and artificial means. Where ceremonies of "initiation" obtain, the bond of initiation, simultaneous or otherwise, connects the boys of the community together on the one hand, and the girls on the other, by a close tie of the *ngiampe* species, and thus the way is prepared for an extension of the prohibition. Fellow-initiates become "brothers" or "sisters." Thus, amongst the Kurnai all the young men who have been initiated at the same time are "brothers" and address each other's "wives" as "wife";[1] this is identical with those cases where fellow-initiates form "guilds."

Such and all terms of relationship, it is to be noted, are in primitive thought also terms of relation. They are both terms of kinship and terms of address. Here may be reconciled a somewhat bitter controversy between those who hold the former and those who hold the latter connotation of classificatory terms. In all ages terms of relationship are terms of relationship,

[1] Fison and Howitt, *op. cit.* 198.

but no less are they, secondarily, terms of address. Of primitive times this is especially true, for "kinship" in primitive thought is a vaguer term than in later culture, not because of any primitive promiscuity, but because the tie of blood had not attained prominence over looser ties of contact and identity of age. To the primitive man such a term as "brother" includes men of his own age, who are in more or less close contact with him, and "sister" includes women in the same way. So with terms like "husband" and "wife." There is also often to be seen a very natural confusion between these two sets of terms. A "wife" is a *woman* of one's own generation, but so is one's *sister*; the same applies to "husband" and "brother," *mutatis mutandis*. This is brought out by the very widely spread use of the words "brother" and "sister" by young people and even by lovers. In Ceram-laut young people call each other "brother" or "sister."[1] Friends in the Aru Islands call each other "brother."[2] In the Babar Islands, lovers call each other "brother" and "sister."[3] Indeed, it seems that early man finds it difficult to rise above the confused notion that all women of his own age are potential "sisters," just as we may infer from many facts cited above a similar difficulty in surmounting the similar idea that any connection with any women of that age is equivalent to marriage. Thus, potentially, brothers and sisters are, in primitive thought, already *married* through having lived together, and therefore, as it were, cannot be married actually. This confusion between "wife" and "sister" is shown by a Kurnai explanation of a practice at initiation. Behind each youth there sits a girl called

[1] Riedel, *De sluik- en kroesharige rassen tusschen Selebes en Papua*, 153.
[2] *Id.* 260.
[3] *Id.* 350.

Krau-un. She is a "comrade" and not a wife; the Kurnai "carefully pointed out that they were like sisters and not like wives." Such girls are often cousins of the boys.[1]

Next as to relationships, beginning with those persons who live together more or less, it is to be noted that habitual proximity and contact is the strongest and most ordinary tie, and is earlier in thought than the tie of blood. The strong conception of the tie of blood, best seen in feudal and semi-civilised societies, is by no means so strong in primitive culture. Identity of "flesh" if not of food, that is, commensality, are both earlier in thought than that of blood. A test case for psychology is perhaps that closest of ties between mother and child; here in all stages of human culture, the idea of the tie of blood is psychologically the last to appear; mutual affection and the relations of help and dependence result from that tie, but psychologically that tie is ignored. Psychologically speaking, relationship develops originally from relations, and in primitive thought, relations are the test of kinship and not *vice versâ*. The relative lateness of the idea of the blood-tie is also indicated by the views held by such early races as the Central Australians, for instance, upon the facts of conception and birth. In the Arunta tribe every member is born "as a reincarnation of the never-dying spirit-part of one of these semi-animal ancestors." This principle is revealed to boys at the second initiation ceremony, and pantomimically acted. The child is not the result of intercourse, which only prepares the mother for its reception. The sacred *Erathipa* stone (= "child") has a hole through which spirit-children look out for women who may pass, and

[1] Fison and Howitt, *op. cit.* 195.

it is believed that visiting the stone will result in conception. "If a young woman has to pass near the stone, and does not wish to have a child, she will carefully disguise her youth, distorting her face and walking with the aid of a stick. She will bend herself double like a very old woman, the tones of whose voice she will imitate, saying, 'Don't come to me, I am an old woman.'" A black line is painted above the hole, and is always renewed by any man who visits it. A similar black line, called by the same name, is painted above the eye of a new-born child to prevent sickness. A man may cause women to be pregnant, even at a distance, by rubbing the stone and repeating a charm. Or, if a man wants to punish his wife for supposed unfaithfulness, he rubs it, saying, "Go quickly and hang on tightly." That is, the child is to remain so long in the woman as to cause her death. If a man and wife desire a child, he ties his hair-girdle round it.[1] The Arunta, who hold these views, count descent through the father. The old superstitious ideas still obtain, though the biological fact is practically admitted. Another indication that the tie of blood is late, is the fact that in some Australian tribes the boys follow the father in "descent," and the girls the mother.[2] Lastly, it is the name, and not the "blood," that in most early societies is the chief test of classificatory or totemic relationship, in maternal and paternal descent alike;[3] and also these very relationships have as their essential purpose not relationship but prevention of marriage.

If one thinks over the matter, it is obvious that the inference of identity of flesh and blood would be a later

[1] Spencer and Gillen, *The Native Tribes of Central Australia*, 338, 339, 265, 337, 338.
[2] *Infra*, 456.
[3] Westermarck, *op. cit.* 111.

achievement than the inference of vague connection between a mother or father and child; and though the biological ties were certain, with the increase of knowledge, to supersede other conceptions and practically were always used, yet there are many facts which point to attempts on the part of other ideas of relation to become conceptions of relationship. It is to be noted also that the idea of the blood-tie cannot explain most of these, except by such forced analogy as is quite impossible.

In the account of *ngia ngiampe* we reviewed the more artificial forms of "relationship." Of other forms, firstly, identity of sex very commonly amounts to a relationship, and where sexual taboo is well-developed, it is perhaps the strongest tie of all. It is a result of sexual solidarity, and assumes various forms. For instance, in several Australian tribes each sex has a totem; in the Port Lincoln tribe a small kind of lizard, the male of which is called *Ibirri*, and the female *Waka*, is said to have divided the sexes in the human species; "an event that would appear not to be much approved of by the natives, since either sex has a mortal hatred against the opposite sex of these little animals, the men always destroying the *Waka* and the women the *Ibirri*."[1] In the Wotjobaluk tribe it is believed that "the life of *Ngunungunut* (the bat) is the life of a man, and the life of *Yartatgurk* (the night-jar) is the life of a woman"; when either is killed, a man or woman dies. Should one of these animals be killed, every man or every woman fears that he or she may be the victim; and this gives rise to numerous fights. "In these fights, men on one side and women on the other, it was not all certain

[1] *Native Tribes of South Australia*, 241.

who would be victorious; for at times the women gave the men a severe drubbing with their yam-sticks, while often the women were injured or killed by spears."[1] In some Victorian tribes the bat is the men's animal, and they "protect it against injury, even to the half-killing of their wives for its sake." The goatsucker belongs to the women, who protect it jealously. "If a man kills one, they are as much enraged as if it was one of their children, and will strike him with their long poles." The *mantis* also belongs to the men, and no woman dares kill it.[2] In the Ta-ta-thi tribes of New South Wales the men have the bat for their sex-totem, and the women the small owl. They address each other as Owls and Bats.[3] In the Mukjarawaint tribe of Western Victoria the bat is the men's totem and the night-jar the women's.[4] The Kulin tribe of Victoria has two pairs of sex-totems, the bat (male) and night-jar (female), and the emu-wren (male) and superb-warbler (female).[5] Amongst the Coast Murring people the men's totem is "man's brother," the women's "woman's sister," phrases which recur in North-West Victoria.[6] The best example is from the Kurnai. All men are descendants of *Yeerung* (emu-wren), and all women of *Djeetgun* (superb-warbler). Emu-wrens are the men's brothers, and superb-warblers the women's sisters. Sometimes if young men were slow to marry, the women went out in the forest and killed some emu-wrens, and casually showed them to the men. An uproar followed. The men were very angry; the *yeerungs* their brothers had been killed; men and girls got sticks and attacked each other. Next day the

[1] *Journ. Anthrop. Inst.* xviii. 58.
[2] Dawson, *op. cit.* 53.
[3] *Journ. Anthrop. Inst.* xiv. 350.
[4] *Id.* xiii. 45.
[5] *Id.* xv. 416.
[6] *Id.* xv. 416.

young men went and killed some of the women's sisters, the birds *djeetgun*, superb-warblers, and the result was a worse fight than before. By and by, an eligible young man would meet a marriageable girl, and would say "Djeetgun," she replied, "Yeerung! What does the Yeerung eat?" This would lead to a marriage. Sons of course follow the father's totem, *Yeerung*, and daughters the mother's, *Djeetgun*.[1]

Sex also supersedes kinship in other ways. A Maori boy inherits the father's, a girl the mother's property.[2] So for teknonymy amongst the Mayas.[3] In Victoria a boy's "nearest relative" is his father, a girl's her mother.[4] In the Ikula tribe, which has four totem-clans, the sons of a *Budera* man and a *Kura* woman are *Budera*, and the daughters are *Kura*.[5]

One of the earliest ties of relationship is that of sharing food together, a natural variation, though not widely spread, being that those to whom the same food is taboo are akin. Such cases form good examples of the action of the principles of contact, and are often connected with the practice according to which young men initiated together, or otherwise associated, habitually take their meals in common. Thus amongst the New Hebrideans there are sets of initiated boys, arranged according to age, and each set mess together and sleep together, and may not eat with other persons.[6] The connection between food and kinship is very clear in early thought, and it is natural that it should be so; the inference being that food produces flesh, and identity of food produces identity of flesh. Amongst the Kamilaroi all things in heaven and earth are

[1] Fison and Howitt, *op. cit.* 201, 215.
[2] *Supra*, 430.
[3] *J.A.I.* xii. 509.
[4] *Journ. Anthrop. Inst.* xix. 99.
[5] Dawson, *op. cit.* 38.
[6] *Id.* xxiii. 6, 7.

assigned to the clan-divisions of the tribe, and to such a question as "What division does a bullock belong to?" the answer is, "It eats grass, therefore it is *Boortwerio*."[1] So the answer to what is practically a proposal of marriage on the part of a young Kurnai was, we saw, "*Yeerung!* (the male totem). What does the *yeerung* eat?" Amongst the Dieri *Murdoo*, which means *taste*, is the term for "family," and the first question asked of a stranger is "What Murdoo?"[2] Again, in the tribes of the Belyando River the "classes" or divisions for purposes of marriage are allowed to eat certain foods only.[3] Amongst the Damaras the word for "marriage division" is *oruzo*, which refers to food, and these divisions are described as "dietaries."[4] Another account states that the "clans" of the Damaras are distinguished by food-taboos. One, for instance, may not eat sheep without bones, another, oxen with certain spots. They will not even touch vessels in which such have been cooked, or go near the smoke of the fire used to cook it.[5] The Gaelic names for family, *teadhloch* and *cuedich*, mean, first, having a common residence, and, secondly, those who eat together.[6] The Arabic and Hebrew words for "flesh" have also the connotation of "kindred" or "clan."[7]

The connection in totemic tribes between identity of food and relationship by totem, those who have the same totem being regarded as akin, is shown in the Narrinyeri tribe. The totems here are called *ngaitye*, which means "friend." All members of a totem-clan are regarded as "relations." This, as is well known,

[1] Fison and Howitt, *op. cit.* 169.

[2] Curr, *op. cit.* ii. 49.

[3] *Id.* iii. 27.

[4] *South African Folklore Journal*, i. 40.

[5] C. J. Andersson, *Lake Ngami*, 222 ff.

[6] McLennan, *Studies in Ancient History*, 123.

[7] Robertson Smith, *op. cit.* 148, 176.

is the case with all totem-clans. In some Australian tribes, however, it is to be noted, totemism has nothing to do with marriage. "The *ngaitye* of the Narrinyeri may be killed and eaten by those who possess it, but they are always careful to destroy the remains, such as bones, feathers, etc., lest an enemy should obtain them and use them for purposes of sorcery. They never marry one who belongs to the same *ngaitye*."[1] When boys are initiated together they become "tribal brothers," and the marriage-bar is thus extended outside the family. In the Torres Straits "initiation mates" may not marry each other's sisters.[2]

Lastly, in connection with food-kinship there is the widely spread custom of forming a tie of "brotherhood" by eating and drinking together. This is a common form of the relation of *ngia ngiampe*, and I need not quote again the examples we have already reviewed. Later than this there arises the same practice with blood as the *kalduke*, and here relations and relationship meet. I may add that amongst the Arabs and elsewhere milk-kinship is equivalent to real kinship.[3] This is due originally not to analogy from motherhood, but to primitive ideas about food. Milk is regarded as equivalent to flesh by the Arabs, and milk-kinship forms one of Muhammad's forbidden degrees.

Again, when friends in the Aru Islands and Ceramlaut call each other "brother" or "sister," and when lovers in the Babar Islands call each other "brother" and "sister,"[4] we see another form of primitive relationship, based on contact and combined with identity of age. It is no analogy, except in terminology, from the real relationship, nor yet does it point to primitive

[1] G. Taplin, in Curr, *op. cit.* ii. 245.

[2] *Journ. Anthrop. Inst.* xix. 411.

[3] Robertson Smith, *op. cit.* 149.

[4] Riedel, *op. cit.* 260, 153, 350.

incest or promiscuity. When lovers and married persons call each "brother and sister"[1] we see that love and marriage are another form of primitive relationship, *i.e.* of *ngiampe*. And here is to be found one reason for the common misconception that marriage ceremonies were intended to make the pair of one kin. In primitive thought relationship is not our relationship. It is rather relation. Relation and relationship are not yet differentiated, that is all. The Cherokees "reckon a friend in the same rank with a brother, both with regard to marriage and any other affair in social life.[2] Amongst the Seminoles two young men would agree to be life-friends, "more than brothers."[3] This is a very common thing in early races.

Again, any form of the *ngia ngiampe* relation is, as we have seen, equivalent to relationship. The disciples of a Buryat *Shaman* are his "sons."[4] Adoption, so common in early peoples, is frequently a bar to marriage, as amongst the Eskimo, Greenlanders, and Andamanese.[5] In European folk-religion there is the rule, sanctioned by the Catholic Church, that godparents become kin to the family, and marriage may not take place between the godparents themselves, between them and members of the family, or the godchildren.[6] Godparents are proxies for the parents, and as such ought to marry, or at least to be married already; the fact that they may not marry proves the primitive ideas both of sexual relation and of relationship, and shows the impossibility of analogy from kinship.

Lastly, there is the well-known form of kinship by name. It is parallel to kinship by totem, and is too

[1] Wright, *op. cit.* ii. 224, 229.
[2] Adair, *op. cit.* 190.
[3] *Fifth Rep. Bur. Eth.* 508.
[4] *J.A.I.* xxiv. 135.
[5] *Ninth Rep. Bur. Eth.* 419; Crantz, *op. cit.* i. 146; *J.A.I.* xii. 126.
[6] Ploss, *Das Kind*, i. 198 ff., 291.

familiar to need illustration. Dr. Westermarck has shown that this is the important point in both maternal and paternal descent.[1] In other words, those who have the same name are *ngia ngiampe* and may not marry.

Primitive relationship, it is clear, is at once stronger and weaker than the civilised tie; weaker, because the bond of blood has not assumed a superiority over other relations, close contact being the test; stronger, because the ideas of contact which characterise these relations have so intense a religious meaning and enforce duty so stringently.

The famous Matriarchal Theory was as exaggerated in its early forms as was the Patriarchal. It is now coming to be recognised that it is simply the tracing of descent through the mother and giving the children her name, though there are a few cases where inheritance of property has later come under the rule, some of these being due to sex. It is a method of tracing genealogy, more convenient in polygamous societies, and more natural in primitive times, when the close connection of mother and child during the early days of infancy emphasises the relation. The system was explained by Bachofen as due to the supremacy of women, and by McLennan as due to doubtful paternity and primitive promiscuity. It is not, however, doubtful paternity which causes maternal genealogy; Dr. Westermarck has shown this, and also that the hypothesis of primitive promiscuity is without any foundation whatever.[2] The last position of the theory of promiscuity will be taken when we discuss "group-marriage" so-called. He has also proved that, though common, "maternal descent" cannot have been either universally or generally a stage through which man has

[1] *Op. cit.* 111.

[2] *Op. cit.* chapters iv. v. vi.

passed. Amongst the lowest tribes in the scale, those of Australia, paternal descent is nearly as common as maternal. It is interesting to notice that the reckoning of descent exclusively through either the maternal or the paternal line, is an example of the influence which sex must necessarily have upon relationships. In those cases where the sons follow the father's clan, and the daughters the mother's, there was a similar phenomenon; here, there is an attempt to make relationship for both sexes follow one sex to the exclusion of the other. In maternal descent, no less than in paternal, however, the relation to the unrepresented side of the house is of course easy to trace. In the islands of Leti, Moa, and Lakor, there is seemingly an attempt to adjust the balance in unisexual relationship, by making the sons follow the mother and the daughters the father,[1] but this is doubtless due to considerations of caste.

Why did not early peoples trace descent in the apparently obvious way, from both father and mother? For the same reason that we, for instance, use the paternal name to trace descent. In the ages before writing, the use of both parents' names and their application to children would be too complicated, as it still is found. This consideration has much to do with "classificatory relationship." But here too sexual taboo has had its influence, and by dividing the family into two parts indefinitely postponed the trial of solutions. A Zulu custom shows the connection of sexual taboo with the paternal system, and has more than a merely casual interest as a savage Salic law. The first-born and second-born sons of the king cannot inherit, because, say the Zulus in a vague way, "they are the sons of the womb."[2] A similar idea shows itself in the

[1] Riedel, *op. cit.* 392, 384.

[2] Arbousset and Daumas, *op. cit.* 149.

objection held by some peoples to the children of two sisters marrying, while they do not object to marriage between the children of two brothers; for instance, in Leti, Moa, Lakor, and Madagascar. With the latter people such marriage is regarded as "incest."[1] Such marriage is of course prevented by the usual exogamous system, whether maternal or paternal, and so is marriage between brothers' children, but the ideas of sex have asserted themselves. It is as if female influence rendered "nearness" of kin too near, while crossing of sex adjusts the balance.

Prof. Tylor has connected the maternal system with the practice whereby the husband takes up his residence with his wife's people. He regards this as the earliest form of setting up an establishment, followed by a transitional method, by which the couple begin married life in the wife's house, but eventually remove.[2] In the first place, Messrs. Spencer and Gillen assert, that as far as they know, it is not the custom in any Australian tribe, maternal or otherwise, for the husband to reside with his wife's people.[3] In the Kunandaburi tribe Messrs. Howitt and Fison remark that, though the maternal system is used, yet the wife goes to her husband's people.[4] In Guinea the maternal system is followed, but the wife goes at once to the husband's home, so in New Britain, and amongst the Arawaks.[5] Again, as to the "transitional" method, it seems at least improbable that the inconvenience of setting up one's residence amongst the wife's people and then setting up another, should have been undergone in

[1] Riedel, *op. cit.* 385; J. Sibree, *Madagascar*, 248.
[2] *Journ. Anthrop. Inst.* xviii. 247 ff.
[3] *Op. cit.* 470.
[4] *Journ. Anthrop. Inst.* xii. 35.
[5] Bosman, *Description of Guinea*, 392, 420; *Journ. Anthrop. Inst.* xviii. 293, 294; *id.* xxi. 230; Brett, *op. cit.* 101.

order to satisfy the maternal system. The inconvenience is certainly put up with, but in most cases it will be found that it is put up with in order to satisfy certain universal feelings of human nature, stronger and more important than is an arbitrary system of kinship. In the first place, it is natural that the marriage should take place, as it often does, both in primitive and modern times, at the "residence" of the bride's parents. Womanly and maternal feelings are not to be denied to the primitive mothers of the race. In many cases early marriage is not a momentary act, but a long process, extending sometimes over several weeks, and during this period the bridegroom resides with his wife's people.

We have seen how in Cambodia a girl's parents are so careful of her happiness that for some time they keep a very strict watch over the son-in-law;[1] also, this natural human feeling often concentrates upon the first delivery of the young bride, and mothers show especial anxiety concerning this. The genial Dobrizhoffer reported of his Abipones: "Mothers are careful of their daughters, and can hardly bear to part with them. Parents after satisfying themselves of the probity of the son-in-law allow the pair to live in a separate house."[2] The Malay bridegroom is "nominally expected to remain under the roof and eye of his mother-in-law for about two years," after which he may remove to a house of his own.[3] The Omaha wife remains for some time with her parents, the husband visiting her, before she goes to live with him;[4] so amongst the Sarae.[5] We have also seen in connection with "marriage by capture" how girls cling to their

[1] *Supra*, 412. [2] *Op. cit.* ii. 208. [3] Skeat, *op. cit.* 384.
[4] James, *Expedition to the Rocky Mountains*, ii. 47. [5] Munzinger, *op. cit.* 387.

home, a feeling naturally enhanced when child-birth approaches—the young wife wishes to be with her mother.[1]

Amongst the Barea the wife returns to her mother's house for her first delivery and there stays three months.[2] Amongst the Adel Bedouin the wife remains in her father's house till she has borne three children.[3] Amongst the Luhtongs the wife lives at her mother's house, the husband sleeping there. After the birth of the first child she goes to his house.[4] Amongst the Bedouins of Sinai the wife stays with her parents till the child is born.[5] So amongst the Khyens and Ainus, Shawanese, Abipones, and Chippeways.[6]

It should be noted here that marriage is often not regarded as complete until a child is born. A birth is indeed a very natural sign of the completion of the marriage tie, and this needs no explanation, though it explains this residing with the bride's parents till the birth, when we take into consideration the affection between mother and daughter, and suspicions of the other sex fostered by sexual taboo. Taboos between the newly married show this, as between themselves; the Miao bride and groom occupy separate bedrooms until the first child is born, afterwards they use one bed.[7] The birth relieves anxiety both maternal and connubial. The Knisteneaux case showed this completion of the marriage.[8] Amongst the Nubians temporary mat huts make a part of every family dwelling. These are occupied by people recently married, for it is "only after the young wife has become a mother that

[1] *Supra*, 354. [2] Munzinger, *op. cit.* 527. [3] Harris, *op. cit.* i. 288.
[4] Colquhoun, *Across Chrysê*, 394. [5] Burckhardt, *op. cit.* 153.
[6] Rowney, *op. cit.* 203; Siebold, *Ethnologische Studien über die Aino*, 31; Klemm, *Culturgeschichte*, ii. 75; Featherman, *op. cit.* iii. 248.
[7] Colquhoun, *Across Chrysê*, 373. [8] *Supra*, 432.

the husband can gain uncontrolled possession of his bride, and he is then allowed to build a stone house for himself in any locality he may choose."[1] As a result of a similar feeling, the ceremony of marriage amongst the Hovas is first celebrated at the house of the bride's parents, then at that of the bridegroom's.[2] The same practice occurs in Nepal.[3]

As to the bride's affection for her old home, which coincides with sexual taboo, we find it commonly satisfied by returning thither. Amongst the Hindus, after a few weeks the bride returns to her paternal home for a visit.[4] Amongst the Bheelalahs the bride's parents take her from her husband back to their house, where she stays for a week.[5] The Turkoman bride returns to her parents after six weeks, to spend a year with them.[6] Amongst the Wa-teita the bride after the three days' seclusion and fasting at her husband's house, which form part of the marriage ceremonial, is conveyed back to her parents' home by a procession of girls. After a while she returns.[7] I do not think that Prof. Tylor allows for these cases.

In more religious form this feeling is satisfied amongst the Larkas by the wife running home after three days of married life. "The most modest course for the wife to follow is to run away from his house and tell her friends that she cannot love him; and the husband must show great anxiety for her, and convey her back by force."[8] Other instances of the same sort of thing we have reviewed when treating of so-called marriage by capture. In more primitive form still, in South Australia the Powell's Creek bride is taken away

[1] Featherman, *op. cit.* v. 260.

[2] *Journ. Anthrop. Inst.* ix. 41.

[3] Oldfield, *Sketches from Nepal*, i. 410.

[4] *Journ. Anthrop. Inst.* ix. 404.

[5] *Id.* ix. 404.

[6] Fraser, *Journey into Khorasan*, ii. 375.

[7] J. Thomson, *op. cit.* 51.

[8] Rowney, *op. cit.* 67.

to a considerable distance after being "purchased or captured" (*sic*) and kept isolated with her husband for some months, until she "settles down to the new order of things." The pair then rejoin the tribe.[1]

Temporary residence with the bride's parents, then, is no survival of continuous residence, but is due to various forms of sexual taboo and parental care. For continuous residence the Ainu practice is instructive; if the girl or her parents propose the match, the pair live in the bride's village, and *vice versâ*.[2]

Nor is the change of residence a transitional method. It takes place, firstly, after the satisfacton of the feelings we have discussed. The Siamese bridegroom builds a room off the house of his wife's parents and there they live for some months, after which he builds a house of his own.[3] In Nukahiva the bridegroom lives with his bride's parents; if, after a time "the pair are still attached to each other," they set up a separate establishment.[4] An Egyptian does not always become a householder at marriage, but may live with his wife in her parents' house.[5] Amongst the Soomoos the groom lives with the bride's people until the girl is old enough to be married.[6] And in New Britain the girl, if very young, stays with her parents; if full-grown, she goes to her husband's house. In New Britain, by the way, descent is through the mother.[7] In Samoa, "a woman does not become a man's wife until he takes her to his own house."[8]

Secondly, the change of residence is due to a very obvious circumstance. In some of the Fiji Islands, after the ceremony of eating together, the girl returned to her parents, where she remained until the marriage

[1] *Journ. Anthrop. Inst.* xxiv. 177.
[2] Batchelor, *op. cit.* 140.
[3] Loubere, *op. cit.* i. 157.
[4] Lisiansky, *op. cit.* 83.
[5] Lane, *op. cit.* ii. 269.
[6] *Journ. Anthrop. Inst.* xxiv. 205.
[7] *Id.* xvid. 289.
[8] Pritchard, *op. cit.* 134.

was consummated, or rather until the bridegroom had built his house.[1] In Leti, Moa, and Lakor, the husband lives with his wife's parents, till he has built a house.[2] In Wetar, the husband lives with his wife's people till he gets a house of his own.[3] Economic causes indeed have always had a good deal to do with marriage. Amongst the Barea a man is "in the power" (*sic*) of his wife's father until he builds a house of his own.[4] Amongst the Cadiacks the bridegroom "pays" for his wife by working for her parents, living with them until the full amount is worked off.[5] The same practice is found amongst the Aleuts, the Arruans of New Guinea, the Klamaths, in Timorlaut, the Kei Islands, Amboina, and the Watubela Islands.[6] Amongst the Arawaks the bride's father expects his son-in-law to do some work for him; the young couple often live with him "until an increasing family renders a separate establishment necessary." These Indians, it is to be noted, are a "maternal" people.[7] Though in origin the "bride-price" is not purchase-money, yet, as commercialism develops, we find cases like that of the Watubela islanders, with whom the children "belong" to the wife's family until the bride-price is fully paid.[8] Many peoples in the East Indies, such as the Battas and Malays, have three forms of marriage:[9] (1) the groom pays "purchase-money"; (2) if he is poor, he works for her parents, living in their house; (3) elopement. In Amboina and Ceram, if the bride-groom cannot pay the "price," he lives with her in her parents' house, and works for them. If he can pay it,

[1] Featherman, *op. cit.* ii. 203.
[2] Riedel, *op. cit.* 390.
[3] *Id.* 448.
[4] Munzinger, *op. cit.* 447.
[5] Lisiansky, *op. cit.* 198.
[6] Featherman, *op. cit.* iii. 467; ii. 33; iii. 329; Riedel, *op. cit.* 301, 236, 63, 132.
[7] Brett, *op. cit.* 101.
[8] Riedel, *op. cit.* 205.
[9] Junghuhn, *op. cit.* ii. 132, 350.

she goes to his house.[1] Lastly, amongst the extinct Tasmanians, supposed to have been the lowest race in the scale known, the husband took his bride to his own *wirlie*, and the system of descent was maternal.[2] The usual Australian custom is for the man to take his wife to his own tribe; and the exception which sometimes occurs amongst the Arunta is natural enough; they are a "paternal" people, but men of other tribes sometimes join them, taking a wife from them and setting up their abode.[3]

We may now proceed to notice the well-known machinery by which exogamy is worked in so many early societies, the "classificatory system." Its origin is perfectly clear. It is in its simplest form of two exogamous intermarrying divisions, consistent with either the paternal or maternal system of descent. It is unnecessary to describe it fully, or to show what has been well shown by Messrs. Fison and Howitt, Spencer and Gillen, that the terms are terms of kinship and not terms of address. As we have seen, however, they are in origin terms of *relation*, and accordingly, so far, terms of address also. For instance, the term *Ipmunna* in Central Australia, which is that used between members of the two subclasses which make up one of two exogamous divisions, would be better described as a term of relation.[4] Relation and relationship are not differentiated in primitive thought. Again, all of the terms *can* be used as terms of address, just as our terms of relationship can be so used, "aunt" and "uncle" for instance, that is, instead of the personal name. In connection with the account of relations already given, an instance typical of all mankind

[1] Riedel, *op. cit.* 68, 132.
[2] Bonwick, *op. cit.* 72.
[3] *Journ. Anthrop. Inst.* xviii. 250; Spencer and Gillen, *op. cit.* 60.
[4] *Id.* 71.

is the modern Egyptian practice; women address aged female friends as "mother," young ones as "sister."[1]

The commonest form of classificatory exogamy is that where the members of the tribe are divided into classes for purposes of marriage, members of one class being forbidden to marry in that class, but bound to marry into the other. Taking the Urabunna tribe as as example, the scheme is as follows, *Matthurie* and *Kirarawa* being the two exogamous classes, and descent being through the mother[2]:—

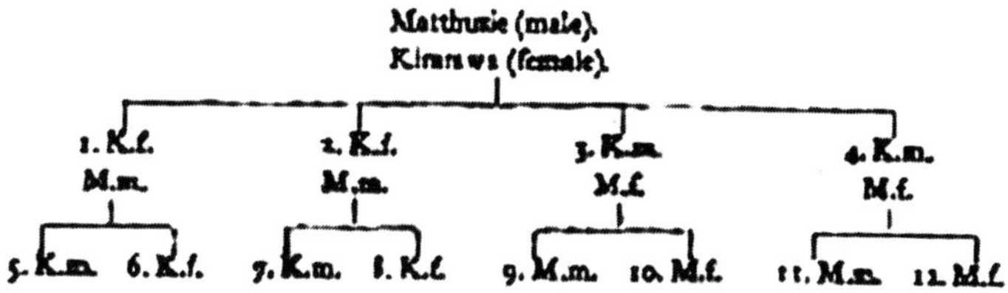

The main point here is, of course, that brothers and sisters may not marry; the system presupposes this when putting them under the same name. The next point is that first cousins, when children of two sisters, as 5 and 8, 6 and 7, or of two brothers, as 9 and 12, 10 and 11, may not marry, this being an accident of the system. Thirdly, first cousins, when children of a brother and sister, as 7 and 10, 8 and 9, may marry, they being of different classes, and in most systems they are indeed expected to marry, as in Australia and Fiji. This species of cousin-marriage Prof. Tylor has well called "cross-cousin-marriage." When this is the case, the system is endogamous as well. Primitive exogamy is in fact also endogamous; and when it is understood that the

[1] Featherman, *op. cit.* v. 265.

[2] Spencer and Gillen, *op. cit.* 60.

essential object of exogamy is to prevent marriage between "brothers" and "sisters," there is no need to tabulate exogamous peoples, for exogamy is practised by every race of mankind, as it is by ourselves, or to search for its origin. As to Prof. Tylor's suggestion that exogamy was due to a desire to secure the survival of the tribe by forming alliances outside, the choice being between marrying-out or dying-out,[1] this is another kind of "exogamy," and one indeed that is sporadic only, though a natural enough practice, as it is between European royal families. Early exogamy proper is a family and not a tribal matter, and is also somewhat too endogamous to include a political exogamy in its origin, and savages do not possess such political insight as would warrant the inference that such was a general cause of exogamy.

Further, each of these marriage-classes is subdivided into several totem-classes, and there is an arrangement as to which totems may intermarry, descent being still through the mother.[2] Thus :—

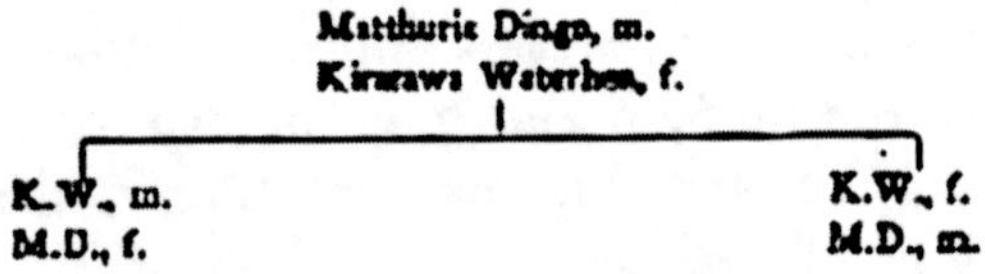

The next form of the classificatory system is one which is common in Australia. Here each of the two exogamous classes is divided into two subclasses. Thus, in the Kamilaroi tribe the two exogamous classes are *Dilbi* and *Kupathin*; *Dilbi* is divided into *Muri* and *Kubi*, *Kupathin* into *Ipai* and *Kumbo*. *Muri* must marry *Kumbo*, and *Kubi Ipai*, no other intermarriage

[1] *Journ. Anthrop. Inst.* xviii. 267.

[2] Spencer and Gillen, *op. cit.* 61.

being allowed. There is the further arrangement that the children belong to the companion subclass of the mother, descent being maternal.[1] Dr. Frazer calls this "indirect female descent."[2] Thus:—

	Male.	*Marries.*	*Children.*
Dilbi	Muri	Kumbo	Ipai.
	Kubi	Ipai	Kumbo.
Kupathin	Ipai	Kubi	Muri.
	Kumbo	Muri	Kubi.

The same system is found in the southern division of the Arunta, though in process of further subdivision as in the northern tribe,[3] and in the Kiabara tribe, both these tribes having paternal descent.[4] When this system is tabulated, it will be found that one difference is produced by it. In the Kiabara tribe *Dilebi* is divided into *Baring* and *Turowine*, *Cubatine* into *Bundah* and *Bulcoin*, and the marriages and descent are as follows:—

Baring, m.
Bundah, f.

Turowine, f. Bulcoin, m.	Turowine, f. Bulcoin, m.	Turowine, m. Bulcoin, f.	Turowine, m. Bulcoin, f.
Bundah, m. Bundah, f.	Bundah, m. Bundah, f.	Baring, m. Baring, f.	Baring, m. Baring, f.
Baring, f. Baring, m.	Baring, f. Baring, m.	Bundah, f. Bundah, m.	Bundah, f. Bundah, m.

The difference is this—the system obviously keeps the marriages within the same generation, *Turowine* and *Bulcoin* alternating with *Bundah* and *Baring*. The children of a given father being put in a separate class, of course, amounts to this.

This result can hardly be counted as accidental when we remember that the savage no less than other men

[1] Fison and Howitt, *Kamilaroi and Kurnai*, 37.
[2] Frazer, *Totemism*, 73.
[3] Spencer and Gillen, *op. cit.* 70.
[4] *Journ. Anthrop. Inst.* xiii. 336.

prefers the natural marriage with one of the same generation. That this feeling should have heen codified, as it were, is an instance of the way in which early man tries to assist nature. The vague fear of the possibility of sexual relation with the mother-in-law, for instance, which sometimes emerges above the complex feelings brought by sexual taboo into that relation, is a case in point; another is the fact, that in some codified marriage-systems, as in our own "Table of Kindred and Affinity," a man is forbidden to marry his grandmother, a grandfather his granddaughter, and so on, each case being one never likely to occur.

There is nothing in these systems except identity of name to prevent children of brothers or of sisters marrying, though some peoples, as the Malagasy, allow children of brothers to marry, but not children of sisters, ideas of sexual taboo probably causing this result; and though other peoples, especially those higher in the scale, often prohibit all cousin-marriage. The old Canon Law of the Church, for instance, did so.[1] In these cases descent is reckoned from father and mother together, cross-cousin marriage being thus prevented as well as the other form.

The third development of the classificatory system is that found in the Northern Arunta tribe, and described by Messrs. Spencer and Gillen.[2] It is a further subdivision of the last form mentioned, and the difference in result produced by it, is clearly that it also prevents cross-cousin marriage. In the Southern Arunta tribe the four subclasses are *Panunga* and *Bulthara*, *Purula* and *Kumara*; in the Northern, *Panunga* is divided into *Panunga* and *Uknaria*, *Purula*

[1] Du Cange, *Glossarium mediæ et infimæ Latinitatis*, s.v. generatio.

[2] *Op. cit.* 71 ff.

into *Purula* and *Ungalla*, *Bulthara* into *Bulthara* and *Appungerta*, *Kumara* into *Kumara* and *Umbitchana*. The system is thus given by Messrs. Spencer and Gillen :—

1.	2.	3.	4.
Panunga	Purula	Appungerta	Kumara.
Uknaria	Ungalla	Bulthara	Umbitchana.
Bulthara	Kumara	Uknaria	Purula.
Appungerta	Umbitchana	Panunga	Ungalla.

Reading across the page, *Panunga* m. (1) marries *Purula* f. (2), and the children are *Appungerta* (3), *Purula* m. (2) marries *Panunga* f. (1), and the children are *Kumara* (4), and so on. By tabulating the system, we see how cross-cousin marriage is prevented :—

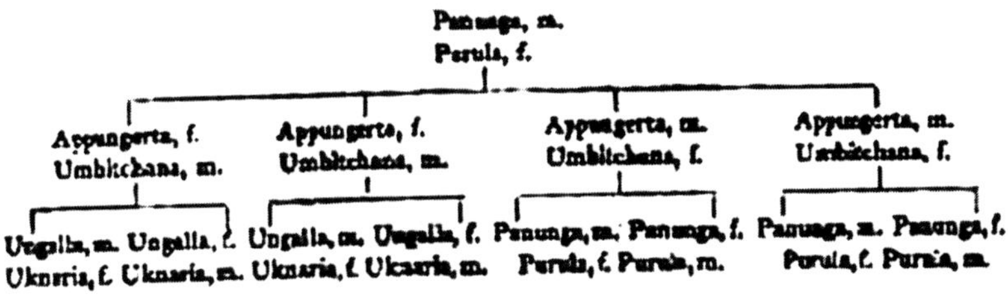

A further point of interest in the Central Australian system is this ; in the Urabunna tribe *nupa* women, *i.e.* women who are marriageable on the system to a particular man, are daughters of his mother's elder brothers, blood or tribal, or of his father's elder sisters, and none others ; a man's wife must belong to the senior side of the tribe. This rule is evidently a codification of the practice found so generally amongst savages, that elder sisters have a prior right to marriage over younger, and is an instance of wise consideration on the part of primitive man.[1] It is a sort of attempt

[1] Spencer and Gillen, *op. cit.* 64, 65.

to assist nature, and is parallel to the preference for marriage within the same generation. In Nias, Halmahera, Java, and China, for example, a younger sister is not allowed to marry before an older one.[1] It is to be noted, that in the Arunta tribe there are, as happens in other classificatory systems, distinct names for elder and younger brothers and sisters, and that when two brothers in blood marry two sisters in blood, the elder brother marries the elder sister; and further, a man may speak freely to his elder sisters in blood, but to tribal elder sisters only at a distance. To younger sisters, blood and tribal, he may not speak.[2] In the Arunta tribe, that is, there is a taboo against women of the junior side, but no fixed rule forbidding marriage with them; in the Urabunna tribe there is such a rule, and we hear of no taboo.

An interesting example of the way in which age influences such relations occurs amongst the Khyoungtha and other Indian hill-tribes, and the Andamanese. With the former, a younger brother may touch and speak to his elder brother's wife; "but it is thought improper for an elder brother even to look at the wife of his younger brother. This is a custom more or less common among all hill-tribes; it is found carried to a preposterous extent among the Santals."[3] An Andamanese may not speak directly but only through a third person to a married woman who is younger than himself. Women are restricted in the same way in relation to their husband's elder brother. Till an Andamanese reaches middle age, he evinces great shyness in the presence of the wife of a younger brother or

[1] Rosenberg, *Der Malayische Archipel*, 155; Riedel, in *Zeitschrift für Ethnologie*, xvii. 76; Winter, in *Tijdschrift voor Nederlandsch-Indië* (1843), i. 566; Gray, *China*, i. 190.

[2] Spencer and Gillen, *op. cit.* 88, 89.

[3] Lewin, *op. cit.* 190.

cousin, and the feeling is reciprocated. His elder brother's wife receives from him the respect due to a mother.[1] In the first case, superiority of age in the male induces the idea of a potentiality of sexual control of a younger female, and with an older woman there is the analogy of the mother, suggested by her greater age. In the second case, the custom is combined with taboos of the mother-in-law species.

We may now consider the last position of the theory that promiscuity was once prevalent amongst early peoples; this is the so-called "group-marriage" of several Australian tribes. Morgan, McLennan, and Lubbock were supported in their hypothesis of primitive promiscuity or community of wives by Messrs. Fison and Howitt, who first adduced the phenomena of "group-marriage." Dr. Westermarck has so ably shown the unscientific character of the promiscuity theory, that it would be unnecessary to add to what he has said, were it not for the fact that Messrs. Spencer and Gillen in their important work have, I think, too easily given their assent to Fison and Howitt's interpretation of "group-marriage" as proving early promiscuity. Indeed they assert that there is no such thing as individual marriage in the Urabunna tribe. It will be clear after we have examined these facts, that Messrs. Spencer and Gillen have misunderstood their origin and meaning, and that their criticism of Dr. Westermarck's condemnation of the promiscuity theory is therefore mistaken. In one detail, that of the so-called *jus primæ noctis*, Dr. Westermarck is wrong, but so are Messrs. Spencer and Gillen.

They say that the facts of the Urabunna system "can only be explained on the theory of the former

[1] Man, in *Journ. Anthrop. Inst.* xli. 136, 355.

existence of group-marriage which has necessarily given rise to the terms of relationship."[1] Now, on the Urabunna system of two exogamous intermarrying classes, the term *mia* for instance, includes not only the meaning of our "mother" but that of "tribal mother," being applied to all women of the same generation in the class to which a man's real mother belongs.[2] But this is an obvious result of the classificatory system, and, apart from the system, it is the regular result of the primitive theory of relationship; the system codifies a combination of relation and relationship, "address" and age. It is the system and not group-marriage, which has given rise to these terms of relationship; these do not in themselves necessarily point to a previous promiscuity or even to a present group-marriage. This "marriageableness" is found also in Fiji, but we do not either there or in Australia find any "right" exercised upon it. We have seen that relation and relationship were not differentiated, and here the classificatory system has stereotyped this confusion. And so when the women of the same generation and class to which a man's real mother belongs are called "mother," and the sisters of his wife in like manner are called "wives," and the brothers of his father are called "father," it no more follows that a man once practised promiscuous marriage with all such "wives," or that he now possesses the right to do so, than that a man once was begotten by all the men who were thus his "fathers," or was born of all the women who were thus his "mothers." Amongst the Kurnai the wife's sister though called "wife" would not sleep in the man's hut, and a *brogan* though calling a man's wife "wife" and though she called him "husband"

[1] Spencer and Gillen, *op. cit.* 59. [2] *Id.* 58.

would have to camp with the young men.[1] So much for the ordinary type of group-marriage. But further, in the Urabunna tribe each man has living with him (Messrs. Spencer and Gillen do not term them wives) certain *nupa* women, that is, women who on the system are tribal-sisters of his wife, and therefore potentially marriageable to him. But this is nothing but actual polygamy. The inference that all such *nupa* women are or once were married to all the men, as group to group, or to one man, is unwarranted; they are simply "marriageable" because of the system. It is possible that a legal-minded savage might draw the inference, but this would not prove such marriage to have been ever actual; there are limits to the polygamous impulse, and the elaborate character of the system is not consistent with a previous confused promiscuity. Promiscuity would not leave, as its results, a system so exact that intermarriage with the wrong class is considered a crime.

Again, there are other women in the relation of *Piraungaru* to every man, like the *Pirauru* of the Dieri tribe, "to whom he has access under certain conditions."[2] The result is, Messrs. Spencer and Gillen state, "that every woman is the special *nupa* of one man, but he has no exclusive right to her, as she is the *Piraungaru* of certain other men who also have the right of access to her" (*i.e.* as *Piraungaru*). "There is no such thing as one man having the exclusive right to one woman. Individual marriage does not exist either in name or in practice in the Urabunna tribe."[3]

In this connection they speak of a "rudimentary

[1] Fison and Howitt, *op. cit.* 210.

[2] Spencer and Gillen, *op. cit.* 62. [3] *Id.* 63.

custom";[1] that is to say, they seem to regard the present system of "rights" as a survival of a fully developed promiscuity. As to this, I would submit that the Urabunna group-marriage has never been more fully developed than it is now, that it is no modified survival, and that it is far from being a "rudimentary" custom. The essence of a "rudimentary" custom should surely be that of a "rudimentary" organ, that is to say, a "rudimentary" custom is one that exists but has no present meaning or use. Now the Urabunna custom seems to have a good deal of meaning still, and to be used in rather a regular way. The term "rudimentary" in this connection both begs the question and stultifies their theory. Again, since Prof. Tylor's *Primitive Culture*, and Darwin's *Origin of Species* were given to the world, there has been too indiscriminate and careless a use of the terms "survival" and "rudimentary"; customs and beliefs of the greatest vitality have been described and condemned as "survivals" or "rudimentary customs"; the form in such cases being of course a survival, but within the form there is a living content, not separable from it, though often changed from its earliest connotation.

As to the *Piraungaru* women of the Urabunna to whom a man has "the right of access"; they have been called "accessory wives," but the term is as misleading as it would be if applied to the wives whom husbands amongst many peoples occasionally "lend" to their guests by way of hospitality. Let us take a similar practice of the Arunta, of which the Urabunna is evidently a development. "Under ordinary circumstances in the Arunta and other tribes," individual

[1] Spencer and Gillen, *op. cit.* 105 ff.

marriage exists, but at certain times a man may have access to other women, sometimes even women of a forbidden class.[1] What are these occasions? First, the well-known savage custom just referred to, by which a man lends his wife to a friend or guest as an act of friendship, gratitude, or hospitality.[2] This is not lightly undertaken, but is an act involving a really religious obligation, as we have seen, and where it is reciprocal it is the highest form of the *ngia ngiampe* relation. In these cases the wife lent has to be of the class marriageable to the man who receives her from his friend. Secondly, a general exchange of wives takes place at certain important festivals.[3] This custom has been already explained. It has nothing whatever to do with the marriage system, except as breaking it for a season, women of forbidden degrees being lent, on the same grounds as conventions and ordinary relations are broken at festivals of the Saturnalia type, the object being to change life and start afresh, by exchanging everything one can, while the very act of exchange coincides with the other desire, to weld the community together. Thirdly, right of access holds at the ceremony whereby young women are made marriageable, that is, is physically prepared for her husband, and which is identical with a marriage ceremony.[4] In the Arunta tribe and others where group-marriage, they say, exists in a "modified form," this right of access does hold, but it simply amounts to a religious duty, whereby the bride is physically prepared for her husband. Various persons in various tribes perform this preliminary act, which is neither *jus primæ noctis* nor "religious prostitution" of the Babylonian type. Here their criticism of Dr. Westermarck is sound, but their own

[1] Spencer and Gillen, *op. cit.* 95. [2] *Id.* 98. [3] *Id.* 96. [4] *Id.* 92-97.

inference that it is a "rudimentary right of marriage" surviving from primitive promiscuity, is more beside the mark still. The act is intended to remove the danger attaching to union (and that the dangerous one of sexual intercourse) for the first time (a dangerous time), with a woman, a dangerous person,—the whole business, in idea and practice, being of the primitive religious stamp, and of the same character as "priestly defloration," and it is quite opposed in theory to the so-called *jus primæ noctis* which, if it ever obtained in Europe (it probably never obtained elsewhere), was simply a barbarous application of feudal rights, and also to religious prostitution. Finally, it is not an "expiation for marriage," as Lubbock thought.

On examining Mr. Howitt's careful description of the Dieri marriage system and the *Pirauru* practice, to which the Urabunna *Piraungaru* practice is compared, we find that in that tribe "license prevails between the intermarrying classes at certain ceremonial times," namely, at initiation ceremonies, and when a marriage takes place between members of different tribes. As to the *Piraurus*, called "paramours" by the white settlers, if a man's own wife is absent he may have marital relations with his *Piraurు*, "but he cannot take her away (from her real husband) unless by his consent, excepting at the above-mentioned ceremonial times." No other occasion of access is mentioned. He adds that the system is not complete promiscuity, for the *Piraurи* "are allotted at some great initiation ceremony."[1] The first part of the above has the same explanation as the Arunta customs; and the *Piraurи* custom is evidently a polyandrous extension, which is often found, of the custom of lending wives, namely,

[1] *Journ. Anthrop. Inst.* xx. 53, 56.

when a husband is absent a particular man may live with her, as in the *Cicisbeate* of South Europe.[1]

The following is Messrs. Spencer and Gillen's account of the *Piraungaru* of the Urabunna. "To women who are the *Piraungaru* of a man (the term is a reciprocal one), the latter has access under certain conditions, so that they may be considered as accessory wives. There is no such thing as one man having the exclusive right to one woman; the elder brothers, or *Nuthie*, of the latter, in whose hands the matter lies, will give one man a preferential right, but at the same time they will give other men of the same group a secondary right to her. Individual marriage does not exist, either in name or in practice, in the Urabunna tribe. The initiation (*sic*) in regard to establishing the relationship of *Piraungaru* between a man and a woman must be taken by the elder brothers, but the arrangement must receive the sanction of the old men of the group before it can take effect. As a matter of actual practice, this relationship is usually established at times when considerable numbers of the tribe are gathered together to perform important ceremonies, and when these and other matters of importance which require the consideration of the old men are discussed and settled. A man may always lend his wife, that is, the woman to whom he has the first right, to another man, provided always he be her *Nupa*, without the relationship of *Piraungaru* existing between the two, but unless this relationship exists, no man has any right of access to a woman. Occasionally, but rarely, it happens that a man attempts to prevent his wife's *Piraungaru* from having access to her, but this leads to a fight and the husband is looked upon as churlish.

[1] Th. Moore, *op. cit.* 64.

When visiting distant groups where, in all likelihood, the husband has no *Piraungaru*, it is customary for other men of his own class to offer him the loan of one or more of their *Nupa* women, and a man, besides lending a woman over whom he has the first right, will also lend his *Piraungaru*."[1] "The relation of *Piraungaru* is established between any woman and men to whom she is *Nupa*—that is, to whom she may be lawfully married, by her *Nuthie* or elder brothers. If a group be camped together, and as a matter of fact groups of individuals who are *Piraungaru* to one another do usually camp together, then in the case of a particular woman her special *Nupa* man has the first right to her, but if he be absent the *Piraungaru* have the right to her; or, if the *Nupa* man be present, the *Piraungaru* have the right to her, subject to his consent, which is practically never withheld."[2]

The very fact that the husband's consent must be obtained proves that he is the woman's husband, and that individual marriage exists, though slightly modified. The *Piraungaru*, like the *Pirauru* practice, is a development, in one aspect, of the practice of lending wives, coinciding with a polyandrous and polygamous tendency, and, in another, of the religious exchange of wives, as is made probable by its connection with tribal meetings. Polyandry, if not polygamy, is an abnormal practice, though found sporadically even in Southern Europe, where the *Cicisbeate* is a close parallel to one side of the Urabunna institution. Lastly, it may be noted that even if this polyandry and polygamy were real "group-marriage," it by no means proves the previous existence of wilder promiscuity for the Urabunna, much less for the rest

[1] Spencer and Gillen, *op. cit.* 62, 63.

[2] *Id.* 110.

of mankind, as a stage through which man has passed. Everything points, on the contrary, to the inference that the Dieri and Urabunna practices are abnormal developments, which have never been more complete than they are now.

Other facts that have been used in the attempt to prove primitive promiscuity and incest have been fully dealt with by Dr. Westermarck. Endogamy and the marriage of cousins have also been so used. It seems unnecessary to refute this. The system of *morongs*, or bachelor-houses, in which the young men live and sleep, has also been used in favour of the promiscuity theory;[1] but there is no ground whatever on which it may be so used; even the illicit intercourse sometimes allowed to boys, is merely either youthful love-making, which is more or less common in all societies, or a custom sanctioned by religious ideas as to its necessity.

It may be confidently assumed that individual marriage has been, as far as we can trace it back, the regular type of union of man and woman. The Promiscuity theory really belongs to the mythological stage of human intelligence, and is on a par with many savage myths concerning the origin of marriage, and the like. These are interesting but of no scientific value. They are cases of mental actualisation of apparently potential states which were really impossible except as abnormal occurrences. When men meditated upon marriage ceremonial and system, they would naturally infer a time when there was not only no rite, but no institution of marriage. Hence the common idea of which the Promiscuity theory is a result, that marriage was ordained to prevent illicit intercourse; this, of course, it does prevent, but it invents it first.

[1] By S. E. Peal, in *Journ. Anthrop. Inst.* xxi. 255.

Taboo and law when they sanction a human normal practice produce the possibility of sin. There was of course a time when there was no marriage ceremony, but the ideas of such were latent in the actual union of man and woman.

The survey of marriage and of sexual relations in early races suggests many thoughts. For instance, one is struck by the high morality of primitive man. Not long ago McLennan could assert confidently that the savage woman was utterly depraved; but a study of the facts shows quite the contrary. The religious character of early human relations, again, gives a sense of tragedy; man seems to feel that he is treading in slippery places, that he is on the brink of precipices, when really his foot standeth right. This sensitive attitude would seem to have assisted the natural development of man. We have also seen the remarkable fact that most of these primitive customs and beliefs are repeated in the average civilised man, not as mere survivals, though their religious content has been narrowed, but springing from functional causes constant in the human organism. Further, it seems to be a probable inference that the functional impulses, not only of man but of at least all higher organisms, have latent in them a potential religious content. This has been noted as especially actualised in the social relations of the individual. The history of psychological processes is the history of the religious consciousness. Lastly, in connection with the main subject, marriage, this diffidence and desire for security and permanence in a world where only change is permanent, has led to certain conceptions of eternal personalities who control and symbolise the marriage tie. Psychologically, the union of man and woman amounts to identification and combination of the two sexes; and in the theological development of this idea, as the Philippine islanders, Chinese, and Yorubas, to quote from what is a large list,[1] have deities who combine the attributes of both sexes, so the Greeks and Romans sometimes included male characteristics in their conception of the Goddess of Love,[2] and lifted marriage to the ideal plane in the conception of the *ἱερὸς γάμος*. More simply, many peoples have thought of a divine trinity of persons to symbolise the family of husband, wife, and child; Christian Europe, for instance, has worshipped the Holy Family for many hundred years. For the male sex an ideal of the Eternal Feminine often satisfies such aspirations, and this survey may fittingly close with a reference to the most prominent ideal personality for modern Europe in this connection, the Maiden-Mother, the Mystical Rose, for her figure enshrines many elemental conceptions of Man and Woman and their relations.

[1] Bowring, *op. cit.* 158; Doolittle, *op. cit.* i. 268; A. B. Ellis, *op. cit.* 41.

[2] Photius, *Bibliotheca*, 151, *b.* 5; Lydus, *De Mensibus*, ii. 10, iv. 95; the Bearded Venus in Cyprus, Macrobius, iii. 8, Servius on Virgil, *Aeneid*, ii. 632, the same in Pamphylia, Lydus, *op. cit.* iv. 44.

INDEX

THE END